MONEY

The Principles of Money and Their Exemplification in Outstanding Chapters of Monetary History

BY

EDWIN WALTER KEMMERER
WALKER PROFESSOR OF INTERNATIONAL FINANCE
PRINCETON UNIVERSITY

NEW YORK
THE MACMILLAN COMPANY
1935

Published November, 1935

SET UP AND ELECTROTYPED BY T. MOREY AND SON

PRINTED IN THE UNITED STATES OF AMERICA

PREFACE

This book developed out of several series of lectures on money and banking given before college classes by the author over a period of about thirty years.

The plan of the book is, first, to explain the fundamental principles of money and bank credit; second, to show how these principles have been exemplified in certain classical chapters in the world's monetary and banking history; and, third, to apply the principles in the light of these experiences to our present-day monetary and banking problems.

The historical chapters represent a "case" treatment. Instead of giving a comprehensive historical discussion of money and banking in which each topic would of necessity be limited to a very brief consideration, the book narrows the historical field covered to a few chapters of outstanding importance in the world's monetary and banking history and discusses these chapters much more fully than does the usual textbook.

This work will consist of two volumes: the present one, dealing chiefly with money, and a second one in process of preparation, dealing chiefly with banking and concluding with chapters on our present-day problems in which the monetary and banking aspects are considered in their intimate interrelationships.

In the preparation of this volume the author has received valuable aid from a large number of his colleagues and former students for which he is deeply grateful. The number is so large as to prevent a citation of their names. In this group, however, he would mention specifically Frank W. Fetter, Frank D. Graham, and Otto Nathan, each of whom gave him valuable criticisms on certain chapters, and Charles R. Whittlesey, who read the entire manuscript and whose suggestions were exceedingly helpful.

E. W. K.

PRINCETON, NEW JERSEY
September, 1935

CONTENTS

PART I

ELEMENTARY FACTS AND PRINCIPLES

PART III

THE PRINCIPLES OF FOREIGN EXCHANGE

CHAPTER VIII

CHAPTER IX

PART IV

SOME SIGNIFICANT CHAPTERS IN THE WORLD'S MONETARY HISTORY

PART I

ELEMENTARY FACTS AND PRINCIPLES

CHAPTER I

MONEY—ITS ORIGIN, FUNCTIONS AND CLASSIFICATION

Barter

Money is a comparatively modern device. Our earliest record of coin money dates back only to the eleventh century before Christ in China, although at that time man had been on the earth probably a million or more years. There are savage people today to whom money is unknown. Goods were exchanged long before money existed, and the origin of exchange was in gifts. One would make a present to another in the hope of obtaining a present in return. In the course of time the *mores* came to demand not only a return present, but one of equivalent value. Our modern customs in regard to Christmas and birthday presents are reminiscent of these primitive forms of exchange.

The exchange of one commodity for another when neither commodity is money is called *barter*. For many thousands of years of the world's history barter was the usual method of exchange. At the present time it is practiced on a large scale in the more backward parts of the world. In advanced countries it is still common. Farmers exchange eggs and butter for groceries, and, in some communities in the United States, still give the local miller grain for grinding their wheat into flour. In time of business depression, when the functioning of the money and credit machinery becomes obstructed, it may become very important. For example, in the world economic depression beginning in 1929 barter played an important rôle in the field of international trade, one illustration of which was the exchange in 1931 by the United States Farm Board of 25,000,000 bushels of wheat for 1,050,000 bags of Brazilian coffee.

In the history of trade, however, as the population grows and the number of goods to be exchanged increases, barter, as a permanent method of exchange, breaks down. It becomes too cumbersome. The chief trouble with it is what is known as "lack of double coincidence" in desires. For effective barter, not only must *A* want what *B* has to give, but *B* must want what *A* has to give; and the wants of each must be for such quantities of the respective articles as to make an exchange possible and profitable for both parties. A good illustration of the difficulty is the following, given by W. Stanley Jevons in his *Money and the Mechanism of Exchange:*

> "Some years since, Mademoiselle Zélie, a singer of the Théâtre Lyrique at Paris, made a professional tour round the world, and gave a concert in the Society Islands. In exchange for an air from *Norma* and a few other songs, she was to receive a third part of the receipts. When counted, her share was found to consist of three pigs, twenty-three turkeys, forty-four chickens, five thousand coca-nuts, besides considerable quantities of bananas, lemons, and oranges. At the Halle in Paris, as the prima donna remarks in her lively letter, printed by M. Wolowski, this amount of live stock and vegetables might have brought four thousand francs, which would have been good remuneration for five songs. In the Society Islands, however, pieces of money were very scarce; and as Mademoiselle could not consume any considerable portion of the receipts herself, it became necessary in the meantime to feed the pigs and poultry with the fruit."

Highly Exchangeable Commodities

Under a barter economy some kinds of articles, in widespread demand, are more easily exchanged than others. Arrowheads and ornamental shells, for example, may be in great demand among a primitive hunting people, cattle and sheep among a pastoral people, and grain among an agricultural people. In each case, the man who has a supply of the most highly desired article is likely to find no difficulty in exchanging it for the other things he wants. It is the man who has the article that very few people want and who wants an article that very few people have who has the most difficulty in a barter régime. His problem is that of marketability. Often his only way of getting the desired article is by a roundabout series of exchanges. This is well illustrated by an incident told by Henry L. Cameron in his book, *All Across Africa:*

> "Syde's agent wished to be paid [for the boat] in ivory of which I had none, but I found that Mohammed Ibu Sahib had ivory and wanted cloth. Since I had no cloth, this did not assist me greatly until I heard that Mohammed Ibu Gharib had cloth and wanted wire. This I fortunately possessed. So I gave Ibu Gharib the requisite amount in wire; whereupon he handed over cloth to Ibu Sahib, who in his turn gave Syde's agent the wished-for ivory. Then he allowed me to have the boat."

In this way people come to see that from the standpoint of getting what one wants by barter it is a wise policy to keep a part of one's wealth always in the form of some of these widely desired and highly exchangeable objects, and this may even be true of people who have no desire to use for their direct needs any more of the particular article. A hunter, for example, may have all the arrowheads he needs for his own hunting and yet be glad to accumulate more for purposes of exchange after he learns that arrowheads are highly exchangeable. In this way, articles of a high degree of exchangeability come to serve as common media of exchange. People receive them for the most part not with the idea of using them directly, but of passing them on to others in exchange for what they want.

Obviously, the highly barterable articles are different among different peoples, and with the same people at different stages in their history. It is common to divide economic history into stages, each stage being characterized by the dominant type of economic production of the period. The three principal stages through which most peoples pass before reaching the modern manufacturing stage are the hunting and fishing stage, the pastoral stage and the agricultural stage. A distinct money economy is generally developed by the time the manufacturing stage is reached.

In the hunting and fishing stage, the highly exchangeable articles are commonly shells, skins, animals' teeth, feathers, spearheads, arrowheads, fishhooks and the like. One of the earliest Chinese books extant uses the expression "a hundred thousand dead shell fishes" as synonymous with riches. Shells were widely used among the early Chinese as articles of ornament, and hence became highly barterable objects. It has been pointed out by W. Vissering,[1] that in the Chinese language "all the words denoting buying, selling, riches, goods, store, property, prices, cheap, dear, and many others referring to money and wealth, are composed of the ideographical sign which denotes the word shell." The high exchangeability possessed by so-called wampum shells among the North American Indians is familiar to all students of American history. Furs were highly barterable objects in the Hudson Bay region at the time of the Hudson Bay Company; beasts' teeth among the Solomon Islanders, animal skulls among the Michinsee, and arrowheads among the North American Indians.

[1] *On Chinese Currency*, pp. 3 and 4.

In the pastoral stage, while the popularity of ornaments may persist, we find new articles standing high in the hierarchy of exchangeability. Cattle, sheep and other domesticated animals become the highly exchangeable goods. So they were among the Hebrews at the time of the Patriarchs, among the Greeks at the time of the Homeric poems, among the ancient Italians and the Kelts. Our modern English words *capital*, *chattel* and *cattle* trace their origin to a time when the principal form of wealth was kine, which, when counted by the head (Latin, *caput*), were called *capitale*. Our English word *pecuniary* from *pecus* (cattle) is a monument to the early importance of cattle in exchange, as is also our word *fee*, which appears to be cognate with the German word *vieh*.

In the agricultural stage, various kinds of agricultural products and implements become highly exchangeable goods: various kinds of grain in early Norway, bunches of rice on the stalk in the Philippines, cacao in early Mexico and Central America, olive oil in the Ionian Islands, rice and tobacco in the early American colonies.

Money Defined

A commodity may be in general demand and be highly barterable without being suitable to be called money. When and how does money emerge in this process of evolution? The best answer to this question is found in a classic passage by Francis A. Walker: [1]

> "Tobacco early became the staple export of that colony [Virginia]. Since tobacco was in unfailing demand for shipment abroad, it was readily taken at the country store. Every planter brought his tobacco thither with perfect assurance, knowing that it would be taken as a matter of course. Every week, or every month, the trader loaded up his teams and sent his stock of tobacco to the sea-shore, where, in the chief towns, it was exchanged against West India goods, dry goods, hardware, etc., imported from abroad. With these the teams returned loaded; and the planters took the rum, the molasses, the cloth, the boots, the tools they wanted, to the amount of the credit given them for their tobacco.
>
> "Such a use of tobacco, however, did not make it money. The transactions thus far described were merely instances of barter . . .
>
> "But the fact that tobacco was thus freely taken at the country store soon led to a further extension of its use in exchange which constituted it money. Since it was so freely taken at the store, in exchange for goods of every kind, it was freely taken between man and man throughout the

[1] *Money in Its Relations to Trade and Industry*, pp. 4 and 5.

community. The lawyer and the physician did not hesitate to receive their pay in tobacco, because tobacco was always good for groceries and dry goods; while the fact that tobacco was taken not only by the store-

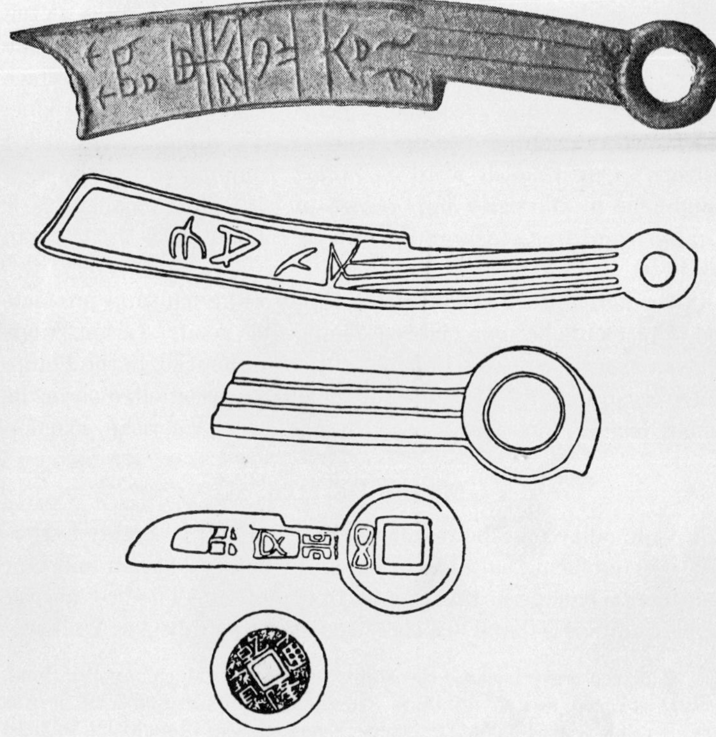

Chinese Knife Money
(Showing the evolution of the modern Chinese coins)

keeper but also by the lawyer and physician, made the farmer who raised corn willing also to take it in exchange for his product.

"And so tobacco became money in Virginia. It was not, however, until pretty much everybody took it, and took it as a matter of course, that it was entitled to be called money."

It is significant that one of the Chinese words for money means "current merchandise."

The constituting quality of money is, therefore, a very high degree of exchangeability; and when, in any country, some one article so clearly surpasses all others in the degree of its exchangeability as to be treated widely as a common medium of exchange, that article attains the right to be called money. Following the lead of Francis A. Walker, therefore, we may define money as a medium of exchange which is commonly accepted in payment for goods and services without reference to the character or credit of the person who offers it. Tersely expressed, "money is as money does."

Transitional Forms of Money

In the development from money, in the form of highly exchangeable commodities which had other uses than monetary uses, to the modern specialized forms of money which can be used for monetary uses alone, there have appeared numerous transitional forms. A few illustrations will make clear their character.

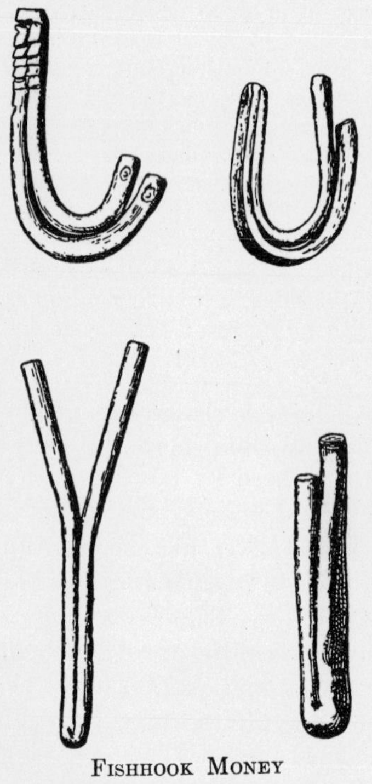

Fishhook Money

In ancient China, knives and pieces of cloth, being objects of widespread demand, attained a very high degree of exchangeability. About the twelfth century B.C., there gradually came into use miniature models of the knives made of metal, which served as media of exchange, but which had no use as commodities. In time the sizes of these miniature knives were so reduced that the entire blade and most of the handle disappeared, leaving nothing but the ring at the end of the handle, which appears to have been the origin of the Chinese "cash." This development is shown by the five graphic reproductions of ancient Chinese money on page 7.[1]

There was a similar development in India and Ceylon from real fishhooks, which were used as money, to bent wires resembling

[1] The first is a copy of a coin in the Princeton University Collection and the other four are copied from William Ridgeway, *The Origin of Metallic Currency and Weight Standards*, p. 157.

fishhooks, but which had no value as fishhooks. Gradually this so-called "fishhook currency" developed into merely a double straight wire, all resemblance to a hook disappearing, as shown by the examples on the opposite page given by Ridgeway.[1]

Precious Metals as Money

Very early in history some of the metals became objects of such universal desire as to attain that high degree of exchangeability which made them money.

> "With the exception of iron," says Jevons,[2] "the principal metals are peculiarly indestructible, and undergo little or no deterioration when hoarded up or handed about. Each kind of metal is approximately homogeneous, piece differing from piece in nothing but weight, the differences of fineness being ascertained and allowed for in the case of gold and silver. The metals are also perfectly divisible, either by the chisel or the crucible, and yet a second melting will always reunite the pieces again with little cost or loss of material. Most of them possess the properties of cognizability and impressibility in the highest degree. Each metal has its characteristic colour, density, and hardness, so that it is easy for a person with very slight experience to distinguish one metal from another. Their malleability enables us to roll, cut, and hammer them into any required form, and to impress a permanent design by means of dies."

But of the various metals which have been used in uncoined forms as money, including iron, tin, lead and copper, the so-called precious metals, silver and gold, have been by far the most important. By reason of their beauty and scarcity and of the universal desire for ornamentation, gold and silver, like the beautifully colored shells of more primitive peoples, very early became objects of wide desire and of high exchangeability. They became money.

According to Vissering, there is evidence of the use of gold bullion as money in China as early as two thousand years before Christ. In ancient Babylonia, Assyria and Egypt, the precious metals, especially silver, circulated as uncoined ingots. They were taken by weight. To this day the bulk of the larger transactions in China are effected by silver cast in the shape of shoes (sycees) which pass by weight.

Many of our words for coins are monuments to the early practice of passing the precious metals by weight. The English *pound*

[1] Ridgeway, William, *The Origin of Metallic Currency and Weight Standards*, p. 28.
[2] *Money and the Mechanism of Exchange*, p. 41.

sterling was originally a pound of silver; similarly, the French *livre*, the Spanish *onza* and the Babylonian *shekel*, were units of weight; while the *drachma* denotes "literally a handful," and meant a handful of small spits or skewers of silver.

Coinage

The use of gold and silver in the form of ingots or of "dust" as media of exchange involved serious inconveniences: first, there was the inconvenience of weighing the ingots or the dust at every transaction; and, second, there was the much greater inconvenience of ascertaining the degree of purity of the metals offered. It is a simple task to weigh a nugget of gold or silver, but a very complicated one to determine its fineness. It was such difficulties and the frauds and uncertainties that they involved that gave rise to the desire for some authoritative stamp to guarantee that the piece of metal, both in quantity and quality, was what it purported to be. Under such a guaranty, with pieces of metal of uniform size, the mere counting of the pieces would be sufficient to determine their value.

While pieces of metal of various shapes were often stamped in very early times by private persons, merchants and others, as a guaranty of their weight and fineness, the task of so stamping them normally fell to the ruler. His stamp or seal would be better and more widely known than that of a private person and would inspire greater confidence. Moreover, from very early in the practice of this "art of coining," profits were realizable, and the ruler naturally seized upon it as a source of revenue. This is the origin of our word *seigniorage*, which meant the amount taken by the seigneur or lord to cover the expenses and the profits connected with the coining of money.

Primary Function of Money

One of the most important things that money does and the thing that constitutes an article money, as previously explained, is to serve as a common medium of exchange for goods and services. Let us now consider the other functions of money.

Secondary Functions of Money

The secondary functions of money are the functions of serving as: (1) a common measure of value, (2) a standard of deferred payments, (3) a storehouse of value and (4) as bank reserves. These four functions are largely derived from the primary function of a common medium of exchange and are dependent upon it.

(1) *A Common Measure of Value.* The monetary unit is a unit of value, and the money which embodies a monetary unit is a common measure of value. As we express length in terms of conventional units of length which we call the foot or the meter, and as we express weight in terms of conventional units of weight which we call the pound or the kilogram, so we express value in terms of a conventional unit of value such as the dollar or the franc.

Just as in mathematics, fractions are reduced to a common denominator in order to make them readily comparable; so in trade, commodities of widely different character are made comparable, as regards the quality of value they possess, by having this value expressed in the value of a conventional unit, such as the dollar, the pound or the franc, of an intermediate commodity called money.

In every exchange, whether it be direct barter or purchase and sale by means of money, each of the two goods exchanged may be said to measure the value of the other. The Indian who exchanges a fox skin for a tomahawk measures the value to himself of the tomahawk in terms of the importance to him, namely, the value to him, of the fox skin. He concludes that the tomahawk is worth to him one fox skin and something more; that "something more" being the motive for the exchange. The other Indian estimates the fox skin as being worth to him one tomahawk and something more; the "something more" in his case likewise being the force which impels the exchange. The man who pays a dollar for a book and the man who sells the book for the dollar both measure the value of the book by the value of the money, and both measure the value of the money by the value of the book.

Any commodity must measure value in order to be exchanged at all. A particular commodity, however, cannot become a *common* measure of value except as it is widely exchanged, and as its value becomes established in the public mind by numerous exchanges. That commodity which is most widely exchanged becomes the common medium of exchange or money, as we have found, and in the process of serving as a common medium of exchange it becomes the common measure of value.

(2) *A Standard of Deferred Payments.* Deferred payments are payments that are postponed. A purchase or sale is a two-sided operation. If the seller receives his money at the time he delivers the goods, we call the transaction a cash transaction; if, on the other hand, he delivers the goods today and does not receive his pay until some time later, a debt is created and this debt is expressed in terms of money. The payment is deferred and the money becomes the standard by which in the meantime the amount of the debt is measured and expressed.

While debts might be expressed in bushels of wheat or tons of coal or any other important commodity, they nearly always are expressed in money. This is true because of the high degree of exchangeability which money possesses. The importance of this standard of deferred payments function will be appreciated if we consider the hundreds of billions of dollars' worth of debts in the world today, comprising such things as bonds and mortgages, insurance contracts, bank deposits, bank loans and book accounts.

(3) *A Storehouse of Value.* The hoarding of money is today usually of little importance, except in countries like India and China where banking facilities are inadequate and often unsafe and where the practice of hoarding is, therefore, still widely prevalent. In more advanced countries, hoarding is often extensively resorted to in times of financial crisis or of business depression, when many people lose confidence in the customary forms of investment and in banks. During the world economic depression beginning in 1929, the amount of hoarded money, particularly gold coin, ran into many billions of dollars.

There is one advantage in keeping one's wealth in the form of hoarded money. It is that money is the most marketable commodity one can possess. In time of stress one may not be able to sell bonds, or land or jewelry; he may not even be able to convert his bank credit into cash or into the goods that he wants. But he can always "sell" his money for commodities. Money is the most "salable" of commodities. The function of serving as a storehouse of value is, therefore, obviously derived largely from that of serving as a common medium of exchange.

The great disadvantage in using money in any considerable quantities as a storehouse of value is its expensiveness. Hoarded money is relatively idle. It does not yield interest, while to keep it safely is often difficult or expensive.

(4) *Bank Reserves.* The fourth and last secondary function of money is that of serving as bank reserves. This is the most important function of money in a modern advanced community, but it is one that can better be understood after we have studied the functions of a bank. Bank deposits and bank notes are usually payable on demand in legal tender money, and banks must, therefore, always have a certain amount of such money available to meet the demands of their creditors. The cash held for this purpose is called "the bank reserve" in the United States and "the cash balance" in England and many other countries. Naturally, a bank holds its reserve in the commodity that is used as a common medium of exchange, namely, money, because the public wishes its deposits paid in the most highly exchangeable commodity possible. A fuller discussion of bank reserves will be given later (pp. 45–47 and 54–56).

Classification of Money

From the functions of money we may derive its classifications. All money serves as a common medium of exchange, possesses value, and, in serving as a common medium of exchange, becomes a common measure of value. In every monetary system there exists a monetary unit, be it a pound of tobacco, an ornamental shell, the dollar, the mark or the franc; *and the kind of money which independently embodies this unit and to which the values of the other kinds of money are assimilated or adjusted is called the standard money.* All other kinds of money are non-standard money. Most non-standard money has its value determined, at least in part, by the fact that it is convertible either directly or indirectly on demand into standard money.

Broadly speaking, there are two important classes of standard money: (1) commodity money (sometimes called primary money), and (2) standard fiduciary money.[1] Commodity money is any kind of money of which the money value and the commodity value are practically the same. Standard fiduciary money is standard money whose value as money is appreciably greater than its value as a commodity.

[1] There is a third class of standard money which is important in the theory of money, but not of great importance in practice. It is standard money which has a value as bullion greater than its value as money and which by stringent laws is prevented from being melted down or exported. For want of a better name, we may call it "depressed value money." For examples, cf., *infra*, pp. 101–103.

Commodity Money

While commodity money may consist of articles of merchandise which have not been given any special form to mark them as money, like the previously described tobacco money of colonial Virginia, the cattle money of Greece in Homeric times, the gold dust money used in many newly opened gold fields, or the sycee silver "shoes" that circulate by weight in China, most of the world's commodity money in recent years has been in the form of coin.

When two kinds of commodity money circulate side by side with essentially equal privileges before the law and are tied together by a fixed legal ratio of equivalence, the monetary system is called *bimetallism*—a subject to be considered later (pp. 83–93). When there is only one kind of standard commodity money, the system is called *monometallism* (pp. 69–81). If two valuable metals like gold and silver, each in substantial proportion, were combined in the standard money unit, the system would be called *symmetallism*—a type of money of interest in monetary theory, but one which has never been used in practice. Occasionally there are instances where two or more kinds of commodity money circulate side by side without being tied together by any legal ratio of equivalence,[1] each kind of money circulating at varying market values in terms of the others. When there are only two kinds of money of this type, the system is called a *dual standard*, and, when there are more than two, we shall call it a *multiple standard*.[2]

Historically speaking, many different metals have been used as standard money: iron in ancient Sparta, tin in ancient Syracuse and probably also in early Egypt, copper in early Palestine and in early Rome, and brass until recently in many parts of China. In modern times, however, monometallism has been based mostly on the so-called precious metals, silver and gold, with an increasing preponderance of gold since the latter part of the last century. Today a true silver standard exists only in Hong Kong and Ethiopia. The legal restrictions on the exportation of silver from

[1] For examples, cf., *infra*, pp. 94–96.

[2] The term *multiple standard* is often used to apply to what is described later (pp. 103–107) under the term *tabular standard*. It is believed that the meaning given to the term *multiple standard* in the text is more appropriate. A word is needed to designate this type of money system, and the expression *multiple standard* is coordinate with the commonly used terms *single standard* and *dual standard*. There is, furthermore, no need of two terms to designate the type of monetary system to which the term *tabular standard* is commonly applied.

China imposed by the Government in 1934 removed China, strictly speaking, from the silver standard. The gold standard is the only monometallic standard of importance in the world today. There is, however, no essential difference (so far as fundamental economic principles are concerned) between the gold standard and the silver standard or any other monometallic commodity standard.

Standard Fiduciary Money

The nature of standard fiduciary money is somewhat more difficult to explain. A fiduciary money standard is one in which the money value of the monetary unit is substantially greater than the value of the material of which the monetary unit is made. India, for example, was on a fiduciary money standard from 1893 to 1898; [1] for the monetary unit during that time, namely, the silver rupee, in which India's prices were expressed, had a money value substantially greater than the value of the silver it contained, while its value was not tied to the value of gold at a fixed rate. During that time the value of the rupee did not change with changes in the value of silver or with changes in the value of gold, but it responded, independently of the value of gold and silver, to variations in the demand for rupees and the supply of rupees. The greenback period of the United States currency from 1862 to 1879 [2] was a period of a fiduciary money standard, and, during the World War, when all gold standard countries gave up the gold standard, fiduciary money standards were in operation nearly everywhere. In September, 1931, when the Bank of England suspended gold payments, England went on a fiduciary money standard, and, at this writing (1935), fiduciary paper money standards exist in the great majority of the countries of the world.

The nature of these different kinds of standard money will be considered later.

Non-Standard Money

Non-standard money is comprised of various kinds of fiduciary money, the value of which reflects the value of the standard money. The supply of non-standard money in circulation is limited. This money, which consists chiefly of bank notes, government notes, fractional coins and unitary fiduciary coins like the American

[1] For a description of this Indian standard, cf., *infra*, pp. 26–29.
[2] Cf., *infra*, pp. 235–260.

silver dollar, is usually convertible on demand into standard money, or its gold or silver bullion equivalent, and is accepted as the equivalent of standard money in payment of taxes and other government dues. In these ways its value is maintained at a par with standard money. In recent years gold coins have practically disappeared from circulation throughout the world and the great bulk of the money in active circulation now consists of non-standard money.

BIBLIOGRAPHY

Du Puy, W. A., "The Geography of Money," *National Geographical Magazine;* December, 1927.

Grierson, P. J. H., *The Silent Trade;* Edinburgh, W. Green & Sons, 1903.

Helfferich, Karl, *Money.* Translated by Louis Infield; 2 volumes; London, Ernest Benn, Ltd., 1927.

Howitt, A. W., *The Native Tribes of South-East Australia;* London and New York, The Macmillan Company, 1904.

Hoyt, Elizabeth E., *Primitive Trade: Its Psychology and Economics;* London, 1926.

Jevons, W. Stanley, *Money and the Mechanism of Exchange;* New York and London, D. Appleton & Company, 1875.

Menger, Karl, "Geld," *Handwörterbuch der Staatswissenschaften;* Jena, Verlag von Gustav Fischer, 1909.

Ridgeway, William, *The Origin of Metallic Currency and Weight Standards;* Cambridge, University Press, 1892.

Sumner, William Graham, *Folkways;* Boston, Ginn & Company, 1907.

Vissering, W., *On Chinese Currency;* Leiden, E. J. Brill, 1877.

Walker, Francis A., *Money in Its Relations to Trade and Industry;* New York, Henry Holt and Company, 1889.

CHAPTER II

PRICES AND THE PRINCIPLES DETERMINING THE VALUE OF MONEY

The central point of economic science—the point at which the forces of production and the forces of consumption are focused—is market price. In this chapter we shall consider in a very elementary way the nature of a market price, the relation of individual market prices to the so-called "price level," and the fundamental forces by which the price level is determined. These subjects are all large and complicated. Concerning their details there is still much controversy among economists, but upon fundamentals there is substantial agreement. In a general discussion of money such as this, only the outstanding principles can be discussed.

Principle of Price Determination

The underlying principle of price determination is the law of demand and supply. In its simplest form this may best be explained by means of a hypothetical illustration. Assume an isolated community to which once a month a supply of horses is driven from neighboring places to be sold in the open market. Assume that the horses brought in at any one time are all alike and that the dealings are all open so that each bid on the part of prospective buyers and each offer on the part of those who have horses to sell are known to all parties interested; and, finally, assume that each person concerned acts on purely selfish motives.

On a certain market day eight horses are brought to the market for sale by eight different persons, whom we shall call prospective sellers and whom we shall designate respectively by the symbols *S1*, *S2*, *S3*, . . . *S8*. On the same day, we shall assume, there come to the market ten prospective buyers whom we shall designate respectively by the symbols *B1*, *B2*, *B3*, . . . *B10*.

Each of these prospective sellers and buyers has his own subjective price for a horse. To each seller the subjective price is the minimum number of dollars which he will take for his horse. He will naturally get all he can, but he will take his horse back home rather than sell it below this minimum. To each buyer the subjective price is the maximum number of dollars which he will pay for a horse. He will try to buy a horse as cheaply as possible, but will bid up to this figure as a limit if necessary in order to get a horse. He will pay no more; beyond that figure he would rather keep his money than buy a horse. A subjective price may be defined, therefore, as an individual's estimate of the value of a commodity to himself in terms of his estimate of the value of money to himself.

A subjective price makes no demand upon the circulating media. A particular seller, *S* for example, may value his horse at $200, but no one else may value it at anything approaching that amount, so that no sale takes place. It is only when someone else, say *B*, a prospective buyer, places a higher valuation on the horse in terms of money than *S* does upon $200; in other words, when some prospective buyer's subjective price for a horse is as high as, or higher than, the seller's subjective price; that a sale of a horse will take place. When two subjective prices overlap, in other words, when both parties believe they would gain by the transaction, a sale takes place. Then a market price emerges. A market price is the number of money units at which an article is actually sold. The proof of the market price is in the sale. Other prices are merely subjective prices; they may be bid prices or asked prices, but, strictly speaking, they are not market prices.

Let us assume that, on a particular market day, the subjective prices, respectively, of the eight prospective sellers of horses and of the ten prospective buyers are as follows:

S1	$100	*B1*	$175
S2	110	*B2*	165
S3	120	*B3*	145
S4	125	*B4*	140
S5	135	*B5*	138
S6	140	*B6*	120
S7	150	*B7*	105
S8	180	*B8*	100
		B9	90
		B10	80

In such a market, a moment's thought will show, the market price for the horses could not be less than $135 nor more than

$138, because it is only within that range that the market would be in equilibrium and that the number of horses offered and the number bid for would be the same. Suppose, for example, that an attempt should be made to fix the market price at $110, the subjective price of *S2*. At that price only two horses would be offered for sale, those of *S1* and *S2*. On the other hand, there would be six buyers (*B1* to *B6*) who would be willing to pay as much as $110 for the horse, and competition of buyers would immediately force the price up.

Suppose, on the other hand, an effort should be made to fix the price at the subjective price of *B3*, namely $145. At that price there would be three buyers and six horses for sale, with the result that competition among sellers would force the price down.

By similar tests it will be found that only between the subjective price of *S5*, namely $135, and that of *B5*, namely $138, will the number of horses offered by the sellers and the number bid for by the buyers be the same. At any price within this so-called "price range," namely, at any price between $138 and $135, there will be the same number of horses offered for sale and bid for—in this illustration, five—and each of five prospective buyers and five prospective sellers would gain by the transaction. The price range is the range of subjective prices within which the market will be in equilibrium and at any point within which there will be an equal number of commodities offered by sellers and bid for by buyers.

The forces which determine the precise point within the price range at which the price will be fixed are similar to those which determine the price range itself. The only difference is that the determining utilities and disutilities which fix the money price within the price range are those incident to the bargaining process itself. They are the psychological disutilities (or possibly pleasures) of higgling and the money advantages of higgling.[1] Within this price range, therefore, the market price is fixed at a point at which both buyers and sellers estimate the disutilities of further higgling to offset the utilities to be gained by such higgling.[2]

[1] For a discussion of this process, cf., article by the writer, "The Higgling of the Market," *Quarterly Journal of Economics*, Vol. 17, pp. 670–677.

[2] When the market is a large one, when many units of a commodity are being offered for sale, and when competition on the part of both buyers and sellers is keen, the price range becomes very narrow and may even contract to a point, namely, to a definite number of dollars and cents.

This is the law of price expressed in its simplest form, as it would apply in a free, selfish, intelligent and perfectly competitive market. It is, perhaps, needless to add that the conditions of exchange in the modern markets of real life are far from meeting these conditions. There are limitations of law, of custom, of ignorance, of altruism, of friendship and of various degrees of monopoly control, that have to be taken into account in the study of individual price movements in any market; but, under them all, this fundamental law is at work and, for the purposes of a brief account of the fundamental forces determining market price, a statement of this underlying principle is sufficient.

Obviously, under the familiar principle of diminishing gratification, the more money a man has, the lower will be his estimate of the value to him of a unit of money and the higher his scale of subjective prices for all kinds of goods, and the greater will be the number of his subjective prices as a buyer that will be translated into market prices; in other words, the greater will be the number of goods he will buy. When a man's money income declines, the reverse is true. On the other hand, the more units of a particular commodity that come into a man's possession, the lower will be his estimate of the value of each unit of the commodity and, consequently, the lower will be his subjective price for that commodity and the more likely will his subjective price as a seller be translated into a market price.

Every change in taste, every alteration in the supply of commodities thrown on the market, every change in the supply of money or of money substitutes and every change in their distribution among the people will cause the subjective prices of buyers and sellers to vary and will, in consequence, bring about changes in market prices. Such factors as these must be taken into account in any explanation of the law of demand and supply.

The Price Level

Let us now turn from the subject of individual market prices to that of the price level, which is a composite of a large number of market prices of different commodities and which is usually expressed in what is known as a *price index number.*

The idea may be expressed figuratively by the illustration of a lake. The lake is deep in some parts and in some parts it is shallow;

its bed is very uneven; its surface is roughened by the wind into waves of different sizes with their alternate crests and troughs. Prices of individual commodities are perpendicular sections of water extending from the bottom of the lake to the top. Some terminate in wave crests, others in wave troughs. Some are in the center where the lake is deep and some are near the shore where it is shallow. The lengths of these perpendicular sections of water are continually changing. Some are rising and some are falling. However, just as there is no lake level except that made by the water in the basin of the lake, so there is no price level apart from the aggregate of individual prices.

The price level, as well as individual prices, is continually changing. When prices rise, the amount of goods which a dollar will buy falls. If the price level should be doubled, the purchasing power or market value of the dollar would have been cut in half; if it should be tripled, the purchasing power of the dollar would have been cut to one-third; and, if the price level should be cut to one-third, the purchasing power of the dollar would have been tripled. The purchasing power of money, therefore, is obviously the reciprocal of the price level. It rises as the price level falls and falls as the price level rises.

Price Index Numbers

A device used for measuring movements in the price level and their reciprocal movements in the purchasing power of money is known as the *index number*, and was apparently first used in 1750 by an Italian economist by the name of G. R. Carli. Carli used it to measure changes in the price level of three commodities, namely, grain, wine and oil. Since this early beginning, there has developed an elaborate technique of index numbers; and index numbers are now used to measure many movements in addition to price levels. Modern price index numbers often cover several hundred commodities. Our leading American wholesale price index number, that of the United States Bureau of Labor Statistics, includes 784 items.

The subject of the construction of index numbers is a large one and hundreds of volumes have been written in recent years concerning it. Some references to a few of the principal works on this subject are cited in the bibliography at the close of this chapter. For the purposes of this book it will be sufficient to show in an elementary way what is meant by an index number, and perhaps the best way of doing this is to construct a very simple one.

Let us take for an illustration four articles of food in a country with a small population, say Chile, during the years 1913–1919. The articles will be flour, sweet potatoes, butter and beans. The prices selected will be prices collected from several leading merchants in each of five important cities in Chile, say Santiago, Valparaiso, Vandivia, Antofagasta and Arica, so as to be representative of an entire country. Care will be taken that the same grade and quality of goods will be used each time, and that all prices will be cash prices. Price figures, it will be assumed, will be collected at frequent intervals, say, once each week for each article in each city. An average price for each article in each city will be computed for each of the years covered by the index numbers, and these average yearly prices for each article in each city will then be combined in a simple average for all five cities to give the average price per year for each of the articles for the country as a whole. The prices for the year 1913 will be taken as the base prices and, in each case, accordingly, the prices for that year will be taken as a price index of 100. The prices for each of the following years will be expressed in the price index in terms of the 1913 price as 100.

Let us assume that, computed in this way, the average annual prices for each of the four commodities for the country as a whole are those given in the following table under the heading of Prices. The price indices for each year are the percentages which the prices of that year bear to the prices of the base year 1913. It happens that in each case the quantity unit taken was 100 kilograms, but, inasmuch as our index numbers are percentage figures, the result would not be at all affected if some of the commodities were quoted in tons, others in meters, and still others by the dozen.

The horizontal column marked Annual Index Number contains the seven annual index numbers for the four commodities. In computing this index number, the price indices of the four commodities are added together and divided by four. In this way all commodities entering the index number are given equal importance. Such an index number is called a simple or unweighted index number.

Construction of Price Index Numbers

Year	Flour 100 Kl.		Potatoes 100 Kl.		Butter 100 Kl.		Beans 100 Kl.		Annual Index Number
	Price Pesos	Index	Price Pesos	Index	Price Pesos	Index	Price Pesos	Index	
1913	26	100	16	100	299	100	29	100	100
1914	43	165	9	56	341	114	35	121	114
1915	58	222	18	112	470	157	48	166	164
1916	35	134	9	56	375	126	48	166	120
1917	40	153	31	194	394	132	53	183	165
1918	43	165	19	119	331	111	45	155	137
1919	52	200	19	119	414	139	56	193	163

In general, however, weighted index numbers are preferable, because, for most problems, different commodities have very different degrees of importance. If, for example, in this instance, we were concerned with the cost of living in a particular class of family, we might find that, on the average, the same amount per adult was spent for butter and for beans, but that the amount spent for potatoes averaged twice as much as that spent for butter or for beans and that the amount spent for flour averaged twice as much as for potatoes. In that case, the index number for the year 1914, for example, would be made up as follows:

Beans	121 × 1 =	121
Butter	114 × 1 =	114
Potatoes	56 × 2 =	112
Flour	165 × 4 =	660
	8 =	1007

Dividing the total 1007 by the sum of the weights, which is 8, we have an index number for 1914 of 126. In carefully prepared index numbers, the system of weighting the different commodities is often a complicated one involving an elaborate study of the relative importance of the different articles for the particular purposes in view.

Then, too, there are numerous methods of combining these simple price indices into general index numbers. In the illustration we have taken a simple average or arithmetic mean; that is, we have added the index numbers together for the different commodities and divided by the number of items in the total. Many other methods may be used for making these combinations. Some are better adapted for certain purposes and others for other purposes. For example, the median is obtained by arranging the individual index numbers in the order of their size, beginning with the smallest number and running up to the largest number and then taking the middle figure—namely, the figure which has an equal number of figures on each side of it. This figure is the median and is taken to represent the series.

Another method is the geometrical mean, where the individual indices are multiplied together and from the result the corresponding root is taken. If eight indices were multiplied together, the eighth root would be taken, and, if twenty were multiplied together, the twentieth root would be taken. For the purposes of this study, we need not go into these refinements. The interested reader will find them discussed in detail in the books on Index Numbers referred to at the end of this chapter.

Experience has shown that, when a large number of commodities is used in computing an index number, running often into the hundreds in our modern index numbers, individual differences in prices tend to be ironed out, so that the different methods of weighting the various commodities and different methods of combining the individual price indices *usually* do not give widely different results.

The Law of Demand and Supply and the Value of Money

The value of money, like the value of every other commodity that is bought and sold in the market, is determined by the law of demand and supply. This is a thoroughly well-established economic law, and, although there are minor differences of interpretation, its fundamental soundness is nearly everywhere admitted. There are a few persons, however, who, while admitting that this law applies to the value of every other commodity, deny its application to the value of money. In a book of this kind, the contentions of this small group of economists need not be discussed further than to say that the burden of the proof is certainly upon those who claim that money alone of all economic goods does not have its value determined by the law of demand and supply.

Principle Illustrated by Cowrie Shell Money

In colonial days, cowrie shells or wampum beads were used both as ornaments and as money among the North American Indians. When used as money, the number of shells required to buy a bear skin, a tomahawk or a dozen arrowheads depended upon the number of bear skins, tomahawks and arrowheads that were available for exchange and equally upon the number of cowrie shells that were available. At times, when, through the discoveries of some fortunate persons, a large additional supply of cowrie shells was thrown on the market, prices of goods in terms of cowrie shells would rise. On the other hand, when the supply of cowrie shells dwindled because few new ones were being found and the old ones were being lost, broken, paid out to other tribes or diverted to uses as ornaments, prices of goods in terms of cowrie shells would fall. If the supply of cowrie shells remained unchanged, while the number of skins, tomahawks, arrowheads and other goods the members of the tribe wanted to buy and sell increased, the prices of these goods would fall, because at the old prices there would not be enough cowrie shells to "go around" in effecting the exchanges of an increased number of goods.

Cowrie shells were first used only as ornaments, such as necklaces, bracelets and bangles, and their use as money was a later development. The universal demand for ornaments among the Indian tribes using them made the cowrie shell a highly exchangeable commodity. In time the shells became a common medium of exchange and therefore money, in trade among the Indians themselves and between the Indians and the colonists. Their value was created by two sorts of demand, the demand for them as ornaments, and the demand for them as media of exchange. With either source of demand removed, their value would have been less. Had the supply of these shells been strictly limited, and had their use as ornaments fallen out of favor, their value would have been reduced, but the money demand alone would have been sufficient to give them a value. That value would have been the resultant of the interaction of the forces of the demand for shell money and the supply of shell money. A sudden increase in the supply of shells would have made shells less valuable in terms of other goods and therefore would have raised prices. A sudden decrease in the supply of shells, on the other hand, would have made shells more valuable in terms of other goods and therefore would have reduced the prices of these other goods. If the supply of goods to be exchanged for shell money increased more rapidly than the supply of shells, prices would have tended to fall, because there would not have been enough shells to go around at the old prices. If the supply of goods, on the other hand, were greatly reduced through forest fire, war or other cause, while the supply of shells was maintained unchanged, prices of goods would have tended to rise.

Briefly, prices rose when the supply of shell money *relative* to the demand for shell money (the number of goods to be exchanged) rose, and prices fell when the supply of shell money *relative* to the demand for shell money fell.

A good method of illustrating how the law of demand and supply functions, in a régime in which money is used, is through a brief examination of a classical chapter in the world's monetary history—the experiences of India during the period 1893 to 1898.

India's Experience, 1893 to 1898

India had been on a silver standard for many years prior to 1893, her monetary unit having been the *rupee*, which contained 180 grains troy of silver consisting of 165 grains of pure silver and 15 grains of copper alloy. This quantity of silver, 180 grains eleven-twelfths fine, was known in India as a *tola*. There was a coinage charge of 2 per cent, which is called *brassage*,[1] upon the payment of which anyone could obtain at the Indian mint a coined rupee for every tola of silver brought. Inasmuch as anyone could have silver bullion in unlimited quantities converted into rupees at the slight expense of 2 per cent for coinage by merely bringing the bullion to the Indian mints, a rupee could obviously not have a value much more than 2 per cent above the market price of a tola of silver. On the other hand, rupees could always be melted down and converted into silver bullion at a very slight expense, and bullion dealers, jewelers and others were accustomed to melt them down for silver bullion whenever it was profitable to do so. The result was that a tola of silver bullion could never be worth much more than a full weight rupee, because full weight rupees were convertible into silver bullion without limit at the slight expense of melting down the coins. Since, therefore, a tola and a rupee were always readily convert-

[1] When the government (or other authority) that coins money charges for the work of coining only enough reasonably to cover the expenses incident to coining, the charge is called *brassage*. When the charge exceeds this amount, so that the coining authority realizes a net profit on the transaction, the term applied is *seigniorage* or *seigniorage profit*.

ible, at a slight expense, the value of a rupee and the value of a tola of silver bullion, in the principal markets of India, were always approximately the same. This system made India a silver standard country.

On June 26, 1893, the Indian Government closed its mints to the coinage of silver on private account, and, after that date, the Indian public was denied the privilege of taking silver bullion to the Indian mints and of having it coined in unlimited quantities into rupees at the rate of one rupee for one tola of silver. The plan was to divorce the gold value of the rupee from the gold value of its silver content, i.e., of a tola of silver, by practically discontinuing the coining of rupees. It was a plan to "starve the circulation," by preventing the supply of money from increasing while the population and trade were growing and the demand for money was accordingly increasing. The Government, in other words, by restricting and controlling the coinage of rupees, planned to prevent the gold value of the rupee from declining as the gold value of its silver content declined, and in fact, to raise the value of the rupee to 16 pence of British money, equivalent to one-fifteenth of a British sovereign. It was an application of the economic principle of monopoly value, the Government in this case enjoying a monopoly upon the supply of an economic necessity, namely, money. The Government decided to regulate the supply of that commodity on the market deliberately to such an extent as to raise the value of that commodity, under the pressure of an increasing economic demand for it, to a gold value of 16 pence.

The Government agreed to give rupees for British gold coin at the rate of one rupee for 16 pence of gold, but it did not agree to give gold for rupees, nor did it have at the time any gold reserve for such a purpose. Immediately upon the closing of the mints, the fluctuations of the gold value of the rupee ceased to run parallel with the fluctuations in the gold value of a tola of silver as they had for many years previous. When the rupee became slightly more valuable than a tola of silver, it was now no longer possible to convert silver bullion into rupees at the rate of one tola to one rupee by bringing silver to the mints and having it coined into rupees, increasing the supply of rupees and thus bringing the value of a rupee down to that of the market value of a tola of silver.

What happened to the gold value of the rupee will be seen from the following chart.[1]

INDIAN CURRENCY REFORM

MONTHLY VARIATIONS IN EXCHANGE AND BULLION VALUES OF RUPEE

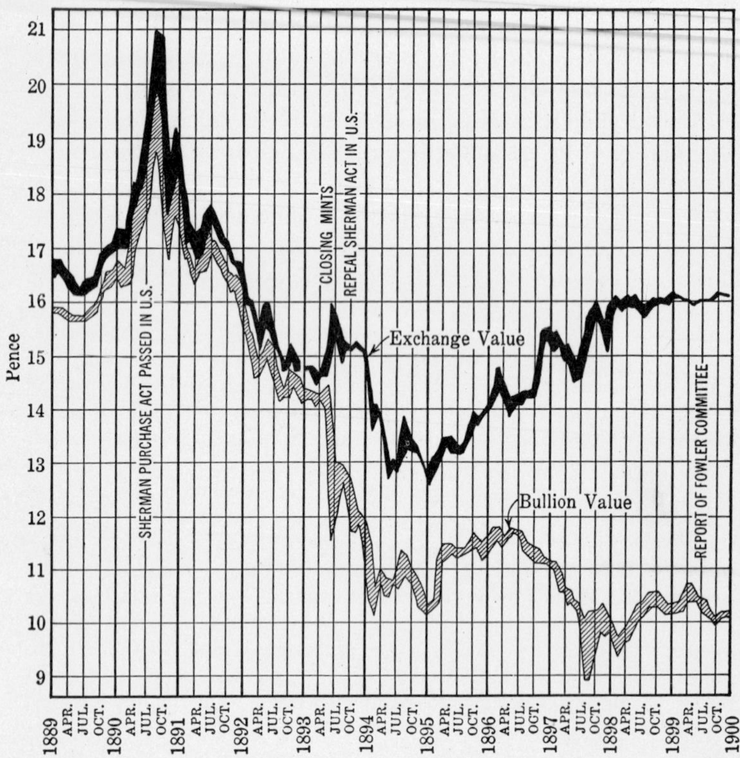

Early in 1894, the gold exchange value of the rupee began to move upward and continued to ascend, with minor interruptions, until 1898; although the gold value of a tola of silver tended downward for most of the period 1893 to 1898. Here was a silver coin whose gold value as money was moving upward, under the pressure of increasing demand for money upon a practically constant supply of money, despite the fact that the gold value of its silver content was rapidly declining and was continually far below the value of the coin. At the beginning of 1898 the gold value of a

[1] The chart is reproduced from the author's *Modern Currency Reforms*, p. 50.

coined rupee touched 16 pence, while the bullion value of a tola of silver was less than 10 pence.

Between 1894 and 1898 the gold value of the rupee as money was raised from 14 pence to 16 pence by this process of starving the circulation; that is, by keeping the monetary supply relatively constant while the monetary demand was increasing. Aside from food prices, which were boosted to extravagantly high figures in India in 1896 and 1897 by a widespread famine, the general tendency of prices in India for the period of 1894 to 1898 was downward, this decline registering an increase in the value of the rupee in comparison with commodities as well as in comparison with gold.

Concerning this experience, the Government of India wrote to the Secretary of State for India, under date of March 3, 1898, as follows:[1]

> "Our experience since 1893 has put beyond doubt one of the main principles upon which the legislation of that year was made—a principle which was challenged at the time—namely, that a contraction of the volume of our silver currency, with reference to the demands of trade, has the direct effect of raising its exchangeable value in relation to gold. Before 1893, while the mints were yet open, the value of the rupee as measured in gold continually declined with the decline in the value of silver; but, since 1893, although the value of silver as a metal has continued, speaking generally, to decrease, the decrease in the value of the rupee has been arrested. The main difference in the conditions of the two periods was that before 1893 the amount of coin in circulation was allowed to increase automatically so as to be sufficient to meet the demands of trade at its reduced value, while since 1893, this automatic increase being stopped, the value of the rupee has been determined rather by the amount of coinage in circulation than by its intrinsic worth."

If, through the process of relative contraction of the currency, namely, contraction relative to trade needs, and without any promise of future redemption in gold whatever, the rupee could have its money value in terms of gold raised to an amount exceeding its value as bullion in terms of gold by 60 per cent, it seems reasonable to believe that by a continuation of the same process its money value could have been raised to still higher figures, even though its bullion value had continued to decline.

[1] Commission on International Exchange, *Stability of International Exchange*, Report of 1903, p. 333.

No Appreciation Except from Relative Scarcity

Just as the value of money may be raised above the value of its bullion content and maintained above that value by preventing the supply of money from increasing when the demand for money is growing, so, similarly, can the value of money be kept below the value of its bullion content by preventing the supply of money from decreasing when the demand for money declines. There have been numerous historical instances of the application of this principle.

On November 17, 1906, for example, the gold value in the London market of the amount of silver contained in a Philippine silver peso was 13.2 per cent above the gold money value at which the peso circulated in the Philippine Islands. The total expense of shipping silver pesos from Manila to London at that time was estimated to be about 1 per cent. Under such circumstances, it would be expected that the large profits that would have been realized by persons who gathered up the pesos from circulation and exported them in substantial quantities to London and New York, where they could be sold as silver bullion, would have quickly reduced the supply of pesos in the Philippine Islands and, thereby, forced the money value of the pesos up to their value as bullion. This is exactly what would have happened, had it been possible to export these coins or to melt them down and export the silver bullion obtained from them. But the Government of the Philippine Islands did not wish to see its coins melted down and sold in the silver market. It had fixed the gold value of these silver coins at 50 cents United States currency and had made them redeemable in gold exchange at approximately that value, and it did not wish to see the supply of coins reduced and their money value pushed up to a point far above their original gold value. The Government, accordingly, took drastic measures to prevent the silver from being melted down or from leaving the country as money, imposing fines and prison penalties upon any persons who should melt down these coins or who should attempt to export them as money. The Philippine police force was so efficient, and the penalties for infraction of the law were so severe that the law proved to be reasonably effective. This explains why for nearly two years the silver coins of the Philippine Islands circulated at a money value considerably below the gold value of their silver content in New York or in London.[1]

Changes in the bullion value of coins can only cause changes in their money value through influencing the supply of money or the demand for money. The law of supply and demand is fundamental. Ricardo's dictum holds true, that "there can be no depreciation except from excess," that is, from "relative redundancy." The reverse of this dictum is likewise true, that there can be no appreciation except from relative scarcity.

The Quantity Theory of Money

Although the market value of every commodity is the resultant of the interaction of the forces of demand and supply, the values of different classes of commodities respond in different ways to the interaction of these forces. To increase the supply of some commodities on the market, for example by 25 per cent, would result in a very small decline in their prices, because the demand for them is so elastic that a slight decline in their prices would stimulate a greatly increased demand for them on the part of the public. This is particularly true of luxuries like jewelry and other forms of ornaments. To increase the marketable supply of other commodities by 25 per cent, however, would result in "breaking the market" and forcing a large reduction in price, because the demand for them is so inelastic that very large price reductions are necessary to stimulate small increases in the demand. This is true of the so-called necessities of life, such as salt and bread.

For some classes of commodities, like fruit and vegetables, the amount produced each year is a very important factor in determining the market price, because the annual production represents practically the entire supply on the market. For other commodities, which are of a highly durable character and of which the marketable supply at any time is the accumulation of many years, as, for example, silver and diamonds, the production for the current year is a very minor factor in the forces determining the market price.

[1] For other illustrations of this principle, see Cairnes, J. E., *Essays in Political Economy*, p. 25; Kemmerer, E. W., "Money and Prices," *American Economic Review*, Supplement, March, 1918, pp. 260–261; and Kemmerer, E. W., and Vissering, G., *Report on the Resumption of Gold Payments by the Union of South Africa*, pp. 536–537.

Inasmuch as money is the most exchangeable of all commodities, its possession gives the owner power to obtain from society any other commodity on the market, provided he has money in sufficient quantity to pay for it. Since man is a creature of unlimited economic wants, money is consequently a commodity of an unlimited and highly elastic demand.

The Equation of Exchange in a Simple Monetary Régime

Demand for money finds expression chiefly in exchange, and, because money is the common medium of exchange, it follows that there is a greater degree of proportionality between the fluctuations in the value of money and the strength of the forces of demand and supply than there is in the value of any other kind of commodity. To illustrate this principle, let us return to our cowrie shell illustration. Assume that the shells are all alike and that they are strung on strings of 10 shells to a string, and that the monetary unit in which all prices are expressed consists of a string of these shells.

Whenever an article is sold, the article passes from the seller to the buyer and the money, in this case strings of cowrie shells, passes from the buyer to the seller. The price is the number of strings of cowrie shells paid for an article. The price level, which we will designate by P, is an average index number weighted according to the volume of the different kinds of goods that are bought and sold in the different years. Designate the number of strings of cowrie shell money in circulation by M.

Obviously, the amount of exchange work a given number of strings of cowrie shells can perform depends upon the number of times the strings exchange hands, or upon what is known as their "velocity" or "rate of turnover." A hundred strings of shells exchanging hands for goods twice in a year and lying idle the rest of the time would do 200 units of money work in a year, while another hundred that exchange hands for goods ten times in a year would do 1,000 units of money work and therefore be five times as efficient as the first hundred strings. The effective shell money supply is obviously increased as truly by increasing the average velocity of turnover, with the quantity of shells constant, as it is by increasing the number of shells, with the average rate of turnover remaining constant.

Let us designate the average number of times the strings of

shells, M, are exchanged in the purchase and sale of goods during the year by V, for "velocity of circulation."

Designate the number of units of goods sold in a year by T, which stands for transactions—a unit of each kind of goods being the physical quantity of it that was worth on the average 10 strings of shells at the prices of the base year.

One could then say that P, or the average price, multiplied by T, the number of goods units sold, would be equal to M, the number of strings of shell money in the community, multiplied by V, the average velocity or rate of turnover of this money for the year. $PT = MV$. Dividing both sides of the equation by T, we have $P = \frac{MV}{T}$. This is the so-called "quantity theory of money" or the "equation of exchange," in its simplest form.

It is only the strings of shells that are passed from hand to hand as money that directly affect prices. Shells used continually as ornaments have no effect on prices, except as their purchase and sale as commodities represent a demand for shell money for making the payments. If, however, prices should fall and shells as money should, therefore, become more valuable than some of the shells used as ornaments, some ornaments would be broken up and the shells taken from them would be strung on strings for money, thereby coming into the money uses. These shells would then influence prices, because they would increase the supply of shell money. The opposite is likewise true. An increased demand for shell ornaments might raise the value of shells in the ornament use above their value in the money use and thereby lead to the transfer of some shells from money uses to ornament uses. This would reduce the supply of shell money, increase the value of a string of shells and thus reduce commodity prices; and the process would continue until the values of shells in both uses were again made equal.

A Gold Coin Régime

So far we have been assuming that all the money in circulation consisted of strings of cowrie shells. A moment's thought, however, will show that the principle would not be at all changed by assuming that the money, instead of consisting of beautiful shells found in the country in limited quantities and useful also as ornaments, consisted of small pieces of gold. We may assume that gold instead of cowrie shells was found in the territory of this isolated tribe, that it was in wide demand for ornaments because of its beauty, and that, because of this demand it became the most highly exchangeable commodity among the members of the tribe and therefore became money. Assume that, to simplify exchanges by means of this money through avoiding the necessity of weighing and testing the gold at each transaction, the chief of the tribe makes provisions for putting up the gold in small round discs of uniform size weighing a little over 23 grains each and bearing his stamp as a guarantee that they are of full weight and pure gold. Assume that anyone who has gold can take it to the chief and have it cut into discs and stamped, without charge, and that there is nothing to prevent the use of these discs for bracelets, necklaces and other ornaments, or to prevent their being melted down for these or other purposes whenever the owner so desires. The conditions then would be practically identical with those assumed for the Indian tribe whose money was exclusively cowrie shells, but we would have a tribe with a gold standard currency and with coined money. The law of demand and supply, as expressed in the quantity theory formula, $P = \frac{MV}{T}$, would apply here just as truly as it did in the case of the cowrie shell money.

For convenience, let us call this gold disc a dollar.[1] Obviously, the value of 23 grains of pure gold and the value of a gold dollar would be practically the same thing under such conditions, just as the value of five strings of cowrie shells as money and of fifty cowrie shells as ornaments would be the same thing, because in both instances they would be interchangeable without loss. Double the amount of gold, other things equal, and its value would go down, and commodity prices would rise. Cut the amount of gold in half, other things equal, and its value would rise, and commodity prices would fall. As long as gold as money and gold as bullion were interchangeable, without expense, 23 grains of gold in one form could not be appreciably more or less valuable than 23 grains in the other. This is what would be called "standard commodity money," and would be essentially like our United States gold coins as they existed prior to March, 1933. The tribe would be on the gold standard—a subject discussed in Chapter VII.

[1] The United States' gold dollar prior to the breakdown of the gold standard in early 1933 contained 23.22 grains of fine gold.

Importance of Velocity Factor

The importance of V in the equation $\left(P=\frac{MV}{T}\right)$ is often not appreciated. Ten thousand gold dollars in circulation in a tribal territory like the one assumed in the illustration, which pass from hand to hand on the average ten times a year, do twice the amount of exchange money work that the same amount of money would do if it passed from hand to hand on an average only five times a year. The efficiency of money, like that of a freight car, depends not only upon the load that it is carrying at any particular time, but also upon the rate at which it is moving.

Broadly speaking, in communities where the population is largely concentrated, where means of communication and transportation are good, where business men are alert and active, and where confidence in the business situation and prospects are strong, the rate of monetary turnover is much greater than in communities where the population is widely scattered, as, for example, agricultural communities, where means of communication and transportation are meager, or in communities where business men are inactive, or confidence in the business situation is low.

Then again, in a community where the money is depreciating rapidly in value and where the public is expecting it to continue to depreciate in the future, the rate of monetary turnover is greatly stimulated, because people wish to get rid of their money quickly before it depreciates in their hands—in other words, to buy goods with their money before prices rise further; and this artificially increased rate of monetary turnover in turn stimulates still further monetary depreciation. While, therefore, increasing business confidence speeds up the circulation of money, decreasing confidence in the money itself also increases the velocity of circulation. In this connection, it is important to distinguish between these two kinds of confidence. When, on the other hand, money is appreciating in value and the price level is falling, people hold back their money in anticipation of a further decline of prices. The rate of monetary turnover is thus artificially retarded and this retardation in turn increases still further the monetary appreciation or the decline in commodity prices (P). Striking examples of this situation occurred in the currency history of Germany,

Austria and Russia during the European War and the years immediately following.

In Chapter IV will be discussed the quantity theory of money as it applies in a régime in which payments are made largely by bank checks.

BIBLIOGRAPHY

THE DETERMINATION OF INDIVIDUAL PRICES

Böhm-Bawerk, Eugen, *The Positive Theory of Capital;* London, Macmillan and Company, 1891.

Fetter, Frank A., *Economic Principles;* New York, The Century Company, 1915.

Hobson, John A., "*Böhm-Bawerk* Positive Theory of Capital," *Economics of Distribution;* New York, The Macmillan Company, 1900

Kemmerer, Edwin Walter, *Money and Prices;* New York, Henry Holt and Company, 1909.

——, "The Higgling of the Market," *Quarterly Journal of Economics,* Vol. XVII, pp. 607–677.

Smart, William, *An Introduction to the Theory of Value;* London, Macmillan and Company, 1891.

INDEX NUMBERS

Brown, Theodore H., *Laboratory Handbook of Statistical Methods;* New York, McGraw-Hill Book Company, 1931.

Chaddock, R. E., *Principles and Methods of Statistics;* New York, Houghton Mifflin Company, 1925.

Copeland, Morris A., "Special Purpose Indexes for the Equation of Exchange for the United States, 1919–1927," *Journal of the American Statistical Association,* June, 1929, p. 109.

Day, E. E., "An Index of the Physical Volume of Production," *Review of Economic Statistics,* September, 1920–January, 1921, Vols. 2 and 3.

Fisher, Irving, *The Making of Index Numbers;* Boston, Houghton Mifflin Company, 1922.

Jerome, Harry, *Statistical Methods;* New York, Harper and Brothers, 1924.

Kelley, Truman L., *Statistical Method;* New York, The Macmillan Company, 1923.

King, Willford I., *Index Numbers Elucidated;* New York, Longmans, Green and Company, 1930.

Mitchell, Wesley C., *Index Numbers of Wholesale Prices in the United States and Foreign Countries, 1921;* United States Government Report (Bureau of Labor Statistics, No. 284, revision of Bulletin No. 173).

Smith, James G., *Elementary Statistics;* New York, Henry Holt and Company, 1934.

Snyder, Carl, *Business Cycles and Business Measurements;* New York, The Macmillan Company, 1927.

FUNDAMENTAL FORCES DETERMINING THE PRICE LEVEL

Anderson, B. M., *The Value of Money;* New York, The Macmillan Company, 1917. (This book is opposed to the position taken in this Chapter.)

Edie, Lionel G., *Money, Bank Credit and Prices;* New York, Harper and Brothers, 1928.

Fisher, Irving, *The Purchasing Power of Money;* New York, The Macmillan Company, 1911.

Kemmerer, Edwin Walter, *Money and Credit Instruments in Their Relation to General Prices*, Second Edition; New York, Henry Holt and Company, 1909.

——, *Modern Currency Reforms;* New York, The Macmillan Company, 1916.

Keynes, John Maynard, *A Treatise on Money*, 2 volumes; New York, Harcourt, Brace and Company, 1930.

Sumner, William G., *A History of American Currency;* New York, Henry Holt and Company, 1874.

Walker, Francis A., *Money;* New York, Henry Holt and Company, 1878.

CHAPTER III

THE ELEMENTARY BANKING FUNCTIONS

This chapter is devoted to a brief explanation of the commercial banking functions of discount, deposit and note issue; and these functions are explained at this point because a knowledge of them is necessary for an understanding of the subjects to be discussed later in this volume. The subject of banking, however, is the field of Volume II.

A commercial bank is a concern which makes a business of receiving the funds of others on general deposit and of using them, together with its own capital funds, as a basis for credit which it lends chiefly in the form of deposits and/or circulating notes. The principal business of a bank is lending credit. It makes funds available in the present and in exchange it takes claims for funds available in the future.

Credit

The word *credit* has a variety of meanings; the Oxford Dictionary distinguishes twenty-one. Etymologically, it comes from the Latin word *credere*, meaning "to believe" or "to trust," and it always carries with it the idea of trust or confidence placed in one person by another. One meaning of the cognate Italian word *credito* is "reputation." Here we are concerned only with the restricted usage of the term *credit* that relates to banking operations.

From the standpoint of a bank, credit may be viewed from two different angles, that of the bank as a creditor and that of the bank as a debtor. As a creditor, the bank is concerned with "the capacity for credit" of its customers, actual and prospective. It wants to know how much it can safely lend to each customer and the amount and character of the collateral it should require. These are questions that call for an understanding of the customer's moral character and business ability and demand a thorough knowledge of the nature of his business and of his assets and liabilities, subjects to be considered later. In this chapter we are concerned only with bank credit from the standpoint of the bank as a debtor.

A bank may lend its credit in a number of ways, of which the principal are: (1) deposits, (2) bank notes, (3) current account credits and (4) acceptances. The subject of bank acceptances will be discussed later. The current account credit, that is, a credit to be utilized by overdrafts on current account, is not employed in the United States, though it is common in most other countries. It will be considered in connection with the subject of banking in other countries. The nature of deposit and bank-note credit may best be explained by assuming a bank comparatively free from governmental restrictions as regards deposits, bank-note issues, and reserves—a bank similar to the First or the Second United States Bank—and by following a few simple operations through the balance sheet.

Deposits [1]

Let us assume that the bank is organized with a million dollars of cash paid-up capital. It expends $150,000 for a banking house and $15,000 for furniture and fixtures. When it opens for business, its balance sheet stands, therefore, as follows:

Resources		Liabilities	
Banking House	$ 150,000	Capital Stock	$1,000,000
Furniture and Fixtures .	$ 15,000		
Cash in Vault	$ 835,000		
Total	$1,000,000	Total	$1,000,000

[1] Classified according to the ownership of the funds, modern banking practice recognizes three broad types of deposits; viz., the general deposit, the special deposit and the specific deposit.

The general deposit is by far the most important class of bank deposits and is the class referred to throughout the text of this chapter. It constitutes a debt payable in lawful money by the bank to the depositor or to the depositor's order. The money which the bank holds as a reserve against its deposits and with which it cashes its deposits belongs to the bank and not to the depositor. Legal title to the money (and other assets of the bank) resides in the bank, but the depositor is a creditor of the bank to the amount of his deposit, which is payable to him according to the terms of the prevailing banking law and banking practice.

A special deposit is essentially a transfer of money or other property to a bank for safe keeping. Legal title continues to reside in the depositor and is not transferred to the bank. A special deposit exists "where the whole contract is that the thing deposited shall be safely kept, and that identical thing returned to the depositor."

A specific deposit arises "when money is deposited to pay a specified check drawn or to be drawn, or for any purpose other than mere safe keeping, or entry on general [deposit] account." In the specific deposit "the title remains in the depositor until the bank pays the person for whom it is intended, or promises to pay it to him. . . . 'A deposit is general unless expressly made special' or specific." Cf., Morse, I, pp. 413–416.

By the end of the first week the bank has received deposits of cash amounting to $140,000; and has discounted for various customers $500,000 of sixty-day notes at 6 per cent, the borrower in each case having left the entire proceeds of his discounted note on deposit with the bank. The cash deposits of $140,000 add that amount to the "cash in vault" as a resource, and the same amount as a deposit on the liability side. A discount charge of $5,000 (amounting to 6 per cent for 60 days) of the $500,000 was made by the bank for discounting the $500,000 of notes. This discount is taken out in advance and the amount is entered as undivided profit among the liabilities and is, like the bank's capital, a liability of the bank to its stockholders. The balance, $495,000, is entered as deposits. The balance sheet then stands as follows:

Resources		Liabilities	
Banking House	$ 150,000	Capital Stock	$1,000,000
Furniture and Fixtures	$ 15,000	Undivided Profit	$ 5,000
Cash in Vault	$ 975,000	Deposits	$ 635,000
Loans and Discounts	$ 500,000		
Total	$1,640,000	Total	$1,640,000

It will be observed that of the $635,000 of deposits, $495,000 represents no cash payment to the bank whatsoever, but is merely a book entry placing to the credit of depositors this amount, which is the proceeds of the promissory notes which the bank has discounted for them. The bank has merely loaned these customers its credit, which they may check against as they will. Suppose that, during the next few days, there are a large number of applications from responsible business men for loans and that the bank discounts for them $2,000,000 of paper, this time all 90-day promissory notes, at 6 per cent, the entire proceeds (amounting to $1,970,000) being left for the time being entirely on deposit. Here the bank is lending and placing to the borrowers' credit on deposit account $1,970,000, although its books showed at the time the loans were made that it had only $975,000 of cash in its possession. These deposits, moreover, are payable in cash on demand. After this operation, the balance sheet stands as follows:

Resources		Liabilities	
Banking House	$ 150,000	Capital Stock	$1,000,000
Furniture and Fixtures	$ 15,000	Undivided Profit	$ 35,000
Cash in Vault	$ 975,000	Deposits	$2,605,000
Loans and Discounts	$2,500,000		
Total	$3,640,000	Total	$3,640,000

The bank has now loaned $2,500,000, although its total receipts of cash from the beginning have been but $1,140,000 and it has spent $165,000 of that for the banking house, furniture and fixtures. It still has on hand $975,000 in cash, but it owes depositors $2,605,000. Obviously, if the depositors should all exercise their legal right to draw out at once the full amount of their deposits, the bank would not have enough money to pay much more than a third of the amount demanded. There are sufficient resources, if they were all turned into cash, to meet all possible demands, paying every dollar of deposits; but the resources are largely in the form of customers' notes that will not be due for some time, while depositors' demands may be for cash.

As a matter of fact, however, the bank knows that there is little likelihood that any very large percentage of deposits will be withdrawn in any one day. It, furthermore, knows that every day there will be receipts as well as withdrawals, since its customers will ordinarily deposit the money and checks they receive over their counters each day. The money the bank receives over its counters in a day will often exceed that which it is called to pay out; while checks on one depositor's account which are deposited by another depositor will cancel each other so far as the balance sheet of the bank is concerned, the transfers being effected merely by debit and credit entries on the books of the bank. The result is that a cash reserve equivalent to a small percentage of deposits is likely to be ample to meet all demands of depositors and to leave an adequate margin of safety.

Ordinarily, a borrower discounting paper at a bank does not leave the entire proceeds of the loan on deposit long. He usually checks against the new credit at once and gradually reduces it; and, as he does so, the bank loses some of its cash and has its percentage of reserve reduced. The bank in our illustration is still carrying a cash reserve against deposits of over 37 per cent, despite its large loans.

Let us assume that, through presentation of checks over the bank's counter, $475,000 of cash is withdrawn. The balance sheet then stands as follows:

Resources		Liabilities	
Banking House	$ 150,000	Capital Stock	$1,000,000
Furniture and Fixtures	$ 15,000	Undivided Profit	$ 35,000
Cash in Vault	$ 500,000	Deposits	$2,130,000
Loans and Discounts	$2,500,000		
Total	$3,165,000	Total	$3,165,000

The percentage reserve is reduced from 37 to about 23.

The less rapidly a borrower reduces the deposit credit representing the proceeds of his loan, and the larger the deposit balance he maintains at the bank, the more profitable his account will be to the bank. In a sense, the bank is having its cake and eating it, too. It is lending the depositor at interest its own credit, namely, the right to draw money on demand, and then keeping part of the credit it has loaned. Borrowers who withdraw the proceeds of their loans quickly and normally carry low deposit balances in proportion to the amounts they borrow are not likely to receive such favorable treatment from banks as customers who keep substantial balances in proportion to their loan accounts. The latter class are the most profitable to the bank. Often banks make the maintenance of a deposit balance of a certain minimum or average amount a condition to granting a certain line of credit.

Bank Notes

The second important form of bank credit is bank-note credit. From the standpoint of the issuing bank, notes of the simplest type of asset currency are essentially the same as demand deposits; although, from the standpoint of the public, there are important differences that will be considered later. Such a bank note is, like the bank deposit, a promise to pay lawful money on demand. Like a deposit, it requires of the bank the maintenance of an adequate cash reserve, and, like a deposit, it is readily transferable from person to person. The deposit is an implied promise to pay, evidenced ordinarily by a pass book, the payment to be made usually against checks properly drawn and signed in accordance with banking law and established practice; the note is a promise to pay engraved on a piece of paper which circulates as money. Like the check, drawn against a deposit, the bank note must be redeemed by the issuing bank in lawful money when presented over its counter for redemption.

Under these circumstances, it should obviously be a matter of little difference to a bank issuing such bank notes, whether a borrower takes the proceeds of his loan in the form of a deposit credit which he can check against or in the form of bank notes which he can use directly as money. The similarity of these two forms of bank credit may be made clearer by carrying through the balance sheet a few operations involving bank notes.

Suppose that, among the customers of the bank, there are several factories employing laborers whom they pay weekly in "cash." These factories, we will suppose, have sold heavily on credit and, finding themselves short of ready funds for their payroll, borrow of the bank $500,000 by discounting their 60-day notes at 6 per cent. They take $300,000 of the proceeds of their loan at once in the form of bank notes, which they pay over entirely to their laborers in the Saturday pay envelopes, and they leave the balance ($195,000) on deposit. The balance sheet of the bank will then stand as follows:

Resources		Liabilities	
Banking House	$ 150,000	Capital Stock	$1,000,000
Furniture and Fixtures	$ 15,000	Undivided Profit	$ 40,000
Cash in Vault	$ 500,000	Deposits	$2,325,000
Loans and Discounts	$3,000,000	Bank Notes	$ 300,000
Total	$3,665,000	Total	$3,665,000

The percentage of reserve against demand liabilities (formerly only against deposits, but now against deposits and bank notes) will be reduced from 23 to about 19. So long as these bank notes remain in circulation, namely, in the tills of merchants and in the pockets of the people, they make no demand on the bank's cash. The bank, in giving its notes to the borrowers, has in effect swapped its non-interest-bearing demand promises to pay, that circulate as money, for the factories' interest-bearing time promises to pay, that do not circulate as money. In this way, the bank lends its credit and realizes its profit. Whether the bank's own demand promises to pay are in the form of its own bank notes or of deposits obviously makes very little difference to the bank. If bank notes to the amount of $200,000 should be deposited at the bank by laborers receiving them, the bank-note item in the balance sheet would be reduced to $200,000 and the deposit item would be increased to $2,525,000; but neither the total demand liabilities nor the cash reserve would be affected, and the reserve percentage would, therefore, remain unchanged at about 19. Returning to the balance sheet as given above, if another factory in the town should need $200,000 for payroll purposes and should obtain them by checking against its deposit account with the bank, deposits would be reduced from $2,325,000 to $2,125,000 and bank notes would be increased from $300,000 to $500,000, but the bank's total liabilities and its reserve percentage would remain entirely unchanged. It is only when bank notes outstanding and deposits combined are raised or lowered in relation to the cash on hand, that reserve percentages are affected. The interchange of deposit liabilities and note liabilities has no effect on the bank's reserve position.[1]

Deposit vs. Bank-Note Credit

Although these two forms of circulating bank credit are fundamentally the same from the bank's point of view, they are different in important particulars from the public point of view. Let a stranger in any city try to make purchases with his checks and he will soon recognize that a check, however good, is a very different thing from a bank note. Or, let anyone compare a check with a bank note in its usefulness for buying a railroad ticket or in buying stamps at the post office. The bank note in a sound and well-organized banking system is accepted everywhere in the country as money, without reference to the character or the credit of the person who is paying it, even though the place of payment may be thousands of miles away from the office of the issuing bank and although the bank may be entirely unknown to the person receiving the note. While this is not true in countries with defective bank-note currency, it is normally true in advanced countries. The check is accepted only when the recipient has confidence in the character and credit of the person paying it. The receiver of the bank note is likely to pass it on to someone else in purchasing goods or paying for services, and so it often remains "away from home" (namely, from the issuing bank)—sometimes very far from home—for long periods of time, passing through the hands of many people who know little or nothing of the standing of the issuing bank or, perhaps, of any other bank. Such a bank note is money.

Bank notes and other forms of money, as contrasted with bank deposits circulating through the instrumentality of checks, so-called "deposit currency," are used much more extensively by the poor than by the well-to-do. Ordinarily, a check makes one payment, is deposited by the recipient at his bank, and is then "kept home" or "sent home" and canceled. Its life is of brief duration. People expect to scrutinize checks when they are offered and, for the purpose of protecting themselves, they usually deposit or cash

[1] This illustration, it should be repeated, refers to a simple type of asset bank-note currency, and the operations mentioned would not be possible in this form, under a bank-note system of the type existing in the United States at the present time.

the checks promptly, thus "sending them home." It would be an unendurable nuisance to trade if bank notes had to be treated in the same way. Bank-note holders, furthermore, are not in so good a position to protect themselves as are depositors. One selects a bank in which to keep his account, presumably with some knowledge of the character of its officers and of its financial standing. When there are many banks of issue, as in the United States, he is not in position to examine the financial standing of all the banks whose bank notes are paid to him. In case of bank failure, the deposit loss is likely to fall in the main on financially broader shoulders than is the bank-note loss; although the average amount of the loss per creditor is likely to be much larger for depositors than for holders of bank notes. Because of these and other differences, from the public point of view, between deposits and bank notes, the government usually throws special safeguards around the issuance of bank notes as a means of protecting the public.

In many jurisdictions bank notes enjoy a prior lien on the assets of the issuing bank so that, in case of bank failure, bank-note holders must receive their pay in full before anything is paid to depositors or stockholders. Special guarantee funds are sometimes set aside for the protection of note holders in case of bank failures. Legal reserve requirements often exist against notes where they do not exist against deposits; and, when they exist for both, they are sometimes higher for notes than for deposits. The pledging with the government of some special form of asset, like the United States bonds against national bank notes in this country, has been a common device for the protection of note holders. In recent years there has been a strong tendency to give a monopoly of the bank-note issue privilege to central banks, which are closely identified with the financial interests of the state, and whose quasi-public character is recognized. This is now the situation in most of the leading countries of the world.

The Bank Reserve

A very important element in bank credit is the bank reserve. The term *bank reserve* in the United States is used loosely and in a variety of meanings. We speak of "cash reserve," "deposited reserve," "legal reserve," "actual reserve" and "secondary reserve." In the strictest and narrowest sense of the term, although not in the sense in which the term is most commonly used, a true bank reserve would consist solely of legal tender money actually in the possession of the bank, for it is only in such money that a bank may legally pay its creditors—depositors and note holders—if they so insist. These obligations, moreover, for the most part are demand obligations, and failure to meet them on demand is an act of insolvency. All kinds of money in the United States today are legal tender.

From the previous discussion of the balance sheet, the function of the bank reserve has been made evident. The term *bank reserve*, therefore, as used in this chapter,[1] means the money which a bank carries in its own vaults and tills for the purpose of meeting demands upon it for cash on the part of its customers. Cash in reserve does not directly yield the bank a profit and therefore, other things equal, the larger the proportion of its assets a bank keeps in the form of "idle" reserve, the less the profit it makes. The profit-making motive, therefore, continually operates to drive reserves down to the minimum. On the other hand, a bank is a credit institution and its own reputation for strength and solvency is its greatest asset. Anything that impairs that reputation drives away customers and tends to reduce profits. The financial standing of a bank in a community is easily weakened and, when once weakened, can only slowly and with difficulty be restored. The failure of a bank to meet the demands of its depositors and note holders (except in times of legal moratoria) is an act of insolvency and, even if it is only temporary, is a serious blow to a bank's prestige. These considerations compel banks to carry sufficient reserves to meet all probable demands and, in addition, to afford a substantial margin of safety. There is here a continual conflict of motives, immediate profits on the one hand and safety, prestige and long-run profits on the other hand.

Because experience has shown that many banks in their zeal for immediate profit will reduce their reserves to dangerously low figures, thereby imperiling the funds entrusted to them and threatening the country's whole delicate credit structure, and because the banks which do this are for a time dangerous competitors of more conservative banks which are better protecting the public interests, we have found it desirable in the United States, as have people in some other countries, to impose by law legal reserve minima. Such minima are enforced by the laws of the

[1] The term will be employed in a broader sense later.

Federal Government and also by the laws of most of our states. They virtually say to the banks: "Each bank must decide for itself above a reasonable limit what percentage of reserve it needs. This percentage will vary from bank to bank, according to the character of its customers and the type of business it chiefly serves. For each bank it will also vary from season to season, according to the seasonal changes in the business needs of the community. But there are limits beyond which no bank can safely go without endangering the public interest, and the rules of the banking game are that those limits shall not be passed, except perhaps temporarily under emergency conditions and subject to certain penalties." In Volume II the facts concerning legal reserves and actual reserves in different classes of banks will be considered. We are here concerned only with the broad general principles involved.

BIBLIOGRAPHY

Dunbar, Charles F., *The Theory and History of Banking;* New York, G. P. Putnam's Sons, 1917.

Morse, John T., Jr., *A Treatise on the Law of Banks and Banking*, Fifth Edition, revised and enlarged by James N. Carter, 2 volumes; Boston, Little, Brown and Company, 1917.

Philipps, Chester A., *Bank Credit;* New York, The Macmillan Company, 1920.

Westerfield, Ray B., *Banking Principles and Practice;* New York, The Ronald Press, 1924.

CHAPTER IV

THE QUANTITY THEORY OF MONEY

This chapter is a continuation of Chapter II, which dealt with the law of demand and supply and the value of money, the further discussion of which was of necessity postponed until the reader could be made familiar with the elementary functions of a bank discussed in Chapter III.

In Chapter II a régime was assumed in which money was the only medium of exchange. This, of course, was an assumption contrary to fact for any modern society, and particularly so for advanced countries where the great bulk of the business is performed by means of credit instruments.

Negotiable Credit Instruments

As regards their relationship to the price level, negotiable credit instruments may be grouped under two heads: (1) instruments of postponed payment, and (2) instruments payable in money on demand.

Negotiable instruments of postponed payment, from the economic point of view, do not pay for goods and services or liquidate debts; rather, they express and carry debts. Typical examples of this kind of credit instrument are promissory notes and time bills of exchange. *A*, for example, buys merchandise of *B*, and gives him a promissory note payable in 90 days. *B* holds the note until maturity, when *A* pays the amount by cash or by check. The note in such a case, from the economic point of view, is not a means of payment but an instrument for postponing payment. The means of payment is the cash or check by which the final settlement is made. Since instruments of postponed payment do not call for payment until a future date, they necessarily involve an element of interest, whether they call for interest on their face or not, because in either case the present value of the instrument is the amount due at maturity discounted at the current rate of interest for the period the instrument has yet to run.

> "Interest-bearing documents," said Jevons, " . . . are held in as large quantities as possible, because the longer they are held the more interest accrues. . . . They may be bought and sold for money, but are not money themselves. They rather necessitate than replace the use of money. . . ." [1]

Negotiable instruments of postponed payment are, therefore, best considered as commodities to be bought and sold, and not as media of exchange. Their prices are elements in the general price level, and vary inversely with market interest and discount rates.[2]

The second class of credit instruments, namely, negotiable instruments payable in money on demand, is the class with which we are especially concerned here. Such instruments consist principally of checks, drafts and sight bills of exchange. Their characters for the purpose at hand are essentially the same. A draft may be looked upon as a check drawn by one bank upon another, and a sight bill of exchange as a check drawn by one individual or corporation upon another, other than a bank. For convenience they will all be included under the term *checks*.

Influence of Credit upon the Price Level

A person can buy goods to the extent of his money and credit combined, and a sound credit demand for goods is just as effective in determining their value as is a like money demand. The statement of John Stuart Mill is apropos.

> "The amount of purchasing power which a person can exercise is composed of all the money in his possession or due to him, and of all his credit. For exercising the whole of this power he finds a sufficient motive only under peculiar circumstances; but he always possesses it; and the portion of it which he at any time does exercise, is the measure of the effect which he produces on price. . . . Credit . . . has exactly the same purchasing power with money; and as money tells upon prices not simply in proportion to its amount, but to its amount multiplied by the number of times it changes hands, so also does credit; and credit transferable from hand to hand is in that proportion more potent, than credit which only performs one purchase." [3]

On the other hand, every exchange performed by means of checks represents an economy in the use of money, and by lessening

[1] *Money and the Mechanism of Exchange*, pp. 240–241.

[2] If, for example, the market rate of discount is 6 per cent, the discounted price of a 90-day note for $1,000 is $985; if the rate is 4 per cent, the discounted price is $990.

[3] *Principles of Political Economy*, Vol. II, pp. 66, 75.

the demand for money affects the money side of the equation, $P = \frac{MV}{T}$. The demand for commodities expressed in the use of checks and the economy effected in the use of money are, other things equal, proportionate to the amount of the checks multiplied by the rapidity of their respective circulations.[1]

Convertible Paper Money

The influence of checks upon prices is not essentially different from the influence of convertible government notes or bank notes. Let us assume, for example, a country with a given amount of business, a given price level, a given rate of monetary circulation, and a circulating medium consisting of $2,500,000,000 of gold coin. Suppose that the government should withdraw from circulation $500,000,000 of this gold coin and make of it a gold reserve against which it should issue $1,500,000,000 of government notes, similar, for example, to the Dominion notes of Canada or to the United States "greenbacks." The notes would be secured by the reserve fund and by the government's credit. The monetary circulation would be suddenly increased by one billion dollars. If the public had confidence in the government and in the business situation, the notes would circulate freely, prices would rise, exchange would turn against the country, and, business remaining otherwise unchanged, an amount of gold somewhat less than $1,000,000,000 would be exported from the country and go into the arts, yielding in return an equivalent amount in foreign commodities and domestic gold products. This return would be a net gain to the community. The billion and a half dollars of government notes would circulate exactly on a par with the gold coins, and, in being exchanged against commodities, would affect their prices in the same way that the gold coins would. The effect of such an issue of circulating notes upon prices would evidently be no different if it were a banking institution instead of the government that established the reserve and issued the notes. Nor would the reason for the existence of the bank's credit any more than that for the

[1] This statement requires one qualification: there are some check transfers, as for example, the cashing of checks and many transfers between banks and between banks and clearing houses, which do not affect the exchange of commodities, but rather owe their existence to the credit mechanism of exchange itself, of which they are part. Such checks should not be included in any statement of the equation of exchange.

existence of the government's credit affect the principle. The important consideration in either case would be, that the public had confidence that the institution, whether government or bank, which issued the notes, always could and always would maintain their parity with gold. Furthermore, the effect upon prices would be no different if the bank, instead of issuing notes against this $500,000,000 gold reserve, should hold the gold as a reserve against deposits, which in turn should give rise to a deposit currency or check circulation equivalent to that represented by the circulation of the government notes or the bank notes in the previous illustrations.

The Equation of Exchange Extended to Include Deposit Currency

If we designate the average price of all economic goods exchanged for money and checks by the symbol P (using the concept of average price described on page 32), if we designate the volume of checks paid for goods and services by C, and the average rate of turnover of the checks so paid (weighted according to their respective amounts) by E, if we designate the number of units of goods sold by T, and if we use the terms M and V in the senses previously described (pp. 32 and 33), the price equation, with the use of checks assumed, would stand as follows:

$$P = \frac{MV + CE}{T}.$$

Most checks make only one purchase and then die. The payee of a check rarely passes another person's check on to a third party in the purchase of goods. Almost always he deposits daily the checks he receives, and makes his payments with his own checks. The percentage of checks drawn that are endorsed by the payee and paid to a third party for purchases is so small as to be negligible. We may, therefore, safely assume that the rate of check turnover, E, is unity, which would transform the price equation to the form:

$$P = \frac{MV + C}{T}.$$

The check is the medium through which a bank deposit circulates, and, in recognition of this fact, check circulation is usually called "deposit currency." The efficiency of bank deposits as media of exchange, like the efficiency of money, must be interpreted in terms of their rate or velocity of turnover. A merchant, depositing daily in his deposit account his money and check receipts, would have a deposit turnover of twelve times a year if his daily credit balance should average $5,000 and his total payments by checks drawn against the account for goods and services for the year should be $60,000. Here we have the concept of "the rate of turnover of bank deposits" or of "bank deposit velocity." If, in the country as a whole, for a given year the average amount of individual and government deposits subject to check, which we shall designate by D, should be $20 billion, and if the volume of checks, C, drawn against these deposits and paid out for goods, should be $600 billion, the rate of deposit turnover (which we shall designate by R) would obviously be 30. This rate of deposit turnover is larger in years of active business than in years of slack business, it is larger when business confidence is high than when it is low, it is larger in times of liquid credit than in times of so-called "frozen credit," it is larger when the value of the monetary unit is rapidly depreciating than when it is stable or appreciating, it is usually many times larger in speculative centers, like the Wall Street district of New York City, than in commercial and manufacturing cities, and is much larger in cities of the latter classes than in agricultural communities.

The following tables show the average annual rate of deposit turnover as computed by the Federal Reserve authorities for: (1) a large group of American cities exclusive of New York City and (2) New York City:[1]

Average Annual Rate of Turnover or Velocity of Bank Deposits

140 Centers (Outside of New York City)

Years	*Average*
1919	34.4
1920	35.8
1921	31.4
1922	30.8
1923	32.4
1924	31.5
1925	32.7
1926	33.9
1927	35.0
1928	37.9

[1] Compare chart, *infra*, p. 113.

AVERAGE ANNUAL RATE OF TURNOVER OR VELOCITY OF BANK DEPOSITS—*Continued*

140 CENTERS (OUTSIDE OF NEW YORK CITY)

Years	*Average*
1929	41.6
1930	34.9
1931	28.8
1932	25.4
1933 [a]	24.9
1934	22.7

NEW YORK CITY

Years	*Average*
1919	54.3
1920	52.4
1921	50.2
1922	55.0
1923	56.3
1924	55.0
1925	61.7
1926	67.1
1927	74.9
1928	93.5
1929	111.9
1930	69.5
1931	46.2
1932	33.1
1933	30.3
1934	27.8

[a] Since "the bank holiday" of early March, 1933, the figures cover only 130 cities.

From the above explanation it will be seen that the C (of the formula as given on page 51) is equal to DR, so that in its finally revised form the formula would read:

$$P = \frac{MV + DR}{T}.$$

RELATIONSHIP BETWEEN VOLUME OF MONEY IN CIRCULATION AND DEPOSITS

What relationship, if any, exists between D and M, namely, between bank deposits subject to check and the amount of money in circulation (exclusive of that held in bank reserves against checking deposits)? More particularly, is there any reason to believe that, as a broad general proposition and under normal conditions, D tends to be a function of M, increasing as M increases and decreasing as M decreases? To this latter question an affirmative answer may be given, both on theoretical grounds and on the evidence of statistical studies that have been made by the writer, by Irving Fisher and by others.[1]

Two facts tend to give deposits a more or less fixed ratio to money in circulation. They are: (1) the fact that the conveniences and customs of the public in a given state of banking development and banking law tend to the maintenance of a constant proportion between the amount of money in active circulation and the amount in bank reserves; and (2) the fact that, under like conditions, the interests of bankers tend to cause them to maintain under given economic conditions fairly constant ratios of cash reserves to deposit liabilities.

Let us consider briefly each of these tendencies. The first tendency has been well stated by Irving Fisher:[2]

> " . . . individuals, firms, and corporations preserve more or less definite ratios between their cash transactions and their check transactions, and also between their money and deposit balances. These ratios are determined by motives of individual convenience and habit. In general, business firms use money for wage payments, and for small miscellaneous transactions included under the term 'petty cash'; while for settlements with each other they usually prefer checks. These preferences are so strong that we could not imagine them overridden except temporarily and to a small degree. A business firm would hardly pay car fares with checks and liquidate its large liabilities with cash. Each person strikes an equilibrium between his use of the two methods of payment, and does not greatly disturb it except for short periods of time. He keeps his stock of money or his bank balance in constant adjustment to the payments he makes in money or by check. Whenever his stock of money becomes relatively small and his bank balance relatively large, he cashes a check. In the opposite event, he deposits cash. In this way he is constantly converting one of the two media of exchange into the other. A private individual usually feeds his purse from his bank account; a retail commercial firm usually feeds its bank account from its till. The bank acts as intermediary for both. . . .
>
> "There is, then, a relation of convenience and custom between check and cash circulation, and a more or less stable ratio between the deposit balance of the average man or corporation and the stock of money kept in pocket or till. . . . If that ratio is disturbed temporarily, there will come into play a tendency to restore it. Individuals will deposit surplus cash, or they will cash surplus deposits."

[1] Cf., Kemmerer, E. W., *Money and Prices*, pp. 139–149; and Fisher, Irving, *The Purchasing Power of Money*, Chap. XII.

[2] *The Purchasing Power of Money*, pp. 50–52.

Relationship of Bank Reserves to Volume of Deposits

Next, let us consider the tendency for the maintenance of a more or less constant percentage of bank reserves to deposits. A bank, we have found, is a concern the principal business of which is to lend its credit. Its profits come largely from the fact that, in any particular period of time, it is called upon to pay only a small proportion of its deposit obligations, and that it can, therefore, lend out at interest a large part of the funds entrusted to it by depositors. The right to receive money from the bank on demand, and the privilege of transferring that right to others by means of checks, are, for most purposes, as valuable to the depositor as the possession of actual money. Inasmuch as money lent out yields the bank interest, while money in the tills (and reserve money deposited in the central bank or banks) does not, the bank's cash reserve and its non-interest-bearing deposited reserve tend to be reduced, by the desire for profits, to the lowest point consistent with safety. The percentage of reserve which a bank needs to hold against its deposits varies with the bank's location, character and the sizes of its individual deposits, its reputation, the general financial condition of the community it serves, the state of business confidence at the time and the reserve requirements, if any, imposed by law. It also varies from season to season according to the seasonal fluctuations in the production and trade of the community the bank serves. But a bank must at all times maintain a sufficient reserve to meet all probable demands. A considerable margin of safety, moreover, is desirable; for failure promptly to meet its obligations means either a damaged reputation or bankruptcy. The result is that banks find it to their advantage to maintain reserves well in excess of the net amounts they are actually likely to be called upon to pay out. These reserves are the necessary conditions to the billions of dollars of check transactions that take place daily. The amount of money continually tied up in bank reserves for the support of bank deposits is withdrawn from the community's active circulating media, and accordingly lessens the supply of money available for cash transactions to the extent of the amount so withdrawn multiplied by what would have been its rate of turnover were it in actual circulation. These bank reserves, or cash balances, are important stones in the foundation upon which our vast superstructure of deposit currency is built. Deposits and checks represent the right to demand money and must be paid in money if the payee so desires. Deposit currency may render money five, ten or a hundred times more efficient, and in doing so may greatly change the value of the money unit; but the fact still remains true, that prices, however high or low they may be, are the value of commodities in terms of the value of this money unit.

Each banker finds from experience what percentage of reserves to deposits it is advisable for him to maintain; and, within the legal reserve limits, if any are imposed, he attempts to order his business so that his reserve shall not depart far, for any considerable time, from this most desirable proportion. If it tends to exceed this proportion, he will, in his desire for profits, reduce his percentage reserve by increasing his loans and buying more securities. If, on the other hand, the percentage of reserve tends to fall below this most desirable proportion, the banker, in the interest of safety, will increase his reserve percentages by curtailing or calling in loans, by rediscounting paper or by selling securities. Experience has shown, however, that this process of adjustment often takes place very slowly, particularly in times of great business depression.

As a result of these forces every bank arrives at what it considers a fairly normal percentage of reserves to deposits—a norm that will be higher in some seasons of the year than in others—and the average of these individual bank normal reserve percentages (weighted according to the respective amounts of money in the different reserves) would give the normal percentage of reserve for the country at any time. In the absence of changes in the banking laws of the country, or of banking practices, or in the relative use of checks and cash as media of exchange, or of business confidence, this normal percentage, with due allowance for seasonal changes, would tend to persist, regardless of changes from year to year in the amount of money in the country or changes in the physical volume of trade.

To use the language of the formula, an increase in M would, other things equal, tend to result in a proportionate increase in the amount of bank reserves; while an increase in the amount of bank reserves, since the percentage of reserves to deposits would tend to persist, would tend to cause a proportionate increase in D through bank loan expansion. If, for example, we suppose M to be doubled, then D would also tend to be doubled and the doubling of M and D would be accompanied by a doubling of P; provided, of course, that the factors V, R and T remained unchanged. The opposite would take place if M were cut in half. There is no reason why a change in M or D should result in *enduring* changes in V, R or T. Except for short transitional periods—a subject to be discussed later (p. 58)—these latter factors are independent variables.

Assumptions Underlying Quantity Theory

Static conditions, like those assumed above, are, of course, never realized in the business world. Changes in banking laws from time to time may result in great changes in normal reserve percentages, as did the banking legislation in the United States which created and developed the Federal Reserve system in 1914 and the years immediately following. Important changes in banking organization, in the character of bank assets, in the average size of banks and in the attitude of the public toward the use of bank checks and cash would, of course, change the normal average percentages of reserves to deposit liabilities. Like any natural law, the quantity theory of money which we are here stating merely tells what will happen under certain assumed conditions. It is a statement of a fundamental principle that works under complex and widely varying economic conditions. To the extent that conditions are different from those assumed, allowance must be made in applying the theory. To the student of money it provides a useful brief formulation of the fundamental factors that directly determine the general price level.

In the proviso, "other things being equal," which must be so strongly emphasized in every statement of the quantity theory, two factors demand special emphasis. One is business confidence in general, and the other is the public's confidence in the country's money itself. These two factors will be considered briefly.

Business Confidence

When business confidence is high, a bank can safely get along with smaller percentage reserve than when it is low. There is little danger of "runs" on the bank at such times, and cash withdrawals are relatively small. Business is profitable and deposit receipts continually tend to exceed withdrawals. Under such conditions, the banks are encouraged to extend their loans and reduce their reserve percentages. When, on the other hand, business confidence is low and the public are pessimistic as to the immediate economic future, banks find it desirable to increase their percentage reserves as a measure of safety. They require more and better collateral for loans and in other respects are more exacting in making advances. The business public, moreover, fearing continued depression, are reluctant to undertake new ventures, extend their capital equipment or accumulate supplies for the future. The business and banking philosophy of the time is to play safe and do little. Funds are piled up in the bank because there is nothing else to do with them. There is a high correlation between movements in business confidence and movements in the ratio of deposit currency to bank reserves.[1] Furthermore, in times of great prosperity and in times of economic stress and strain during which there are pronounced movements in business confidence, there is a strong correlation between the movements of business confidence and of bank deposit velocities.[2] These velocities and business confidence, for example, were both very high during the boom years 1928 and 1929, and very low during the depression years 1930–1935. It is to a large extent through such influences of variations in business confidence upon reserve ratios and, probably more importantly, upon deposit currency velocities, that the variations in the relative supply of the circulating media are caused which explain the cyclical fluctuations in the general price level with which the student of the business cycle is primarily concerned.

A moderate rise in the price level often stimulates business confidence itself and this in turn may increase temporarily the rates of money and deposit turnover (V and R) and the supply of goods sold (T). It was such a temporary stimulus that David Hume apparently had in mind when he said in his *Essays, Moral, Political and Literary* (published in 1742):

> "Accordingly we find that, in every kingdom into which money begins to flow in greater abundance than formerly, everything takes a new phase: labor and industry gain life; the merchant becomes more enterprising, the manufacturer more diligent and skillful, and even the farmer follows his plough with greater alacrity and attendance."

[1] Cf., Kemmerer, E. W., *Money and Prices*, pp. 121–126, 144–145; Persons, W. M., "Quantity Theory as Tested by Kemmerer," *Quarterly Journal of Economics*, February, 1908, p. 287; and Fisher, Irving, *The Purchasing Power of Money*, pp. 276–279, 430–432.

[2] *Supra*, p. 35, and Kemmerer, E. W., "Controlled Inflation," *American Economic Review*, Supplement, March, 1934, pp. 90–100.

Public Confidence in Money

The second factor for which allowance must be made under the "other things equal" in interpreting and applying the equation of exchange is the variations in the public's confidence in the money itself or in the public's expectations concerning the future value of the money. These variations find expression chiefly through changes in the various factors in the right-hand side of the price equation. The fundamental fact here is that, with money as with any other commodity, people quickly drop things that they believe are going to depreciate and cling to things which they believe are going to appreciate. The point may be made clear by a few illustrations.

Prospects of Convertibility

Assume that the money of a country consists entirely of government paper notes like our greenbacks of the years 1862–1878.[1] Assume that these notes were originally convertible into gold on demand, but that convertibility was discontinued some years ago and that the notes are now circulating at a value of 65 cents' worth of gold to the dollar, that there are no prospects at the moment for a resumption of gold payments, and that this 65-cent gold value is entirely the resultant of the interplay of the forces of monetary demand and monetary supply. Assume that the government of the country is a strong one with a well-balanced budget, and enjoying the confidence of the public. Assume further that this government's credit is such that it can borrow very substantial sums of money in the domestic market at 5 per cent.

Now change the situation in one respect. Have the government suddenly announce to the public that five years from the date of the announcement it will resume gold payments at par and that, in the interim, it will not increase the amount of money in circulation. Assume that the public believe that this announcement will be carried out.

On the above assumptions every dollar of paper money, in addition to being paper money, becomes a promissory note to pay one dollar gold, without interest, five years from date; and every day that passes after that announcement, the date of maturity comes one day nearer. Inasmuch as by hypothesis these notes are the only money in the country, if the demand for money increases

[1] Cf., *infra*, Chapter XIII.

while the supply remains constant, the value of the paper dollar will rise toward gold parity, under the force of the monetary demand.[1] This promise of redemption five years hence, however, has placed a lower limit to a paper dollar's gold value, a limit below which it cannot go appreciably at any time during these five years, and that limit is the present value of the right to draw a gold dollar on the date when gold payments will be resumed, computed at the current market rate of interest, which we have assumed to be 5 per cent. The present value of such a right to draw a gold dollar in the future is:

	Cents Gold
5 years hence	78.4
4 " "	82.3
3 " "	86.4
2 " "	90.7
1 year "	95.2

The notes would be worth these values in gold as an investment at the current rate of interest, and, if as money the notes should fall below these present discounted values, they would yield more than the current rate of return on other equally safe investments to anyone withdrawing them from circulation and holding them to the date when gold payments would be made. Whenever the gold values of the notes as money fell below these investment values, quantities of the notes would be withdrawn from circulation and held as investments. This would reduce the M of the equation and, as a consequence, tend to reduce P, or, in other words, to raise the money value of the paper dollar up to the investment value; but, it should be noted that this increase in the money value of the dollar would be effected only through a reduction in M or (if one prefers to consider hoarded money as money in circulation with a zero rate of turnover) by a reduction in V, in harmony with the principle of the quantity theory.

A Flight from Money

Let us now view the subject from the standpoint of an anticipated depreciation in the value of the monetary unit. Anything that causes the public to believe that the value of money is going to fall rapidly, or, in other words, that prices are going to rise sub-

[1] *Supra*, pp. 26–29.

stantially for a considerable period of time, tends to increase the rate of money and deposit turnover (V and R). If you believe that the value of money is going down rapidly in terms of goods, or, stated otherwise, that the prices of goods are going up rapidly, it is good policy "to drop your goods and hang on to your money and bank deposits."

In Mexico in 1916, when the so-called Vera Cruz and Constitutional Army paper money was depreciating rapidly and when the Government was discriminating against the notes of the larger denominations, but was forcing merchants to take the money under heavy penalties for refusal, there was a mad rush to get rid of this money quickly. Holders of the notes rushed to the stores to buy with them anything they could, without much regard to prices. Merchants, however, who charged unduly high prices, were subject to heavy penalties. Stories were told in Mexico City of people crowding the stores and waiting on themselves. In one store it was reported people took shoes in boxes from the shelves, paying the prices named with little or no regard to the sizes of the shoes or to the kinds—men's, women's or children's. Merchants, on the other hand, cut down their clerical force during these days and clerks who remained on duty in numerous cases were instructed to waste all the time they could in waiting on customers.

Similar situations existed in many European countries during the period of rapid currency depreciation after the World War. People in Germany, Austria and Russia rushed to the shops to spend their money as rapidly as possible to prevent its value from fading away in their hands, for often in the short period of a few hours prices rose by large percentages. At this time velocities of money and of bank deposits were very high and were rapidly increasing.

A pertinent illustration of the principle is the experience of Germany with the paper mark in the latter part of 1923, at the time of the introduction of the *rentenmark*, as described by Karl Helfferich.[1] Before the depreciated notes of the Reichsbank were stabilized at the rate of a trillion to one by the establishment of the Rentenbank,[2] the public were losing confidence in the notes so rapidly that the rate of monetary turnover increased enormously, with the result that the gold value of the notes depreciated much

[1] *Statist* (London), February 2, March 1 and March 8, 1924.
[2] *Infra*, pp. 315 and 316.

more rapidly than the rate of increase in the money supply and, in consequence, the gold value of the total amount of money in circulation dropped precipitously. When confidence in the currency was restored by the establishment of the Rentenbank, the abnormal and overstimulated rate of monetary turnover declined, with the result that there was not nearly enough money in circulation at the new and lower rate of turnover to maintain current business at the existing price level, so that a substantial increase in the amount of money in circulation was required to prevent a great fall in prices. Speaking of this experience, Helfferich said:

> "Therefore it appears that in the first quarter of the stabilization of the German standard, the circulation of money rose from 450 million to about 2,350 million of gold marks—a five-fold increase—whereas the circulation of money combined with the giro credit at the Reichsbank rose from 670 million to 3,050 million gold marks—a 4½-fold increase. The stabilization of the German standard therefore was not brought about by a contraction of the money in circulation; on the contrary the stabilization process was accompanied by an enormous increase in the monetary circulation."

It should be added that the stabilization was accompanied by an enormous reduction in the rate of the monetary turnover, which, according to the principle of the quantity theory, was equivalent to a reduction in the monetary supply. In other words, a great reduction in V and D of the formula caused by a return of confidence in the money had to be compensated by an increase in M and D in order to prevent a fall in P. Always, therefore, in the interpretation of the quantity theory as expressed in the equation of exchange, and in the application of the equation to monetary problems, the two forces, business confidence in general and the public's confidence in its money in particular, must be taken into account.

The Interest Rate and the Price Level

An influence that affects directly every factor on the right side of the quantity theory formula and which is in turn directly affected by all the factors of the formula is the interest rate. This influence of variations in the interest rate upon the factors that determine the price level is one whose importance is only recently becoming adequately appreciated by economists, and one which offers a fruitful field for future studies.

The bank-note element in M of the formula and the factor D are circulating media whose volume is to a large extent determined by the volume of bank loans. They grow out of bank loans and, in a high degree, consist of non-interest-bearing circulating bank debits, which the banks have given in exchange for the interest-bearing non-circulating debits of their customers. In a country like the United States, in which probably over 90 per cent of the media of exchange consists of bank deposits circulating through checks and in which bank notes constitute the principal element in the money circulation (M), the great influence of variations in the interest and discount rates charged by banks upon the supply of the circulating media is obvious.

When, as a result of increasing bank reserves or for other reasons, the interest and discount rates charged by banks decline, or, in other words, the "rental price of short-time capital" to the banks' customers becomes cheaper, borrowing is encouraged, bank-note and deposit currency tend to expand, the demands for capital goods tend to increase and an upward pressure is exerted on the price level. A rising price level, in turn, tends to increase business confidence and thereby to increase the velocities of M and D. It also stimulates the physical volume of business, T, but more slowly. The result is an upward tendency in prices (P).[1] In this price advance wages and many fixed charges lag behind most commodity prices—a fact that tends to increase profits, stimulate the demand for capital and thereby raise interest rates.

Rising commodity prices are synonymous with a declining value of the dollar, and this means that loans contracted during a period of rising prices give promise of being paid in a less valuable dollar than the one loaned. Depreciation of the dollar eats into interest, and sometimes consumes it entirely. It may even devour part of the principal, resulting in what is known as negative interest.[2]

[1] Low and declining interest rates may continue for a considerable length of time without actually causing a rise in commodity prices, as repeated experiences have shown. If, for example, the low interest rates are a factor in an economic and financial policy on the part of the Government which the business world considers dangerous, this policy may depress business confidence and thereby greatly reduce the velocities of circulation of both money and deposits (V and R). This reduction may more than compensate the expansion of M and D that was caused by the low and declining interest rates. This subject will be considered more fully in the final chapter of Volume II, with particular reference to American experience during the economic depression beginning in 1929. Cf., Kemmerer, E. W., "Controlled Inflation," *American Economic Review*, Supplement, March, 1934; and "Federal Reserve Policy," *ibid.*, March, 1933, pp. 132–134.

[2] Cf., Fisher, Irving, *The Theory of Interest*, pp. 40–44, and 493 and 494.

Under such conditions and prospects borrowers become increasingly urgent in their demands for loans, and lenders increasingly reluctant to lend, with the result that the rate of interest required to equilibrate supply and demand rises.

Rising interest rates tend to have exactly the opposite effects on the factors in the quantity theory formula which declining interest rates have. They tend to contract bank loans and thereby M and D. They thus tend to depress P and thereby to weaken business confidence, which in turn reduces the velocities, V and R, with consequent further declines in P.

While declining interest rates are a force exerted in the direction of checking a fall in commodity prices and causing a rise, and while rising interest rates, *per contra*, are a force exerted in the direction of checking a rise in commodity prices and causing a fall, there are numerous other forces both economic and political always at work, and what actually happens is the resultant of all of the forces.

As a matter of recent historical experience, the movements of commodity prices and of interest rates have frequently shown a considerable direct correlation. For this the outstanding cause is probably the facts that high business confidence stimulates the velocities of M and D and thereby pushes up prices, while rising prices stimulate the demand for capital and push up interest rates. On the other hand, low business confidence reduces the velocities and thereby depresses prices. Declining prices, in turn, weaken the demand for capital and depress interest rates.

With the background of this discussion of the relationship of variations in confidence and in interest rates to the price level, we are now prepared for a final statement of the quantity theory.

Quantity Theory Restated

Other things equal and business confidence and public confidence in the country's money remaining the same, an increase in the quantity of money in circulation will result in a proportionate increase in bank reserves; and an increase in bank reserves will result in a proportionate increase in bank deposits. A decline in the quantity of money in circulation will have the opposite effect. The D of the formula is, therefore, a function of M, and, other things equal, tends to increase and decrease as M increases and decreases and in the same proportion. This being true, the quantity theory of money, in spite of all the complexities of the modern credit régime, still holds true as a general principle.

Changes in the quantity of money in circulation require time to work out their influence on the price level, the principal buffers being V and R. Of course, the "lag" is very different for different classes of prices and for the prices of different commodities. Wholesale prices normally respond more quickly than retail prices and retail prices more quickly than wages. Moreover, among the commodities of each group there are widely different degrees of lag. Prices that are regulated by government, like those for railway freight and passenger services, or for gas, water, electricity, street car fares and the like, are often the last to respond to enduring alterations in the relative money supply. The effect of temporary alterations in the monetary supply is often limited almost entirely to a few kinds of commodities which at the particular time happen to be the most sensitive. Like a pebble dropped into a lake, the ripples it causes are imperceptible beyond a very responsive and closely adjacent area.

The question of the relationship of money and credit instruments to the price level has been a controversial one in the United States for several generations. It cannot be said today that there is general agreement among the majority of American economists as regards the details of this problem. There are economists of high standard in America who lean strongly towards the bullionist school, as, for example, the late Professor James Laurence Laughlin.[1] There are others, like Dr. B. M. Anderson, Jr., who accept a so-called "social value theory" and see no truth whatever in the main contention of the advocates of the quantity theory. There are others who look upon the quantity theory formula as true, but as merely a mechanical statement of a self-evident fact and therefore of little use. And there are still others who believe that the direction of causation is usually from the left-hand side of the formula to the right; namely, from prices (P) to the relative monetary and circulating credit supply $\left(\frac{MV = DR}{T}\right)$, and not in the opposite direction as here maintained. Readers interested in

[1] Briefly stated, the members of the bullionist school believe that the value of the dollar is determined fundamentally by the value of the bullion content of the commodity money dollar, and that when a country's money is not convertible on demand in commodity money or bullion, its value depends upon and varies with the prospects of such convertibility in the future.

this controversy should read the references given in the bibliography at the end of this chapter.

Despite much disagreement on the subject and many minor variations in the form of expressing the quantity theory, I think it can be said, without fear of successful contradiction, that a large majority of scientific economists, both in the United States and abroad, who have worked intensively in the field of monetary theory, accept some form of the quantity theory of money; although most economists believe that the problem of the relationship between money, credit and prices is one that demands much further study. On this subject, doubtless, the last word has not yet been said.

We are now prepared to consider the principal types of monetary standards, and this task will occupy the next three chapters and Chapter IX. First, we will consider the Monometallic Standard.

BIBLIOGRAPHY

American Economic Association Publications, Third Series, Vol. VI, No. 1, pp. 84–115.

Anderson, B. M., *The Value of Money;* New York, The Macmillan Company, 1917.

Edie, Lionel G., *Money, Bank Credit and Prices;* New York, Harper and Brothers, 1928.

Fisher, Irving, *The Purchasing Power of Money;* New York, The Macmillan Company, 1911.

——, *The Theory of Interest;* New York, The Macmillan Company, 1930.

Kemmerer, Edwin Walter, "Controlled Inflation," *American Economic Review*, Supplement, March, 1934.

——, *Money and Credit Instruments in Their Relation to General Prices*, Second Edition; New York, Henry Holt and Company, 1909.

Keynes, J. M., *Monetary Reform;* London, The Macmillan Company, 1924.

——, *A Treatise on Money*, 2 volumes; New York, Harcourt, Brace and Company, 1930.

Knight, Frank K., "Interest," *The Encyclopaedia of the Social Sciences*, Vol. VIII; New York, The Macmillan Company, 1932.

Laughlin, J. Laurence, *The Principles of Money;* New York, Charles Scribner's Sons, 1903.

——, *Money and Prices;* New York, Charles Scribner's Sons, 1919.

Marshall, Alfred, *Money, Credit and Commerce;* London, The Macmillan Company, Ltd., 1924; especially Chaps. 2–4.

Scott, William A., *Money and Banking;* New York, Henry Holt and Company, 1926.

Walker, Francis A., *Discussions in Economics and Statistics;* edited by Davis R. Dewey, New York, Vols. I and II.

PART II

MONETARY STANDARDS

CHAPTER V

THE MONOMETALLIC STANDARD

Monometallism Defined

Under a monometallic standard the unit of value consists of the value of a fixed quantity of some one metal, in modern times usually gold or silver. The metal constituting the unit is the standard metal, and all kinds of money are assimilated in value to the standard unit. Their denominations are expressed in terms of multiples or fractions of this unit.

The monetary unit in the United States, for example, prior to the breakdown of the gold standard in early March, 1933, was a gold dollar containing 23.22 grains of pure gold combined with 2.58 grains of copper alloy to give it proper wearing qualities when coined. The gold monetary unit, therefore, had a gross weight of 25.8 grains and a millesimal fineness of .900. Prior to 1893 India was on the silver standard, and her monetary unit, the *rupee*, consisted of 165 grains of pure silver combined with 15 grains of copper alloy. In the United States, under the gold standard, all the different kinds of money (paper money, silver, nickel and copper coins) were kept at a parity with the gold dollar, and a dollar of any kind of money was equivalent to a dollar of gold. Likewise, in India prior to 1893, all the different kinds of money (rupee notes, fractional silver coins and copper coins) were kept at a parity with the silver rupee.

While, historically speaking, the world has had a much longer experience with silver monometallism than with gold monometallism—the English currency of 1821 having been the first national currency in the world to be both legally and actually on a gold monometallic basis—silver monometallism is no longer of any importance in the world, the only two strictly silver standard countries remaining being Ethiopia and the British colony of Hong Kong. Except for China, moreover, which at least technically gave it up in 1934, the silver standard has been of comparatively little importance in the world since the latter part of the nineteenth century. The principles of monometallism may, therefore, best be explained and illustrated by reference to the gold standard. The reader should bear in mind, however, that the same fundamental principles apply also to silver monometallism.

There are a number of varieties of gold monometallism, the principal of which will be described later, but the automatic gold coin standard is the form of gold monometallism best adapted as a starting point in an explanation of fundamental principles. This, with minor qualifications, is the form of the gold standard used in the United States, England, France, Germany and many other countries prior to the World War. In most of its essentials, moreover, it was the monetary standard of the United States from the end of the War until March 3, 1933.

The Gold Coin Standard

Under the gold coin standard, the unit of value is the value of a fixed quantity of gold in a free gold market, and this gold is coined, without appreciable coinage charge, into money which circulates freely. For example, in the United States in 1932 the unit of value was the gold dollar, consisting of 25.8 grains of gold, .900 fine. This dollar was coined in gold pieces of the denominations of $2.50, $5, $10 and $20. Gold pieces representing a single unit or dollar were coined from 1849 to 1889, but after the latter date none were coined, except a few memorial pieces. There was no brassage charge for the process of converting standard gold bullion (i.e., bullion .900 fine) into gold coin.[1]

Our mint and assay offices made charges to depositors of gold bullion sufficient to cover such costs as those for melting, refining and alloy.[2] Anyone could take standard gold bullion to any American mint and have it coined into gold coin, and receive for his bullion the full amount of the coin into which it was coined (less the above-mentioned charges); in other words, he could get $18.60 of gold coin for each ounce of standard gold bullion he brought to the mint. This was the equivalent of $20.67 for each ounce of fine gold. Holders of gold bullion could have it converted into gold coins or exchanged for gold coins or their equivalent in gold certificates at the rate of $18.60 an ounce of standard gold at any of the ten mint-service institutions operating in the United States. Furthermore, owners of standard gold bars could sell them at

[1] There was a small charge of 1/5 of 1 per cent for a time prior to January 14, 1873.
[2] Revised Statutes of the United States, Section 3524.

practical gold parity for Federal Reserve notes at any of our twelve Federal Reserve banks.

There were in the United States no restrictions or tariff duties of any kind on the importation or exportation of gold.

Under such conditions gold coins in the United States could not be worth appreciably more than the market value of the gold bullion they contained. In other words, $18.60 in gold coin could not be worth appreciably more than the market value of an ounce of standard gold in the free markets of the world, because the United States would give anyone gold coin in unlimited quantities for standard gold bullion at this price, and gold bullion could be freely imported and converted into United States gold coins.

It was equally true that $18.60 of gold coins could not be worth appreciably less in the American market than the market price of an ounce of standard gold bullion in the international gold market, because anyone having unworn gold coins in the United States could melt them down and convert them into standard gold bars, and could get an ounce of standard gold out of each $18.60 worth of gold coin he melted down. These gold bars, or the gold coins themselves, could be exported from the United States in unlimited quantities and without any restrictions or tariff duties whatsoever.

If gold bullion could always be converted into gold coin, and gold coin into gold bullion, in unlimited quantities at this rate of $18.60 for an ounce of standard gold, without appreciable expense, and if both the coin and the bullion could be exported and imported without restrictions, it is obvious that, in terms of market value, an ounce of standard gold would always be practically the same thing as $18.60. In other words, $18.60 of gold coin would be a name for an ounce of standard gold with the Government's mint stamp upon it. Anything that affected the value of gold in the world's free gold markets would affect the value of every ounce of gold in the United States and therefore of every dollar of United States gold coin. If, as a result of new gold discoveries, the supply of gold on the world's market should increase greatly relative to the demand for gold, the value of gold bullion in the world's markets would decline, and with it the value of all American gold coins; and, *per contra*, if the demand for gold in the world for money, jewelry, plate, etc., should increase relative to the supply, the value of gold bullion in the world's markets would rise, and with it the value of every American gold coin. But, whether the value of gold rose or fell, an ounce of standard gold in the United States was always equivalent to $18.60, and an ounce of pure gold always equivalent to $20.67. The value of gold in terms of goods and services continually changes; but in a country that is squarely on the gold standard, the price of gold never changes to any appreciable extent. To say that the price of an ounce of standard gold in the United States in 1932 was always $18.60 is an identical proposition. It is like saying that a foot is always twelve inches long.

Under the typical gold coin standard, just as the gold monetary unit, say, the gold dollar or the sovereign, is always maintained at a value practically equivalent to the value in a free market of the gold bullion it contains, so, likewise, all the different kinds of money in the country—namely, all kinds of paper money, silver coins and minor coins of nickel and copper—are kept at a parity with the gold monetary unit. Ten dollars of any kind of the nation's money, for example, is always maintained at a value equal to ten dollars of any other kind of money.

Devices for Maintaining Parity of Different Kinds of Money

For the maintenance of this parity four devices are commonly used. They are:

(1) Limitation of the supply of fiduciary money. If any kind of money is issued to excess relative to trade needs, it tends to depreciate in terms of other kinds of money; as, for example, the famous Wood's pennies in Ireland in the early part of the eighteenth century,[1] and fractional silver coins in many parts of China in recent years, coins which have been issued in such excessive quantities that it takes from twelve to thirteen ten-cent pieces to equal a silver dollar. Special provisions are often incorporated in the monetary law to prevent excessive issues of fiduciary coins, in addition to the provisions of law restricting the issues of bank notes and government paper money. Examples of such provisions are: (a) a legal per capita limit, or a maximum total-amount limit of such money that can be issued; (b) a provision that the amount of such money in circulation can only be increased against the

[1] Dodd, A. F., *History of Money in the British Empire and the United States*, p. 171.

presentation to the government of an equivalent amount of gold; (c) a legal requirement that the central bank shall accept such money at par in unlimited amounts, sometimes coupled with the stipulation that no increase in the circulation of such money shall be made by the government without the approval of the board of directors of the central bank.

(2) A second device used to maintain the parity of fiduciary money is the simple one of making it interchangeable on demand with gold at government or central bank offices. Thus, for example, United States notes (greenbacks) and Federal Reserve notes prior to March 3, 1933, were redeemable on demand in gold coin at the United States Treasury in Washington.

(3) A third device is to make all such money acceptable in unlimited quantities in payment for taxes and other government dues, so that, if it is issued to excess, it quickly comes back to the government. Provisions to this effect are found in the monetary laws of Chile and Peru.

(4) A fourth device is to make such money legal tender—usually to a limited extent in any one payment—for private debts.

In the United States there was a general provision in the law (Act of March 14, 1900, Section 1), effective until the breakdown of the gold standard in the spring of 1933, that "all forms of money issued or coined by the United States shall be maintained at a parity with this standard [gold dollar], and it shall be the duty of the Secretary of the Treasury to maintain such parity."

Characteristics of Gold in Its Relations to the Gold Standard

Gold in its relation to a gold standard currency has three important characteristics, one of which, its fixed price, was explained earlier in this chapter. The second is, that it has in the currency system an unlimited market; and the third is, that the amount produced tends to vary inversely as the general price level.

In a typical gold coin standard system, the mints offer to gold producers and gold dealers a market, at a fixed price, for their entire supply of gold, no matter how large it may be. Under our former free coinage system, for example, in the United States, our American mints were obligated to buy at the rate of $18.60 for an ounce of standard gold (or $20.67 for an ounce of fine gold) all the gold that was brought to them and this was true whether the amount were only a few thousand ounces, as it was for the year 1917, or over ten million ounces, as it was for the year 1904. Gold in a gold standard country under a free coinage system and silver in a silver standard country under a free coinage system are the only instances we have in our modern, advanced communities of an indefinitely continued, unlimited demand for a commodity at a fixed price.

The third characteristic of gold in its relation to the gold standard is that the production of gold tends to vary, not with the "price of gold," as the production of other commodities varies with their prices, but with the prices of other commodities—namely, with the general price level.

The value of gold is expressed in its purchasing power over goods, that is, in the general price level. When the general price level, expressed in terms of gold standard money, declines, say, 23.5 per cent, as it did approximately in the United States between 1929 and 1934, the value of gold increases about 31 per cent; in other words, a dollar, or any other given weight of gold, say, an ounce or a gram, buys 31 per cent more goods (of the kinds covered by the general price index number) than it did before. This means dearer gold and cheaper goods. On the other hand, when the general price level rises, say, 93 per cent, as it did in the United States from 1913 to 1920, the value of gold declines 48 per cent and a given weight of gold—a dollar, or an ounce—buys only about half as much as it did before. This means cheaper gold and dearer goods.

A rising price level means that the supply of gold is increasing relative to the demand, and that the value of gold is falling. When the value of any commodity other than gold, in a gold standard country, declines, its price falls and producers' profits tend to decline, with the result that declining profits tend to reduce its production and the falling price tends to stimulate its consumption. These two forces react on the price and tend to bring it back into equilibrium, or keep it in equilibrium, with the prices of other commodities. When the value of gold falls, similar forces come into play, but, since gold is the standard of value, these forces appear in reverse form. The price of gold does not fall, but the expenses of producing gold, e.g., the prices of cyanides, explosives and machinery and the wages of laborers in the mines, all tend to rise, and this advance in the expenses of production reduces profits and automatically reduces the production of gold, thereby ultimately lessening the supply on the market relative to the demand and forcing up the value of gold; in other words, forcing down commodity prices including the prices of mining supplies and equipment and also wages.

Furthermore, when the value of gold falls and the commodity price level rises, the price of the gold itself used in jewelry, plate, etc., does not rise, although the cost of labor and other costs involved in their manufacture and marketing will advance. This means that the prices of articles made largely of gold do not advance in times of rising price level as rapidly as do the prices of most other things, or as rapidly as do most wages and salaries. Gold jewelry and other gold articles, therefore, at such times appear cheap as compared with other goods and this fact stimulates demand for them, thereby increasing the flow of new gold into the arts and diverting old gold from monetary uses into the arts. At such times the hoarding of gold is also stimulated, particularly in countries like India and China. All this tends to hold down general prices and to force up the value of gold until profits in the gold mining industry again become normal.

But if the gold producer loses when the value of gold falls, that is, when the commodity price level rises, it is equally true that he gains when the value of gold rises, that is, when the commodity price level falls. His day of prosperity is the time when other industries are suffering from falling prices. At such times, prior to the disruption of our American gold standard in March, 1933, the gold producers had still in the United States an unlimited market at the mints and assay offices for selling their gold at the fixed price of $18.60 an ounce of standard gold, while all their expenses of production tended downward. This chapter was begun in 1932, in the midst of the great world depression, and the gold mining industry at that time was about the only important industry in the world that was exceptionally prosperous.

Falling prices mean that the supply of gold has failed to keep pace with the demand, and that as a consequence gold is becoming increasingly valuable in terms of goods.[1] In periods of falling prices natural forces, the reverse of those mentioned above, assert

[1] The increased demand may be an enduring one or it may be purely temporary, as, for example, a demand expressed in the form of widespread hoarding of gold resulting from an economic crisis.

themselves and ultimately force up prices by stimulating the production of gold and by diverting large and increasing proportions of the gold on the market away from the arts and into the money uses. The rising profits of gold producers stimulate gold production, while the fact that the price of gold remains unchanged when other prices and wages are falling means that gold manufactures do not fall in price as rapidly as do most other things. This makes them appear dear to the consuming public, and therefore lessens the demand for jewelry, plate, etc., and diverts into the money uses much gold that would otherwise go into the arts. Gold in the money uses is thereby made more plentiful and therefore cheapened, and the commodity price level is given an upward push.

Characteristics of Gold as a Commodity

Gold, in addition to its characteristics just described *vis à vis* the gold standard, has as a commodity certain other characteristics which have an important bearing upon its use as a standard money metal. These are: (1) scarcity, (2) durability, (3) elasticity of demand and (4) variability in production.

(1) *Scarcity.* Largely by reason of its beauty, gold very early in the history of the human race became an object of keen and widespread demand for ornament. The fact, however, that, although gold is found almost everywhere throughout the world, both on land and sea, it usually can be obtained in substantial quantities only by much effort and that nature is very niggardly in her offering of gold to man, except in a few limited parts of the world, makes gold a very scarce commodity. The entire twelve billion dollars of monetary gold in the world today would represent a cube only about 32.1 feet on a side. A universal demand for gold for ornament and a widespread demand for gold for monetary uses, coupled with this very limited supply, spell scarcity and high values.

(2) *Durability.* Gold is a very durable metal, especially when alloyed with a baser metal like copper, as it usually is. There is gold in the world today that men extracted from nature thousands of years before Christ. Ancient gold ornaments and coins may be seen in almost any of the world's leading museums. Gold in one form is continually being melted down to reappear in another form. Doubtless there are modern gold coins and gold watches

in the world today that contain gold that was dug out of the earth thousands of years ago. Although the permanent losses of gold through abrasion, shipwreck and similar causes, are substantial, it should be remembered that, because of their high value, one's gold possessions are usually guarded carefully. The world's present total known supply of gold, therefore, is the accumulation of the ages. Inasmuch, however, as the world's gold production was comparatively small until the Californian and Australian gold discoveries of about the middle of the last century, by far the greater part of the world's present supply of gold has been produced since 1840. This point is illustrated by the following figures.

World's Production of Gold
(Millions of Fine Ounces)

Period	Average Annual Production	Total	
		Number of Yrs.	Amount
1493–1840	.38	348	132.34
1841–1890	4.98	50	249.00
1891–1934	17.63	44	775.50
1493–1934	2.67	442	1,180.54

Gold being such a durable object and the world's present stock being the accumulation of the ages, the production of any one year is a small percentage of the total stock. Furthermore, since a large part of the world's known stock of gold—much more than half—is in relatively unspecialized forms, such as coins and bars, forms into which very little labor has been wrought, the major part of the world's accumulated gold at any time is a potential supply on the market. It therefore takes a relatively long time for changes in the amount of gold produced annually to affect materially the market supply. The production of gold, for example, in 1934, which was the largest annual production in the world's history, was only about 4 per cent of the world's stock of monetary gold at that time.

(3) *Elasticity of Demand.* Gold is a commodity of highly elastic demand; in fact, it has the most elastic demand of any commodity on the market in a gold standard country. The demand elasticity of a commodity is an expression of the degree to which an increased supply of the commodity can be thrown on the market without depressing its market value, and, *per contra*, the degree to which supplies can be removed from the market without raising its

market value. The coefficient of demand elasticity expresses the resistance of an article to changes in its market value when the supply of the article on the market changes. All three of the principal kinds of demand for gold are highly elastic; namely: (1) monetary demands, (2) demands for ornamentation (including jewelry) and (3) hoarding demands.

The monetary demand is obviously highly elastic, when the mints of the country will buy all the gold presented to them at any time, when the gold market is a world market and the costs of shipping gold are small, and when the new gold appearing on the market each year is such a small percentage of the total gold stock.

It should be added, however, that, in times of economic crisis and financial tension, when the maintenance of the gold standard itself is in jeopardy, this elasticity of demand is temporarily greatly reduced. Small withdrawals of gold from the market and small increases in the supply of gold thrown on the market at such times may exercise a substantial influence on the value of gold.

The second important source of demand, namely, ornamentation, is likewise highly elastic. Primitive man's first form of clothing was probably some form of paint or mud on his skin—in other words, ornament. Clothing for protection came later. The desire for ornamentation from that day to this has been universal. Gold is the most widely treasured article of beauty. Most people in the world would like to have more gold ornaments than they now possess and would buy more if they should become cheaper. Very small reductions in the value of gold ornaments (as compared with other goods), therefore, quickly stimulate an increased demand and this demand acts as a buffer to depreciation.

The third important source of demand, hoarding, especially in India and China, is likewise highly elastic. Gold to these people who hoard it is the symbol of wealth in general. A given quantity of gold jewelry is not only a commodity which gives direct enjoyment to the Hindu farmer, but is also a blank check which he can fill in at any time with the name of any commodity he may want at its market price and which he can cash on demand. The capacity of India and China to absorb gold and silver in hoards is well known. For many generations India was known as the "sink" of the precious metal. Since 1931, however, when India went off the gold standard and the price of gold in terms of Indian rupees advanced greatly, India's hoarded gold has been poured onto the world's markets at rates even greater than those at which it was previously accumulated.

This high degree of elasticity of demand is an important factor in maintaining such stability of value as gold possesses.

The forces just described making for stability in the value of gold are countered by other forces making for instability. Among the latter is the fourth characteristic of gold which we shall describe, namely, the wide variability of its production when viewed over any considerable period of time.

(4) *Variability in Production.* Only about 15 per cent of the world's gold production since the discovery of America took place prior to 1850, so that we are primarily concerned with the gold production since that date. From the following table it will be seen that the production was nearly four times as great for the decade beginning 1851 as it was for the preceding decade. This was due to the enormous production of gold that came from the newly discovered gold fields of California and Australia. During the next decade, production fell off rapidly and then, during the last decade of the century, thanks chiefly to the gold discoveries in South Africa and Alaska, it practically doubled. Gold produc-

VARIATIONS IN WORLD'S GOLD PRODUCTION

PERIOD	AVERAGE ANNUAL PRODUCTION 000,000 FINE OUNCES	REMARKS
1801–1810	0.57	
1811–1820	0.37	
1821–1830	0.46	
1831–1840	0.65	
1841–1850	1.76	
1851–1860	6.45	Californian and Australian gold discoveries.
1861–1870	6.11	
1871–1880	5.57	
1881–1890	5.13	
1891–1900	101.60	South African gold discoveries.
1901–1910	182.9	
1911–1920	207.9	
1921–1930	185.2	Decline caused by depreciation of gold consequent upon the World War.
1931–1934	244.3	Advance caused by increase in value growing out of "scramble for gold" during world economic depression.

Data taken from Annual Report of U. S. Director of Mint.

tion increased 80 per cent during the next decade, and, despite the immediately repressing effects of the World War on gold production, it increased over 12 per cent during the decade 1911–1920. War-time and post-war inflation greatly reduced the value of gold, with the result that production was lowered during the next decade. With the increasing demand for gold resulting from the return of many countries to the gold standard after the War, the value of gold again rose. Gold production has been increasing continually since 1923. It is now well above its pre-war maximum and has been greatly stimulated by the high value of gold resulting from the world-wide scramble for gold growing out of the world depression.

These wide variations in the world's production of gold are an important factor in explaining the rather pronounced secular movements in the value of gold which constitute the principal defect of our modern gold standard and which will be discussed later in this book.

The Gold Bullion Standard

So far in this chapter we have been discussing that variety of the gold standard called the gold coin standard, which was the principal form of the gold standard employed in the leading countries of the world prior to the World War. During the decade following the War, when most of the world returned to the gold standard, many countries, including Great Britain, substituted for the gold coin standard the so-called gold bullion standard. In the gold bullion standard, as in the gold coin standard, all the different kinds of money are kept at a parity with each other by the devices previously explained (pp. 72 and 73). Furthermore, all are kept at a parity with the gold monetary unit, which consists of the value of a fixed quantity of gold. The paper money of the country is usually made interchangeable with gold bullion in the form of gold bars at one or more central offices. Redemption is usually authorized only in substantial amounts, the minimum being normally equivalent to several thousand dollars. The importation and exportation of gold bars is permitted without restriction. The gold bullion standard is, thus, in all essentials, a form of the gold standard, although it dispenses with the minting and circulation of gold coins, and thereby effects substantial economies in the monetary use of gold.

Another form of the gold standard without a gold currency which has come into prominence in recent years is the so-called "gold exchange standard." Since, however, an understanding of this monetary system involves an understanding of the principles of foreign exchange, which are discussed later (Chapter VIII), our study of the gold exchange standard will be postponed until Chapter IX.

BIBLIOGRAPHY

Cannan, Edwin, *The Paper Pound of 1797–1821;* London, P. S. King & Son, 1919.

Director of the Mint of the United States, Annual Reports, *passim;* Washington, Superintendent of Documents.

Edie, Lionel G., *Money, Bank Credit and Prices;* New York, Harper and Brothers, 1928.

Graton, L. C., "Future Gold Production: The Geological Outlook," *Transactions American Institute of Mining and Metallurgical Engineers*, 1931.

Gregory, T. E., *The Gold Standard and Its Future*, Third Edition; New York, E. P. Dutton & Co., 1935.

International Gold Problem, Collected Papers—A Record of the Discussions of a Study of Members of the Royal Institute of International Affairs, 1929–1931; London, Oxford University Press, 1931.

Jevons, W. Stanley, *Money and the Mechanism of Exchange;* New York, D. Appleton & Co., 1875.

Kemmerer, Edwin Walter, "Gold and the Gold Standard," *Proceedings of the American Philosophical Society*, Vol. 71, No. 3, 1932.

——, *Kemmerer on Money*, Second Edition; Philadelphia, Pa., The John C. Winston Company, 1934.

Kemmerer, Edwin Walter, and Vissering, Gerard, *Report on the Resumption of Gold Payments by the Union of South Africa;* Pretoria, Government Printing and Stationery Office, 1925.

Keynes, John Maynard, *Essays in Persuasion;* New York, Harcourt, Brace and Company, 1932.

——, *A Treatise on Money*, 2 volumes; New York, Harcourt, Brace and Company, 1930.

Launay, Louis de, *L'Or dans le Monde;* Paris, 1907. Translated by O. C. Williams under title, "The World's Gold"; London, 1908.

League of Nations:

First Interim Report of the Gold Delegation of the Financial Committee; Geneva, 1930. *Second Interim Report of the Gold Delegation of the Financial Committee;* Geneva, 1931. *Selected Documents on the Distribution of Gold submitted to the Gold Delegation;* Geneva, 1931.

Lehfeldt, R. A., *Gold, Prices and the Witwatersrand;* London, P. S. King & Son, 1919.

Macmillan, H. P., and Others, *Report of the Committee on Finance and Industry;* London, H. M. Stationery Office, 1931.

Ricardo, David, *Works;* edited by J. R. McCulloch; London, John Murray, 1888.

Rogers, James Harvey, *America Weighs Her Gold;* New Haven, Yale University Press, 1931.

Scott, William A., *Money and Banking;* New York, Henry Holt and Company, 1926.

Soetbeer, Adolf, *Materialien zur Erlänterung und Beurteilung der wirtschaftlichen Edelmetalverhältuisse und der Währungsfrage;* Second Edition; Berlin, 1886.

Touzet, André, *Emplois Industriels des Métaux Précieux;* Paris, V. Giard & E. Brière, 1911.

CHAPTER VI

THE BIMETALLIC STANDARD [1]

Bimetallism Defined

Although gold and silver had been used contemporaneously as money in different parts of the world for many centuries, true bimetallism can hardly be said to have existed prior to the early years of the nineteenth century. Previous to that time silver and gold had frequently circulated side by side—originally uncoined and later in the form of coins—as a sort of dual standard. From the dawn of the modern era, however, down to the fore part of the nineteenth century, silver was nearly everywhere the prevailing commodity money standard, and gold, when used as money, usually circulated to a much smaller extent and rather as a highly exchangeable commodity at continually varying ratings in terms of silver. True bimetallism, moreover, existed in practice for many years in the nineteenth century before any thoroughgoing theory of bimetallism was worked out. In fact, the theory of bimetallism was largely developed out of the controversies over the relative merits of bimetallism and the single gold standard that were waged in Europe, America and part of Asia during the last third of the nineteenth century.

True bimetallism, in the usual sense of the word, exists when a country opens its mints to the free and unlimited coinage of gold and silver, at a fixed ratio of equivalence called the mint ratio, giving to the coins of both metals (other than the fractional coins whose coinage is usually limited) a like standing before the law. The coins that enjoy the free coinage privilege are usually made unlimited legal tender. Although bimetallism under a gold and silver bullion standard, without the coinage of either gold or silver standard money but with the interconvertibility of paper money

[1] This chapter deals with the theory of bimetallism, while Chapters XIV and XV discuss the experiences of France with bimetallism from 1803 to 1873, the experiences of the United States from 1791 to 1873 and the silver controversy in the United States, culminating in the Bryan "16 to 1" campaign of 1896. The reader desiring at this point a comprehensive picture of the bimetallic controversy down to the economic crisis of 1929 should read the latter two chapters after reading the present one.

with gold and silver bullion at fixed rates of equivalence, has never existed, such a system is possible and would be entitled to be called "true bimetallism." Just as we can have a gold standard without the coinage of standard gold coins, so, likewise, we could have a bimetallic standard without the coinage of standard gold and silver coins.

The Compensatory Principle

The fundamental theory of bimetallism is found in the so-called "compensatory principle," which may best be explained by the use of a hypothetical illustration. Let us first consider one country by itself, so-called "national bimetallism," and then a number of countries leagued together with the same mint ratio, so-called "international bimetallism."

Assume that the weights of all gold and silver coins (other than fractional coins) are those that existed under our American law prior to the monetary legislation of 1933; namely, 25.8 grains of standard gold (i.e., gold .900 fine) to the dollar and 412.5 grains of standard silver (i.e., silver .900 fine) to the dollar. These weights would give a mint ratio of 16 to 1 $\left(\text{because } \frac{412.5}{25.8} = 16\right)$[1]. That means that anyone taking to the mint standard gold can obtain one dollar of gold for each 25.8 grains of standard gold which he brings, and anyone, similarly, taking standard silver to the mint can obtain a silver dollar for each 412.5 grains of standard silver. At these rates an ounce of standard gold would coin into $18.60 $\left(\frac{480 \text{ grains}}{25.8 \text{ grains}}\right)$, and an ounce of standard silver would coin into $1.16 $\left(\frac{4.80 \text{ grains}}{412.5 \text{ grains}}\right)$.

In order to simplify the illustration, let us assume that the United States is one of nine countries in the world—all equally important from the monetary point of view. Assume that each country has a monetary circulation (in addition to its subsidiary and minor coins) of two billion dollars. Assume that four of the countries are gold standard countries, each with two billion dollars of gold coin (or gold certificates against which 100 per cent gold is

[1] The exact ratio they give is 15.9888 to 1. Here, as throughout this illustration, slight fractions will be ignored to simplify the illustration. In actual practice, under the bimetallic system, calculations must be made very exact, since slight fluctuations are often of great consequence in the movement of the two metals.

held in reserve); that four of them are silver standard countries, each with two billion dollars of silver coin (or silver certificates supported by 100 per cent silver reserve); and that one country, the United States, is bimetallic, one-half of its standard money being gold coin (or gold certificates) and the other half silver dollars (or silver certificates).

Adapting an illustration used by Francis A. Walker, let us designate these countries by letter: gold standard, *A*, *B*, *C*, *D;* bimetallic standard, *E;* silver standard, *F*, *G*, *H*, *I*.

Let us assume at the beginning that the market ratio of gold to silver is the same as the mint ratio; in other words, that in the open market an ounce of standard gold costs just 16 times as much as an ounce of standard silver. Anyone, therefore, can bring gold to any of the mints in unlimited quantities and receive $18.60 of gold coin for each ounce of standard gold, and anyone can take silver to any of the mints in unlimited quantities and receive $1.16 for each ounce of standard silver; while, in the open bullion market, standard gold bullion can be bought for $18.60 an ounce and standard silver bullion for $1.16, whether the bullion is paid for in gold coin or silver coin.

If, under these conditions, there should be a great increase in the production of gold (without at least an equal increase in the demand for gold or a proportionate decrease in the demand for silver) relative to the production of silver—such, for example, as took place in California and Australia in the middle of the last century—the value of gold would fall in terms of the value of silver; in other words, the market ratio would decline below 16 to 1. To simplify the figures of our illustration, let us make the extreme assumption that the market ratio would temporarily decline to 15 to 1. This would mean that an ounce of standard gold would exchange in the market as the equivalent of 15 ounces of standard silver (or at approximately $17.40), but that at the mint it would be received as the equivalent of 16 ounces of standard silver (or at approximately $18.60). Stated in the reverse way, it would mean that an ounce of standard silver in the market would be equivalent to one-fifteenth of an ounce of gold, while at the mint it would be received as the equivalent of only one-sixteenth of an ounce of gold. Inasmuch as every commodity tends to seek the best market, newly mined gold would come to the mint where it was greatly overvalued in terms of silver as compared with the open market, while newly mined silver would go to the open market where it was greatly overvalued in terms of gold as compared with the mint. Furthermore, anyone could buy sixteen silver dollars in circulation for sixteen dollars of gold coin and then melt down the silver dollars and sell in the silver market the silver bullion thereby obtained, at the rate of fifteen silver dollars in bullion for sixteen dollars in gold, making a nice profit on the transaction and repeating it over and over again.[1] The existing silver coins would thus be melted down and the silver would go into the arts at home or would be exported; while their place in circulation would be filled by new gold coins minted in part from newly mined gold, and in part from a heavy importation of gold bullion and of foreign gold coins that would be brought into the country to be sold at this relatively high mint price for gold.

The circulation of silver dollars (and/or silver certificates) would rapidly decline, and that of gold coin (and/or gold certificates) would rapidly increase. Here would be an exemplification of the principle of Gresham's Law, the cheaper money, gold, driving out of circulation the dearer money, silver.

How long could this process continue? The obvious answer is: "Until the bimetallic country's billion of silver dollars were all replaced by gold, at which time the country would find itself on a *de facto* gold standard." This is true, but this process of replacing silver money by gold money would be retarded by two important forces; namely: (1) the effect on the market value of gold of this increasing use of gold money in the bimetallic country; and (2) the effect on the market value of silver of the dumping on the silver market of the vast quantity of silver coins withdrawn from circulation and melted down in the bimetallic country. The market ratio, which was assumed at the beginning to have gone to 15 to 1, would

[1] Why this would be so is easily seen. A bullion dealer could withdraw from circulation, say, $1,000 in silver dollars which (subject to allowance for abrasion that we shall here ignore) upon being melted down would yield approximately 859 ounces of standard silver. The market ratio being 15 to 1, the dealer would sell that silver in the market at the rate of $^1/_{15}$ the mint price for an ounce of standard gold ($18.60), which would be $1.24 instead of $1.16, and which would give him on the 859 ounces of standard silver sold $1,065, representing a gross profit of approximately 6½ per cent on the transaction. From this a few small expenses covering abrasion, melting charges, transportation, etc., would have to be deducted. The bullion dealer could now repeat the transaction, this time using the $1,065 he had received instead of the $1,000 used in the first instance, and this would bring him an additional 6½ per cent gross profit, which he could again compound in the same way, and so on so long as silver coins continued in circulation on a parity with gold. Of course, there would not be one but many playing the game.

obviously be raised as the bimetallic country demanded more and more gold, and supplied the market with more and more silver. The market value of gold would go up and the market value of silver would go down. As more gold was taken into circulation and more silver thrown out, therefore, the ratio would rise toward 16 to 1, and if it should reach that figure before the bimetallic country lost all of its silver dollars, the process would be discontinued, there being no longer any profit to bullion dealers in continuing it; and the country would still be on the bimetallic basis, although with a much larger percentage of its money in the form of gold coin (and/or gold certificates) than formerly, and a much smaller percentage in the form of silver dollars (and/or silver certificates).

In the above illustration we have assumed that the market ratio originally dropped to 15 to 1, while the mint ratio was 16 to 1. As a matter of fact, such a large difference would be utterly impossible as long as bimetallism were maintained. A drop to 15.9 to 1 would be more than sufficient to set the above forces vigorously into operation.

If our bimetallic country could draw in enough gold and throw out enough silver to restore the mint ratio before its supply of silver dollars was exhausted, we would have an example of successful national bimetallism. Its ability to do this would obviously depend upon: (1) its relative monetary strength, namely, the amount of gold it could draw in and the amount of silver it could pay out, relative to the world's stocks of these metals, and (2) the strength of the outside forces operating to change the market ratio, namely, the variations in the proportions of gold and silver produced from year to year and the variations in the relative demands for the two metals, both for use as money and for use in the arts.

The process above described would be reversed if silver instead of gold were to become cheaper; say, as a result of a great increase in the production of the white metal or a great decline in the demand for it in the arts. If, under such circumstances, the market ratio should rise materially above the mint ratio, for example, to 17 to 1, silver, the cheaper and overvalued metal, would be drawn into circulation, and gold, the dearer and undervalued one, would be forced out, with the result that an ever increasing proportion of the country's money would be silver dollars (and/or silver certificates) and an ever decreasing proportion would be gold coins (and/or gold certificates). This process would continue until either the market ratio were brought back to the 16 to 1 mint ratio, or all the country's gold money were driven out and bimetallism gave way to the silver standard.

International Bimetallism

During the great bimetallic controversy of the last three decades of the nineteenth century, few economists of standing believed that national bimetallism, that is, the maintenance of a bimetallic standard by one nation alone, was feasible, although many economists of standing believed in the economic soundness of the arguments for international bimetallism based upon the compensatory principle. Many of these, however, doubted the political expediency of even international bimetallism.

International bimetallism differs from national bimetallism in only one important respect; that is, instead of one nation's undertaking it alone, several nations are leagued together in a monetary union by an agreement according to which each member of the union maintains a bimetallic standard at one and the same mint ratio as all the others. Of course, the larger the number of countries that enter into such a monetary union and the stronger that the countries are from the monetary point of view, the stronger will be the bimetallic standard they will establish.

Reverting to our previous illustration of nine countries equally strong from the monetary point of view, each with a circulation of two billion dollars of standard commodity money, let us assume that two of the formerly gold standard countries, *C* and *D*, and two of the formerly silver standard countries, *F* and *G*, join with *E* to form an international bimetallic union at a mint ratio of 16 to 1. The line-up would then be as follows:

Gold Standard Countries	*Bimetallic Standard Countries*	*Silver Standard Countries*
A B	*C D E F G*	*H I*

This would be a powerful bimetallic union and under it bimetallism would be many times as strong as when conducted by one country alone. Why this is so a minute's thought will make evident. Let us assume that, after this bimetallic monetary union is established, an enormous increase in the world's production of gold should occur (the world's production of silver remaining fairly constant). This would make gold cheaper in terms of silver and would force the market ratio below the mint ratio, say (again using an extreme illustration), from 16 to 1 to 15 to 1. Gold would now be the overvalued metal at the mints and, being worth more as money than as bullion, would move toward its best market, that is, toward the mints of the five bimetallic countries. They would all be saying that an ounce of gold was worth sixteen ounces of silver, while the markets of the world everywhere else would be saying that an ounce of gold was worth only fifteen ounces of silver. Conversely, the mints of all five bimetallic countries would be saying that an ounce of silver was worth only 1/16 of an ounce of gold, while all other markets in the world would be saying that an ounce of silver was worth 1/15 of an ounce of gold. In the bimetallic countries silver would be worth more as bullion and gold would be worth more as money.

In response to the profit-motivated operations of bullion dealers previously described, silver dollars would be melted down and thrown on the market, while gold bullion would be drawn into the bimetallic countries from the world's markets and coined into money to take the place of the silver coins that were being melted down and exported. Note, however, how much stronger would be the position of the bimetallic standard here under international bimetallism than it was in the case of national bimetallism. Instead of one country withdrawing from circulation quantities of the dearer metal, silver, and throwing it on the market to make it cheaper and to force the market ratio back to 16 to 1, there would now be five countries and they could throw this dearer metal out up to the limit of five billion dollars—five times as much as under national bimetallism—before the supply would be completely exhausted and the bimetallic standard entirely broken down.

Secondly, the league of five bimetallic countries would have five times the demand for the cheaper metal, gold, that one country alone would have had, and it could now absorb new gold up to the maximum limit of five billion dollars before its supply of silver would be exhausted.

Thirdly, in throwing out the dearer and undervalued metal, silver, these five bimetallic countries would throw it into a much smaller market than would one country under national bimetallism. Now, the monetary demand for silver as standard money would come from only two silver standard countries (*H* and *I*), instead of from four (*F*, *G*, *H* and *I*), from which it previously came, and a given supply thrown on the market would for that reason much more quickly depress the price.

Fourthly, in drawing in the cheaper and overvalued metal, in this instance gold, the demand would be exerted on a much smaller supply of monetary gold than before, in this case on the supply of only two gold standard countries (*A* and *B*, instead of as formerly, *A*, *B*, *C* and *D*).

This mechanism of shifting the monetary demand of five important countries from whichever of the two metals at any time tends to be dearer than the other, in terms of the mint ratio, and of throwing vast quantities of that metal on the world market; and of transferring that monetary demand to the metal which tends to be cheaper, thereby absorbing from the world's market into the circulation of the bimetallic countries vast quantities of the cheaper metal; would tend at all times to hold the market ratio close to the mint ratio. The market ratio would, of course, fluctuate now on one side and now on the other side of the mint ratio, but, bimetallists maintain, it could not move very far away from that ratio.

International bimetallism would not be an attempt, as some critics claim, to nullify by governmental action the law of demand and supply; it would be rather a utilization of that law. By continually shifting the brunt of the monetary demand of the bimetallic countries to the metal which was cheaper, according to the mint ratio, and by withdrawing it from the metal which was dearer, the mint ratio and the market ratio would be forced closer together. Whether a given mint ratio could actually be maintained would of course depend upon the strength of the bimetallic forces above described, and upon the nearness with which the mint ratio chosen approximated the real market ratio. If it were in the public interest that the prices of potatoes and rice be kept in a fixed relationship to each other, and if many millions of people would shift from the use of potatoes as their chief vegetable to the use of rice when the price of potatoes was above this fixed ratio with the price of rice, and if they would shift from rice to potatoes whenever the price of rice should be unduly high relative to that of potatoes, a comparatively fixed relationship could be maintained (in the absence of any revolutionary changes in the production of the two commodities); provided, of course, that the ratio fixed were not an unreasonable one. The maintenance of such a ratio would be easier, moreover, in the case of gold and silver than in the case of potatoes and rice, because, as previously pointed out, the annual production of the precious metals is such a small percentage of the total supply potentially available in the market that variations in production from year to year have relatively little influence on their value.

The two chief advantages claimed for bimetallism over monometallism are: (1) it provides a more stable monetary unit and therefore eliminates or greatly lessens the evils of fluctuating prices; and (2) it maintains fixed pars of exchange between countries on different metallic standards.

Argument that Bimetallism Provides a More Stable Monetary Unit than Monometallism

(1) Silver and gold, when tied together so that their values in terms of commodities must move together, give a broader monetary base than does either one of them separately. The mass of value to be influenced is greater. A commonly used illustration of this argument for bimetallism was that of two tanks. It is used in a simple form by Jevons in his *Money and the Mechanism of Exchange*. He says:[1]

> "Imagine two reservoirs of water, each subject to independent variations of supply and demand. In the absence of any connecting pipe the level of the water in each reservoir will be subject to its own fluctuations only. But if we open a connection, the water in both will assume a certain mean level, and the effects of any excessive supply or demand will be distributed over the whole area of both reservoirs. The mass of metals, gold and silver, circulating in Western Europe in late years, is exactly represented by the water in these reservoirs, and the connecting pipe is . . . [the French Bimetallic Law] which enables one metal to take the place of another as an unlimited legal tender."

In further support of this argument, bimetallists point out that gold and silver are produced under very different conditions, and that as a matter of history the periods of heavy production of one metal have often been periods of small production of the other, so that there has frequently been an equalizing process that made for the stability of a standard based upon the two metals.

[1] P. 138.

The Fixed Par of Exchange Argument

(2) The service of bimetallism in giving the world relatively fixed pars of exchange was a valuable one. It can better be understood after we have studied the subject of foreign exchange (Chapter VIII). It will be sufficient here to note that, during the period of the bimetallic controversy of the latter part of the nineteenth century, there were a number of important silver standard countries in the world, as well as of gold standard countries. In the gold standard countries, the price levels rose and fell with the fall and rise in the value of gold, and in the silver standard countries they rose and fell with the fall and rise in the value of silver. The value of silver and the value of gold were frequently moving in opposite directions, and the value of each metal in terms of the other fluctuated widely. British prices, for example, were quoted in terms of gold and Indian prices in terms of silver. The Indian rupee price of a gold standard shilling and the British shilling price of a silver standard rupee were continually fluctuating and often very widely. This was disturbing to the trade between gold standard and silver standard countries, and also to the international movement of investments. Under an effective system of bimetallism the values of gold and silver would be tied together and, if the ratio were, for example, 16 to 1, a given weight of standard gold coin in any country would always have a value in the international markets of the world approximately equal to 16 times the same weight of standard silver coin in any silver standard country. This linking together of the values of gold and silver, therefore, not only gave bimetallic countries approximately fixed rates of exchange between themselves, but gave them fixed pars of exchange with all gold standard countries and all silver standard countries, and likewise gave all gold standard countries and all silver standard countries fixed pars of exchange with each other. This would obviously be a great advantage to all in the stabilization of international trade and international investments. At the present time this argument is of very little weight because the only true silver standard countries in the world are Hong Kong and Ethiopia.[1]

A further consideration of the arguments for and against bi-

[1] China's monetary system is very close to being a silver standard, but since the Chinese Government in 1934 imposed duties and other restrictions on the exportation of silver, China's currency has not been a true silver standard.

metallism will be found in the chapters that deal with the history of bimetallism in France and the United States and with the subsequent silver controversy (Chapters XV and XVI).

BIBLIOGRAPHY

Darwin, Leonard, *Bimetallism;* New York, D. Appleton & Company, 1898.

Giffen, Robert, *The Case Against Bimetallism,* Fourth Edition, London, 1896.

Helfferich, Karl, *Money.* Translated from the German by Louis Infield; 2 volumes; London, Ernest Benn, Ltd., 1927.

International Monetary Conference Held in Paris, in August, 1878; Washington, Government Printing Office, 1879. Contains also Proceedings of the International Monetary Conference of 1867.

International Monetary Conference Held at Brussels in 1892; Washington, Government Printing Office, 1893.

Jevons, W. Stanley, *Investigations in Currency and Finance;* London, Macmillan and Company, Ltd., 1909.

Johnson, Joseph French, *Money and Currency;* Boston, Ginn & Company, 1905.

Laughlin, J. Laurence, *The History of Bimetallism in the United States;* New York, D. Appleton & Company.

de Laveleye, Emil, *La Monnaie et Bimetallisme International;* Paris, Felix Alcan, 1891.

Nicholson, J. Shield, *A Treatise on Money,* Third Edition; London, Adam and Charles Black, 1895.

Reports of the Silver Commission of 1876; Washington, Government Printing Office, 1887.

Report of the Monetary Commission of the Indianapolis Convention; Chicago, University of Chicago Press, 1898.

Walker, Francis A., *International Bimetallism;* New York, Henry Holt and Company, 1897.

——, *Money in Its Relation to Trade and Industry;* New York, Henry Holt and Company, 1889.

CHAPTER VII

OTHER MONETARY STANDARDS

In addition to monometallic standards and the bimetallic standard, there are a number of other kinds of monetary standards, with some of which the world has had very extensive experience, with others only a limited experience, and with still others no experience at all up to the present time. A few of these types of monetary standards will be briefly studied in this chapter.

Multiple Standard

The term "multiple standard" is frequently used as synonymous with the term "tabular standard." This, in my judgment, is the wasting of a good name on a concept already well named.[1]

Here the term "multiple standard" will be used rather in contrast with the terms "single standard" and "dual standard." When one commodity, as in the case of gold in France, silver in Hong Kong or tobacco in colonial Virginia, is the standard, we call it a "single standard," and, if the commodity is a metal, we call it a "monometallic standard." If two metals tied together at a fixed mint ratio constitute the standard, we call it a "bimetallic standard"; if two commodities serve as standards at the same time, each separately, we call the system a "dual standard"; and, if more than two commodities so serve, we should logically call the system a "multiple standard." A multiple standard may consist of different kinds of standard metallic money, or of different commodities, or of different kinds of standard paper money, or even of several kinds of money belonging, respectively, to two or more of these classes. In colonial Virginia, for example, at one time tobacco, Spanish coins and British coins all served as standard money at the same time.

Probably the best examples of the multiple standard in the world are to be found in various parts of China. In Shanghai, China, for example, in 1929 there existed side by side: (1) "Big money," which consisted of large silver dollars and of paper money

[1] For a discussion of the tabular standard, see pp. 103–107.

10-cent and 20-cent pieces, which were divisions of the "big dollar" and which constituted a silver standard system. (2) "Little money," which consisted of 20-cent and 10-cent silver pieces containing relatively much less silver to the dollar than did the "big dollar." These small denomination coins were not divisions of the big dollar, but circulated at from $1.20 to $1.30 to the big dollar according to the scarcity or redundancy of the two kinds of money. Some kinds of goods were usually quoted in terms of big money, and others in terms of little money. The small transactions of the market places were mostly carried on with "little money" and copper coins. (3) Sycee silver, which consisted of silver bullion put up in the form of so-called "shoes" that circulated by weight, the weight being expressed in various units represented by different kinds of so-called "taels." Large wholesale business transactions were usually effected in terms of silver bullion expressed in terms of taels, and the value of each of the different kinds of taels, which was continually changing, was daily quoted in terms of big money. Big money, little money and sycee silver each represented a variety of the silver standard. (4) A large proportion of the petty transactions of the Chinese in Shanghai, as well as in most other parts of China, were effected by means of copper coin. These coins were minted freely in different parts of China and their values tended to vary with the variations in the value of copper. They were practically a copper standard and the number of copper cents to the silver dollar varied daily. Each day the Shanghai press quoted the number of copper cents which were equivalent to a big dollar and a little dollar. In 1929, in Shanghai, a little dollar was quoted a good share of the time in the neighborhood of 320 to 330 cents. In many parts of China today most of the transactions in the market places and the petty shops are effected by means of copper coins on the copper standard. (5) Another kind of money in Shanghai (and other port cities of China), introduced in 1930, is the Chinese customs gold unit, which is a strictly gold standard unit in terms of which customs duties are payable.

In 1930 all these kinds of money circulated side by side; each was quoted daily, at continually changing prices, in the Chinese markets in terms of all the others. The "cheaper" money did not drive out the "dearer," because no one kind was cheaper. Each circulated at its current market exchange value in terms of the other. Obviously, here was not one standard, but many standards, namely, a "multiple standard."

Dual Standard

The dual standard exists when currencies on two different standards and without any permanent legal value ratio between them circulate side by side, each independently of the other at market rates varying one with the other. During the seventeenth and eighteenth centuries, gold and silver coins frequently circulated side by side in this way in Europe. Silver usually dominated, but gold was quoted in terms of silver and many transactions were effected with gold. In 1919 the writer saw such a dual system in full operation in the city of Guatemala in Central America. Here the principal money at that time consisted of depreciated bank notes—fiduciary standard money—issued by a few local banks and circulating in the neighborhood of three to four cents United States currency to the peso. Along with them there circulated large quantities of United States money, the peso value of the United States dollar varying from day to day and the exchange rate being regularly quoted in the daily press. In buying goods, one could pay in one or the other money as he desired at the current market rate of the day. In the early days of the American occupancy of the Philippine Islands and of Puerto Rico, there existed such dual currencies, the local silver standard or fiduciary standard money of the country circulating side by side with United States gold standard money.

Multiple and dual standard currency systems are inconvenient and confusing, and are not to be advocated. They often exist for short periods of time during the transitional periods from one currency to another. They have played an important rôle in monetary history and the manner in which they have functioned throws light on a number of controversial questions in monetary theory.[1]

Fiduciary Money Standards

Fiduciary money standards have played an important rôle in the world's monetary systems—in fact, nearly every country in the world has experimented with them—and at this writing (1935)

[1] Cf., Kemmerer, E. W., *Modern Currency Reforms*, pp. 171–177, 279–290 and 324–346.

most of the leading countries of the world are on fiduciary paper money standards. Under a fiduciary money standard, the standard unit of value consists of a monetary unit whose value is substantially greater than the value of the material of which the unit is made, and varies, for the most part, independently of variations in the value of that material. The unit of value may be embodied in a coin or in paper money. In both cases the underlying principle determining the value of the money unit is the same, namely, the so-called principle of monopoly value. The nature of the fiduciary standard can, perhaps, best be explained by reference to the fiduciary coin standard.

A good example of a fiduciary coin standard is the Indian rupee from the closing of the Indian mints to the free coinage of silver June 26, 1893, down to the virtual establishment of a 16d. gold par in 1899. As previously explained (pp. 26–29), during this period the supply of money in India was kept fairly constant and as the demand for money increased during a considerable part of this period, with increasing population and increasing business, the value of the money unit rose. Although the silver rupee was not redeemable in gold during this period, its money value as measured either by sterling exchange rates or by commodity prices, rose far above the bullion value of its silver content, and fluctuated for most of the time without appreciable regard to the fluctuations in the value of silver. During these years the rupee was not a silver standard coin, because its value did not vary with the value of silver as it had previous to the closing of the Indian mints; nor was it a gold standard coin for its value did not depend upon the value of gold or vary with the value of gold as it came to do later. It was a case of scarcity value. As the amount of business to be done increased, while the supply of rupees was kept down, the gold value of the rupee rose and commodity prices fell. This was true, although for most of the time the gold value of the silver content of the rupee was falling; and for part of the time the world value of gold itself was rising.

There is no evidence that the vague prospects that the rupee would at some indefinite future time be given a fixed gold value of 16d. materially affected the money value of the rupee during the greater part of the period 1893 to 1898.[1]

[1] A more detailed account of India's experiences with the fiduciary standard at this time is given in the author's book on *Modern Currency Reforms*, pp. 35–71.

Prospectively Convertible Fiduciary Standard Money

Prospects for future convertibility, however, may be elements in the demand for fiduciary money that affects its value. Such prospects may affect the acceptability of money among some people, and therefore the extent of its use and the rate of its turnover. Prospectively convertible fiduciary standard coins cannot depreciate in value materially below their present worth as an investment, according to the estimates of the market, just as they cannot, in a free and open market, depreciate materially below the bullion value of their constituent material. In the latter case, they would cease to be money through being melted down and sold as bullion, and, in the former, they would cease to function as money through being withdrawn from circulation and held as an investment. The point will be made clear by the following illustration.

Assume that a country adjoining the United States, say Mexico, has a monetary circulation consisting entirely of silver coins and of silver certificates (against which silver coins, dollar for dollar, are kept in reserve); assume that all coins contain ¾ of an ounce of pure silver to the dollar; that the silver standard prevails with free and unlimited coinage of silver, that the gold price of silver bullion in the United States is ruling at about $1.00 an ounce, and that the United States is on the gold standard as it prevailed prior to March, 1933. Under such circumstances, the Mexican dollar would be worth approximately 75 cents United States gold. At this stage assume that Mexico decides to adopt gradually the gold standard, as India did from 1893 to 1899, and, to this end, closes her mints to all further coinage, limiting her monetary circulation absolutely to the circulation of the date on which the mints are closed. Assume that on closing the mints the Mexican Government announced that, beginning five years hence, the Government would make all silver coins convertible into new Mexican gold standard coins on demand, the new gold standard coins to be of the same weight and fineness as the former gold coins of the United States.

If the population of Mexico should grow rapidly during these five years and if business should increase greatly, the gold value of the Mexican dollar would rise above 75 cents of United States gold coin, under the pressure alone of an increasing demand for money against a constant supply. Even were the gold price of silver to fall, during this period, far below $1.00 an ounce and were the promise of future convertibility to be revoked, such an increasing demand against a constant supply would force up the gold value of the Mexican silver dollar (assuming the value of gold itself to remain stable) and would force down the Mexican commodity price level. The gold value of the Mexican dollar might in this way even be forced up beyond the value of a United States gold dollar and American exchange in Mexico go to a discount.

If the Mexican Government should agree, however, to give new silver dollars on demand at any time for United States gold coins or their gold bullion equivalent, dollar for dollar, the Mexican dollar would not rise appreciably in its gold value above a United States gold dollar, because the supply of Mexican dollars could be increased indefinitely, after this point were once reached, by the presentation of gold.

If, on the other hand, immediately after the mints were closed and the promise of redemption in gold five years hence was made, there should occur a strong business reaction in Mexico with a consequent great decline in the demand for money, the gold value of the silver dollars would tend to depreciate, and, if it became less than the gold value of the silver bullion in the dollar, these silver dollars would be melted down.

Under these circumstances, what limit, if any, would there be to the possible depreciation of these dollars, assuming that no restrictions were placed upon their being melted or exported? Obviously, there would be two possible lower limits, and depreciation could not go appreciably below whichever of the two was at that particular time the higher. These limits would be: (1) the gold value of the bullion content of the dollar in the local market; and (2) the investment value of the Government's promise to redeem the silver dollars in gold in the future.

If two years after the mints were closed the gold price of an ounce of fine silver fell to 60 cents United States currency, the Mexican silver dollar could not depreciate in its gold value appreciably below 45 cents United States currency, because it would be worth approximately that amount melted down as silver bullion. On the other hand, if the Mexican Government's promise to redeem in gold at a date now only three years distant were considered by the market to be absolutely good, and if the market rate of interest in the community on an investment of that kind and estimated degree of safety were 5 per cent, the Mexican dollar could not depreciate below the present worth at 5 per cent of a promise to pay one gold dollar three years hence, which, at interest compounded semi-annually, would be approximately 86 cents United States gold. If it should fall below this gold value, anyone withdrawing Mexican dollars from circulation at such a low value and holding them for three years would presumably realize upon his investment more than the current market rate of return (assumed to be 5 per cent). Dollars would accordingly be quickly withdrawn for investment purposes until the decrease of the supply in circulation should force their gold value up to at least this investment value minimum. In other words, the supply of money would be reduced relative to the demand and the value of the money would rise.

If the value of the bullion content of the dollar should be higher than the investment value, that bullion content value would determine the lower limit of possible depreciation and, if the investment value should be the higher, that would determine this limit. Neither of these factors, however, would fix an upper limit to the possible appreciation of the silver dollar and it is perfectly possible that the monetary demand might be so strong as to raise the money value of the Mexican silver dollar in terms of gold and commodities so far above either the bullion value or the investment value that neither of these values would exercise any influence whatsoever upon the value of the silver dollar. They might merely fix lower limits to the possible depreciation of money which had actually appreciated far above those limits and of whose future depreciation the public had no fears.

Rarely is there a definite promise to redeem a fiduciary money upon and after a certain definite future date, although in most fiduciary monetary systems future redemption has been expected. The investment value in such cases is determined by the varying estimates of the market as to the time and conditions of redemption. This estimated investment value of the market may or may not be a factor in determining the purchasing power of the money. If it is, its influence is made effective through decreasing or increasing the supply of money in circulation.

The principles underlying the circulation and value of fiduciary standard paper money are essentially the same as those just explained for fiduciary standard coin, except for the fact that the paper money possesses no value in the substance of which it is made corresponding to the bullion value of fiduciary coins. In the case of all kinds of fiduciary standard money future depreciation or appreciation is sometimes discounted. If the public anticipates a decline in the value as a result of prospective new issues or for other reasons, it attempts to pass on its money to others by increased purchases of commodities, gold bullion and exchange before the decline takes place. This increases the rate of monetary turnover and hastens the depreciation. The opposite takes place when a sudden rise in value is expected.

In later chapters some historical examples of fiduciary paper money standards will be considered (Chapters X–XIII). At this writing, with the widespread breakdown of the gold standard, fiduciary standards exist in most of the countries of the world. The term "managed currency," so widely used today, usually (though not necessarily [1]) refers to a fiduciary money standard.

The Depressed Value Coin Standard

Another kind of standard of which monetary history contains a few examples, all of brief duration and for periods of temporary currency maladjustment, is what we may call for lack of a better name "the depressed value standard." This is the opposite of a fiduciary standard, where the value of the monetary unit is maintained above the value of the bullion of which the unit is made by keeping the money supply relatively scarce. Here there is a superfluity value instead of a scarcity value. Ordinarily, for example, when the value of the silver bullion in a silver dollar becomes worth more in the open market than the dollar itself is worth as a coin or when the value of the gold in a gold dollar becomes worth as bullion more than a dollar of gold coin is worth, the coins are melted down or exported, and this melting or exportation reduces the monetary supply and thereby raises the value of the dollar as money to parity with the market value of its bullion content. It sometimes happens, however, that governments, in order to prevent their coins from being melted or ex-

[1] In modern times even gold standard currencies are nearly all more or less managed through central bank operations such as changing discount rates, "open market operations" and the manipulation of exchange funds.

ported at such times, impose heavy penalties on melting or exportation and thereby maintain the monetary supply at an artificially high level.[1] A good example of such a depressed value coin standard is the experience of the Union of South Africa from 1917 to 1920.

On July 9, 1917, a law went into effect in the Union of South Africa prohibiting the use of gold other than as currency, and on August 28, 1917, an Executive Proclamation was issued prohibiting, with certain qualifications and except with the permission of the Controller of Imports and Exports, the exportation of gold in the form of coin, bullion or ornament. Meanwhile, the gold sovereign continued to be the monetary unit of the Union of South Africa, gold coins continued to circulate freely, and the paper money of the country, although it was being issued in very large quantities, continued to be convertible on demand in gold sovereigns. However, since the exportation of gold coin was rigidly restricted—although there was considerable smuggling out of the country—gold coin was dammed up in the country and not permitted to flow out into the world market. Its value in the Union of South Africa was artificially depressed, and with it the value of the other kinds of money, which were being maintained at a parity

[1] An experience of this kind in the Philippine Islands in 1906 has already been cited (p. 30). Another striking illustration of the principle was encountered by the author in Mexico in 1917.

During the autumn of 1917 in Mexico there circulated freely throughout the Republic, at par with Mexican gold coins (which at that time were circulating at a scarcity value), silver half pesos, and fractional silver coins of lower denominations. The principal silver coin in Mexico was the *tostone* or half peso. On September 20, 1917, two tostones in Mexico circulated everywhere as the equivalent of one gold peso, but the silver they contained was worth in the New York silver market at the current market price of silver 70 cents of United States money. Here then was a situation in which silver coins containing 70 cents' worth of silver were circulating, peso for peso, as the equivalent of gold coins containing approximately 50 cents' worth of gold and which were themselves circulating at a value equivalent, according to New York exchange rates, to approximately 56 cents gold. Just as the gold coins could not depreciate to their bullion value because they were so scarce, their supply being strictly limited, so the silver coins could not appreciate to their bullion value because they were so plentiful, their melting down or exportation being prohibited under heavy penalties. Their supply could not be reduced and so they circulated at the value determined by demand and supply, with little or no regard to the value of their bullion content. Cf., *The American Economic Review*, Supplement of March, 1918, pp. 258–262.

Both the Philippine experience and the Mexican experience cited here show how money may have a superfluity value as well as a scarcity value; but in the Philippine instance the money possessing this superfluity value was not the standard money, and in the Mexican case silver coins possessing a superfluity value circulated along with gold coins having a scarcity value, and the standard itself was really a fiduciary gold coin standard. While the two experiences, therefore, illustrate well the nature of superfluity value, they are not examples of a depressed value coin standard.

with gold coins. Professor C. S. Richards of the University of the Witwatersrand of the Union of South Africa says concerning this experience:

> "Throughout 1919 the banks were agitating for the Government to issue a proclamation making their notes inconvertible, for during all this time, owing to the continuous depreciation of paper due to its over-issue, the banks had been increasingly called on to honour their promises to pay, and the sovereigns thus obtained were smuggled abroad and sold for more than the foreign currency equivalent of a South African pound. In order to meet this demand for sovereigns the banks were obliged to buy raw gold in London at a premium, that is, paying more than a South African pound for each 113 grains, and getting it coined in the usual way at the London mint. In other words, the penalty which they had to pay for issuing too much paper was that they had to buy a certain number of sovereigns at 26s. or 28s. and pay them out at 20s. The exchange position was also naturally affected." [1]

Here, the monetary unit did not consist of a fixed quantity of gold in a free market, but of a gold coin whose value was depressed by excessive issue of convertible paper money accompanied by restrictions on the exportation of gold. Its value was far below the bullion value of its gold content in a free market. Here was a clear case of a depressed value coin standard.

The Tabular Standard

The tabular standard is a device for giving a stable standard of value for the payment of debts, particularly long-time debts. It is concerned directly only with the standard of deferred payment function of money, and may be employed while any other kind of monetary standard is serving for the medium of exchange.

Suggestions for the use of some standard, other than the medium of exchange standard, for deferred payments have been made from time to time over a period of centuries by writers on economic subjects. Most of the earlier suggestions for such a different standard contemplated the use of only one commodity. Adam Smith thought that he had discovered in labor a stable standard of deferred payments. Labor, he said, "never varying in its own value, is alone the ultimate and real standard by which the value of all commodities can at all times and places be estimated." Smith realized to some extent, however, the practical difficulties in the

[1] Report submitted by Edwin Walter Kemmerer and Gerard Vissering on *The Resumption of Gold Payments by the Union of South Africa*, p. 537.

way of employing in current business such an abstract standard, for he said later:

> "... the current prices of labour at distant times and places can scarce ever be known with any degree of exactness. Those of corn, though they have in few places been regularly recorded, are in general better known and have been more frequently taken notice of by historians and other writers. We must generally, therefore, content ourselves with them, not as being always exactly in the same proportions as the current prices of labour, but as being the nearest approximation which can commonly be had to that proportion."

Accordingly, he measured the variations in the value of silver by fluctuations in the price of grain, being convinced that over long periods of time the value of grain was the more stable of the two.

As a result of such causes as the impairment of coins through clipping, plugging and sweating, debasement of the unit of value by governments and wide fluctuations in the value of silver and gold, we find that in the seventeenth and eighteenth centuries resort was occasionally made to some other commodity than gold and silver as a standard of deferred payments. For example, an act of Parliament in 1576 (18 Elizabeth, cap. 6) declared that

> "For the better maintenance of learning and the better relief of scholars in the Universities of Cambridge and Oxford, and the colleges of Winchester and Eton. . . . no Master or chief ruler of any college . . . after the end of this present session of Parliament, shall make any lease for life, lives, or years, of any farm, or any their lands, tenements, [etc.] . . . except that the one-third part at the least of the old rent be reserved and paid in corn for the said colleges . . . that is to say, [paid] in good wheat after six shillings and eightpence the quarter or under, and good malt at five shillings the quarter or under, to be delivered yearly, . . ."

Subsequent to that time the price of wheat rose greatly with the result of making those colleges far richer than they would otherwise have been, the rents and endowments expressed in money having sunk to a fraction of their ancient value.[1]

In the latter part of the eighteenth century and the fore part of the nineteenth, we find a number of economic writers referring to the use of a group of commodities, instead of money or one commodity, as a standard for long-time debts. One of the clearest of these early statements was that of G. Poulett Scrope in 1833.[2] Scrope called his plan a tabular standard, and in describing it laid

[1] Jevons, W. Stanley, *Investigations in Currency and Finance*, pp. 92 and 93.
[2] *Principles of Political Economy*, p. 406.

down all the essentials of the tabular standard as it is understood today.

The plan, broadly speaking, is to have prepared by the government an official index number of prices of a group of staple commodities. This index number should be published at short intervals, say, weekly or monthly. The law would then permit or require time contracts calling for the payment of money to be adjusted on the basis of these index numbers. If, for example, the index number should rise from 100 January 1, 1933, to 125 January 1, 1938, a loan for $1,000 contracted on the former date and due on the latter would call for a payment of $1,250 (in addition to interest) on January 1, 1938, because, according to the index number, it would require $1,250 on the latter date to buy the same quantity of the commodities covered by the index number as $1,000 bought when the contract was made five years before. The borrower, in other words, would be paying to the lender 25 per cent more dollars than he borrowed, but the same purchasing power in terms of the official index number. If the index number, on the other hand, should fall during the five years from 100 to 80, the borrower would cancel the principal of his obligation at maturity by the repayment of only $800. The amount of interest due periodically would also be adjusted on this index number basis.

We have had in this country at least two actual experiences in the use of such a standard, although rather crude ones. The two experiences were in Massachusetts during the eighteenth century and were the outcome of evils arising from depreciated paper money. The first of these was with Governor Shirley's *so-called* "equity bills of 1742," and the second was with the *so-called* "Massachusetts depreciation notes of 1780." [1]

Advantages of Tabular Standard

The two chief advantages of a tabular standard are:

(1) It would assure a more stable income in purchasing power to persons and institutions having funded incomes, such as interest on bonds and mortgages, dividends on preferred stock, pensions and annuities. To such people and institutions the rising cost of

[1] The reader interested in these interesting experiments with the tabular standard will find a detailed description of them in an article written by Willard C. Fisher, "The Tabular Standard in Massachusetts History," *Quarterly Journal of Economics*, Vol. XXVII (1912–1913), pp. 417–461.

living would have its teeth drawn. The purchasing power of their principal and income would be comparatively constant.

The purchasing power income of life insurance would likewise be stabilized, and a man who took out insurance for the protection of his family would be freed from the present danger that is so discomforting that an amount of insurance that may seem adequate when taken out may prove altogether inadequate when paid to the beneficiaries, because of being whittled away year by year through a possible depreciation in the value of the monetary unit.

(2) It would tend to lessen the frequency and the severity of economic crises and depressions. Under present conditions, a depreciating dollar, as expressed in rising prices, unduly stimulates industry, increases demand for capital, and leads to excessive speculation, which in turn leads to collapse and panic. Then come periods of liquidation, stagnation and readjustment, followed by overexpansion, again culminating in overspeculation and panic. On the other hand, when the dollar appreciates and prices fall, the debtor classes are burdened, business is depressed, and there follow long periods of comparative stagnation in business enterprise. Under the tabular standard these alternate periods of fever and chills would tend to become of less importance. When prices fell, the debtor would pay less dollars in settlement of his debts, and the creditor would need less. When prices rose, the creditor would receive more dollars in payment of his credits, and the debtor would be able to pay more.

Defects of Tabular Standard

(1) The tabular standard is more complicated and cumbersome than any of our present monetary standards of deferred payments, and cannot be so readily understood by the masses of the people. The use of such a standard in long-time contracts has been possible for many years, since there have existed in this country and in most other advanced countries carefully prepared price index numbers readily available to the public. There is nothing, for example, to prevent men today from making loan contracts agreeing that, at the maturity of the loans one or more years hence, the number of dollars shall be repaid that, according to the Bureau of Labor Statistics index numbers of wholesale prices, shall then have the same purchasing power over commodities as that possessed by the amount loaned when the loan was made. And yet,

despite the recognized evils of rapidly rising and rapidly falling prices as concerns the equities between debtor and creditor in long-time contracts, very few, if any, such contracts have been made in recent times.

(2) A second difficulty is that it would cause confusion and hardship in setting a different standard for long-time credits from that used in cash transactions and short-time credits. A manufacturer who was selling his products for cash and providing his capital by borrowing money on tabular standard contracts would frequently experience great difficulties in meeting obligations which he could not calculate in advance. Imagine the difficulties of railroad companies if they were compelled to pay their bonds on a tabular standard basis, while their incomes came mostly in cash, and their freight and passenger rates were controlled by government commissions. It would be difficult to fix wages on a tabular basis, and, if they were not so fixed, the laboring man whose mortgage was fixed on such a basis would suffer when the price index number was rising rapidly, and benefit when it was rapidly falling. His wages would usually lag behind these price movements both on the rise and the fall. The compulsory adoption of this plan for long-time debts would probably bring into business a larger amount of uncertainty, risk and confusion than it would eliminate.

(3) A third difficulty concerns the relations of the trade of the tabular standard country with other countries. The adoption of a tabular standard in the United States, for example, if Europe were on the gold standard, would bring an element of uncertainty and risk into our foreign trade, foreign credit and debit relations and the international exchanges. To be broadly successful the tabular standard would need to be adopted by all the leading commercial nations of the world, on the basis of an international agreement, and an international index number would need to be agreed upon. At present there is not the remotest prospect of any such action being taken.

If anything ever comes of the tabular standard, it is likely to develop out of the gradual but optional adoption of such a standard in individual contracts. There is no tendency in that direction at the present time. In saying this, however, it is not meant to imply that general price index numbers may not some day become important factors in regulating the value of the standard monetary unit. That is another story.

The Commodity Dollar [1]

The concept of a "commodity dollar" in the sense in which the term is usually employed today has been suggested from time to time over a period covering more than a hundred years.

The American astronomer, Simon Newcomb, suggested a commodity dollar plan in 1879, and an Englishman, Aneurin Williams, worked out such a plan in considerable detail twelve years later. Little attention, however, was given to these early proposals. Irving Fisher formulated a commodity dollar plan independently in 1911 and he, more than anyone else, is responsible for the subsequent development of the plan and for arousing public interest in it. Although a number of varieties of the commodity dollar plan appear in present-day discussions, the plan as developed by Fisher in his book on *Stabilizing the Dollar* is the one that is best known. It is the plan considered in this chapter. The formulation of the plan runs briefly as follows.

A Plan to Give the Dollar a Fixed Value

Our present unit of weight is a fixed weight, the pound; our unit of length is a fixed length, the foot; and our unit of content is a fixed content, the quart. But for our unit of value prior to 1933, when we were on the gold coin standard, we used not a fixed value, but whatever value happened to attach at the time to a fixed weight of gold, namely, to 23.22 grains of pure gold, which was the gold content of the dollar. Since the value of gold is continually changing under the impact of world forces of demand and supply, our gold unit of value was not fixed but variable, and this instability in the value of our monetary unit was a serious defect.

To meet this difficulty the commodity dollar plan provides that the weight of the dollar shall be changed from time to time, with the object of making the dollar always buy approximately the same quantity of goods; in other words, of giving it a fixed value or purchasing power. To the minds of the advocates of the commodity dollar it is a misnomer to call it a "rubber dollar." In fact, their object is to transfer "the rubber" from the *value* of the dollar, which is its most important quality, to the *weight*, which in itself is comparatively unimportant.

[1] This discussion of the commodity dollar is a reproduction, with some revision, of the chapter on this subject contained in the author's book, *Kemmerer on Money*, Second Edition.

The commodity dollar at the beginning would be made equivalent to a certain weight of gold. It would not be coined, but would circulate in the form of notes which would be convertible on demand into varying amounts of gold bullion known as "the bullion dollar."

How the Value of the Commodity Dollar Would Be Determined

The government would maintain a price index number covering the principal commodities in our economic life. At stated regular intervals, perhaps every two months, this index number would be published. When it rose, the weight of the bullion dollar would be increased, and when it fell, the weight of the bullion dollar would be decreased. For example, if the plan were inaugurated with a bullion dollar of 23.22 grains of gold, and if at the end of the first two months the price index number was found to have risen from 100 to 101, so that it would then require $101 to buy the same composite group of commodities that could have been bought by $100 two months before, the bullion dollar would be increased in weight, say, by 1 per cent, or from 23.22 grains of pure gold to 23.452 grains, and all bullion dollar notes would now become convertible into a bullion dollar of this increased weight. If at the end of the next two months the commodity price index number showed another advance, the weight of the bullion dollar would again be increased and this process would be continued every two months until the advance in commodity prices was checked and the price index number was forced back to 100. On the other hand, whenever the commodity price index at the end of any two-months period was found to be below 100, the weight of the bullion dollar would be decreased, and a reduction would be made every two months until the index number was forced back to 100.

> "How can we know," asks Fisher, "that if the index number is one per cent above par, a one per cent increase in the weight of the gold dollar will be *just* sufficient to drive the index number back to par? The answer is we *do not* know, any more than we know, when the steering wheel of an automobile is turned, that it will prove to have been turned *just* enough and not too much."

If the first correction is not enough or if it is too much, the index number when next computed will tell the story, and the necessary corrections will be continued every two months until they accomplish their purpose.

The government would purchase gold bullion, paying for it by bullion dollar notes at its reserve fund offices at the rate of one bullion dollar note for each bullion dollar, and, on the other hand, it would sell bullion dollars on demand for bullion dollar notes at a price slightly higher than a one dollar note for one bullion dollar. This difference between the government's buying rate for bullion dollars and its selling rate, which it is proposed at the beginning should be 1 per cent, is intended to prevent dangerous speculation in gold in anticipation of a rise or fall in the gold content of the bullion dollar. The requirement that the weight of the bullion dollar should not be raised or lowered more than 1 per cent at a time is intended to prevent excessive speculation in gold in anticipation of a rise or fall in the gold content of the bullion dollar. This 1 per cent charge, Fisher maintains, would eat up all the profits a speculator might otherwise expect to make by buying gold from the government just before an anticipated reduction in the size of the bullion dollar and selling it back after the reduction; or by selling gold to the government just before an anticipated rise in the bullion dollar and buying it back after the rise. Fisher believes that the expenses and risks involved in any extensive speculation in bullion dollars for a longer period than two months would not be justified by the probable gain.

Criticisms of the Plan

Since Fisher first put forth his plan in 1911, there has been a large amount of controversy over it. It has been vigorously assailed by economists in this country and in Europe and has been ably defended by Fisher and by a number of other economists. The plan has been modified from time to time to meet objections that have been raised. A detailed and critical presentation of the objections to the plan is impossible within the limits of this book. I shall confine myself, therefore, to a brief summary of what I believe to be the principal valid objections to the plan.

A Long Period of Rising Prices Would Dangerously Deplete the Gold Reserve

The ratio of the bullion dollar reserve to the volume of notes in circulation would continually decline during periods when the commodity price level was tending upward, for, as the weight of the bullion dollar was increased, the number of bullion dollars represented by the gold reserve existing at the time the increases were made would decline. Experience has shown that rising prices may continue over long periods of time. Furthermore, the price advances that would need to be checked might often be very pronounced from year to year, or even from month to month. Our wholesale price level, for example, rose almost continually from 1896 to the summer of 1920, reaching a maximum in May, 1920, of 260 per cent above that of the year 1896. Within that period there were at least three months in which the monthly rise was 6 per cent or over and at least six months in which it was over 4 per cent. Of course, the opposite would take place when commodity prices were falling and the weight of the bullion dollar was being progressively reduced. Then the percentage reserve would be increased.

Speculation in Gold Would Tend to Defeat Plan

A second objection that has been frequently urged is that, at times when the commodity price level was tending strongly upward or downward, the plan would give rise to heavy speculation in the bullion dollar that would render impossible the price adjustments sought. The proposed difference of 1 per cent between the government's buying and selling price for the bullion dollar and the restriction of changes in the price to 1 per cent every two months were incorporated in the plan to meet this difficulty, but it is very doubtful if they would prove effective at times when the commodity price level was tending strongly in one direction or the other over substantial periods. This difficulty is discussed at some length by Dr. B. M. Anderson in his article, "On the Practical Impossibility of a Commodity Dollar," published in the *Chase Economic Bulletin* of December 13, 1933, from which the following quotation shows the general line of reasoning:

> "We take first the case of falling prices. We shall assume that prices have fallen 2 or 3 per cent and that the tendency is still downward, so that we can confidently expect that for the next two or three months the redeeming authority will progressively lighten the gold content. Will not foreigners withdraw their money from our markets, turning their cash in American banks into gold in order to avoid the loss of 2 or 3 per cent which they can clearly anticipate? Will not speculators rush to turn in their dollars for gold, anticipating that at a later time they can turn back the same gold to the redeeming authority and get more dollars for it? Will not everyone, who has foreign payments to

make, hasten to purchase foreign exchange, thereby increasing the foreign drain upon our gold? And will not all of these transactions operate to reduce the money supply of the country—since it is by turning in paper money that the gold is obtained from the central authority? And will not all these operations withdraw money from bank reserves, tightening the money market, raising rates of interest on short loans, reducing the credit available for the carrying of commodities and securities? But is tightening the money market the correct procedure when one wishes to raise prices?"

Commodity Dollar Would Bring Great Instability into Our Foreign Trade

If the plan were a national one, in effect only in the United States, its operation would bring a large element of uncertainty and speculation in all of our foreign trade. Fluctuations in exchange rates between the United States and other countries would be wide. From the standpoint of foreign commerce, we would be in much the position of a country like China a few years ago, which was on the silver standard when most of the rest of the world with which it carried on trade was on a gold standard. This difficulty would be largely overcome if the plan were adopted, on the basis of an international price index number, by all the leading commercial nations of the world, but the prospect of such an international adoption is exceedingly remote. Twenty-one years ago, in answering this and other criticisms of the plan, Fisher said: [1]

> "I am sure I am under no illusions as to the possibility of the early adoption of any plan to standardize the dollar. This may require centuries . . ."

On the other hand, if the plan were made international in scope, changes in the bullion content of the commodity dollar would affect prices much more slowly than under a purely national system. The reason would be that foreign trade among the nations concerned would not be materially affected by changes in the gold content of the dollar, through the stimulus to exports and the retardation of imports that a reduction in the gold content of the dollar would cause under a purely national system, and through the stimulus to imports and the retardation of exports that an increase in the dollar's gold content would cause.[2]

[1] *The American Economic Review*, Supplement, March, 1913, p. 46.
[2] *Infra*, pp. 136–139.

Powerful Psychological Factors That Affect Price Movements Are Ignored by Plan

Perhaps the most weighty objection to the plan is that it involves a highly mechanistic theory of the relation of money and bank credit to prices, and in doing so underestimates the great influence of changing human emotions, feelings and prejudices, hopes and fears on the movements of our commodity price level, particularly in periods of economic and political stress and strain.

In Chapter IV it was pointed out that the price level was the resultant of the interaction of the supply of our circulating media,

Annual Rate of Turnover of Bank Deposits

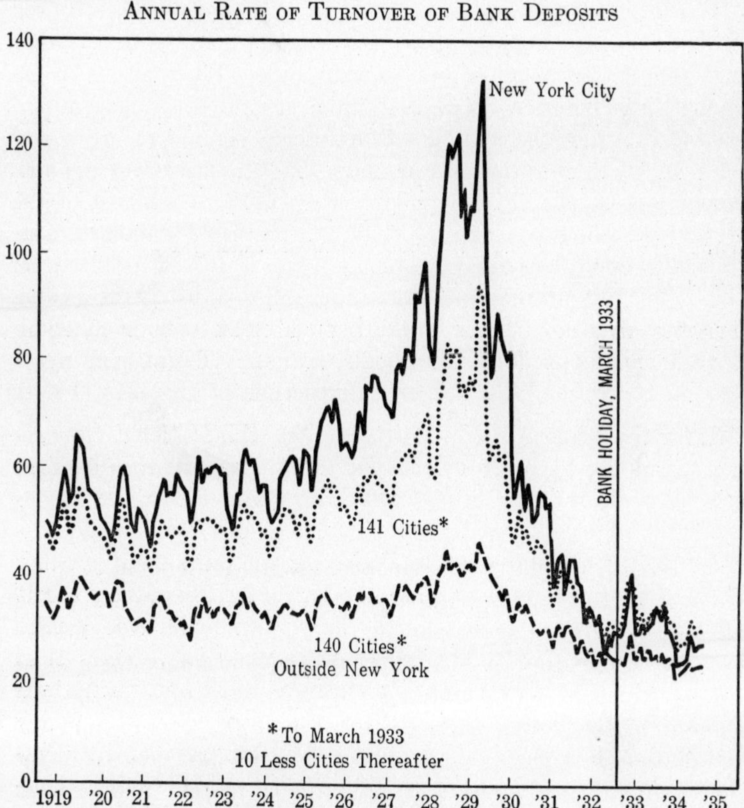

consisting of money and of bank deposits subject to check, and of the demand for these circulating media represented by the physical volume of goods and services to be exchanged, and it was noted that the supply of the circulating media was not only a question of the volume of money and of bank deposits, but also of the velocities at which this money and these bank deposits circulate. We have figures in the United States on a monthly basis covering approximately sixteen years that show the velocities at which the demand deposits of member banks in some 141 cities have circulated.[1] These figures vary widely from city to city and from time to time in each city. As previously noted, they are high when business is active and when the confidence of business men in the economic situation and prospects is strong. They are low in times of business depression and when the business public is full of doubts as to the economic outlook. In times of boom or of crisis and business depression, they move up and down with the movements of business confidence.[2] Deposits that are not moving are similar to money that is hoarded, so far as their influence upon prices is concerned. The preceding chart shows the movements of velocities for New York City, for 140 important cities exclusive of New York City and for these 140 cities and New York City combined. The fluctuations during the last seven years have been enormous.

Efforts to Expand the Volume of Money and of Deposit Currency and Thereby to Raise Prices Nullified by Declining Velocities

Since the crises of 1929 and early 1930, the National Government and the Federal Reserve authorities have made vigorous efforts to check declining prices and bring about a price advance by means of heavy, open-market purchases of Government securities by the Federal Reserve banks, for the purpose of glutting the member banks with reserve funds and of forcing a strong credit expansion. The supply of money in circulation for a long time has been larger than it was in the boom year 1929. Rediscount rates at the Federal Reserve banks have long been maintained at an extremely low figure, and a most liberal rediscount policy has been followed in order to enforce credit expansion. The National Government, through the Reconstruction Finance Corporation and numerous other governmental agencies, has made

[1] Since the "bank holiday" of March, 1933, the figures cover only 131 cities.

[2] For a study of the relationship between business confidence, deposit velocities and prices, see the author's article on "Controlled Inflation," *American Economic Review*, Supplement, March, 1934. See also *supra*, pp. 57 and 58.

enormous advances of credit to the public, with the hope of bringing about a strong rise in commodity prices. Except for a few months, however, chiefly in the fore part of the year 1933, business confidence continued very low from the collapse of October, 1929 to the end of the year 1933, and the velocities of bank deposits moved strongly downward. During most of this period the efforts at deposit currency expansion were more than nullified by the rapidly declining velocities, and, despite all these efforts, prices continued downward almost continuously from 1929 to the spring of 1933.

Here is an excellent illustration of the difficulty of controlling commodity prices merely by the mechanics of increasing the volume of money in circulation and the volume of reserve bank credit. "You can lead a horse to water, but you can't make him drink." Even if bank credit is cheap and plentiful, responsible business men will not use it if they have little confidence in the business situation and prospects, and if, in their judgment, extending their business gives promise of losses rather than profits. The Government and the Federal Reserve banks may to a considerable extent control the volume of money and of deposit currency in an inconvertible paper money régime, but they cannot control the velocities. These velocities are questions of business confidence and prospects,[1] of hopes and fears, of emotions and prejudices. They are matters of class feeling and of mass psychology. This is the principal reason why in critical times like those of the years 1930–1935 the commodity price level could not be controlled through regulating the supply of money by changing from time to time the weight of a bullion dollar.

Politics and the Commodity Dollar

Closely related to this obstacle to a successful functioning of a commodity dollar standard is the political obstacle. Commodity prices are affected with tremendous public and class interests. Their ups and downs are matters of vital concern to every class in the community—the farmer, the manufacturer, the business man, the professional man and the housewife. Taking human nature as it is today and American politics as it is, any board at

[1] Here we are speaking of confidence in the business situation and prospects. Confidence in a country's money is a different thing. When confidence in business is low, velocities are low, but when confidence in a country's money is very low, velocities tend to be high. Then we have "a flight from money." See pp. 60–62.

Washington that should try to control our commodity price level in the manner contemplated by the proponents of the commodity dollar would find itself continually under heavy political pressure, both from Congress and the public at large. Under this pressure a scientific and disinterested administration of such a plan would frequently break down. The commodity price index number, which the authorities would be trying to maintain at approximately 100, would be made up of the prices of a larger number of individual commodities. At all times the prices of some of these commodities would be rising and those of others would be falling. Producers of goods whose prices were falling at a time when the general price level was rising would resist by strong political pressure action by the authorities at Washington to increase the weight of the bullion dollar and thereby to push down the price level, which would tend to drag down still further the already declining prices of their products. What would happen, for example, in a case where the Government's price index numbers were rising while the prices of wheat and cotton, under the influence of unusually large crops or of unfavorable markets, were rapidly falling?

Conclusion

All in all, under present-day economic and political conditions in America, a price level anchored to a commodity of universal demand, such as gold—a commodity of which there is always an enormous marketable supply, and of which the annual product is but a petty percentage of the world's accumulated stock—is likely to be much more stable and dependable than a price level controlled by any such mechanism as that of the commodity dollar. Such a dollar may work in a model state of a distant utopian future. It would have hard sledding in the United States of today.

BIBLIOGRAPHY

Anderson, B. M., "On the Practical Impossibility of a Commodity Dollar," *Chase Economic Bulletin;* New York, Chase National Bank, 1933.

Fisher, Irving, *Stabilizing the Dollar;* New York, The Macmillan Company, 1925. (Contains a valuable bibliography on the commodity dollar.)

Fisher, Irving, and Others, "A Remedy for the Rising Cost of Living—Standardizing the Dollar," *The American Economic Review*, Supplement; Princeton, N. J., March, 1913.

Fisher, Willard C., "The Tabular Standard in Massachusetts History," *Quarterly Journal of Economics*, XXVII (1912–1913).

Kemmerer, Edwin Walter, *Modern Currency Reforms;* New York, The Macmillan Company, 1916.

Kemmerer, Edwin Walter, and Others, *Project of Law for the Gradual Introduction of a Gold Standard System in China, together with a Report in Support Thereof;* submitted to National Government of China by the Commission of Financial Experts, Shanghai, 1929.

Reed, Harold L., *The Commodity Dollar;* New York, Farrar and Rinehart, 1934.

Scrope, G. Poulett, *Principles of Political Economy;* London, 1833.

PART III

THE PRINCIPLES OF FOREIGN EXCHANGE

CHAPTER VIII

THE PRINCIPLES OF FOREIGN EXCHANGE

The subject of exchange divides itself into two parts, foreign exchange and domestic exchange. The first concerns itself with payments between different countries, and the second with payments between places within the home country. Inasmuch as political boundaries do not limit the operation of economic laws, the fundamental economic principles that govern foreign exchange are the same as those that govern domestic exchange. Persons familiar with foreign exchange, therefore, will have no difficulty in understanding domestic exchange. Although a few comments on domestic exchange will be made in this chapter, the chief concern here will be with foreign exchange. Further consideration of the subject of domestic exchange will be given later (in Volume II) under the discussion of the clearing and collection system of the Federal Reserve banks. The subject of foreign exchange itself may be divided into two parts: first, exchange between countries on the same standard; and, second, exchange between countries on different standards. In this chapter we shall study these two general types of foreign exchange in their order, including in the discussion of exchange between countries on the same standard certain general facts and principles that apply to both.

EXCHANGE BETWEEN COUNTRIES ON THE SAME STANDARD

Classes of Goods in Foreign Trade

Importers must pay for what they buy abroad, and exporters must be paid for what they sell abroad. It is in making these payments that the foreign exchange business functions. From the standpoint of foreign exchange, five broad classes of exports and imports may be distinguished, which may be designated as: commodities, securities, services, treasure and travel.[1]

[1] The United States Department of Commerce publishes every year a *Trade Information Bulletin* on "The Balance of Payments of the United States," in which the volumes of the various items in America's international balance sheet for the preceding year are estimated.

(1) *Commodities* (using the term in its narrower meaning) covers agricultural, forestry, mineral and animal products and manufactures. These comprise the bulk of the so-called "visible" items of foreign trade and, aside from "treasure," are the only items included in the usual statistics of imports and exports.

(2) *Securities.* As here used, the term covers stocks, bonds, debentures, long-time notes and the various kinds of short-time notes, government treasury bills, certificates of indebtedness and acceptances which are bought and sold in the international markets. Interest figures large in this item; so, also, do dividends. Most of these securities represent physical goods. A thousand shares of Pennsylvania Railroad stock, for example, constitute a certificate of ownership (subject to the liens of the Company's creditors) of $\frac{1}{13,163}$ of the property of the Pennsylvania Railroad Company, consisting in large part of roadbeds, tracks, stations and rolling stock; while $500,000 in Pennsylvania Railroad bonds constitute a lien on this same property to the amount of the bonds. In both cases, however, the value is more than that of the physical property. It is the value of a going concern, in which the physical property is an important factor. The exportation of these securities, therefore, from the standpoint of foreign exchange, is equivalent to the exportation of a part of the Pennsylvania Railroad.

(3) *Services.* Services are important items in foreign trade. Foreign ships and railroads, for example, in 1933, rendered us approximately $65 million of freight services for carrying American goods. Such services were imports for the United States and exports for the foreign countries rendering them, as truly as would have been the shipment to American merchants of an equivalent value in English woolen goods or Colombian coffee. An important service which England exports is marine insurance; another one is certain banking services rendered foreigners by England's great international banking houses. When American engineers render professional services in South America worth a million dollars, those services are as truly exports from the United States that must be paid for by South Americans as are shipments of a million dollars' worth of locomotives. Some of their compensation will be received by the engineers while they are in South America and used up by them for expenses incurred there; but the greater part will probably be remitted by them to the home land.

Under this head comes one of the principal items in our so-called "invisible trade"; namely, a substantial part of the services of recent immigrants. There are millions of immigrants in the United States who remit funds back home every year. They give labor services in the United States, for which they receive a wage compensation. Much of this compensation, however, they do not use up in the United States, but send home to dependents or for their own saving and investment. The value of their services over and above the part they consume and retain in the United States is, from the standpoint of foreign exchange, an American import from their respective home countries, which we must pay for by some kind of export. The amount of these remittances for the depression year 1934 was approximately $124 million.

(4) *Travel.* The fourth type of export and import arises from international travel. If an Englishman should receive from a French dealer a case of wine worth two thousand francs, it would clearly be an import for England and an export for France of a value of approximately two thousand francs.[1] In some way or other a remittance of this amount would have to be made from England to France. Suppose, however, that the Englishman, who, we will assume, has been in the habit of importing a case of this wine every year, spends a vacation this year in Paris, buys his case of wine there and consumes it there. It would not then figure in the import statistics of England or the export statistics of France; but, from the standpoint of foreign exchange it would be equivalent to a shipment of a case of wine from France to England (less shipping charges, etc.). It would require payment by the Englishman as truly as if he imported it into England and, since he is assumed to be on a vacation in France and therefore to be rendering the French people no equivalent economic services, the means of payment would have to come directly or indirectly from England. The goods and services consumed abroad by American travelers in the depression year 1934 are estimated to have amounted to $292 million. These are American imports "headed off," as it were, and consumed without getting here. From the standpoint of foreign exchange, they are important items of importation for the United States and of exportation for foreign countries. Euro-

[1] The Englishman, of course, receives somewhat more than the Frenchman exports, because to the value of the wine in France must be added the value represented by shipping and insurance expenses, customs charges and the like.

peans traveling in the United States give rise to similar exports by the United States and imports by Europe, but this item is relatively small, having amounted in 1933 to only $71 million. In some countries, as, for example, Switzerland and Egypt, where the tourist travel is large, one of the principal items of export consists of goods and services consumed by foreign travelers.

(5) *Treasure.* Gold and silver bullion constitute the principal items under this head; in fact, the only items under the term "treasure" as that term is usually employed in trade statistics. Gold and silver are commodities as truly as are the goods mentioned in the first group and, like them, move from the cheaper market to the dearer market under the impetus of the same fundamental economic forces. They are referred to separately because they are the world's principal standard money metals and, as such, perform functions worthy of special consideration. During the World War and for a number of years thereafter, there was a considerable international movement of paper money. Such money in international trade may best be classified as treasure, although this is a highly euphemistic term for some of it.

Means of Payment

Obviously, every export is also an import and every import an export. They are the same thing viewed from opposite angles. In every case of foreign trade, under normally functioning business, the exporter must be paid for the goods exported and the importer must pay for them. How are these payments made and received? The answer in its simplest form can best be given by limiting ourselves for the time being to the trade between two places, say, New York City and London, and by inquiring concerning the various methods that might be used, bearing in mind that in actual practice the major part of these payments are effected in a very small number of ways. The discussion will be based upon conditions as they existed prior to the departure of England and the United States from the gold standard during the period 1931–1933.

If payments were made directly in gold, vast quantities of gold would be continually in transit, ships carrying gold from New York to London passing ships carrying gold from London to New York. The expenses by way of interest during time of transit, packing, cartage, freight, insurance and abrasion would be very large.

Because this method of making payments in gold is so expensive, merchants in international trade many centuries ago devised methods of making payment through the machinery of written bills of exchange; and later, when the cable and the radio came into operation, also through the use of "cable and radio bills of exchange" or transfers. This is a refined form of barter and requires the shipment of relatively little gold.

If exporter *A* in New York were shipping $100,000 of cotton to importer *B* in London, and if importer *B* in London were shipping £20,000 of cloth (pounds sterling being taken in the illustration for convenience at a round figure of $5.00) to *A* in New York, it is easy to see how the one transaction would offset the other. It would be a case of simple barter. Or, suppose *A* in New York were shipping cotton to *B* in London, and *B* in London were shipping the cloth to *C* in New York, the settlement of both accounts could be made without the shipment of any cash, if *B* would instruct *C* to pay *A* the $100,000 that *C* owes *B* for the cloth. This process might be made a more roundabout one involving many others, say, *D*, *E*, *F* and *G;* but the principle would be the same.

Three different types of difficulties would arise from this method of making payment: (1) the amount due in one direction would almost never be equal to the amount due in the other. *B*, for example, might owe *A* $100,000, but *A* might owe *B* only $50,000 (£10,000). The dates when the obligations came due would also be likely to be different, one transaction being perhaps a cash transaction and the other one calling for payment, say, in ninety days. (2) The different parties in the import trade and export trade would often not know each other; *A* would not know *C*, nor would he know *D* and *E* to whom *B* would be shipping goods. Unless *B* were shipping to him, he might not even know that *B* was shipping goods to the United States. (3) If *A* knew that *B* was shipping goods to the United States and knew *C*, the party to whom he was shipping, he might not be willing to accept an order of payment from *B* on *C* in lieu of a direct payment from *B*.

Such difficulties are easily met in practice through the use of middle men in each country, namely, bankers and exchange brokers, who make a business of buying and selling bills of exchange and who, therefore, furnish a market for bills of different kinds and amounts. This is the foreign exchange market.

The Bill of Exchange

A bill of exchange is defined by the American Uniform Negotiable Instruments Law as "an unconditional order in writing addressed by one person to another signed by the person giving it, requiring the person to whom it is addressed to pay on demand or at a fixed or determinable future time a certain sum in money to order or to bearer." The following is an illustration of a simple trade bill:

New York, N. Y.
September 10, 1935

£10,000

Ninety days after sight of this First of Exchange (Second unpaid) pay to the order of The Thirtieth National Bank of New York City Ten Thousand Pounds Sterling. Value received and charge to our account.

The Royal Textile Company,
London, England.

United States Cotton Export Company,
New York City.

In this bill the United States Cotton Export Company, the drawer, which has exported £10,000 worth of raw cotton to the Royal Textile Company of London, the drawee, orders the drawee to pay, ninety days after this bill is presented to it for its O. K. or acceptance, the £10,000 it owes the United States Cotton Export Company, to the order of the Thirtieth National Bank of New York, which is the payee. The drawer is selling the bill to the Thirtieth National Bank and hence makes that bank the payee.

Bankers buy the bills of exchange offered by exporters in New York and send them to their foreign branches or representatives in London, who present them to the drawees for acceptance and ultimate payment or for immediate payment if the bill so requires. The bills bought by the American banks may be in amounts varying respectively from a few dollars to many millions of dollars. The proceeds realized when the bills are paid, or discounted in advance of payment, in London are paid to the credit of the New York bank's account with its London representative.

The New York bank is supposed to know what persons to trust and to what extent it is reasonable to trust them in the purchase of their bills of exchange, because the buying and selling of credits is its business and it has a credit department whose chief function is the studying of the credit standing and responsibility of the bank's customers, actual and prospective. In the analysis of the safety of a particular bill of exchange the bank also has the benefit of the advice of its London representative, which is in a position to pass judgment on the credit standing of the London importer.

The funds paid in London at maturity, or in discount in advance of maturity, of those London bills bought by the New York bank provide funds in London to the credit of the New York bank against which it may sell its own drafts on London to importers in New York who have payments to make in London. These drafts may obviously be made out for any amount within the limit of the funds available in London.

In this way bills of exchange calling for payment for exports and bank drafts used in paying for imports are made to offset each other through the intermediation of banks, with the result that international trade becomes, to a large extent, a process of bartering exports for imports. The mechanisms by which this bartering process is effected, of course, take a variety of forms. The above description represents one of the simplest and commonest.[1]

Rates of Exchange

A rate of exchange is merely one kind of price. It is usually the amount of money of one country charged for a bill of exchange per unit of the money of a second country in which the bill is payable. A sterling rate of 4.87, for example, means $4.87 for each pound sterling covered by the bill.[2]

[1] For a description of the various kinds of bills of exchange, and an account of the legal responsibilities of the parties to the bill, namely, drawer, drawee, payee and the different endorsees, the reader should consult a book treating the Law of Negotiable Instruments.

A classic work in this field is Daniels on *Negotiable Instruments*. For most students, however, the brief discussion of negotiable instruments in E. W. Huffcutt's *Elements of Business Law*, or that in C. H. Bush's *Uniform Business Law*, will be adequate.

[2] The methods of quoting exchange are different in different countries. Rates are sometimes quoted in terms of the foreign money. Prior to the World War, for example, French exchange in the United States was usually quoted in terms of the number of francs to the dollar. Sometimes two methods are used for the same exchange in a given country. Moreover, the methods of quoting are changed from time to time. The student should familiarize himself with the methods employed for the exchanges in which he is interested.

It is, however, fortunately becoming increasingly the custom in the United States to quote all the foreign exchanges in terms of the number of United States cents to the foreign unit and for this reason it is now much simpler to understand tables of foreign exchange rates than it was a few years ago.

Mint Par

The fundamental rate in the exchanges of all countries actually upon a gold basis is the so-called "mint par," which is the ratio of the pure gold content of the monetary unit of one country to that of the monetary unit of another country. For example, the sterling mint par prior to September 21, 1931, was obtained by dividing the number of grains of pure gold contained in the sovereign, namely, 113.00156, by the number contained in a dollar of United States gold money, namely, 23.22, which gave a mint par of 4.8665.[1]

Factors Determining Exchange Rates

We are now prepared to consider some of the basic factors in the determination of an exchange rate. For the sake of clearness, let us begin with the cable rate, because it involves no interest; although we should recognize that for most exchanges the demand rate is the dominant rate. Assume for the moment a condition contrary to fact, that all international payments are made through cable transfers. Assume that the time is the middle of August and that, in the broad sense of the terms, exports and imports are approximately equal. As autumn approaches and the exports of our American cereal and cotton crops take on larger and larger proportions, an increasing amount of sterling exchange is thrown on the New York market.

In other words, those selling cotton, wheat and other American commodities to London merchants sell them for English money and therefore have pounds sterling coming to them. *Sell goods to people in England, sell English money*, is the normal rule. The rate of exchange is merely the United States currency price in New York for a pound sterling of English money to be delivered in England at a certain time, in the case of cable transfers immediately.

In the fall our exports normally greatly exceed our imports; exporters, therefore, we may assume, had more pounds sterling to sell than importers cared to buy at the mint par rate of, say, 4.8665. The New York price of a pound sterling, therefore, moved

[1] Calculated in the same way, the French mint par at that time was 3.9179; the German, 23.82; and the Italian, 5.2632. The mint pars of the principal countries of the world, together with the recent movements of New York exchange rates in these countries, are published by the Federal Reserve Board each month in the *Federal Reserve Bulletin*.

downward. It went from 4.8665 to 4.8660, then to 4.8600, etc., until it reached 4.8465, which we will assume to have been the gold-import point rate at that time for cable transfers. Beyond this point the cable rate could not go, under the conditions assumed, in an unrestricted market for gold.

Gold-Import Point

What is meant by the gold-import point? When the exporter was selling his sterling bill for $4.8465, he was virtually selling British gold at a discount of 2/5 of 1 per cent (exactly 2 cents on the equivalent of $4.8665), since the pound sterling, which was coined in the form of the British sovereign, contained 4.8665 times as much pure gold as the United States dollar. Under the conditions assumed, two American cents to the amount of gold in a sovereign was sufficient to pay all the expenses incident to shipping gold bars from London to New York and of there converting them into United States money; that is, the expenses for packing, carting, shipping, insurance and interest during the time of transit of the gold from London to New York, and of converting the gold bars into United States money in New York. The result was that, if the American exporter of wheat were compelled to sell in New York, by cable, for immediate delivery in London, the pounds sterling due him there for less than $4.8465 to the pound, he could more profitably have obtained his pay in London in Bank of England notes, converted them into gold bars in London, had the gold bars shipped to New York and then had the bars exchanged for United States money at the Federal Reserve Bank. In actual practice the exporter of wheat did not do this, but there were banks and bullion brokerage houses which made a business of importing gold whenever the exchange rates were such as to yield them a reasonable profit on its importation. And this is true today, although England is no longer on the gold standard, and gold is not now permitted to circulate in the United States.

The gold-import point is not a fixed point. It declines as interest rates and shipping and insurance expenses rise, and it rises as they fall. It is affected by mint charges (when coinage is involved), brokerage charges, taxes and other minor expenses, all of which vary from time to time. Some concerns, moreover, are able to import gold at slightly lower expenses than others, and some will work on a smaller margin of profit than others.[1] Gold embargoes, moreover, and other less open restrictions, are sometimes imposed by the authorities against the free exportation of gold when the exchange market would be otherwise favorable to such exportation. Sometimes gold is imported, it is claimed, at a loss on the transaction itself, with the expectation on the part of those importing it of realizing a profit on stock exchange operations as a result of the "bullish" effect on the stock market which gold importations frequently have.

At this writing in 1935 there are few countries on the gold standard and the free markets for gold in the world are very limited.

Gold-Export Point

The gold-export point comes into play under conditions essentially the opposite of those described in connection with the gold-import point. When imports of goods are large relative to exports and American buyers of British goods are making heavy purchases of pounds sterling in order to pay in England the British money they owe for the goods they are importing, the price of a pound sterling, namely, the rate of exchange, rises. *Buy goods in England, buy pounds sterling.*

When both England and the United States were on the gold standard, the more pounds sterling importers bought, other things equal, the higher the price of a pound sterling. Under those conditions, when the demand for pounds sterling on the part of American importers exceeded the supply of pounds sterling thrown on the market by American exporters at the current rate the dollar price of a pound sterling rose; in other words, the rate of exchange advanced toward the gold export point. If, for purposes of illustration, we assume that it costs two cents to ship the amount of gold in a sovereign (the equivalent of $4.8665 United States gold coin) from New York to London,[2] that is, 2/5 of 1 per cent, then, when the cable rate in New York on London advanced above this point, say, to 4.8865, it became profitable for foreign exchange

[1] Most standard books on foreign exchange contain itemized computations of the costs that enter into the determination of the gold shipping points. See, for example, A. C. Whitaker, *Foreign Exchange*, Chap. XX; and Ira B. Cross, *Domestic and Foreign Exchange*, Chap. XI.

[2] Actually the expenses of shipping gold from New York to London were often different from those of shipping it from London to New York.

operators to ship gold from New York to London, selling it on the London gold market for British money and selling cable exchange in New York against the British money so received. Importers having large payments to make in London could afford to make their payments through the instrumentality of shipping gold to London (incurring all the expenses of making such shipments), rather than pay cable transfer rates appreciably above $4.8865. In practice, of course, it was not the merchants but the bullion brokerage houses and large exchange banks that made such shipments.

Gold movements in a free market in international trade take place under fundamentally the same conditions as do the movements of other commodities. It is simply a case of a commodity seeking the best market, gold differing from other commodities chiefly in the fact that it is the most salable commodity in the international market, a fact that makes it the money of international trade.

Assuming 4.8465 to have been the gold-import point and 4.8865 to have been the gold-export point, it will be observed that gold was imported when it was more valuable in the United States than in London by about 0.4 per cent, that is, by enough to pay all shipping expenses and yield a profit; for, obviously, if $4.8465 of United States money bought English money with a gold equivalent of $4.8665 of United States money, a given amount of gold in the form of United States money was worth more than in the form of English money. Other goods are imported under exactly the same conditions; that is, when they are dearer in the United States than abroad by an amount sufficient to pay shipping expenses and to yield the importer a reasonable profit. On the other hand, the gold-export point, assumed to have been 4.8865, meant that in the form of money it took 4.8865 of our dollars to buy the amount of gold in a sovereign, which was the quantity of gold contained in $4.8665 of our gold coin. Gold in London, therefore, in the form of standard gold bars was more valuable than gold in New York by about 0.4 per cent and, since this difference was enough to cover all shipping expenses and to yield a reasonable profit to the shipper, gold moved from the cheaper market, New York, to the dearer market, London, until the lessened supply in the United States and the increased supply in England made further shipments unprofitable.

If the United States exported gold to England at a rate of 4.8865, then England imported gold from the United States at 4.8865 (equivalent to about 4s.1.14d. to the dollar), so that rate was our gold-export point and England's gold-import point. In the same way, 4.8465 (equivalent to 4s.1.24d. to the dollar) was our gold-import point and England's gold-export point.

Demand and Usance Exchange

So far in the discussion of foreign exchange, we have been assuming cable rates, in order to eliminate as far as practicable for the time being two other factors contained in most exchange rates, namely, insurance and interest. In doing this, however, we should note that in practice the demand rate and not the cable rate is the dominant sterling rate. It is now time to consider briefly these two factors.

(1) *Insurance.* Whenever a period of time elapses between the purchase of a bill of exchange and its payment, an element of risk enters. If *A* in New York draws a clean bill (a bill without documents attached as security) at sixty days' sight upon *B* in London for £10,000 and offers to sell it, before it is accepted by *B*, to Bank *X* in New York, Bank *X* will obviously not wish to buy it unless it believes *A* to be good for the amount of the bill. The bank will naturally pay a better price for a bill drawn by a concern of high financial standing than for one drawn by one of lower standing. The risk involved in such a purchase is reduced after *B* accepts the bill, provided *B* is looked upon as a concern of high financial responsibility. Banks, however, often place their sole reliance upon the financial standing of the drawer of the bill, whom they usually know, rather than upon the drawee in a foreign country, whom they often do not know. Endorsements on the bill also lessen the risk involved in buying it as they increase the number of persons contingently liable for its payment. In this connection, one financially important name may be of much more consequence than half a dozen unimportant ones. Even large concerns, however, may find their paper discriminated against in the form of unfavorable rates when they throw an unduly large amount of it on the market. The larger the risk involved in buying a bill, according to the estimate of the market, the lower the rate, other things equal, that will be paid for the bill. This difference represents a sort of insurance charge for protection against proba-

ble loss in handling bills and commonly goes by the name of insurance.[1]

A large part of the bills in the market are documentary bills; that is, bills with documents attached, such as warehouse receipts, bills of lading, insurance papers, invoices, government inspectors' certificates and securities. These documents protect the purchaser of the bill in the control of the merchandise or securities during the process of shipment until the bill is paid by the drawee or, at least, until the drawee assumes responsibility by accepting it. In the case of demand bills, documents are released only on payment; in the case of time bills they may be released on acceptance or only on payment according to the instructions on the bill. Whether the documents shall be released on acceptance or only on payment depends largely upon the financial reputation of the drawee. Of course, the character of the goods being shipped and the character of the protection to the purchaser of the bill otherwise given by the documents attached are important factors in the insurance element of the exchange rate.

(2) *Interest.* The third element in the exchange rate is interest. Whenever an appreciable period of time elapses between the date when the bill is sold and the date when it is payable, an item of interest is involved whether it is expressed in the contract or not. Interest figures even in demand bills, because time is required for the transit of the bill. Interest for time of transit is a large item when the places are distant, as, for example, in the case of a bill drawn in Manila on New York City. A ninety-day sight bill in New York on London may require anywhere from five to fifteen days to reach London and be accepted, depending upon the frequency of sailings, the speed of the steamer on which the bill travels and the delays at both ends of the trip. If we assume seven days as the normal time and add the three days of grace

[1] "The price which is paid to a merchant of undoubted position for his sixty days' sight bill on a foreign country, will be higher than that which is granted for a second-rate bill on the same place. The purchasers of bills must be induced, by a concession in price, to take an article of inferior security. They must be indemnified for the greater risk. Credit is a very important element to be considered in the rate of exchange; and so notorious is this amongst those engaged in international trade, that the price at which exporting houses can sell their foreign bills, is looked upon as an unerring test of the credit which they enjoy among their neighbours. Thus credit causes a difference in the value even of such foreign bills as are drawn on the same day, rendering it difficult to give any exact or definite quotation of the price of long-dated paper; and, further, it operates on exchanges generally in times of commercial panic or excitement, and causes the prices of all bills to fall." Goschen. Viscount, *Theory of the Foreign Exchanges*, p. 56.

customary in England on time bills, we arrive at a hundred days between the time of purchase by the New York bank and the time of payment by the drawee in London. This would mean that, if the New York bank should wait for its funds in London until the ninety-day bill matured, it would be deprived for 100 days of the use of the money it paid for the bill. Clearly, then, it should pay a lower rate for a bill drawn on the same concern and with the same security payable in a hundred days than one payable by cable, and the difference should be equivalent to the market interest on the dollar value of a pound sterling for 100 days. Inasmuch as a sight bill requires the same time in transit as a ninety-day sight bill, which we have assumed to be seven days, the ninety-day sight bill should have a rate lower than the sight bill by the amount of interest on the dollar equivalent of a pound sterling for ninety-three days. There are no days of grace on a sight bill.

For what market should the rate of interest be taken, New York or London? Since the bill in the illustration is assumed to be payable in London and to be discounted there, it is the London rate that controls. If it were dollar exchange drawn in London on New York, payable in dollars and discounted in the New York market, it would be the New York discount rate that would control.

In every bill of exchange, then, involving any appreciable time before payment there are three elements: (1) pure exchange, that is, the premium or discount from the mint par represented by the cable rate; (2) insurance against risk; (3) interest at the market rate, usually that of the place where the bill is payable.[1]

Our future comparisons will be based upon the sight rate, which, although containing a few days' interest, is, as previously noted, in practice, usually the basic rate.

Foreign Exchange and the Discount Market

Foreign exchange rates and discount rates are closely related. The differences between the rates for demand bills and the rates for time bills are chiefly a matter of the interest for the life of the bill; and "the spreads" between time rates and the demand rate,

[1] In every rate of exchange there is also a fourth element, an administrative expense to compensate the banks or exchange brokers for their services in connection with the transaction. On large transactions this item is of comparatively little importance.

therefore, vary with the market rate of discount. This is inevitable, for, if the ninety-day rate were lower than the sight rate by more than the amount of the discount on a pound sterling for ninety-three days at the current rate of discount in London, bankers would profit by buying ninety-day bills, discounting them and selling demand drafts against the proceeds, thereby forcing up the ninety-day rate and forcing down the demand rate until they were again in equilibrium; that is, until they differed by only the interest on a pound sterling for ninety-three days at the current rate. If, on the other hand, the ninety-day sight rate were not lower than the sight rate by as much as the interest for ninety-three days on a pound sterling at the current rate of discount, bankers would make a profit by selling ninety-day sight bills, buying demand bills with the proceeds and lending the proceeds of the demand bills in London, at the market rate of discount. This would soon restore equilibrium by forcing down the rate for ninety-day sight bills and forcing up the rate for demand drafts. A high discount rate in London attracts money to London for investment, thereby increasing the demand for sight drafts, and decreasing the supply through decreasing the discounting of long bills in London, thus pushing up the demand rate. A low discount rate has the opposite effect. It reduces the flow of money to London for investment and increases the flow of London funds to other places where higher money rates prevail.

Dollar Exchange

Prior to the War most of the exchange operations in connection with our trade with the Orient and Latin America were conducted by a triangular process through London.[1] The effecting of these American exchange operations through the instrumentality of the London exchange market was due chiefly to the fact that there was a good discount market in London for such bills and a well-organized system of acceptance houses and exchange banks for carrying on the business. Neither of these existed in New York. As a result, bills drawn on London were more salable in Latin America or in the Orient, or salable on better terms, than bills drawn on New York or on any other financial center. After the War, however, this situation changed and dollar exchange, that

[1] For a typical example of such an exchange operation, see Escher, *Foreign Exchange Explained*, Chap. XIV.

is, exchange drawn in dollars and discounted in New York, assumed greater importance. This was brought about chiefly by three forces: (1) the establishment of the Federal Reserve system, which furthered the development of an American discount market; (2) the enacting of new laws in the United States favorable to the acceptance of bills by banks, so-called "bank acceptances"; and (3) the influence of the War on the relative credit positions of New York and London.

Some Monetary Forces in Foreign Trade

Between two countries like the United States and England the fundamental monetary forces operating in the exchange market may be seen if one isolates the two countries and asks himself what forces would come into play to prevent one of them, say the United States, from being denuded of its money supply if it should for some time import from the other, say England, more merchandise, securities and services than it should export to her. It is assumed that both countries are squarely on the gold standard and that there are no restrictions upon the flow of gold between them. The more important forces at work are shown in the following table:

United States	*England*
(1) Excess imports into the United States from England will push *up* the demand exchange rate from, say, the old mint par 4.8665 toward the gold-export point, say, 4.8865. All other exchange rates in the United States on England will tend to move upward, in harmony with the basic demand rate.	(1) Excess exports from England to the United States will push *down* the demand exchange rate from the mint par 4.8665 toward the gold-import point 4.8865. All other exchange rates in England on the United States will tend to move downward in harmony with the basic demand rate.
(2) As the exchange rate rises (from 4.8665 to 4.8865) American importers, who make their payments through the purchase of London drafts, will incur an increasing expense in the fact that they will be compelled to pay a continually higher price in American money for the pounds sterling required of them to pay for the goods they are importing. This will tend to reduce	(2) Decreased American imports are decreased British exports. As the exchange rate falls (from 4.8665 to 4.8865) those few British exporters who obtain payment by selling in London drafts drawn in dollars on the United States, will suffer slightly, because they will be compelled to give an increasing amount of United States money for each pound sterling they obtain. This

United States	*England*
the imports of the kinds of merchandise, securities and services on which the margin of profit normally realized is very small.	will tend to reduce the exports of the kinds of merchandise, securities and services on which the margin of profit normally realized is very small.
(3) A rising exchange rate will give a slightly additional profit to American exporters, who obtain their pay by selling in New York the pounds sterling due them in London (i.e., their sterling bills), for they will receive an increasing amount of American money for each pound sterling due them. This will tend slightly to increase exports, particularly of the kinds of merchandise, securities and services on which the margin of profit normally realized is very small.	(3) Increased American exports are increased British imports. As the exchange rate falls (from 4.8665 to 4.8865) those few British importers who make their payments in the United States by buying in England dollar drafts on the United States, will realize a slightly additional profit through the larger amount of American money they will receive for each pound sterling. This will tend slightly to increase imports of merchandise, securities and services of the kinds on which the margin of profit normally realized is very small.
(4) Relatively large demands in the United States for pounds sterling in London, namely, for sterling drafts, or relatively large payments by American importers against dollar exchange drawn upon them or for their account by British exporters, cause a flow of funds to New York exchange banks, strengthening bank reserves and thereby tending to reduce call rates of interest and, more tardily, time rates.	(4) Relatively large payments by London banks to British exporters against sterling drafts drawn by American banks on their London correspondents, or against the sale to London banks of dollar exchange drawn by or for the account of British exporters, decrease the supply of bank funds in England, reduce bank reserves and thereby tend to increase interest rates on demand loans, and, more tardily, on time loans.
Obviously, a large part of these payments to New York banks represent merely transfers of funds from one bank account to another, and the actual increase of banking funds that takes place is represented solely by the net flow of money from active circulation into the banks.	Obviously, a large part of these payments by London banks to British exporters represent merely transfers of funds from one bank account to another, and the actual decrease of banking funds that takes place is represented solely by the net flow of money from the banks into active circulation.
(5) Increasing bank reserves induce New York banks to reduce their	(5) Reduced bank reserves cause London banks to call in loans made

United States	*England*
indebtedness to the Federal Reserve Bank and, in turn, encourage reductions in the New York Federal Reserve Bank's discount rates.	to discount houses, acceptance houses and similar institutions, which, in turn, increase the demands on the part of those institutions for loans at the Bank of England and encourage advances in the Bank of England's discount rates.
(6) Increasing bank reserves and declining interest and discount rates spell an easier money market. This causes a rise in business confidence, stimulates business activity and increases the rates of monetary and deposit turnover (*V* and *R* of the equation of exchange).	(6) Decreasing bank reserves and rising interest and discount rates spell a tighter money market. This causes a fall in business confidence, retards business activity and decreases the rates of monetary and deposit turnover.
(7) Declining interest rates, rising business confidence and increasing rates of monetary and deposit turnover stimulate speculation, encourage increased purchases of securities and commodities, and thereby force up the prices of the more sensitive securities and of staple articles of produce and later of those which are less sensitive.	(7) Rising interest rates, declining business confidence and decreasing rates of monetary and deposit turnover retard speculation, reduce purchases of securities and commodities, and thereby force down the prices of the more sensitive securities and staple articles of produce and later of those which are less sensitive.
(8) Rising security and commodity prices encourage increasing purchases in the cheaper market, England, and still further accentuate the forces already mentioned.	(8) Declining security and commodity prices encourage increasing sales in the better market, the United States, and still further accentuate the forces already mentioned.
On the other hand, a counter force is set up in the form of increasing sales and exportation of United States securities and of certain American export commodities to British speculators, investors and merchants, who buy in anticipation of further price advances.	On the other hand, a counter force is set up in the form of increasing purchases and importation of United States securities and staple American import products by British speculators, investors and merchants, who buy in anticipation of further price advances.
(9) The decline of interest and discount rates in the United States tends to cause a flow of loanable funds out of the country.	(9) The rise of interest and discount rates in England tends to cause a flow of loanable funds into England.

United States

(10) Low interest and discount rates, large bank reserves, high rates of monetary and deposit turnover, high security and commodity prices, and high exchange rates, all spell relatively redundant money, and therefore relatively cheap money. Such money seeks a better market, exchange rates finally reach the gold-export point, and gold is exported.

(11) The outflow of gold reduces bank reserves and possibly also monetary circulation. It tends to increase interest and discount rates. It exercises a depressing influence on business confidence and therefore tends to reduce rates of deposit and monetary turnover and to lessen speculation and business activity. It tends to decrease prices, at first of the more sensitive securities and staple commodities of international trade, and later of the less sensitive securities and commodities. The high gold-export point exchange rate puts a slight additional burden on imports and gives a slight exchange premium to exports. All these are forces which tend to discourage imports and to encourage exports.

Of course, if at the time gold is being exported the Federal Reserve Bank replaces the gold that is going out of the country by the expansion of Federal Reserve notes and circulating deposit credit, through extending its open-market purchases and its rediscounts, the forces above mentioned may be thereby weakened or possibly even entirely offset by this policy.

England

(10) High interest and discount rates, low bank reserves, low rates of monetary and deposit turnover, low security and commodity prices, and low exchange rates, all spell relatively scarce money and therefore relatively dear money. Such a market attracts money from abroad, exchange rates finally reach the gold-import point, and gold is imported.

(11) The inflow of gold increases bank reserves and tends to decrease interest and discount rates. It tends to increase business confidence and therefore rates of deposit and monetary turnover. It stimulates speculation and business activity. It tends to increase prices, at first of the more sensitive securities and staple commodities of international trade, and later of the less sensitive securities and commodities. The low gold-import point exchange rate puts a slight additional burden on exports and gives a slight exchange premium to imports. All these are forces which tend to discourage exports and to encourage imports.

Of course, if at the time gold is being imported the Bank of England adopts a policy of impounding gold and of refusing to expand bank note and deposit credit upon it, the new gold will be sterilized and the forces above mentioned will be weakened or possibly even entirely offset by this policy.

Every force mentioned in the above table is at all times an actual or potential factor in the exchange situation. Although exchange rates and prices are never in complete equilibrium, a movement in any direction tends to set up corrective movements in the opposite direction, so that there is always going on a struggle of forces working toward the establishment of equilibrium. It may happen, of course, that forces in one direction may be so strong that any particular gold standard system—or any other monetary system, for that matter—will break down before counter forces have come into play with sufficient strength to turn the tide.

The condition assumed in preparing the above tabular statement, namely, that the United States and England were isolated from the rest of the world, each carrying on foreign trade solely with the other, is, of course, contrary to fact. The trade of these two countries is only part of a world-wide international trade situation, the different parts of which are always tending toward equilibrium. Money markets in both countries are influenced greatly by conditions in places in other parts of the world, so that it is common for interest rates and price movements to move sympathetically in England and the United States, rather than oppositely, and even a slight lag is likely to be quickly corrected by arbitrage transactions. None the less, the forces brought out in the above statement—albeit in an exaggerated way—are continually at work, and it is such forces that under normal conditions maintain an orderly functioning of foreign exchange markets and prevent currency systems from breaking down as a result of international transactions.

Arbitrage

Arbitrage, in the field of foreign exchange, consists of the payment of money from one country to another country, through the intermediation of a payment to and a payment from a third country. It is a roundabout method of payment resorted to because it is found to be cheaper than the direct method on occasions where the exchanges are out of equilibrium. Obviously, equilibrium tends to be restored by such transactions. Sometimes there may be more than one intermediary country. Payments to Paris and Berlin are often made by remittances through London; and, in the past, payments from the United States to London were frequently made through Paris, and sometimes through Berlin and Amsterdam.

The character of a simple arbitrage transaction is shown in the following illustration, which is assumed to have taken place in early 1931.

Suppose a St. Louis banker wished to remit 125,000 francs to Paris, and that the best rate he could obtain in St. Louis on Paris was 3.91 cents to the franc, so that 125,000 × 3.91 cents, or $4,887.50, would have been required to make the remittance. Suppose that he found that demand drafts in St. Louis on London were selling for 4.84, and that cable reports from London gave the London selling rate for checks on Paris as 125 francs to the pound sterling. For £1,000 in London he could buy a check on Paris for the desired amount, i.e., 125,000 francs; while at 4.84 the cost in St. Louis of the check on London would be but $4,840. This is less than the $4,887.50, the cost of remitting directly, by $47.50. From this gross profit there would be slight deductions for commission to the London bank through which the London part of the transaction was effected, for revenue stamps in London and for interest on extra time required.

Arbitrage bankers watch the international exchange rates very closely, eager to take advantage of every slight variation from equilibrium. Since the amounts transmitted are often large, and the transactions normally require but very short periods of time—sometimes an important arbitrage transaction can be effected by cable within a few minutes—a slight margin of profit, say, 1/64 of 1 per cent, or even less, often yields a substantial profit.

Exchange Futures

Most exchange contracts are "spot" contracts, that is, contracts for immediate delivery of the draft, bill or cable transfer; but in our principal exchange markets a large business in futures is continually being transacted. A future has been defined by Whitaker as follows: [1]

> ". . . a contract under which one of the parties agrees to deliver, and the other to take a stipulated amount and kind of exchange (as £10,000 bankers' sight sterling) at an agreed future time, for a price (*i.e.*, at a rate) *determined upon when the contract is made, but payable on the future date when the exchange is actually delivered.* The motive of either party may be to make an outright speculation, or it may be only to make a hedge against some risk of exchange assumed in connection with an

[1] Whitaker, *Foreign Exchange*, p. 286.

independent transaction already put through or decided upon: and one of the parties may have the speculative motive and the other the motive of hedging."

Futures are more important in exchange between countries on different monetary standards, where fluctuations in rates are wide, than between countries on the same standard, where the range of possible variations in rates is narrowly limited by the shipping points. This subject will be discussed later in this chapter.

EXCHANGE BETWEEN COUNTRIES ON DIFFERENT STANDARDS

In exchanges between a country on the gold standard and a country on the silver standard, or between a country on the gold or silver standard and one on a fiduciary money standard, or between two countries on different fiduciary money standards, there are no narrow limits of possible fluctuations like those fixed by the "gold points" in exchanges between two gold standard countries, or the "silver points" in exchanges between two silver standard countries. Between such countries the fluctuations in exchange rates that may take place are practically limitless, and those that do take place within short periods of time are often wide. These variations give rise to problems that justify a separate consideration of the exchanges between countries on different monetary standards.

Exchange between a Gold Standard Country and a Silver Standard Country

In exchanges between a gold standard country and a silver standard country, there are no fixed mint pars of exchange and the limits of the possible fluctuations of exchange rates vary widely and are fixed roughly by the market price of silver in gold standard countries and the market price of gold in silver standard countries. Since there are no limits to the possible fluctuations in these prices, there are no limits to the possible fluctuations in exchange rates. When there are no restrictions on the exportation and importation of gold and silver, and when coinage is free in both the gold standard country and the silver standard country, exchange rates in a gold standard country on a silver standard country move roughly with the gold price of silver, rising when the price of silver rises and falling when it falls. In a silver standard country, similarly, rates on a gold standard country move roughly with the movements in the silver price of gold. Silver moves into and out of a silver standard country and into and out of the monetary circulation in such a way as to tend to keep the value of a given quantity of silver approximately the same within the country and abroad and approximately the same in the form of coin and in the form of bullion. If the value of silver in the world's silver market goes down, more silver is shipped to the silver standard country and more is coined, for more money is needed to give expression in monetary form to this reduced value of silver, with the result that the price level rises. If, on the other hand, the value of silver in the world's market rises, the inflow of silver to the mints of the silver standard countries falls off and silver coins are exported or melted, thereby reducing circulation and bringing down the price level, for, obviously, less money is needed in silver standard countries to do a given amount of money work when the value of silver, and therefore of silver money, rises.

Since 1873, when effective bimetallism ceased to exist in the world, the price of silver in terms of gold has fluctuated widely,[1] and, as a consequence, there has been great instability in exchange rates between silver standard countries and gold standard countries. The evil effects on trade of widely fluctuating exchange rates, whether they be in silver exchanges or in paper-money exchanges, are partly mitigated by the practice of exporters and importers of fixing their exchange forward and of the banks in covering forward exchange purchases by forward exchange sales, or by "hedging."

An idea of some of the evil effects of wide exchange fluctuations and of a common method of meeting them may be had from the following hypothetical illustration, adapted from the writer's book on *Modern Currency Reforms.*[2]

[1] *Infra,* p. 350.

[2] The only important silver exchanges in the world for many years have been those of China and the British colony of Hong Kong. The National Government of China in 1934, by placing taxes and other restrictions on the exportation of silver, discontinued, strictly speaking, the silver standard in China. Furthermore, since the Chinese exchanges are very complicated, they do not submit themselves readily to purposes of clear illustration of the fundamental principles with which we are here concerned. For this reason I have chosen for illustration the simpler silver standard system that existed in the Philippine Islands at about the time of the American occupation. Since 1903 the Philippines for most of the time have been on the gold standard. During the silver standard period, exchange rates in Manila

Prior to 1903 the monetary unit of the Philippines was the Mexican silver dollar, containing approximately 79 per cent of an ounce of fine silver (or 85 per cent of an ounce of British standard silver, i.e., silver .925 fine). Under this silver standard régime, let us suppose that on January 1st a hemp dealer in the Philippines contracts to deliver a given quantity of hemp in New York by the fore part of April at a total price of $10,000 payable in New York City,[1] to be forwarded so as to arrive in New York at about the time of the arrival of the hemp.[2] Suppose also that, at the time these arrangements are being made, the Manila bank's buying price for such demand bills is Pfs. 2.50; that is, they will give Pfs. 2.50 for each dollar of the bill. At this rate, the exporter would receive for his hemp bill Pfs. 25,000. Assume that he knows at about what price he can buy the hemp in the Philippines and that he calculates that he can buy it and deliver it in New York at a total cost in the Philippines of Pfs. 23,000. This would leave him a net profit of Pfs. 2,000. Accordingly, he buys the hemp as planned during January and February, obtaining the funds by means of an overdraft at his Manila bank, secured by a pledge of the hemp as purchased. He ships it the first of March, drawing at the same time a sight bill on the consignee for $10,000, and offers to sell this bill to his Manila bank. Meanwhile, however, let us assume that the price of silver has risen and that New York exchange has, therefore, fallen, so that the rate now for such demand bills is Pfs. 2.20, instead of the Pfs. 2.50 upon which the merchant had based his calculations. Being compelled to sell at Pfs. 2.20, that is, to receive only Pfs. 2.20 for each dollar coming to him, instead of the Pfs. 2.50 which he expected, he obtains for his bill of $10,000 only Pfs. 22,000, instead of his estimated 25,000. Thus, his expected profit of Pfs. 2,000 is changed into a loss of Pfs. 1,000, and this, despite the fact that he bought the hemp

were usually quoted in terms of the number of foreign money units to the Philippine peso, as, for example, a shilling and seven pence to the peso, or forty cents United States money to the peso. To simplify the illustration and avoid confusion, the rates will be quoted here in the form most widely used in the United States today, namely, the number of units of local money to each unit of foreign money, in this case the number of Philippine pesos and centavos to a dollar of United States money.

[1] Throughout this illustration, the dollar mark ($) will signify United States dollars, and the symbol Pfs. (officially used in the Philippines) will signify Philippine silver standard pesos.

[2] In practice such a transaction would usually have been financed through a sterling letter of credit opened in London by the consignee through his New York bank.

at the calculated price and definitely contracted for its sale before he purchased it.

If, however, in the interim, the gold price of silver had fallen and the exchange had risen from Pfs. 2.50 to, say Pfs. 2.80, he would have received Pfs. 28,000 for his $10,000 bill, and his profit would have been increased from his expected Pfs. 2,000 to Pfs. 5,000. The hemp exporter would thus gain by a rise in exchange and lose by a fall; but he would run a great risk and such risk-taking as this is not his business. He is a hemp dealer, not an exchange speculator.

Let us take a similar illustration from the side of the importer. A Manila wholesale shoe merchant buys by cable order, on January 1st, 5,000 pairs of cheap shoes in the United States at $2.00 a pair, when exchange is at Pfs. 2.50. The shoes are to be delivered in Manila in sixty days, and the merchant is to pay for them by cable in New York funds thirty days after their delivery. The local market for shoes of this kind, let us assume, is such that the merchant can sell them at Pfs. 6.00 a pair, which would yield him a gross profit of a peso per pair or a total of Pfs. 5,000. Allowing Pfs. 2,000 for expenses, he would have a net profit on the transaction of Pfs. 3,000 (which would be equivalent with exchange at Pfs. 2.50 to $1,200). He closes his contracts on both sides; that is, he buys the 5,000 pairs of shoes at $2.00 a pair and agrees to deliver them to Philippine retailers at Pfs. 6.00 a pair. But, during the next three months, let us assume, there is a substantial drop in the price of silver and a corresponding rise in New York exchange, the price of cables rising from Pfs. 2.50 to Pfs. 3.00. The merchant has realized Pfs. 30,000 for the shoes, and he now goes to his Manila bank to purchase his cable transfer on New York in favor of the shoe manufacturer for $10,000. At an exchange rate of Pfs. 3.00, however, this sum costs him Pfs. 30,000, instead of the Pfs. 25,000 which he had counted upon in figuring exchange at the earlier rate of Pfs. 2.50. When he adds to this the Pfs. 2,000 for expenses, he finds that his anticipated net profit of Pfs. 3,000 has been transformed into an actual net loss of Pfs. 2,000.

Even had he not contracted in advance for the sale of the shoes in Manila for Pfs. 6.00 a pair, he would probably have suffered, because the mere fact of a rise in exchange does not make it possible to sell the shoes at a higher price. The local currency wages and incomes of most persons who buy shoes have not been appreciably affected by this sudden rise in exchange, nor is their demand for shoes thereby increased. In the course of time such a rise in exchange (resulting from a depreciation of silver), if it were permanent, would influence the supply of shoes on the market through lessening their importation and thereby tend to raise the local currency price of shoes. But at best this influence works slowly—often too slowly to be of much benefit to the merchant who has already imported a large stock—for of imported goods like shoes there is usually a considerable supply kept on hand. Then, too, there may be the alternative of importing the goods from silver standard countries with which exchange has remained practically constant. One must not assume, as Americans thinking in terms of United States currency so commonly did when the Philippines were on the silver standard, that the price of shoes would rise promptly and in exact proportion to the fall in exchange. The responsiveness of prices, even of goods imported from gold standard countries, was usually slow. Retail and wholesale prices cannot fluctuate with daily, or even weekly or monthly, movements of exchange—and that is particularly true in an oriental and tropical country like the Philippines where inertia and custom play such important rôles.

If, in the above illustration, exchange had fallen to Pfs. 2.00, instead of rising to Pfs. 3.00, the importer would have been able to buy his $10,000 cable transfer to New York for only Pfs. 20,000, thereby raising his anticipated net profit from Pfs. 3,000 to Pfs. 8,000—an increase in the net profit as measured in United States currency from an anticipated $1,200 to an actual $4,000.

Obviously, the fall in exchange which was so harmful to the exporter was *pro tanto* favorable to the importer; while the rise in exchange which was so favorable to the exporter was *pro tanto* harmful to the importer. A rising exchange stimulated exportation and inhibited importation; a falling exchange stimulated importation and inhibited exportation. Either called for an adjustment in currency shipments; and either tended toward a one-sided and artificial stimulus to trade which was not in the interest of healthy trade development.[1]

[1] Cf., "The Influence of Falling Exchange upon the Returns Received for National Products." Argument submitted to the Monetary Commission of the Republic of Mexico, April 18, 1903, by Charles A. Conant, Jeremiah W. Jenks and Edward Brush. Printed in *Report of Commission on International Exchange, 1903*, pp. 431–439.

Forward Exchange Contracts

The above illustrations, although representing a common interpretation of the handicaps under which Philippine foreign trade was conducted during the period of the silver standard, greatly exaggerate those handicaps. As a matter of fact, the exporter of hemp, unless he deliberately planned to speculate in exchange, would have gone to his bank at about the time that he contracted with the New York merchant for the sale of his hemp and would have made a contract for the forward sale of his hemp bill at a definite price. He would have agreed in January to sell his hemp to the New York merchant at so many dollars per bale, and at the same time would have agreed with his Manila bank to sell the dollars he was to receive in New York, i.e., his New York bill of exchange, at a definite price in local currency, say, at a rate of Pfs. 2.40 to the dollar. Then, no matter what happened to exchange, he would have been safe. If exchange fell to Pfs. 2.20, he would not have suffered—that would have been the bank's affair, not his. If it rose to Pfs. 2.60, he would not have profited. He is not a speculator in silver, but a dealer in hemp, and he would have shifted this speculative risk to the shoulders of those whose business it is to handle risks. A similar policy would have been followed by the importer of shoes. When in January he made his contract to buy the shoes in New York for $10,000, he would have made a forward contract with the bank for the purchase of $10,000 to be laid down in New York, say 90 days hence, when payment for the shoes should fall due, at the exchange rate of, say, Pfs. 2.60. If, in the interim, exchange rose to, say, Pfs. 2.80, he would not thereby have lost, and, if it fell to, say, Pfs. 2.40, he would not have gained. The price at which he was to buy his New York dollars would have been fixed, and the risk of loss or chance of profit arising from exchange fluctuations would have been shifted to the bank.

The bank itself, however, in making these two forward contracts, one for the delivery by the bank three months hence of a cable transfer of $10,000 on New York, and one for the delivery to the bank in Manila of a demand bill which would be paid in New York three months hence, would also have avoided the risk arising from exchange fluctuations. It would have "hedged." The $10,000 bought from the exporter at the rate of a dollar for each Pfs. 2.40

it would have sold to the importer at the rate of Pfs. 2.60. The profit to the bank would have consisted in the difference between the buying rate and the selling rate—here, for simplicity of illustration, assumed to be much larger than would normally have been the case.[1]

Let us now turn to the paper money standard exchanges.

Paper Money Standards

Prior to the World War the paper money exchanges, although considerable in number, were comparatively unimportant, for the great bulk of the world's foreign trade was between gold standard countries. During the War and for some time thereafter, most of the world was on some form of a managed paper money standard. Between 1922 and 1929 nearly all of the leading countries returned to the gold basis. Then, beginning in 1930, under the pressure of the world economic crisis, a large part of the world again abandoned the gold standard and at this writing most countries are on a depreciated paper money standard. The evils of this situation are so serious that it is reasonable to expect a return on the part of the leading countries to a fixed gold basis within a few years. For the time being, however, the paper money exchanges are of great importance.

With countries on different paper money standards, there are no fixed pars of exchange and no shipping points that correspond to the gold points of gold standard countries. The value of the paper money unit is a question of the supply of money relative to the demand. There are no limits to the possible fluctuations in the value of such inconvertible paper money determined by the stuff out of which the money is made. "The sky is the limit," there-

[1] It should be repeated that the transactions were generally nothing like so simple in practice as in the above hypothetical illustrations. Most of the exchange business at that time (but not now) was done through London and comparatively little directly with New York. Sterling exchange dominated the market. Exports, moreover, were financed largely by time bills, which were later discounted in London, not by demand bills. The banks did not "cover" each day their forward contracts for the purchase of exchange with forward contracts in like amount for its sale. Each bank studied its own situation and made its forward contracts according to its own circumstances and its anticipation of the future silver and exchange market. If the bank was conservative, it kept both sides of the account about equal, that is, it covered all of its forward contracts with reasonable promptness. On the other hand, if it was willing to speculate—and oriental banks generally did speculate in exchange—it oversold sterling when it expected silver to rise, thereby expecting to receive its pay in an appreciating local peso; and it overbought sterling when it expected silver to fall, thereby expecting to pay for its sterling in a depreciating local peso.

fore, of possible variations in exchange rates when one or both of the countries concerned have paper money standards—a fact that will be realized if one studies the fluctuations of exchange rates in New York on, say, Berlin or Vienna, for a few years after the Armistice.

Exchange rates are very sensitive prices. If a country issues paper money to excess, one of the first signs of depreciation will be a rise in exchange rates above the gold-export point, followed by heavy exportations of gold. Prices of most other things do not respond to excessive issues of paper money anything like as quickly as do the prices of foreign monetary units, such as pounds, francs and marks, prices which we call exchange rates. Furthermore, different classes of prices, as, for example, wholesale prices, retail prices, wages (i.e., the prices of labor), interest rates (i.e., the rental prices of capital) and rates of public service corporations, respond differently to the influence of increasing issues of paper money, as do also the prices of different articles within each of these groups.[1] Given sufficient time, the prices of all goods and services will rise (under the influence of paper money issues) until they reach a new equilibrium at a level at which they will bear roughly the same relationship to each other that they bore before the paper money depreciation began. But the speed with which different prices in a paper money country adjust themselves to this new equilibrium level varies greatly, and the prices of gold and of foreign moneys (i.e., foreign exchange rates)—articles which are bought and sold in large quantities under keen competition in a world's market—respond very quickly.

It is these varying degrees of lag in the responses of different prices to variations in the relative volume of paper money circulation that cause the great disturbances in international trade that take place during periods of international monetary instability.

A Paper Money Standard Country and a Gold Standard Country

This point may be illustrated by reference to the exchange situation between France and the United States before the War and in July, 1921. In 1913 both countries were on a gold standard and had been for many years. Their commodity prices were, therefore, in approximate equilibrium, so far as goods entering the in-

[1] Cf., pp. 246–250 and 290–295.

ternational markets were concerned. A franc had a gold equivalent of 19.3 cents United States money, so that, broadly speaking, commodity prices in France expressed in francs were numerically about five times as high as they were in the United States where they were expressed in dollars.

The value of gold (as measured by its purchasing power over commodities at wholesale in the United States) was about 32 per cent less in July, 1921 than for the year 1913. This means that, had France still been on a gold basis, her price level, like that of the United States, should have been 47 per cent higher in July, 1921 than it was for the year 1913.[1] But France was on a paper money basis in July, 1921 and the gold value of the paper franc, as measured by New York exchange rates on Paris (bankers' checks), averaged about 7.77 cents for the month. If French prices had risen from 1913 to July, 1921 proportionately to the depreciation of the gold value of the paper franc, they would have been in July, 1921, $\frac{1.47 \times 19.3}{7.77}$, or 3.65 times as high as they were in 1913; and they would have been $\frac{19.3}{7.77}$, or 2.48 times the July, 1921 level of United States prices, as expressed in index numbers. These figures would represent what Gustav Cassel has named "the purchasing power parity." Average wholesale prices in France in July, 1921 were actually only 3.32 times as high as they were in 1913, and only 2.24 times as high as they were in the United States in July, 1921.[2] Retail prices in Paris were only 3.06 times as high in July, 1921 as they were in July, 1914.[3] Wages in general and the prices of a great many articles of home production had not advanced anything like as much as had the general price level.

Here is a situation that placed a substantial premium on exports from France to the United States. Whereas, in 1913, we received a franc for every 19.3 cents of our money, in July, 1921 we received 2.48 francs for this amount, but wholesale prices in general had only risen to 2.24 times what they were in 1913, giving an average additional profit due to the lag in price adjustments of nearly 10 per cent, and a much greater exchange profit in the

[1] If the dollar was worth 32 per cent less in purchasing power, it was a 68 per cent dollar as compared with 1913, and with a 68 per cent dollar prices should have been 47 per cent higher because the reciprocal of .68 is approximately 1.47.

[2] Cf., Index numbers of *Bulletin de la Statistique Générale*.

[3] There was practically no change in the price level between 1913 and July, 1914.

numerous cases where the lag was greater than the average. This extra profit gave an artificial stimulus to exports from France to the United States, thereby tending to force up prices of home products in France until they were brought into equilibrium with the new level of exchange rates, at which time the extra exchange profit would disappear.

On the other hand, this lag in price adjustments to rising exchange rates severely handicapped the import trade of France with the United States. French money had a greater purchasing power at home than abroad. The people of France in July, 1921 had to pay on an average 2.48 francs for 19.3 cents of United States money, whereas they should have paid only 2.24 francs if they were to get the full value of their money as measured by its purchasing power at home. Prices in gold standard countries seemed to them unreasonably high, and they accordingly tended to curtail their imports. This created a scarcity of goods in France and lessened the outflow of funds for the payment of imports, both of which forces tended to force up home prices to the new equilibrium set by exchange rates.

This retardation of imports and stimulus to exports would have been more effective in these early post-war years in France and in other paper money countries, in restoring the price equilibria, had it not been for two impeding forces: (1) the great need for foreign-produced raw materials to get industry started after the ravages of war, and (2) the continuation by governments and by banks of an inflationary policy for a long time after the Armistice.

Later, after the United States gave up the gold standard in the spring of 1933, and subsequently (in January, 1934) stabilized the gold value of her dollar at approximately 59 per cent of its former value, while France remained on the gold standard at the pre-depression gold value of the franc, the situation just described was reversed. In the United States the prices of gold and of French exchange quickly rose about 69 per cent (the reciprocal of .59 is 1.69) above what they were in February, 1933 (the last month in which the United States was on the old gold standard). Commodity prices in general, however, advanced much more slowly. Between February, 1933 and January, 1935, for example, wholesale prices in France declined approximately in the ratio of 100 to 86.5, and had the wholesale commodity price index number in the United States "taken up the slack" represented by the reduction of the gold content of the dollar to 59 per cent of its former weight, the American price index number should have been 69 per cent higher in January, 1935 than the corresponding price index number of France. Using February, 1933 as a base of 100, it should have been 1.69 × 86.5, that is, 146, which is 46 per cent above the American index number of February, 1933. It actually was only 32 per cent higher. In other words, commodity prices were far out of equilibrium as between France and the United States. Our American price level was too low for "a 59-cent dollar." In terms of purchasing power gold was worth much more in the United States than it was worth in France. American prices to the Frenchman seemed low as compared with what they were formerly, while French prices to the American seemed high. Exports from the United States to France were thus stimulated, and the French people were encouraged to travel in the United States where "a franc goes much farther than it used to." On the other hand, commodity imports from France into the United States were discouraged and American tourists' travel to France was falling off greatly. On every side American travelers were saying that "a dollar doesn't go anything like so far in Paris as it used to." At the same time, there was a strong flow of gold from the cheaper gold market, France, to the dearer gold market, the United States. All this tended to bring the commodity price levels in the two countries back into equilibrium with the exchange rates, in other words, to bring back to parity the internal and the external purchasing power of the dollar, but this process takes time.

Two Paper Money Countries

The principle above discussed applies equally between two paper money countries, in one of which depreciation is more rapid than in the other. Temporarily, in such cases, exports are stimulated from the country with the more rapidly depreciating monetary unit and the imports to that country are retarded. A case in point was that of France and Germany in the fall of 1921. Then the rapidly declining German exchange rate in Paris stimulated the importation of German products into France and retarded the exportation of French products into Germany.

When paper money becomes scarcer and exchange rates fall, there is the same sort of lag in the declines of different classes of prices and of different prices in each class. At such a time the phenomena described above are reversed. Exchange rates in the home paper money country give a higher gold value to the monetary unit than that expressed in the home price level. Local prices are temporarily out of equilibrium with world gold prices—they are too high. Imports are stimulated and exports are retarded until the prices adjust themselves to the newer and lower equilibrium.

All maladjustments, it should be emphasized, are but temporary, and they automatically correct themselves unless prevented from doing so by artificial restrictions placed on the flow of goods, securities, or specie, or by progressive inflation or deflation.

BIBLIOGRAPHY

Angell, James W., *The Theory of International Prices;* Cambridge, Mass., Harvard University Press, 1926.

Cassel, Gustav, *Money and Foreign Exchange after 1914;* London, The Macmillan Company, 1922.

Commission on International Exchange, *Reports*, 2 volumes; Washington, U. S. Government Printing Office, 1903 and 1904.

Cross, Ira B., *Domestic and Foreign Exchange;* New York, The Macmillan Company, 1923.

Daniel, John Warwick, *A Treatise on the Law of Negotiable Instruments;* Re-edited and enlarged by Thomas H. Calvert, Sixth Edition, 2 volumes; New York, Baker, Voorhis & Co., 1919.

Escher, Franklin, *Modern Foreign Exchange;* New York, The Macmillan Company, 1932.

Furniss, Edgar S., *Foreign Exchange;* Boston, Houghton Mifflin Company, 1922.

Goschen, Viscount, *The Theory of the Foreign Exchanges;* London, Effingham Wilson, 1906.

Kemmerer, Edwin Walter, *Modern Currency Reforms;* New York, The Macmillan Company, 1916.

——, "The Theory of Foreign Investments," *Annals* of American Academy of Political and Social Science, November, 1916.

Spalding, W. F., *Eastern Exchange, Currency and Finance;* London, Sir Isaac Pitman & Sons, 1924.

——, *Foreign Exchange and Foreign Bills;* London, Sir Isaac Pitman & Sons, 1915.

Whitaker, A. C., *Foreign Exchange*, Second Edition; New York, D. Appleton & Company, 1933.

Young, John Parke, *European Currency and Finance;* Commission of Gold and Silver Inquiry, United States Senate; 2 volumes; Washington, U. S. Government Printing Office, 1925.

CHAPTER IX

THE GOLD EXCHANGE STANDARD

The gold exchange standard is a variety of the gold standard, since the unit of value is the value of a fixed quantity of gold in a free gold market. Its outstanding characteristic is, that it provides for redemption of the various forms of fiduciary money in drafts on gold funds located abroad, rather than in gold coin or gold bullion at home. The gold exchange standard is a monetary standard that has come into prominence since the beginning of the present century, although instances of practices closely akin to those of the modern gold exchange standard are found over a century ago.[1] At the time of the outbreak of the World War, the gold exchange standard was in operation in India, the Philippine Islands, Java, the Straits Settlements, Nicaragua and a few other countries.

All varieties of the gold standard broke down during the period of the World War. With the world's gradual return to the gold standard during the decade after the War, the gold exchange standard became very popular, and the principles of the gold exchange standard were incorporated in varying degrees in the currency systems of a majority of the gold standard countries of the world. The gold exchange standard was favored by the Financial Commission of the International Conference held at Genoa in 1922.

Object of Gold Exchange Standard

The object of the gold exchange standard is the extension of the principal advantages of the gold standard to countries not financially able or, for other reasons, not willing to use gold coins, in any considerable degree, as media of exchange, or to redeem their fiduciary money in gold bars. The gold exchange standard is essentially a mechanism for providing a gold standard without a gold currency. Usually in gold exchange standard countries the money in circulation is mostly paper and silver.

[1] Cf., for example, the currency plan for British colonies and dependencies outlined in a Treasury Minute of February 11, 1825, described by E. H. D. Arndt in his *Banking and Currency Development in South Africa*, p. 45.

The Principle of the Gold Exchange Standard as Exemplified in the Experience of the Philippine Islands

Probably the nearest approach to the "Simon-pure" gold exchange standard which the world has seen was the currency of the Philippine Islands as it was administered from 1905 to about 1910, under the Philippine Gold Standard Act of October 10, 1903. This system will, therefore, serve well for purposes of illustration.[1]

At the beginning of this period the currency of the Philippine Islands consisted chiefly of fiduciary silver pesos, fractional silver coins, minor coins of nickel and copper, silver certificates issued by the Government and supported by a 100 per cent reserve of silver pesos held in the vaults of the Government Treasury, and a few million pesos of bank notes. There was some United States money in circulation, but gold coin was rarely seen. Under American control no Philippine gold coins were minted and those which had been minted many years before, under the Spanish régime, had long since disappeared from circulation.

The Philippine Coinage Act, passed by the United States Congress March 2, 1903, had declared that the unit of value of the Philippine Islands should be a theoretical gold peso (not coined) consisting of 12.9 grains of gold, .900 fine, and therefore exactly equivalent to 50 cents of United States gold coin, and had required that the silver peso and all the fractional coins of the Islands should be kept at parity with this gold monetary unit.

For maintaining the parity of Philippine silver coins with gold at this rate, the Philippine Gold Standard Act of 1903 created a special reserve fund known as the Gold Standard Fund. This fund was composed of the proceeds of a loan which the Philippine Government floated for the purpose, of all seigniorage profits realized in the coinage of the new money, and of certain other profits incidental to the administration of the currency. It was a trust fund, kept separate from all other government funds, and to be used exclusively for the maintenance of the gold parity of

[1] Unfortunately, for a time during later years, every fundamental principle of the gold exchange standard was ignored by those in authority in the Philippine Islands, with the result that the Philippine gold exchange standard suffered severely. The system was later restored, however, and today is functioning in a manner similar to that of this earlier period. Cf., E. W. Kemmerer, *Modern Currency Reforms*, pp. 314–323 and 365–382, and George F. Luthringer, *The Gold Exchange Standard in the Philippines*.

the Philippine currency. The law provided that part of the fund should be kept in Manila and part in New York.

For the maintenance of the parity three forms of redemption were provided in the law, the principal one—the only one that concerns us here—being mandatory, and the other two incidental and optional with the Government.[1] The principal form of redemption was in gold drafts on New York. The Philippine Treasurer was directed to sell, on demand, for Philippine currency, drafts (in sums of $5,000 or more) on that part of the Gold Standard Fund kept on deposit in New York banks, charging for the same a premium of three-fourths of 1 per cent for demand drafts and of 1⅛ per cent for telegraphic transfers. It was likewise provided in the law that the bank in New York, which acted as the depository of the Gold Standard Fund should sell drafts (in sums of ₱10,000 or more) on that part of the Gold Standard Fund held in the Treasury vaults in Manila, payable in Philippine currency, charging for them the same premium rates.

All Philippine currency brought to the Philippine Treasury for the purchase of exchange on New York, pursuant to the above provisions of law, was required immediately to be withdrawn from circulation, and *physically kept in the Treasury vaults.* The money so withdrawn from circulation—with certain qualifications that do not concern us here—could not be paid out again, except in response to drafts drawn by the Gold Standard Fund depository bank in New York, on the fund in Manila, or for the purchase of silver to provide a needed increase in coinage.

The object of the sale of drafts was to provide a means for the maintenance of the parity, and, to that end, of automatically adjusting the currency supply to the varying demands of trade, without the necessity of introducing gold coins into circulation; in other words, to create "a gold standard without a gold currency." Every legitimate function of a gold currency, except that of shipment to and from other countries in making international trade payments, could be performed as well by the Philippine silver and paper currency as by gold coin. In fact, this Philippine silver and paper currency was better adapted than gold coins would have been to the needs of Philippine trade and to the tastes

[1] For a more detailed account of this system including an explanation of the other two forms of redemption, cf., the author's *Modern Currency Reforms*, pp. 317–323.

of the great majority of the Filipino people. Some provision, however, had to be made for the performance of this function of money of making international trade payments that could not be performed by Philippine fiduciary money. This function of money, or of bullion promptly exchangeable for money on demand, is not only important because it provides a means by which foreign trade payments are made, but it is still more important because it is through the performance of this function that the currency supply is adjusted to the currency demand, and that the parity of the currency is maintained by a reduction in the circulation in times of relative redundancy of the currency and an increase in times of relative scarcity.

When, in the trade among gold standard countries, the balance of payments becomes strongly unfavorable in one of them, exchange rates rise to the gold-export point, registering a relative redundancy of the home currency, and gold is exported. Likewise, when in the trade among gold standard countries the balance of payments becomes strongly favorable in one of them, exchange rates fall to the gold-import point, registering a relative scarcity of the home currency, and gold is imported. All the expenses of shipping gold, including packing, cartage, freight, insurance, interest and loss from abrasion are borne by the shipper.

Under the gold exchange standard, as it existed in the Philippines in 1905, this fundamental principle was recognized. The premium charged by the Government in Manila for dollar exchange on New York, and the premium charged by the Government's depository bank in New York for peso exchange on Manila, were fixed to represent as nearly as possible the actual commercial costs of shipping gold bars between the two cities.[1]

When, for example, exchange rates in Manila on New York rose to the gold-export point, the actual gold was not exported, as it would have been under similar circumstances in the United States, and other gold coin or gold bullion standard countries, but the Philippine Government gave the would-be gold exporter, in exchange for his Philippine currency in Manila, a draft entitling him to the gold credit in New York, and charged him as a premium

[1] Shortly after the Philippine Gold Standard Act was passed, the rates charged in New York for peso exchange on Manila were reduced, to prevent settlements being made by the shipment to Manila of United States paper currency, which could be imported into the Philippines more cheaply than could gold bars and which circulated in the Islands.

for the draft simply the amount which the actual exportation of the equivalent in gold bars from Manila to New York would have cost him, had he exported the gold himself.

The Philippine pesos paid to the Government for the draft (exclusive of the premium) were equivalent to the amount of gold he would have shipped. They (including the premium charged) were withdrawn from circulation by the Government and stored away in the vaults of the Gold Standard Fund—a procedure which reduced the circulation of Philippine currency as effectively as the actual exportation of an equivalent amount of Philippine coins would have done.

When, on the other hand, exchange rates in Manila on New York fell to Manila's gold-import point (which would mean that in New York rates on Manila had risen to New York's gold-export point), the depository of the Philippine Gold Standard Fund in New York gave the would-be gold exporter in New York, in exchange for his gold (or its equivalent in United States currency) a draft entitling him to the equivalent in Philippine pesos laid down in Manila, and charged him (for the credit of the Philippine Gold Standard Fund) a premium sufficient to cover the expenses that he would have incurred under the gold coin standard, had he actually shipped the equivalent in gold bars from New York to Manila. When the drafts on the Gold Standard Fund were presented in Manila for payment, they were paid in pesos, *physically withdrawn from the vaults* of the Gold Standard Fund, and this payment increased the Philippine currency circulation as truly as would the importation into the Islands of an equivalent amount of Philippine gold coins.

The system was just as automatic in its regulation of the money supply to the needs of trade as a gold coin or gold bullion standard would have been, although there was no gold coin in circulation in the Philippines, and no gold reserve was required there. Aside from such official transfers as those for the army and navy (which in practice interfered somewhat with the perfect functioning of the system), the Government had nothing to do with commercial exchange, except at the gold (or currency) shipping-point rates. These points represented the limits of fluctuation in the gold exchange value of the peso which the Government imposed. When exchange rates rose to the gold-export point, the Philippine Government virtually said: "So far they may rise and no farther. A further advance would signify a depreciation of our peso below its legal gold par if we were on a gold coin standard, and it will be so interpreted under the gold exchange standard; therefore, we will sell on demand gold drafts on New York (in sums of $5,000 and multiples thereof) in unlimited quantities at these gold-export-point rates, and will relieve the currency redundancy by withdrawing from circulation the pesos paid to us for these drafts." On the other hand, when exchange rates in Manila fell to the gold-import point (later the United States paper currency import point), the Government virtually said: "So far they may fall and no farther; a further decline would signify an appreciation of our peso above its legal gold par if we were on a gold coin standard, and it will be so interpreted under the gold exchange standard; therefore, we will sell on demand pesos laid down in Manila (in sums of ₱10,000, and multiples thereof) in unlimited quantities at these gold (or currency) import point rates, to be paid for by gold or its equivalent in New York. This will relieve the currency scarcity in the Islands by pouring pesos into circulation from the Gold Standard Fund." Commercial exchange rates, therefore, could not rise or fall appreciably beyond these respective limits; and between them the Government had nothing to do with exchange. That was the exclusive field of the banks.

Advantages of Gold Exchange Standard

The advantages of the gold exchange standard over a strict gold standard for a country like the Philippines are twofold.

First is the advantage previously mentioned, that the gold exchange standard enables such a country to have a circulating medium of the kind best adapted to its needs. Gold coin is not well fitted to the needs of a country the great bulk of whose transactions are small. Silver and paper are much better.

The second advantage is that of economy, and this is a matter of great importance for many countries, which cannot afford the luxury of a gold coin or even of a gold bullion standard. Although possibly a larger gold reserve is needed under the gold exchange standard than would be needed under a strictly gold coin standard in a country having a large circulation of gold coin along with its fiduciary money, the net expense is not proportionately so large. This is true for several reasons: (a) The money of circulation is all fiduciary money and therefore much less expensive than if a large part of it were full-weight gold coins. No gold coin and no gold bars are hoarded, and no gold reserve is maintained in the country to meet the possible demands of would-be hoarders. Conversion of local money into gold is made only through foreign drafts of which the minimum amount sold is the equivalent of $5,000. (b) Under the gold exchange standard the reserve is more effective than under the gold coin standard, being all in one reservoir (e.g., the Gold Standard Fund), where every dollar can be immediately used in time of need; whereas gold coin in circulation and gold bars in private hands may be difficult to mobilize in emergencies, for the very emergency that creates the demand for the gold is likely to cause the public to cling to it more tightly. (c) The premiums realized by the Government on exchange ordinarily yield the reserve fund a good profit. For example, the premiums on exchange realized by the Philippine Government for the six fiscal years 1905–1906 to 1910–1911 were ₱1,106,768 on an average circulation of about ₱41,700,000. (d) Part of the reserve fund is capable of earning interest—namely, that part deposited abroad. The Philippine Government, for example, realized as high as 4 per cent on that part of the Gold Standard Fund kept on deposit in the United States, and its interest earnings on that part of the fund for the five years ending June 30, 1910, amounted to ₱1,437,942.

Except under unusual circumstances, the reserve fund under the gold exchange standard continually increases in amount. This is true, because (aside from the slight expenses connected with the currency administration that are usually charged to the reserve fund) money is never paid out of the fund except in return for a larger sum paid in. A demand draft on New York for $10,000 sold in Manila by the Government, when the premium was three-fourths of 1 per cent, reduced the fund in New York by $10,000, but increased the fund in Manila by ₱20,150; and, vice versa, a New York draft on the fund in Manila for ₱20,000 decreased the fund in Manila by ₱20,000, but increased the fund in New York by $10,075. When the fund is temporarily reduced for the purchase of silver (or nickel or copper) to meet the need of new coinage, the fund is later increased by the amount withdrawn and by the net seigniorage profit on the coinage in addition.[1]

[1] Losses incurred on the recoinage of worn coins are usually chargeable to the reserve fund, but this item is small when all the coins are fiduciary, as they usually are in gold exchange standard countries.

The only times when the reserve fund is materially depleted in amount (aside from remotely possible losses by theft or by failure of the depository bank or banks) are times of extreme business depression, when, because of a great decline in business, the currency needs of the country may fall off decidedly and remain far below normal for a considerable period of time. Under such contingencies, the silver peso reserve in Manila (continuing our illustration) might be greatly increased as a result of continually heavy purchases in Manila of drafts on New York, and the gold part of the fund in New York might be correspondingly depleted by the payment of these drafts. If the depression were so severe that the movement was not checked by the usual forces before the danger point were reached, the gold fund in New York could be replenished through the forward sale in New York by cable from Manila of a few million ounces of silver to be obtained by the Government through the breaking up of the excess pesos held in the peso part of the fund in Manila. The gold proceeds of this sale of silver bullion would be deposited to the credit of the fund in New York. Here the fund would suffer a loss of the difference between the nominal or money value of the pesos broken up and sold and the price obtained for the silver bullion, to which would be added the expenses of the transaction. It would be the opposite of a seigniorage profit—a sort of negative seigniorage. Such a measure would be adopted only as a last resort, and the need of doing so would be evidence that for existing trade needs too many pesos had been coined.

Under ordinary circumstances the depletion of the gold fund in New York would be checked before it had gone far by forces analagous to those that prevent an undue exportation of gold from a gold coin or gold bullion standard country. They are notably: (1) a tightening of the money market in Manila through the withdrawal from active circulation and from bank reserves of the large quantities of pesos physically deposited in the Gold Standard Fund's vaults in Manila; (2) the stimulus given to merchandise exports by the prevailing high exchange rates; and (3) the retardation of merchandise imports caused by the same high rates.

The Qualified Gold Exchange Standard

A qualified form of the gold exchange standard, which assumed great importance after the War, is one that is administered not by the government but by the central bank. In this form, the principal money of the country consists of notes issued by the central bank, and the only central reserve used for maintaining the gold parity of the currency is that of the central bank, a large part of which is kept in foreign financial centers, such as New York and London, in the form of bank deposits and of highly liquid, short-time paper, such, for example, as bankers' acceptances. Under this system, the central bank obligates itself to sell drafts on say New York, at all times on demand, at the gold-export point, and provides for the sale of drafts by its agent in say New York, on the central bank at home, at all times on demand at the gold-import point. These gold points mark the limits, as in the gold coin or gold bullion standard, beyond which exchange is not permitted to go. Between these points, the central bank, like any other bank, may, of course, conduct an ordinary foreign exchange business.

Under this system, in order to assure a contraction of the currency when heavy sales of drafts at the gold-export point are depleting the gold reserves held abroad, the law usually provides that the central bank must pay a tax which increases progressively as its percentage of gold reserves declines below a certain point, and that the equivalent of this tax must be added to the bank's discount rates. These requirements tend to enforce a contraction of the currency when the currency is relatively redundant and when, under the gold coin or gold bullion standard, currency contraction would be effected by gold exports. Under such requirements, the central bank can expand its credit and increase its note circulation, when its reserves are low and declining, only at a progressively increasing expense to the borrowers and at a progressively declining rate of profit to itself.

Peru's Qualified Gold Exchange Standard of 1931

The following provision of the Law of 1931 creating the Central Reserve Bank of Peru—a law which has since been modified in certain particulars under the influence of the economic depression—will serve as an illustration of a typical qualified gold exchange standard.

The Central Reserve Bank of Peru had a monopoly of the note issue privilege in Peru and was required by law to maintain the parity of its notes with gold at the rate of the equivalent of 28 cents United States gold to the monetary unit, the *sol*. For this purpose, the Bank was required to maintain "a normal legal minimum reserve of 50 per cent of its notes outstanding and deposits combined." Aside from a small amount of silver coin which might be included, the reserve consisted of "any or all of the following items" in such proportions as the Board of Directors may decide: (1) gold bars and gold coin in Peru, and "earmarked" gold held in banks of high standing situated abroad; (2) deposits payable in gold or its equivalent on demand in banks of high standing in New York and/or London; (3) bankers' acceptances of high standing maturing in not more than ninety days from the date of acquisition by the Central Reserve Bank of Peru and enjoying a ready market in New York and/or London. (Not more than two-fifths of the normal legal minimum reserve could be invested in this form.)

The notes of the Bank were redeemable on demand at the Bank's head office in one or both of the following forms, the particular form or the proportion of the two forms in which redemption was made being at the option of the Bank: (1) gold bars at parity; (2) demand drafts on New York or London, payable in gold or the equivalent. On said drafts the Bank was permitted to charge premia above the gold parity of the *sol* with the United States gold dollar and the pound sterling respectively, which did not exceed the amount necessary to cover all expenses involved in shipping gold bars in substantial quantities from Lima to New York or London, as the case might be.

The law also required that "to avoid appreciation in the gold value of the Peruvian monetary unit, the Central Reserve Bank of Peru shall pay out its own notes on demand in exchange for: (a) gold bars of approximately 100 per cent fineness" and foreign gold coins at their gold parity weight in pure gold; and (b) against foreign gold credit paid to the account of the Central Reserve Bank's legal reserves in the banks of New York and London in which the Bank maintained such reserve accounts; "Provided, that, for each payment of notes in Lima against the aforementioned deposits abroad of gold and its equivalent, the Bank may charge a premium sufficient to cover the expenses that would be involved in shipping gold bars in substantial quantities from said foreign cities to Lima."

The Peruvian Law provided a tax on reserve deficiencies, the rate of which increased progressively as the reserve declined below the normal legal minimum of 50 per cent. Whenever this reserve deficiency tax was imposed, the Law provided that there should be added to the respective rediscount rates, discount rates and interest rates charged by the Bank, in addition to whatever increase in such rates might be necessary to raise the lowest rate to 7 per cent per annum, a percentage equal to at least one-half of the percentage rate of the tax imposed upon the reserve deficiency. This tax and these enforced advances in the Bank's discount rates, it will be observed, put progressive brakes upon currency and credit inflation.

The gold exchange standard, as we have noted, possesses certain real advantages over the gold coin or the gold bullion standards. It is less expensive, in that it avoids the tying up in central bank vaults or government vaults of proportionately such large reserves of gold as does the gold standard, reserves that do not yield a return in interest, and in that it makes difficult the obtaining of gold for hoarding, which so often involves an economic waste. In economizing the use of gold, the gold exchange standard not only serves the country which adopts it, but may well render an international public service in the future, if we should reach a time, as some fear, when the world's gold production shall prove inadequate for the world's monetary needs. For many countries, particularly those in which revolutionary upheavals are likely to be frequent, the gold reserve of the central bank would actually be safer if kept abroad than it would be if kept in the central bank's own vault at home.

Disadvantages of the Gold Exchange Standard

Despite these obvious advantages, the gold exchange standard has, since the economic crisis of 1929, lost much of the prestige which it formerly enjoyed. The principal criticisms that may be raised against it are the following.

(1) In effecting an economy in the use of gold, critics claim that it often carries too far the pyramiding of gold reserves. Take, for example, a small country on the gold exchange standard in which the normal legal minimum gold reserve of the central bank against its notes and deposits is 40 per cent and in which commercial banks are required to maintain in the central bank deposited reserves of 15 per cent against their own demand deposits. Assume that the demand deposits of the commercial banks of the country are $100

million and that the bank notes outstanding issued by the central bank are likewise $100 million.

If the central bank were required to hold its entire legal gold reserve in its own vaults, it would need $40 million in gold reserve for its notes and $6 million (40 per cent of $15 million) for its deposits, a total of $46 million, or an average gold reserve against central bank notes outstanding and demand deposits of commercial banks combined of 23 per cent.

Assume that, under the gold exchange standard, the central bank is permitted to keep all of its own normal legal minimum reserve in a New York City national bank and that it actually does so. The $40 million reserve required against the notes would be deposited in the New York City bank, which, under American law, would hold against this deposit a 13 per cent reserve, or $5.2 million; but this reserve would be in the form of a deposit in the New York Federal Reserve Bank, against which the New York Federal Reserve Bank would be required by law to hold a reserve of 35 per cent in lawful money, which we will assume to be gold, as in practice it would largely have been prior to 1933. Thirty-five per cent of $5,200,000 is $1,820,000. The actual gold reserve "held somewhere" against the $100 million of bank notes outstanding in the country having the gold exchange standard would, therefore, be 1.82 per cent, as contrasted with the 40 per cent required under the gold coin or gold bullion standard.

As regards deposits, the central bank in the gold exchange standard country would deposit its $6 million gold reserve in the New York City national bank, which would, in turn, maintain a 13 per cent reserve against this deposit, or $780,000. This reserve, however, would be in the form of a demand deposit in the New York Federal Reserve Bank, against which that Bank would be required to hold a reserve of 35 per cent, or of $273,000. The amount of gold reserve "held somewhere," therefore, against the $100 million of deposits in the commercial banks of the gold exchange standard country would be $273,000, as contrasted with $6,000,000 under the gold coin or gold bullion standard. The decline would have been from 6 per cent under the gold coin or gold bullion standard to less than .3 per cent under the gold exchange standard.

Combining note liabilities of the central bank and deposit liabilities of the commercial banks, the percentage of gold reserve actually held somewhere under the gold coin or gold bullion standard would have been 23, and under the gold exchange standard 1.0465—a percentage nearly 22 times as large under the gold coin or gold bullion standard as under the gold exchange standard.

Of course, this estimate needs certain qualifications, to give an accurate picture. The commercial banks of the gold exchange standard country would in practice have kept some till money in addition to their deposited legal reserve and the central bank would likewise in practice have kept some till money at home (in addition to its available unissued bank notes) and would normally have kept a deposited reserve abroad somewhat in excess of the 40 per cent legal requirement. Furthermore, the New York City bank would normally have held a reserve somewhat above the legal requirement and the New York Federal Reserve Bank would, in turn, usually have carried a gold reserve very substantially above the normal legal minimum. It should be remembered, however, that, under the gold coin or gold bullion standard, some excess reserve likewise would also have been kept.

The illustration is a fairly representative one and, when all necessary qualifications are made, probably does not much exaggerate the greater degree of pyramiding which is done under the gold exchange standard than under the gold coin or the gold bullion standard. In some qualified gold exchange standard countries the law permits only part of the legal gold reserve of the central bank to be held on deposit abroad and requires part—sometimes a major part—to be maintained in physical gold at home or in earmarked gold abroad. In such countries the amount of gold legally required to support a given volume of note and deposit liabilities is substantially increased over that required in countries where all the legal reserve may be a deposited reserve.

(2) The second objection to the gold exchange standard is, that it does not automatically function so effectively, that is, does not set up as efficient a set of forces of checks and balances in "the foreign country" as does the gold coin or the gold bullion standard. In the home country, the gold exchange standard may be as automatic and as efficient in its functioning as the gold coin or gold bullion standard, but not in the foreign country. Under the gold coin or gold bullion standard, one country exports gold at its gold-export point and another country receives the gold at its gold-import point. The currency is contracted in the country exporting the gold and expanded in the country importing it.

Under the gold exchange standard, the currency is normally contracted in the country selling the drafts on its gold standard reserve located abroad, but is not expanded in the country in which the reserves are held. Furthermore, when exchange goes to the gold-import point, the currency of the gold exchange standard country is normally expanded under the gold exchange standard as effectively as it would be under the gold coin or gold bullion standard, but the currency of the foreign country in which the bank is located that holds the gold reserve is not decreased when the bank sells a gold exchange standard draft on the gold exchange standard country. In the foreign country these operations usually mean merely the debiting of one bank deposit account and the crediting of another.[1]

(3) A third objection—or more correctly, a group of objections—to the gold exchange standard grows out of the fact, that the gold reserves of a country are less in control of its own authorities when the reserves are deposited or otherwise invested abroad than when they are kept physically in the home country. This fact may mean sometimes greater insecurity for the gold reserves.

The legal title to gold in a central bank's own vaults resides in the bank and the gold itself is in the bank's own control. The legal title to the bank's gold reserves that are deposited in a foreign bank (aside from "earmarked" gold) resides in that foreign bank and the home central bank is merely a creditor of the foreign bank for the amount deposited on deposit account. The foreign bank invests the funds and usually invests them in the country where it is located. If the foreign bank fails, the home central bank merely participates in the ultimate distribution of the assets *pro rata* like any other creditor. Furthermore, the foreign deposit is payable in the money of the country in which the depository bank is located. If that country's currency should depreciate, the depositing central bank would lose. In this way, many gold exchange standard countries suffered severely—the losses amounting to tens of millions of dollars—when England suspended gold payments in September, 1931 and their deposited gold reserves suddenly ceased to be payable in gold and became payable in a greatly depreciated paper pound. Similar losses by foreign central banks,

[1] For a further elucidation of this difficulty, the reader is referred to the *Report* of the Gold Delegation of the Financial Committee of the League of Nations, pp. 13 and 14.

although on a much smaller scale, were suffered when the United States gave up the gold standard in 1933. These experiences were the greatest shock which the gold exchange standard had ever received.

Moreover, the deposits in any country representing the reserves of foreign central banks are likely to be highly volatile. The amounts of the individual deposits are usually large and are ordinarily concentrated in a few markets, notably New York and London. Most of them, furthermore, are demand deposits. Heavy pressure for gold redemption (purchase of gold standard reserve drafts) often arises suddenly, perhaps from an economic or political crisis, so that the large calls upon gold reserves cannot always be anticipated by the depository banks. If the crisis should be international in character, the strain upon gold reserves deposited in a world money market would be still further aggravated. This sort of drain on London was the immediate cause of the breakdown of the gold standard in England in the autumn of 1931. Two generations ago, the eminent British economist, Walter Bagehot, after saying that recently London had become the sole great settling-house of exchange transactions in Europe, added, "and we may reasonably presume that in proportion as we augment the deposits of cash by foreigners in London, we augment both the chances and the disasters of a run upon England."

Another phase of the problem is the claim, that funds in a foreign market will always be administered with primary reference to the needs of that market rather than to the needs of the country which deposited the funds. These needs are sometimes in conflict. India, for example, with its qualified gold exchange standard, normally had very large reserve funds in the London market. The immediate interests of the London market as to discount rates, sale of Council Bills and other financial policies were very different on occasion from those of India in relation to India's enormous reserves. This was the source of vigorous criticisms on many occasions by Indian economists and financiers. For example, S. V. Doraiswami a few years ago said:[1]

> *". . . the three hundred and fifteen millions of Indians do not exist for the benefit of London bankers. . . . This manipulation of India's exchange and currency, not for the benefit of India but solely for the benefit of London joint-stock bankers exchange bankers and bullion dealers should no longer be tolerated."*

[1] *Indian Finance, Currency and Banking*, pp. 36–37.

Then there is the matter of political risk. A country naturally hesitates before locating its gold reserve—the foundation stones of its currency and credit system—in a foreign country. What would happen, it asks, if the country in which our gold reserve is located should go to war with us? Would it not at once seize our gold reserve and bring down in a crash the currency and credit structure built upon it? The experiences of the Great War were not very reassuring on this point. It is a point that has been frequently stressed in discussions of the gold exchange standard for China. Of course, this danger ordinarily does not apply in the case of a colony or dependency which keeps its reserve in the mother country, and it has little weight in cases where danger of war between the two countries is remote.

Future of the Gold Exchange Standard

The gold exchange standard has certain decided merits, of which economy is the most important. It also, as we have just seen, has certain shortcomings. Its future is in doubt. Probably, however, it will continue to be used extensively by smaller states and by colonies and dependencies, and will be to a large extent given up by the great nations of Europe. The practice followed by many countries on the qualified gold exchange standard—for example, Germany, Poland and Colombia (from 1923 to 1930)—of requiring a certain proportion of the gold reserve to be kept physically in the form of gold will probably be increasingly followed in the future. It is, moreover, desirable that the peculiarly volatile character of deposited foreign gold standard reserves be recognized both by law and by banking practice. Banks holding such deposited reserves should be required to maintain against them larger percentages of reserves than they are required to hold against ordinary domestic deposits. As in the past, these reserves will be deposited chiefly in commercial banks, rather than in the central bank, because of the all-important fact that commercial banks can pay interest on such deposits, while it is generally considered unsound banking policy for a central bank to pay such interest.

BIBLIOGRAPHY

Fowler Committee, Indian Currency Committee of 1898, *Evidence*, Questions 3275–4303; London, Eyre & Spottiswood, 1899.

Gold Delegation, Financial Committee of the League of Nations, *Report;* Geneva, 1932.

Gold Delegation, Financial Committee of the League of Nations, *Selected Documents;* Geneva, 1931.

Kemmerer, Edwin Walter, *Modern Currency Reforms;* New York, The Macmillan Company, 1916.

Laughlin, J. Laurence, "The Gold Exchange Standard," *The Quarterly Journal of Economics,* Vol. XLI, 1926–1927.

Lindsay, A. M., *Ricardo's Exchange Remedy;* London, Effingham, Wilson & Co., 1892.

Luthringer, George F., *The Gold-Exchange Standard in the Philippines;* Princeton, N. J., Princeton University Press, 1934.

Royal Institute of International Affairs, *The International Gold Problem—Collected Papers;* London, Oxford University Press, 1931.

PART IV

SOME SIGNIFICANT CHAPTERS IN THE WORLD'S MONETARY HISTORY

CHAPTER X

THE FRENCH ASSIGNATS

The French Assignats of 1789–1796 are the classical example of a fiduciary paper money standard. Here, in the brief space of seven years, France made a series of experiments with paper money in which most of the numerous devices that the world has invented down to the present time for preventing the depreciation of inconvertible paper money were tried and tried vigorously. Many of the monetary panaceas so widely advocated in the United States during the economic depression of 1929–1935 were tried out in France during these years.

To the student of monetary science it is an illuminating chapter in monetary history, although as "a laboratory experiment" it suffers from a lack of much of the important data which advanced countries now have and which are so desirable as aids in interpreting such monetary experiences—such data as index numbers of prices, wages and the physical volume of production, and figures for volume of credit, interest rates and trade movements.

Conditions Preceding the Issue of the Assignats

France, during the greater part of the eighteenth century, had both silver and gold in circulation, but silver greatly preponderated. In 1726 the legal ratio had been fixed at $14\frac{5}{8}$ to 1, but this ratio had for some time undervalued gold, and had led to its gradual disappearance. In 1785, therefore, the ratio was changed to approximately $15\frac{1}{2}$ to 1, with the object of attracting more gold; and the existing gold coins were recoined at this ratio. The metallic monetary unit was the silver *livre* (franc), which was divided into 20 *sous*. Gold was coined by the Government and circulated along with silver, but there was no free coinage of gold. The system was that of a dual currency.

The year 1788 was economically unfavorable for France. A hail storm had severely damaged the crops, and manufacturing industries were depressed, while the Government's finances were in a weak condition. Grain transactions were being regulated by the

Government and coined money was being widely hoarded. At about this time the amount of money in circulation, including that in hoards, was estimated at approximately two billion livres.

The immense proportion of the nation's wealth in the hands of the privileged classes consisting of the Church and the nobility—classes whose members amounted to something like 270,000 out of a total French population of about 25 million—was increasingly arousing the jealousy and exciting the wrath of the populace. The estimates of M. de la Gorce place the wealth of the Church in 1789 at approximately three billion livres and the annual income at about 85 million livres. But this sum "was nearly doubled by the dues levied on the faithful . . ." [1] The State, being in severe financial straits, seized this vast Church property in October, 1789.

Threatened by war from abroad, facing a popular upheaval at home arising in part from excessive taxes, and suddenly coming into possession of such a valuable domain, the State naturally looked about for some method of "cashing in" on its new possessions. Obviously, it could not sell the lands on any large scale, for the very Revolution that led to their seizure was threatening the property and security of the wealthy classes—the only people who would normally have the means of buying. The return to be received by the State's working the lands itself would be uncertain and slow. What could be more natural under such circumstances than proposals that the Government provide itself with revenue by issuing paper money on the security of these lands?

It is true that a couple of generations before France had suffered disastrously from John Law's paper money schemes and that after that experience her people were determined never again to be drawn into the paper money whirlpool. Of this experience, Andrew D. White said: [2]

> " . . . There were then sitting in the National Assembly of France many who owed the poverty of their families to those issues of paper. Hardly a child in the country had not heard the men who issued that paper cursed as the authors of the most frightful catastrophe France had then known. It was no mere attempt at theatrical display, but a natural impulse, which led a thoughtful statesman, during this debate, to hold up in the Assembly a piece of paper money, and to declare that it was moistened with the blood and tears of their fathers."

[1] Madelin, Louis, *The French Revolution*, p. 8.
[2] *Paper Money Inflation in France*, p. 5.

The memory of people, however, is short. They may remember yesterday, but they forget the day before. In nothing is this more true than in regard to paper money disasters. Conditions are always "so different" that the "previous experiences afford no lessons." And this is what happened in France.

The first serious threat of paper money was an edict of the King dated August 16, 1788, creating a form of short-time, interest-bearing paper, intended to circulate as money. It met such a storm of public protest, however, that it was revoked within a month. Thereafter, for the better part of a year, frequent suggestions of paper money encountered vigorous opposition. With the outbreak of the Revolution, however, the advocates of paper money became much stronger and the opposition gradually weakened.

Mirabeau, who previously, as an opponent of paper money, had declared: "Paper money is a hold-up, or a loan made at the point of the sword," now became one of its strongest advocates. He could see no other way effectively to finance the early stages of the Revolution, and he urged vigorously the issue of paper money, despite dire prophesies of disaster on the part of the opposition. Of this advocacy the historian, von Sybel, says: [1] his "only object was to gain breathing time for the formation of a strong government."

The popular argument, which has been almost universally put forth throughout history, when paper money issues have been under consideration—the argument of money scarcity—was repeatedly advanced. Every man knew that he himself did not have enough money, and, from this fact, the conclusion was natural that there was not enough money in circulation. Clavière maintained that there was an urgent need for more money in circulation, and Martineau said that business was stagnant and that the sole cause was lack of sufficient money in circulation.

First Issue of Assignats

The first issue, which was for 400 million livres, was decreed by the National Assembly December 19, 1789; the second issue, also for 400 million livres, came in April, 1790; and, by the end of

[1] von Sybel, Heinrich, *History of the French Revolution*, in four volumes, translated by Walter C. Perry, Vol. I, p. 146.

1791, the total amount issued (less the amount withdrawn and burned) was 1,490 million livres.

According to White,[1] the Assignats

> "were engraved in the best style of the art. To stimulate loyalty, the portrait of the King was placed in the centre; to stimulate patriotism, patriotic legends and emblems surrounded him; to stimulate public cupidity, the amount of interest which the note would yield each day to its holder was printed in the margin; and the whole was duly garnished with stamps and signatures, showing that it was under careful registration and control."

Being interest-bearing, these early Assignats were not a true form of paper money. They were for the most part in large denominations; namely, in notes of 1,000, 500 and 200 livres, respectively. The need for money of smaller denominations for ordinary retail trade and wages had to be met for some time by small denominations of coined money and by *billets de confiance*—a form of paper money issued in small denominations by various municipalities. Decrees of October, 1790 and May, 1791 authorized issues of Assignats in denominations of 50 and 5 livres. By December, 1791, however, the agitation for Assignats of the smaller denominations had become so strong that the Assembly approved issues in denominations of 50, 25, 15 and 10 sous.

Early Issues Bore Interest

The Assignats of the first issue bore interest at the rate of 5 per cent per annum, and they were not legal tender. The Assignats of the second issue, that of April 17, 1790, were made legal tender, but, since they bore interest at 3 per cent per annum, they had a substantial investment character. After October 1, 1790, the payment of interest on all Assignats ceased, and, from that time forward, the Assignats were full-fledged paper money.

Assignats Secured by Land

For the security of the Assignats, the vast domains of the Church lands were pledged, and, at a later date, to these pledged domains were added the seized domains of the *émigrés*. The Assignats were made redeemable in these lands. When paid in for the purchase of State lands, they were to be withdrawn from circulation and destroyed. Mirabeau maintained that the Assignats

[1] *Op. cit.*, p. 7.

were in their essentials bills of exchange, payable in land at sight,[1] were "in essence territorial," [2] and were "representations of the national domain, which itself is the foundation of wealth." In the debate in August, 1790, Chabroux said:

> "The Assignats are of the essential symbol of the land which is the source of all value. . . . Therefore it is evident that the creditors of the State will not suffer loss from accepting them." [3]

As the Revolution progressed and it became increasingly important for its success that the financial interests of the agricultural classes should be identified with it, the further issue of Assignats was justified also as a means of getting the land into the hands of the people. This, it was agreed, would turn the new landlord class against the old privileged classes and cement it to the Revolution.

The land was sold on the installment plan, payments being extended over long periods of time, and much of it was sold in very small parcels to poor people. Land sales accounted for the retirement of large quantities of Assignats during the years 1790 to 1792.

The Measurement of Fluctuations in the Value of the Assignats

In a study of the Assignats, as in the study of any other currency, one of the first questions to raise is: How stable was their value? Obviously, stability in value is one of the first criteria of the goodness of any money.

There are, broadly speaking, three different methods of measuring the extent of the depreciation of the Assignats; namely: (1) the market prices in terms of Assignats at which gold and silver were bought and sold in France; (2) the exchange rates in France on countries with a metallic money standard; and (3) the prices of staple commodities in France. Unfortunately, the statistical data available for all three of these criteria are very inadequate. Furthermore, in none of them did there exist anything approaching a free market throughout most of the life of the Assignats.

[1] *Gazette National ou Moniteur universel*, Sept. 28, 1790, p. 1121.
[2] *Ibid.*, Aug. 28, 1790, pp. 990–991.
[3] *Ibid.*, Aug. 29, 1790, p. 996.

The Price of Gold and Silver

Early in the Revolution the Government prohibited the exportation of gold and silver bullion and coin, and this prohibition was maintained, with heavy penalties, at a time when there was a pronounced flight of capital out of the country seeking refuge from the dangers of the Revolution. This prohibition tended to dam up specie within the country and, by restraining its natural flow to the best foreign markets, to depress its value. On the other hand, the extreme insecurity in which property of all kinds found itself during the Revolution stimulated greatly the demand for forms of property such as gold and silver, which embodied large values in small bulk and which, therefore, could be easily hidden and would presumably maintain their values substantially, regardless of political events in France, and be readily marketable when conditions should again become normal. There was, therefore, a scramble for gold and silver for hoarding throughout the Revolution analogous to the scramble for gold of the period of the world crisis of 1929–1935 which pushed up the value of gold throughout the world. Hoarding of gold and silver became so common in France that at one time for a brief period it was made punishable by death, and, in the latter part of 1792, according to White,[1] "even the bell-metal sous, obtained by melting down the bells, appear to have been driven out of circulation." But we are getting ahead of our story, for the depreciation of the Assignat down to the end of 1791, as measured by any of the criteria available, was not large. These instances are given merely to show that the prices of gold and silver in terms of Assignats were not the prices of a reasonably free world market, and were not, therefore, a safe criterion of the fluctuations in the value of the Assignat.

Foreign Exchange Rates

Much the same should be said of rates of exchange on the principal foreign markets, London, Amsterdam and Hamburg. Since international movements of gold and silver were not free and since both foreign commerce and foreign exchange operations were greatly restricted—during the Reign of Terror, for example, the banks had to turn over to the Government all of their available foreign credits and the Government took over control of the

[1] P. 27.

export and import trade—foreign exchange rates did not afford a true picture of the value of the Assignat.

Commodity Prices

The best criterion of variations in the value of money is to be found in scientifically prepared price index numbers covering a wide and representative group of commodities and services. Unfortunately, this period was before there was an appreciable development of the use of price index numbers, and none were compiled in France at the time. However, in April, 1796, the Council, in connection with its efforts to solve the problem of providing a basis for the equitable settlement of debts, adopted a resolution calling for the construction of local tables of depreciation, a resolution that became law in June, 1797. M. Caron has recently published these original tables, and, on the basis of them, Harris has constructed a number of series of depreciation indices for various Departments separately and for the 83 Departments combined. These are the indices here used.[1]

The Treasury reported to each Department the values of gold and silver, and each was instructed to obtain information as to the local prices of land, merchandise, food, gold and silver. These price quotations served as the basis for computing the local values of the Assignat and the Mandat. The period covered was 1791 to 1796.

By reason of the limited amount of the price data collected, of the controlled and artificial character of many of these prices, of the differences in the qualities of the same commodity at different times and in different Departments, and of the widely different prices often existing at the same time in the different Departments, these price indices are far from satisfactory as a measure of the fluctuations in the value of the Assignat.

Taken together, these three classes of figures (i.e., the price of specie, foreign exchange rates and commodity prices) are the best criteria we have. Moreover, broadly speaking and during the major part of the period 1791 to 1796, the three series of figures tell essentially the same story, although the extent of the depreciation shown by the local price tables rules somewhat less than that shown by the Treasury tables for deprecia-

[1] A description of the method of constructing these indices and graphs representing them will be found in Harris, *The Assignats*, Chap. V.

tion in terms of specie. There are, moreover, a number of instances of temporary differences of considerable magnitude in the direction of the movements shown by the three series of figures.

Into a detailed discussion of the reasons for the major fluctuations in the value of the Assignats—a highly controversial subject—and of the decline of this value to practically zero by 1796, limitations of space prevent us from going.[1]

Six Periods in the History of the Assignat

The life of the Assignats may be conveniently divided into six periods for which the following table gives the outstanding facts as to the volume of notes issued, the amounts in circulation and their value.[2]

Table I. Depreciation of the Assignat

Period	Notes Emitted by End of Period (000,000)	Notes in Circulation at End of Period (000,000)	Value at End of Period: According to Local Price Tables (% of 1790 Value)	Value at End of Period: Treasury Figures for Specie Value (% of 1790 Value)
	Livres	*Livres*	*Livres*	*Livres*
(1) 1790–1791	1,860	1,490	86	77
(2) Jan.–May, 1792	2,200	1,660	72	58
(3) June–Dec., 1792	2,750	2,250	75	72
(4) Jan.–Aug., 1793	4,950	4,050	39	22
(5) Sept., 1793–July, 1794	8,450	7,200	41	34
(6) Aug., 1794–Nov., 1795	——	19,700	.8	.8

I am indebted to Professor Harris for the privilege of reproducing here his chart showing the course of the depreciation of the Assignat.[3]

[1] A table giving the monthly figures from March, 1790 to March, 1793 and from August, 1795 to March, 1796 for the price of specie in Paris, for Paris exchange rates on Amsterdam and for Paris exchange on London is given by C. U. Falkner in his *Das Papiergeld der französischen Revolution, 1789–1797*, pp. 36–37. A chart showing the movement of exchange rates in Hamburg on Paris, for the period January, 1789 to June, 1796, will be found in Hermann Illig, *Das Geldwesen Frankreichs zur Zeit der Ersten Revolution bis zum Ende der Papiergeldwährung*, p. 63.

[2] Harris, pp. 166–187.

[3] For the purpose of reproducing the chart it was necessary to redraw it. In mechanical make-up it has been slightly changed.

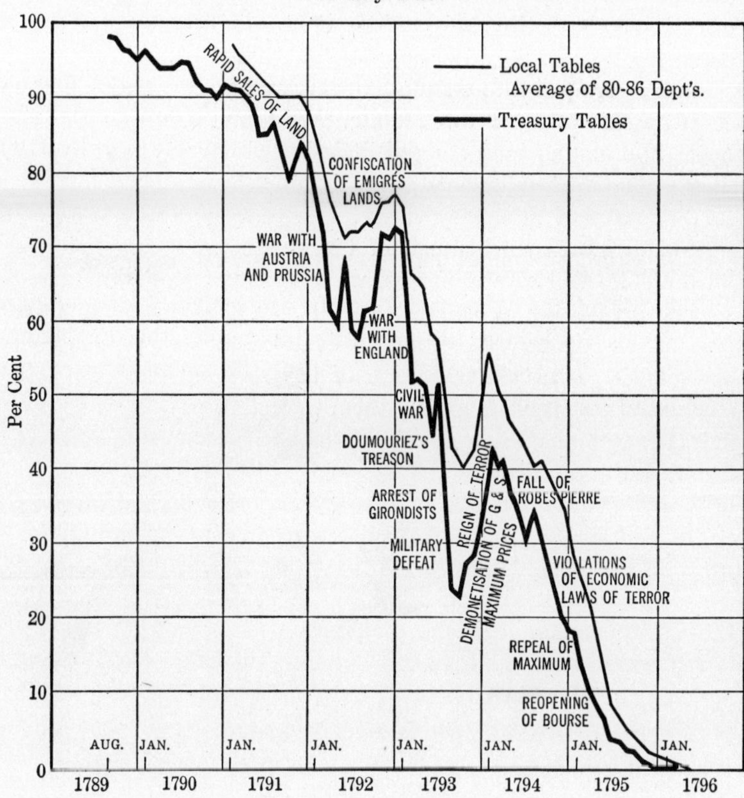

First Period

Reasons for Early Stability. As has been so frequently the case in other countries with issues of inconvertible paper money, the early issues maintained their value remarkably well. The depreciation from 1789 to the end of 1791 was very moderate and most of it took place in 1791.

Variations in the value of money, we have found,[1] must be explained by the interaction of the forces representing the supply of money and the demand for money. Prominent among these factors are those representing the amount of money in circulation, the rate of monetary turnover, the extent to which credit instru-

[1] *Supra*, Chaps. IV and VI.

ments are used as media of exchange and the physical volume of business to be transacted. For France during this period and, in fact, during the entire period of the Assignats, we have no satisfactory figures for any of these factors. We know how many Assignats were put into circulation, but we have no idea to what extent specie continued to circulate. We have no measure of the physical volume of business and little knowledge of the extent of the use of credit instruments as media of exchange. About all we know of rates of monetary turnover is that the rate for specie tended downward since much of the specie was being hoarded and therefore had a rate of zero, while the rate for the Assignats rose enormously when confidence in them was declining rapidly. Without attempting, therefore, to evaluate the various factors that tended to sustain the value of the Assignats during these early years, we may cite among them the following:

(1) *Demand for Money.* The demand for money as represented by the physical volume of business to be done was apparently well maintained during these years. Food markets were normal and agriculture was stimulated by freedom from taxation and from many feudal exactions that were lifted by the Revolution. Jaurès maintains that industry held its own, but on this point there is much difference of opinion.[1]

(2) *Coins Withdrawn from Circulation.* Under the forces which express themselves in Gresham's Law, increasing amounts of the metallic money of the country were withdrawn from circulation and hoarded during this period, and, except for the coins of small denominations, the coins that circulated had in general a low rate of circulation. The rest between jumps from one hoarder to another was usually a long one. This meant that the Assignats did not represent a net increase in the volume of money in circulation, but were to a large extent during this period a substitute for the coins that were withdrawn.

(3) *Early Assignats Bore Interest.* During a great part of this period, the Assignats were interest-bearing obligations of the State rather than money in the true sense of the word, and, since they yielded interest to the person who retained them, there was a tendency to hold them as investments. This fact made their rate of circulation or velocity lower than it otherwise would have been.

[1] Cf., Harris, p. 169.

(4) *Assignats Chiefly in Large Denominations.* The great bulk of the Assignats during much of this period were in the form of notes of large denominations, denominations of 1,000, 500 and 200 livres, and it was not until October 8, 1790, that the Government authorized the manufacture of the modest sum of 140 million livres in denominations below 100 livres. Money of large denominations proverbially circulates more slowly than money of small denominations. All are familiar with the English expressions, "the nimble sixpence" and "the slothful sovereign." These Assignat notes of large denominations must have been inconvenient for most transactions and therefore must have circulated on the average very slowly. A reasonable number of notes of such high denominations, for use in large transactions and in reserves, makes for monetary efficiency; too large a proportion of a country's currency in large denominations, however, makes for inefficiency.

(5) *Acceptability for Purchase of Public Lands.* Possibly the acceptability of the Assignats in the payment of public lands may have had some influence on the willingness of the public to receive them and hold them and therefore on the demand for them, and in this way to have supported their value during this period. It is certain that many people at the time believed that such acceptability for the purchase of land was a force in upholding the value of the Assignats. It is easy, however, to exaggerate this influence, and many economists, such, for example, as William Nassau Senior, Edwin Cannan and H. Illig, believe that this acceptability for the purchase of land was not a factor in the demand. To a large percentage of the public even at this day, "a dollar is a dollar"; which means that they look upon the value of money as fixed, and believe that all changes of prices are due to changes in the values of the goods that are bought and sold. The great bulk of the people in France who received Assignats paid them out again promptly. They could not afford to hold them and they were not interested in the purchase of land. They were only concerned with the fact that the "other fellows" should receive them at current prices. Few accumulated them for the purchase of land and those few probably would have accumulated metallic money for the same purpose, had there been no Assignats and had the Government otherwise offered its land for sale on equally favorable terms. The convertibility of the Assignats into land resulted in the withdrawal from circulation of many Assignats,

but the net volume of Assignats in circulation was continually increasing, and one of the justifications for the increase was this very convertibility. As the Assignat depreciated, the prices of the land were raised. Moreover, no matter what kind of money was in circulation, it would have been used to purchase public lands and other goods at current prices, and, even without the Assignats, a price-fixing policy like the Maximum would presumably have been tried. It seems very doubtful, therefore, whether the convertibility of the Assignats into land either created an additional demand for money or on balance, reduced the supply of money in ways materially to sustain their value.

Second Period

From January to May, 1792, the volume of the circulation increased only moderately and, although, during these five months, economic conditions in many respects improved, the Assignats continued to depreciate during most of the period. Concerning this period Harris says: [1]

> "After January it became apparent that the outbreak of war was imminent. Hence the public disbursed their Assignats quickly and hoarded commodities. The same fear induced the farmers and traders to hoard their supplies. The results . . . were food riots everywhere, impeded circulation of products, and higher prices. . . . People were beginning to lose confidence in the paper money. The Minister of War complained in January of the refusal of the meat contractors to accept the Assignats. . . . The Minister of Interior received complaints from a local official of the refusal of workers to accept them. The Committee of Agriculture and Commerce was informed in April that farmers were selling grain at prices reduced by one-half, upon the condition that payments be made in gold and silver."

Third Period

The third period extended from June to December, 1792. During these seven months, the volume of Assignats in circulation increased about 40 per cent, but the value of the Assignat, as measured by recorded local prices, prices of gold and silver, and foreign exchange rates, was well sustained. This period was characterized by military successes for France and by the seizure and "placing back of the Assignats" of the vast domains of the *émigrés* who had left France before July 14, 1789, and had not

[1] Pp. 171 and 172.

returned. There were frequent riots and some eight hundred people were massacred in Paris on August 10. In the same month came the deposition of the King. Orderly marketing under such conditions was utterly impossible and food supplies were everywhere hoarded. Quoted prices of staple commodities were largely nominal and speculation was widespread.

Fourth Period

This period extending from January to August, 1793 was characterized by an increase of over 100 per cent in the volume of Assignat circulation and by an enormous depreciation in value, although there was a small increase in value during the latter part of the period.

Describing the general background of these eight months, Harris says:[1]

> "The faith in the French Republic fell to a new low point during this period. January brought the execution of the king, and February the bread riots and the opening of hostilities with England. . . . Three decisive military defeats were the lot of the Government in the month of July, which also saw the introduction of the Reign of Terror. And finally in August came the surrender of the largest fleet of France with the capitulation of Toulon, as well as the uprising in Lyons."

From a monetary point of view, the most significant events of this period were the introduction of "the Maximum," the increasing tendency to hoard commodities and specie, the growth of capital investments, and the demonetization of Assignats of the larger denominations. Each of these items will be considered briefly.

The Maximum. During 1792 and early 1793, as we have seen, prices had been rising rapidly, and this was particularly true of grains and other staple food supplies. The result was a heavy burden on the Government in its purchases of provisions for the army, and great hardships to the general public. There were numerous food riots, and mobs in Paris repeatedly seized supplies of food from the shops. The washerwomen of Paris, protesting against the high price of soap, urged that all merchants who were refusing to sell goods for Assignats at fair prices should be punished by death. On April 18 the fixing by law of maximum prices was proposed by representatives of the Department of Paris, and early in May the Convention agreed on the Maximum laws. The decrees

[1] P. 176.

authorized districts to make requisitions on municipalities and communes, and authorized municipalities and communes to make requisitions on individuals. These requisitions were to be made at fixed prices. The Maximum for grain in each locality was based upon the average price of grain in that locality for the period from January to April, 1793. The Maximum was to be a decreasing one and farmers were to receive for their grain prices that decreased progressively during successive months. By the end of the year the principle of the Maximum was extended to many other necessities, including foods, fuel, cloth and leather. How this worked will be discussed in connection with later developments.[1]

The Forestalling or Hoarding of Commodities. The introduction of the Maximum accentuated a practice that had already become common, namely, the withholding of commodities from the market. Farmers were refusing to sell and were hiding their produce. Vigorous laws against this practice were passed, but they had little effect.

> "In the same way as corn, all other goods now began to avoid the market: the *cafés* in Paris, e.g. were suddenly without sugar, because no dealer dared to confess that he had a supply sufficient for the demand. It was still more alarming that there were good reasons for fearing that the same thing would happen in the case of bread, at no great distance of time. . . . On the 15th of August, therefore, direct compulsion was added to indirect, and powers were given to the conventional commissioners to make a certain requisition of corn from every acre of land." [2]

Large Capital Investments. A third phenomenon of this period of inflation, one that was very common in Germany during the inflation period following the World War, was the strong movement for investments in durable goods. The prices of all classes of commodities were tending strongly upward, but the law, with the aid of heavy penalties, was striving to hold down the prices of staple goods. The export of capital from France and the hoarding of gold and silver were prohibited under heavy penalties. The value of paper money faded away rapidly in one's hands. What was more natural than to invest one's money quickly in durable goods, like land, buildings, furniture and jewelry? Referring to this "exceedingly brisk trade in all kinds of permanent property," White says: [3]

[1] *Infra*, pp. 190–191.
[2] von Sybel, Vol. III, pp. 173 and 174.
[3] P. 35.

> "It was simply a feverish activity caused by the intense desire of a large number of the more shrewd class, to convert their paper-money into any thing and every thing which they could hold and hoard until the collapse, which they foresaw, should take place. . . . It was the 'unloading' of the assignats by the cunning upon the mass of the people."

During this period, the sale of public lands declined because of an increasing fear that a counter-revolution might render titles to these lands insecure.

Restrictions on Use of Specie. During this period, still further restrictions were placed on the use of gold and silver, which resulted in increased hoarding. On April 11, 1793, a decree was passed which prohibited the buying of gold and silver at a premium, under a penalty of six years' imprisonment in irons, and which required all money obligations to be paid in Assignats. The law was strengthened with an increased penalty in August, and in September the death penalty was imposed for its infraction.

Increased Velocity of Monetary Circulation. A striking fact in the history of the Assignats—a fact that has been prominent in many of the world's recent paper money experiences—is the great increase in the velocity of circulation when confidence in the currency was waning. While the velocity of circulation of the Assignats did not reach its height until early in 1796, it none the less increased very much in this fourth period. From the end of December, 1792 to the end of August, 1793, the volume of Assignats in circulation increased from 2,250 million to 4,050 million livres; but the values of this volume of money in terms of the livre of 1790 declined at the same time from 1,688 million livres to 1,580 million livres, when measured by local price tables, and from 1,620 million livres to 891 million livres, when measured by the Treasury figures for specie values. In other words, confidence in the Assignats had so declined in that period that, although the amount of Assignats in circulation was nearly doubled, the value of that amount actually declined. A situation like this is called hyper-inflation. It is largely a phenomenon of increased velocity of circulation. When goods are going up in value rapidly in terms of the money unit, or the money unit is going down in value in terms of goods—in other words, when commodity prices are rising—the tendency everywhere is to buy goods today because they will be dearer tomorrow, to get the appreciating goods and to drop the depreciating money. But the people who have the goods are reluctant to sell under such circumstances, while the people who have the money are keen to buy. The result is that prices must rise enormously in order to move the goods, and the velocity of monetary circulation advances in an increasingly speculative market.[1]

As early as 1790 an American citizen, on the basis of recent American paper money experiences, warned the National Assembly that the Assignats would circulate so rapidly that long before a volume of circulation equivalent to the pre-Revolutionary volume of money in circulation was reached, the Assignats would depreciate.[2] In the fore part of 1792, a Parliamentary Committee in a report to the Assembly said:[3]

> "Your committee are thoroughly persuaded that the amount of circulating medium before the Revolution was greater than that of the assignats to-day; but then the money circulated slowly, and now it passes rapidly, so that one thousand million assignats do the work of two thousand millions of specie."

Cailhasson, in giving an extract of a report previously made to the Assembly in the name of the extraordinary Committee of Finance, said:[4]

> "The assignats now circulate at a much greater velocity than formerly."

This he attributed to their more rapid rate of depreciation, saying that a money which changes owners often will suffer a larger number of changes in value than one that remains for a longer time in the same hands. If one assumes for illustration, he said, that under existing conditions, the velocity of circulation of the Assignats had been doubled, a billion livres in Assignats would now facilitate as many transactions as two billion livres in coin.

It was recognized that the velocity of circulation was to a large extent a question of public confidence in the Assignat, and Mallet du Pan had said as early as August, 1790: "If there is doubt as to the success of the Assignats the cause of the Assignats is lost."[5]

Other Measures to Keep Down the Circulation. As the Assignat depreciated, it became increasingly apparent to the leaders that the volume of circulation must be kept down or the Assignat

[1] For an account of a similar experience in Germany after the World War, see *infra*, pp. 289–294.

[2] Cf., Harris, p. 16.

[3] Cf., White, p. 26.

[4] *Moniteur*, May 1, 1792, No. 122, Vol. IV, p. 500.

[5] Mallet, Bernard, *Mallet du Pan and the French Revolution*, p. 112.

would become worthless. In pursuance of this policy, the Government, in the spring of 1793, in place of an equivalent issue of Assignats, levied upon the rich a forced loan of a million livres, and in July the Government decided to force the creditors of the Army to accept their pay in the future in the form of *reconnaissances de finance*, a non-circulating form of credit. In July the credit of the nation was disgraced and weakened by the demonetization of all Assignats of the denominations of 100 livres or more that had been put out before August, 1792. An "interconvertibility scheme" between Assignats and a 5 per cent debt of the nation was tried out in August, 1793, but failed.[1]

Fifth Period

The fifth period, extending from September, 1793 to July, 1794, covers most of the period of the Reign of Terror (which extended from June, 1793 to July, 1794). During this fifth period of 11 months, the volume of Assignats in circulation increased from 4,050 million livres to 7,200 million livres. From September, 1793 until early in 1794 the value of the Assignat as expressed in the prices of the precious metals and in local commodity price tables advanced sharply, and thereafter declined substantially to the end of the period. The value of the Assignat ruled higher during this period than it did just preceding or at any time thereafter. For reasons that will be made clear later, it is doubtful if the commodity price and specie price figures used for measuring the value of the Assignats give even an approximately fair picture of the true value of the Assignat during these months of the Terror.

This was a period of tremendous social disturbance and of economic and political repression. The Government vigorously undertook to maintain maximum prices of all "necessities" and to ration supplies. It became itself an enormous purchaser of supplies, and in its purchases it enforced the principle of the Maximum. It determined practically both the prices of all necessities of life and the respective amounts that could be bought. The Bourse was closed, and foreign trade was brought to a standstill.[2] The death penalty was imposed for hoarding commodities,

[1] White, p. 33.

[2] Speaking of the foreign trade of France at this time, our American Minister to France, Gouverneur Morris, writing somewhat later to President Washington, said: "At the same time the total suspension of foreign commerce shut up all remaining commodities within the country and the permission to export was only granted in

for refusing to accept Assignats or for accepting them at a discount. The public was warned that gold and silver found hidden would be confiscated; one-half of the hoarded treasure was to go to the informer and one-half to the Government. It was reported that twelve men were guillotined for hoarding gold and silver, although the Court pretended that the evidence pointed to treason by reason of an intention to transmit it to the enemy.

The Government's Finances. Mallet du Pan in his *Mémoires* gives the following excellent summary of the fiscal situation:[1]

> " . . . The income is drawn from taxes demanded in a usurious fashion, and paid only by the proprietors. They alone assume the taxes; the people properly so-called pay nothing, and no one thinks of obliging them to pay. The usufruct of the unsold national possessions forms another branch of revenue; but they are mere drops in the ocean. The latter with the aid of arbitrary local taxes, especially on those with visible fortunes, suffice for the decreased current expenses. This decrease results from the gradual extinction of rentes, from the discontinuance of the pensions and salaries allowed the Clergy, and from the opportunity afforded by the Grande-Livre to know of the possessions of suspects, and thus to destroy any part of the public debt. Finally, the expenses of the 'culte' are nil, and many other expenses such as charitable donations, the maintenance of public establishments, and the support of roads are equally suppressed or very much reduced.
>
> "The extraordinary expenses are met from the extraordinary sources, which have increased five times in the last year. These resources consist in the creation of Assignats, in the confiscation of private wealth, in spoliation of all kinds, and in the forced loan of a milliard."

Methods of Evading Price Fixing. While the system of the Maximum with its heavy penalties undoubtedly exercised a great influence during this period of the Terror and in particular provided the mechanism through which the Government requisitioned enormous supplies at very low prices, it none the less caused great hardship and at times was evaded extensively. Its enforcement in some parts of the country was much more effective than in others. In fact, local governments at times are reported to have competed with one another in laxity of administration, because, the more lax the administration, the more supplies a particular local government could obtain.

exchange for articles wanted by the Government, which gave its paper for those things which it obliged the owner to sell, and which all but its agents were prohibited from buying, by the very same means which compelled the sale. Mankind were pretty generally the dupes of these appearances." *Diary and Letters of Gouveneur Morris*, edited by Anne Cary Morris, two volumes, Vol. II, p. 149.

[1] Quoted by Harris, pp. 44 and 45.

Among the methods employed for evading this price-fixing system the following may be cited: the withdrawal of goods from the market and the failure to produce new supplies when the existing stocks were exhausted; the production and sale of goods of inferior quality; the feeding of grain to farm animals at times when the prices of grain were subject to the Maximum and the prices of live animals were not; the milling of wheat into flour by the farmers when the price of wheat was controlled and the price of flour was not. Farmers sold their produce at home clandestinely, instead of bringing it to market. When the prices of raw materials were controlled, the prices of manufactured articles frequently rose abnormally, and, when the prices of necessities were held down, the prices of luxuries soared. Evasion of the law yielded large profits, while the penalties for evasion, if one were caught, were extreme. This led to much official corruption. The supply of goods available in the markets at the controlled prices was often very inadequate and the queue, as in Russian cities of today, became a familiar institution.

Alleged Depreciation in Value of Specie. Some authorities on the Assignats, as, for example, Hawtrey [1] and Harris,[2] believe that the substantial increase in the value of the Assignat during the Terror was due in part to depreciation in the value of gold and silver, a depreciation which resulted from the laws against the hoarding of treasure and against the use of gold and silver as money "at values which discriminated against the Assignats." Their arguments on this point are not convincing. There was no market at this time in France in which prices of commodities were quoted in terms of gold and silver, and there is no evidence based upon open-market prices that gold and silver depreciated in terms of commodities. It is true that at such times the demand for gold and silver for monetary purposes becomes practically negligible, and it is also true that during the Reign of Terror hoarders of specie, *when caught,* often suffered extreme penalties; but it is equally true that,

[1] "Economic or uneconomic regulations might be evaded or ignored under the Gironde and afterwards under the Directorate, but under the Terror even economic regulations were not to be trifled with. The prospects of France and the prospects of the Revolution rose. In November, 1793, the assignat was at 33, or 50 per cent. above the panic quotations of August. In December it leapt up to 48. . . . Like the low level of August this rise was in part artificial. Gold and silver themselves were depressed in value in consequence of a law against hoarding; hidden treasure was liable to be confiscated, half to the Government and half to the informer." Hawtrey, pp. 303 and 304.

[2] P. 181.

despite all penalties against the hoarding of the precious metals, they are usually hoarded in large quantities at times of great political disturbances and economic insecurity. Of all commodities of widespread demand the precious metals carry the largest value in the smallest bulk. They are, therefore, the commodities that are the easiest to hide. Moreover, they are of all commodities the ones most certain to retain their value through critical periods and to be salable at high values when such periods are over. At these times, therefore, the increased demand for them to serve as a storehouse of value may more than compensate for the reduced demand for them as media of exchange. The world had a similar experience during the long economic crisis and depression beginning with the crash of 1929. At that time, although the world's gold production was increasing continually, the demand for gold for monetary purposes declined enormously because a large part of the world went off the gold standard. There was, however, such a scramble for gold for hoarding and for otherwise serving as a storehouse of value in those years of insecurity that the value of gold in terms of commodities everywhere exhibited a great rise.

A more plausible explanation of the apparent increase in the value of the Assignat during this fifth period would seem to be the repressive influence of governmental price regulations under the Terror and the largely nominal character of many of the quoted prices under such conditions.

With the execution of Robespierre at the end of July, 1794, the Reign of Terror ended and the Assignats, whose value had been declining since early in the year, continued declining at an even faster rate. This brings us to the sixth and last period of the Assignats.

Sixth Period

The sixth and last stage in the hectic career of the Assignats extended from August, 1794 to November, 1795, when they vanished into thin air.

Their decline was continuous. Madelin, describing the situation existing in the fall of 1795, when the Directory assumed power, says: [1]

> "The coffers of the State were empty: the Nation had ceased to pay the taxes. So there must be a fresh issue of assignats: 36 billion, 603 million

[1] P. 497. In making this quotation I have not used the italics which the author uses.

livres in the Year IV. The result was a state of discredit that soon became fabulous. On the day the Directors assumed their functions the gold louis (24 livres) was worth 3,400 livres in paper money: on the 15th Brumaire it was worth 4,000 livres. Six months later Charles de Constant found it was worth 12,000 livres. The peasants, when they refused this paper money, would say, 'We would take it if the horses would eat it.' Benjamin Constant writes: 'The assignats are going completely to the devil.' "

According to John Stuart Mill,[1] the final result was "that it at last required an assignat of five hundred francs to pay for a cup of coffee."

Hyper-Inflation. During this period hyper-inflation set in with a vengeance, and the velocity of circulation of the Assignats rose to extravagant figures. Harris says that by December, 1795 the depreciation was at least twelve times "as great as might be expected from a survey of quantities in circulation." [2] According to von Sybel: [3]

"Money, which was formerly sought by every one, was now passed from hand to hand like a piece of hot iron: every man endeavoured to get rid of it, in any legal way, for a tolerably secure possession."

Some notes were hoarded, however, for the purpose of meeting later installments on purchases of public lands.

Decline in Business. Although the Maximum was not repealed until the latter part of December, 1794, its effectiveness practically ceased several months before. After the fall of Robespierre, it "became at once a dead letter, when the transgression of it was no longer punished by death or transportation." [4] During this period the nation's economic activity reached a low ebb.[5]

Credit. There was little credit, public or private, and that which was granted was at interest rates that appeared to be extremely high, but which in fact usually proved to be low when the transaction was in terms of paper money, because of the rapid depreciation of the Assignats between the time loans were made and the date on which they were paid. Debtors, fearing a return to a specie basis, frequently paid their debts before maturity, and this gave rise to so much opposition that, in July, 1795, the Government took action prohibiting such pre-maturity payments.

[1] *Principles of Political Economy*, Vol. II, p. 95.
[2] P. 201.
[3] Vol. IV, p. 334.
[4] von Sybel, Vol. IV, p. 222.
[5] Harris, pp. 190 and 191.

Labor and Wages. Although the supply of labor was greatly reduced by the large numbers absorbed in the army, wages in general did not rise anything like as rapidly as the cost of living. The result was much hardship for the laboring classes. Of this situation White says: [1]

> "Under the universal doubt and discouragement, commerce and manufactures were checked or destroyed. As a consequence, the demand for labor was stopped; laboring-men were thrown out of employment, and, under the operation of the simplest law of supply and demand, the price of labor—the daily wages of the laboring class—went down . . ."

Extravagance. One effect of the rapid depreciation of the Assignat—and another phase of the high velocity of its circulation—was the stimulus it gave to extravagant living. If one kept his money, it faded away in his hands; if he loaned it at interest, the interest and principal were repaid in Assignats of much less value than those he loaned; if he invested it in Government lands, he was not certain that his title to the land would be subsequently sustained. The natural conclusion was, to spend all one received and to spend it quickly. Speaking of this, von Sybel says: [2]

> It was "accounted a folly to curtail the pleasures of the moment, to acquire or save for an uncertain future . . . Whoever possessed a handful of *assignats* or silver coins, hastened to spend them in keen enjoyment, and the eager desire to catch at every passing pleasure filled each heart with wild pulsations. In the autumn all the theatres had been reopened, and were frequented with untiring zeal. . . . The *cabarets* and *cafés* were no less filled than the theatres. Evening after evening every quarter of the city resounded with music and dancing. . . . These enjoyments, too, received a peculiar coloring—glaring lights and gloomy shadows—from the recollections and feelings of the Revolution. . . . In other circles no one was received who had not lost a relative by the guillotine; the fashionable ball-dress imitated the cropped hair and the turned-back collar of those who were led to execution; and the gentlemen challenged their partners to the dance with a peculiar nod, intended to remind them of the fall of the severed head."

Speculation. Speculation was widespread and all classes participated. As always under such conditions, the middle and poorer classes suffered heavily.

> "Before the end of the year the paper money was almost exclusively in the hands of the proletaries, the officials, and the small *rentiers*, whose property was not large enough to invest in stores of goods, or national lands." [3]

[1] P. 43. [2] Vol. IV, pp. 222–223. [3] von Sybel, Vol. IV, p. 335.

Of this situation White says:[1]

> "The financiers and men of large means, though they suffered terribly, were shrewd enough to put much of their property into objects of permanent value. The working-classes had no such foresight, or skill, or means. On them finally came the great, crushing weight of the loss."

Issuance of Assignats Discontinued

Early in 1795 various proposals were made, to return to a metallic money basis. In April of that year a law was passed authorizing business operations in gold and silver, and from then on specie in substantial quantities worked its way back into circulation from abroad and from hoards within the country.

Early in 1796 the value of Assignats of the more popular denominations became worth less than the cost of their manufacture and on February 19, by Government authority, the engraving plates and the presses used in printing the Assignats were publicly destroyed.

Mandats

Reminiscent of the frequent attempts previously made in the American colonies to restore a rapidly depreciating paper money by replacing it with an issue of "new tenor" notes, the French Government in 1796 authorized an enormous issue of a new kind of paper money called the *promesses de mandats* and popularly known as Mandats. These Mandats were, on their face, orders for the transfer to the bearer of portions of the national domain specified on the note. Authority was given to the Directory by the Legislature to issue 2,400 million livres of these Mandats; one-fourth of this sum was to be exchanged for the Assignats at the rate of 30 to 1; one-fourth was to be used for current government expenses; and the remaining 1,200 million livres was to be used for future exigencies. The new money was made legal tender. It was issued between April and September, 1796. The public had no faith in the Mandats and they rapidly depreciated. Within a year's time they had become practically worthless.[2]

[1] P. 37.

[2] A detailed history of the Mandats will be found in E. L. Hargreaves, *Restoring Currency Standards*, pp. 34–72.

Return to a Specie Basis

As the paper money disappeared, specie came back into circulation. Of this Falkner says: [1]

> "Now the metal that had been hidden in trunks and chests suddenly began to perform the function of money once again. Thus coin was payable in Assignats at many times its nominal value . . . As for the source whence this supply of specie was obtained, the speed and completeness with which the circulation of specie was restored demonstrated that the disappearance of the precious metals from circulation had been due almost entirely to their having been hoarded by the French, rather than to a flight abroad which the contemporary economists had so feared." [2]

A similar phenomenon of a sudden return to circulation of specie from hoards after an extended experience with paper money inflation occurred in Mexico in 1916 after the *infalsificables* had become practically worthless.

Conclusion

The evil effects of the Assignats have been narrated in some detail. The Assignats robbed the creditor classes of billions of livres of property and imposed heavy losses and hardships on both the peasants of the country and the laborers of the cities. They broke down the business morality of the people and led to frenzied speculation. They greatly weakened thrift and put a premium on wastefulness and extravagance. The experience with the Assignats gave rise to the French saying: "The guillotine follows the paper money press—the two machines are complementary one to the other."

BIBLIOGRAPHY

Courtois, Alph, *Histoire de la Banque de France et des Principales Institutions Françaises de Crédit depuis 1716;* Paris, Libraire de Guillaumin et Cie., 1875.

Falkner, C. U., *Das Papiergeld der französischen Revolution, 1789–1797;* Munich, Duncker & Humblot, 1924.

Hargreaves, E. L., *Restoring Currency Standards;* London, P. S. King & Son, 1926.

Harris, S. E., *The Assignats;* Cambridge, Mass., Harvard University Press, 1930.

[1] P. 53.

[2] Harris thinks that Falkner overestimated the speed with which the specie came back. Compare, pp. 219 *et seq.*

Hawtrey, R. G., *Currency and Credit;* new impression; London, Longmans, Green and Company, 1930.

Illig, Hermann, *Das Geldwesen Frankreichs zur Zeit der Ersten Revolution bis zum Ende der Papiergeldwährung;* Strassburg, Verlag von Karl J. Trubner, 1914.

Madelin, Louis, *The French Revolution;* New York, G. P. Putnam's Sons, 1923.

Stourm, René, *Les Finances de l'Ancien Régime et de la Révolution,* 2 volumes; Paris, Guillaumin et Cie., 1885.

von Sybel, Heinrich, *History of the French Revolution.* Translated from the Third Edition of the original German work by W. C. Perry; 4 volumes; London, John Murray, 1867.

White, Andrew D., *Paper-Money Inflation in France: How It Came, What It Brought, and How It Ended; revised;* New York, The Society for Political Education, 1882.

CHAPTER XI

THE PAPER MONEY STANDARD IN ENGLAND, 1797–1821

The experiment with a paper money standard in England between 1797 and 1821 is of particular interest to students of money for two reasons: the first, because it represents a long-continued and a reasonably well-controlled experiment with a managed paper currency standard, by an advanced nation; and the second, because the so-called "bullion controversy" which grew out of this experience gave the world a classic presentation of certain monetary theories which at that time were understood and accepted by comparatively few persons, and which later became the world's "orthodox" philosophy of money. A knowledge of the outstanding facts and controversies of this period, therefore, should be a part of the equipment of every student of monetary science.

Currency and Banking Conditions in England Prior to Outbreak of War with France in 1793

During the latter years of the eighteenth century in England, although silver was looked upon as the legal standard of value, with gold rated to it at a legal ratio, there was free coinage of both gold and silver, and from 1783 to 1798 coins of both metals were unlimited legal tender. The mint ratio, however, since the recoinage of 1696, had overvalued gold and undervalued silver, as compared with both the market ratio and the mint ratio in France. Consequently, almost no silver had been coined in England and, when the war broke out in 1793, the silver coin circulating in England was small in volume and generally badly worn. In 1798 a decline in the gold value of silver led to the fear that silver might return to circulation in excessive quantities and drive out gold, and resulted in the passage of a law suspending the free coinage of silver and reënacting a provision of a law repealed in 1783, limiting to £25, in one payment, the legal tender quality of silver coin. In the payment of wages and for retail trade at this time (1793–1797), gold coins of the denominations of one guinea, half guinea and a third of a guinea were widely used. There were no coins representing a pound, but the gold equivalent of a pound was 123¼ grains of gold, $^{11}/_{12}$ fine. Gold was freely convertible into coin at the mint or, on slightly less favorable terms, at the Bullion Office of the Bank of England. Although the exportation of English gold coin or of gold bullion obtained from melting down the coin was forbidden by law, the law was rather extensively flouted. At times when gold was moving out of England, there developed a premium on gold bullion and foreign gold coins that were legally exportable. This premium was always small, and, referring to it, Bosanquet in his *Practical Observations* concerning the Report of the Bullion Committee said in 1810: "The conscience of the exporter and the value of a false oath [regarding the origin of the gold being exported] are correctly stated by the Committee at four and one-half per cent."

Bank Notes. The paper money of England consisted entirely of bank notes, and none of these notes enjoyed the legal tender privilege. After 1742 the Bank of England enjoyed a monopoly on the privilege of issuing bank notes in England, subject to the qualification that the note-issue privilege was still permitted to banks having less than six partners. A result of this restriction was that most concerns of wealth and high standing were prevented from issuing notes. The weak banks, on the other hand, found it the more advantageous to issue their bank notes and, since the country could not obtain a supply of paper money from strong institutions, it obtained it from the weak ones.

> "A number of shopkeepers, chemists, tailors and bakers, taking advantage of the clause authorising banks formed by less than six persons, became bankers and flooded the country with worthless paper. In 1750 there were not 12 banks outside London: In 1793 there were 400. Some of these 400 banks were no doubt well-established. . . ." [1]

Many of them, however, were weak and bank failures at this time were common. These were the so-called "country banks." Their notes, which were in denominations of £5 and upwards, circulated only in their respective communities.

Long before 1793, private banks had ceased issuing notes in London. On the other hand, the circulation of Bank of England notes was for the most part limited to London and its immediate

[1] Andréadès, pp. 171–172.

vicinity. Up to 1795, no notes of the Bank of England were issued in denominations of less than £10.

There were no restrictions on the receipt of deposits by country banks and by the private banks of London or on their circulation through bank checks, and the use of deposit currency was becoming increasingly important in England during the latter half of the eighteenth and early nineteenth centuries.[1]

From the Outbreak of the War to the Restriction Act of 1797

England declared war on France in February, 1793. Four years later specie payments were suspended by the Bank of England. Great Britain was at war until 1815 and the suspension of specie payments by the Bank, which was expected to be but temporary, actually continued for twenty-four years.

After beginnings favorable to England and her allies in the early part of 1793, the tide of war turned and, during the remainder of this period, the French were almost continually victorious. By 1797 England's allies had all been compelled to make separate treaties of peace with France, and England, as the sole surviving enemy of France, faced Napoleon. The military situation during the latter part of this period looked black for England. The country was threatened by a French invasion, and in 1796 a small body of French troops actually disembarked in Wales. Early in 1797 the sailors of two British fleets mutinied in home waters.

The internal economic situation during these four years was unstable. In the early part of 1793, there was a strong business recession, followed by a panic, with many bank failures. The Government came to the temporary relief of hard-pressed merchants by making loans of £5 million in exchequer bills. During the summer the panic subsided and was followed by a depression which continued throughout the year 1794. The year 1795 was, on the whole, a period of economic recovery, but was marked by deficient crops and high prices. The year 1796 was a year of abundant harvest, but low agricultural prices; it was a time of very active foreign trade. There was a stringent money market,

[1] In May, 1810, the Inspector of the London Clearing House testified before the Bullion Committee that 46 banks cleared their checks there every evening and that the average amount of checks cleared daily, exclusive of settling days, was about £4,700,000. *Bullion Committee Report*, p. 151.

however, and much economic hardship among the people. The year 1797 was characterized by poor crops, business inactivity and a financial panic.

Such was the general background of the suspension of gold payments. We may now consider briefly a few of the more important factors that directly contributed to the breakdown of the *de facto* gold standard.

Heavy Fiscal Demands. First and foremost were the heavy demands made by the Government upon the Bank of England for advances with which to meet the extraordinary expenditures of the war, a large part of which had to be transferred to the Continent.

The total expenditures of the National Government in 1793 were £30.6 million sterling, of which about one-third was for war services. These expenditures increased continually and by 1797 amounted to £71.6 million, of which the expenditures for war services alone amounted to £29.4 million, or nearly three times what they were in 1793.[1] The total net income of the National Government increased from £31.0 million in 1793 to £74.6 million in 1797; while of these sums the amount borrowed increased from £12.4 million in 1793 to £53.1 million in 1797.[2] Not only did England have her own war expenses to meet; but she was making loans and paying subsidies to her allies, Austria, Prussia, Spain and Sardinia, and these payments alone from 1793 to 1797, inclusive, amounted to approximately £13.7 million.[3] It is apparent that for financing the early years of the war the nation relied chiefly upon borrowing. A greater dependence upon customs duties and internal taxes for financing these years was doubtless prevented by the unfavorable economic conditions in the country previously noted, by the obstacles which the war placed in the way of foreign trade, and by the fact that the new industries that were just beginning to develop in England in these early days of the Industrial Revolution were still "infant industries" and hardly in position to stand heavy taxes.

A law was passed in 1793 which removed certain restrictions that had previously been imposed on government borrowing from the Bank of England, and which thereby left to the discretion of the Directors the whole matter of loans to the Government. As a matter of fact, however, it was impossible in a time of war for the directors of a central bank, situated as was the Bank of England

[1] Silberling, p. 215. [2] *Ibid.*, p. 217. [3] *Ibid.*, p. 227.

at that time, to refuse any demands for advances which the Government might see fit to make. It was the custom at the time for the British military and naval authorities located abroad to obtain the funds needed for their financial operations by drawing and selling abroad bills on the Paymaster General or on the Treasurer of the Navy, made payable at the Bank of England. When the bills were presented at the Bank, it was expected to provide the funds for paying them.

The demands of Pitt upon the Bank for advances increased for some time, much to the anxiety of the Bank's Directors; and they finally became so great that the Directors, on December 11, 1794, made a protest to Pitt, and later, in January, 1795, they protested again and declared that they could not allow advances on Treasury bills at any time to exceed a liberal figure which they mentioned. Pitt agreed to comply with their request, but failed to do so, and the advances he required mounted to progressively higher figures. Finally, the Directors, in a resolution of December 31, 1795, formally recognized the paramount claim of the Government and resolved that the amount to be devoted to discounts for the public should be fixed from day to day, and that any demands from the public over and above the amount allotted were to be dealt with by returning "a *pro rata* proportion of such bills in each parcel as are not otherwise objectionable . . . without regard to the respectability of the party sending in the bills or the solidity of the bills themselves."

In addition to this pressure on the Bank for funds for the Government for meeting military, naval and political expenditures on the Continent, there were in 1795 and 1796 substantial demands for advances to the Government for importing naval stores, foodstuffs and other needed supplies. The home expenditures of the Government were also greatly increased by the war.

Another force that tended to pull specie out of England was the return of France to a specie basis in 1795 and 1796, after her disastrous experiences with the Assignats and Mandats.[1] During the early years of this paper money experience, specie in large quantities had flowed from France for safety to England and other neighboring countries. With the conclusion of the French Revolution and the restoration of law and order in France, much of this specie was drawn home again.

[1] *Supra*, pp. 195–196.

Banking Situation within the Country. During most of the first two years of the war, the principal foreign exchanges were favorable to London, and specie was flowing to England from the Continent—a fact which was evidenced by the unusually heavy purchases of foreign gold for the Mint in 1793 and 1794.[1] This increase in the supply of monetary gold coupled with the crisis and subsequent depression of these two years, which reduced the demand for money, led to a substantial reduction in the bank-note circulation of the country, and this reduction applied both to the notes of the Bank of England and to those of the country banks.[2] Throughout 1794 the Bank's reserve position continued strong. In late 1795, however, the Bank of England, as well as the country banks, experienced heavy demands upon their reserves. From August, 1795 to August, 1796 the Bank's stock of bullion declined from £5.1 million to £2.1 million, while its notes in circulation declined only from £10.9 million to £9.2 million, and its deposits from £8.2 million to £6.7 million. By February, 1797 the bullion had reached the low figure of £1.1 million, while the circulation stood at £9.7 million and the deposits at £4.9 million.[3]

The uncertain political situation early in 1797 and the gloomy military outlook led country banks to make heavy demands for specie on the Bank of England. Exchange became strongly unfavorable the latter part of 1794, and by May, 1795 the gold-export point was reached. There was a strong outward movement of specie throughout the remainder of 1795 and throughout the year 1796, a movement to Paris, Hamburg and Lisbon. Thus England experienced at one time a heavy internal demand for gold and a

TABLE I. IMPORTANT ITEMS IN BANK OF ENGLAND'S BALANCE SHEET

	Feb. 1795	Aug. 1795	Feb. 1796	Aug. 1796	Feb. 1797
	£ 000,000	£ 000,000	£ 000,000	£ 000,000	£ 000,000
Notes in Circulation	14.0	10.9	10.7	9.2	9.7
Deposits	6.0	8.2	5.7	6.7	4.9
Bullion	6.1	5.1	2.5	2.1	1.1
Private Securities	3.6	3.7	4.2	6.2	5.1
Public Securities	13.2	13.3	13.0	10.9	11.7

[1] Hawtrey, p. 326.
[2] Andréadès, p. 194.
[3] *Report on the Bank of England Charter*, Appendix 5, p. 17.

powerful foreign drain. This gold drain reduced the Bank's note circulation and its deposits, but during this period the Bank expanded its private credit. The figures are as shown in Table I, on page 203.[1]

The specie reserve had reached such a low figure by February, 1797 and the drain was continuing so strongly, that the Directors notified Pitt that the situation was desperate. Pitt responded on February 26 with a Council resolution declaring it to be

> "the unanimous opinion of the Board that it is indispensably necessary for the public service that the Directors of the Bank of England should forbear issuing any cash in payment until the sense of Parliament can be taken on that subject and the proper measures adopted thereupon for maintaining the means of circulation and supporting the public and commercial credit of the Kingdom at this important conjuncture."

The resolution further required the Directors "on the grounds of the exigency of the case to conform thereto until the sense of Parliament can be taken . . ." [2] This resolution was passed and the Bank was notified on Sunday. Monday morning the Bank opened as usual. It notified the public of what had been done by merely posting the resolution, along with the following notice:

> "The Governor, Deputy-Governor, and Directors of the Bank of England think it their duty to inform the proprietors of Bank Stock as well as the Public at large that the general concerns of the Bank are in the most affluent and prosperous situation, and such as to preclude every doubt as to the security of its notes. The Directors mean to continue their usual discounts for the accommodation of the commercial interest, paying the amount in bank-notes, and the dividend warrants will be paid in the same manner." [3]

Later on the same day, a meeting of merchants and bankers was held in London, which passed a resolution agreeing to accept Bank of England notes. Eventually some 4,000 persons signed this resolution. The bank notes, it will be remembered, though receivable by the Government for all government dues, were not at this time legal tender.

The above Order in Council was enacted into law on May 3, 1797, by Parliament under the name of the "Bank Restriction Act" (Geo. III, c. 45). This act was looked upon as a temporary emergency measure and was to terminate on June 24 of that year.

[1] *Ibid.*, p. 17. [2] Cannan, p. xi. [3] *Ibid.*, pp. xi and xii.

A few days before, a law was passed allowing the issue of bank notes in denominations under £5, but not under £1.

From the time at which the news of the Order in Council reached the provincial banks, these banks assumed that the Restriction Act required them as well as the Bank of England to discontinue specie payments. But, unlike the Bank of England, they did not claim to be able to insist on paying out nothing except their own notes. On the contrary, they felt under obligation to continue to redeem their own notes in Bank of England notes or in drafts on London. Thus their powers of bank-note expansion continued to be restricted. The Bank of England, however, was relieved from all obligation to redeem its notes in any other kind of money.

Gold coin promptly disappeared from circulation. Large quantities were exported surreptitiously, or falsely sworn off,[1] and much found its way into private hoards. As previously noted, there was little British silver in circulation, and the need for small coin was met in part by the use of foreign silver coins, many of which were stamped with the King's head.

Years of Comparative Monetary Stability

The events of the next dozen years may be passed over rapidly. After a brief period of excitement and tension following the suspension of specie payments, confidence in the currency and the banks recovered. The years 1798 to 1801, inclusive, were years of almost continuous depression. There was a recovery beginning the latter part of 1801 and lasting for about two years. The latter part of 1803 and the year 1804 were again poor years. Then followed two years of prosperity and two years of depression. England was at war during the entire period.

The expenditures of the National Government stood at £72 million in 1797 and, except for a sharp one-year rise in 1801, continued in this neighborhood through 1804. They then advanced substantially, reaching £129 million in 1810.[2]

Following the Restriction Act, the Government adopted a much more vigorous taxation policy, and, as time went on, placed relatively less and less dependence upon borrowing. The proportion of the total net income of the Government which was obtained from borrowing was at its highest in 1797, when it stood at 71 per cent. It dropped sharply the next year, and from 1798 to

[1] *Supra*, p. 199.

[2] Silberling, p. 215.

1810 the percentage exceeded 60 in only one year and it was less than 50 in seven years.[1] This highly creditable fiscal record on the part of the Government did much to strengthen public confidence during these trying years.

A rough idea of the extent to which the Bank expanded its credit during the years from 1797 to 1810 can be obtained from the following table:[2]

TABLE II. IMPORTANT ITEMS IN BANK OF ENGLAND'S BALANCE SHEET FOR MONTHS OF FEBRUARY AND AUGUST, 1797–1821

Year and Month	Notes in Circulation	Deposits	Bullion	Private Securities	Public Securities
1797 F	9.7	4.9	1.1	5.1	11.7
A	11.1	7.8	4.1	9.5	8.8
1798 F	13.1	6.1	5.8	5.6	11.2
A	12.2	8.3	6.5	6.4	10.9
1799 F	13.0	8.1	7.6	5.5	11.5
A	13.4	7.6	7.0	7.5	9.5
1800 F	16.8	7.1	6.1	7.4	14.0
A	15.0	8.3	5.2	8.6	13.6
1801 F	16.2	10.7	4.6	10.5	16.0
A	14.6	8.1	4.3	10.3	11.9
1802 F	15.2	6.9	4.2	7.8	14.2
A	17.1	9.7	3.9	13.6	13.5
1803 F	15.3	8.1	3.8	14.5	9.4
A	16.0	9.8	3.6	13.6	13.3
1804 F	17.1	8.7	3.4	12.3	14.7
A	17.2	9.7	5.9	10.8	15.0
1805 F	17.9	12.1	5.9	11.8	16.9
A	16.4	14.0	7.6	16.4	11.4
1806 F	17.7	10.0	6.0	11.8	14.8
A	21.0	9.6	6.2	15.3	14.2
1807 F	17.0	11.8	6.1	14.0	13.5
A	19.7	11.8	6.5	16.5	13.4
1808 F	18.2	12.0	7.9	13.2	14.1
A	17.1	13.0	6.0	14.3	15.0
1809 F	18.5	10.0	4.5	14.4	14.7
A	19.6	12.3	3.7	18.1	15.3
1810 F	21.0	12.5	3.5	21.1	14.3
A	24.8	13.6	3.2	23.8	17.2
1811 F	23.4	11.4	3.4	19.9	17.2
A	23.2	11.1	3.2	15.2	21.9
1812 F	23.4	11.6	3.0	15.9	22.1
A	23.0	11.8	3.1	17.0	21.2
1813 F	23.2	11.3	2.9	12.9	25.0
A	24.8	11.2	2.7	14.5	25.6

[1] *Ibid.*, p. 218.

[2] This table is based upon figures given in the Bank-Charter Commission's Report of 1831–1832 (Appendix 5).

TABLE II. IMPORTANT ITEMS IN BANK OF ENGLAND'S BALANCE SHEET FOR MONTHS OF FEBRUARY AND AUGUST, 1797–1821
(*Continued*)

YEAR AND MONTH	NOTES IN CIRCULATION	DEPOSITS	BULLION	PRIVATE SECURITIES	PUBLIC SECURITIES
1814 F	24.8	12.5	2.2	18.4	23.6
A	28.4	14.8	2.1	13.4	35.0
1815 F	27.3	11.7	2.0	17.0	27.5
A	27.2	12.7	3.4	20.7	24.2
1816 F	27.0	12.4	4.6	24.0	19.4
A	26.8	11.9	7.6	11.2	26.1
1817 F	27.4	10.8	9.7	8.7	25.5
A	29.5	9.1	11.7	5.5	27.1
1818 F	27.8	8.0	10.1	4.0	26.9
A	26.2	7.9	6.4	5.1	27.3
1819 F	25.1	6.4	4.2	9.1	23.4
A	25.3	6.3	3.6	6.3	25.4
1820 F	23.5	4.1	4.9	4.5	21.7
A	24.3	4.4	8.2	4.7	19.2
1821 F	23.9	5.6	11.9	4.8	16.0
A	20.3	5.8	11.2	2.7	15.8

Despite the suspension of gold payments, the value of the paper pound, measured in terms of gold or of silver in England, or in terms of the principal specie exchanges, namely, Paris and Hamburg, showed a fair degree of stability down to 1808. Another criterion which tells a similar story is the movement of commodity prices in England.

The following table on page 208 shows the fluctuations in the value of the pound in terms of these different indices during these years.[1]

It will be observed that the fluctuations in the value of the pound were small by whatever criterion measured during the eleven years ending 1808, as compared with fluctuations which the world has experienced since that time in the purchasing powers of both gold and silver.

It was not until after the crisis of 1800 that the public began to suspect that the rise in the price of bullion and the decline in

[1] The table is based chiefly upon figures given by Hawtrey, p. 335. The commodity price index number covering 35 articles is that prepared by Silberling and given in the *Harvard Review of Economic Statistics*, October, 1923, p. 232. To make possible a comparison with changes in the price level in the United States, which at this time (except for the years 1814–1817) was upon a specie basis, I have added a column, giving the wholesale price index numbers for the United States prepared by Alvin H. Hansen and published in the *Monthly Labor Review* of February, 1927, pp. 166 and 167.

Table III. Fluctuations in the Value of the Paper Pound as Evidenced by Prices of Specie, Foreign Exchange Rates and Commodity Prices, 1797–1819

Year	1[a]	2[a]	3	4	5	6
1797	100.0	102.6	—	98	141	—
1798	100.0	100.1	—	96	149	—
1799	—	106.7	—	103	156	—
1800	107.0	113.5	—	113	159	—
1801	109.0	117.3	—	113	166	162
1802	—	113.7	105.7	109	143	133
1803	—	111.9	102.9	105	156	136
1804	103.0	108.3	100.1	101	153	147
1805	103.0	107.4	98.8	103	160	151
1806	—	110.5	103.0	105	157	148
1807	—	110.2	103.5	104	152	139
1808	—	107.1	108.4	106	166	136
1809	—	110.4	123.3	121	176	143
1810	—	113.9	121.6	120	176	156
1811	123.9	120.7	139.1	144	158	152
1812	130.2	126.5	131.2	128	163	154
1813	136.4	136.7	128.6	130	185	179
1814	124.4	124.3	116.4	119	198	224
1815	118.7	117.5	115.6	114	166	176
1816	102.9	100.9	99.6	100	135	150
1817	102.2	104.3	102.0	102	143	151
1818	104.6	106.5	104.3	105	150	148
1819	102.3	104.7	102.7	102	136	130

Headings of above columns:

1—Gold, Index Numbers, Par = £3 17s. 10½d. per oz. = 100.
2—Silver, Index Numbers, Par = 60·84d. per oz. = 100.
3—Exchange on Paris, Index Numbers, Par = 25·22 Fr. per £ = 100.
4—Exchange on Hamburg, Index Numbers, Par = 36s. banco per £ = 100.
5—Commodity Prices in England, Year 1790 = 100.
6—United States Wholesale Price Index, Year 1913 = 100.

[a] Quotations for the price of gold are very incomplete, because for several long stretches of time there was no established market. The bulk of England's trade at this time was with silver standard countries, and there exists a practically continuous series of quotations for silver. For this reason, the price of silver, or more specifically the average price per ounce of Spanish dollars, is probably the best criterion of the price of specie (Silberling, p. 230). The variations during these years in the gold-silver market ratio were not large. Soetbeer's annual figures for this ratio at Hamburg showed a range for this entire period (1797–1810) of only a little over 5 per cent.

the foreign exchanges were evidence of a depreciation in the specie value of the bank note. During the next few years, however, this view was frequently expressed, both in Parliament and outside.[1]

[1] Among those who early took this position were Walter Boyd, Charles James Fox, Henry Thornton and Lord Peter King.

A well-reasoned statement showing a realization of the variability of the value of gold itself as well as of the fact of the depreciation in the gold value of the Bank of England notes was given in King, *Thoughts on the Effects of the Bank Restrictions.*

A substantial rise in the price of bullion, with sharp declines in the foreign exchanges and pronounced advances in commodity prices, in 1809, accompanied by a speculative expansion into South America, brought the subject of the state of the currency again prominently to public attention. The facts, moreover, that this apparent depreciation of the bank-note currency was accompanied by an increase in the bank-note circulation, a large increase in the Bank's holdings of private securities, and a pronounced decline in its specie reserve, directed public criticism toward the Bank.

Ricardo's Letters to "The Morning Chronicle"

David Ricardo, an exchange broker in London, who in the course of his business had been having extensive transactions with the Bank of England, on August 29, 1809, wrote a letter to *The Morning Chronicle* of London on "The Price of Gold." This letter was vigorously attacked by other correspondents of the paper, and Ricardo replied to the attacks in two subsequent letters, one on September 20 and one on November 23.[1] The monetary philosophy set forth in these letters was further elaborated by Ricardo and published under the title, "The High Price of Bullion, A Proof of the Depreciation of Bank Notes," the first edition of which was dated December 1, 1809. These letters to the *Chronicle* represented David Ricardo's first public appearance as an economist. His position may be briefly summarized as follows:

The *de facto* monetary standard of England prior to the suspension of specie payments in 1797 was gold. The value of gold itself, as expressed in its purchasing power over commodities, varies with the scarcity or abundance of gold; it is a question of demand and supply. The market price of gold, however, remains comparatively fixed so long as the country is on the gold standard, and "no scarcity, however great, can raise the market price much above the mint price, unless it be measured by a depreciated currency." The approximate parity of gold bullion and Bank of England notes at the mint price of gold was maintained, while the gold standard prevailed, by the fact that dealers could exchange their notes at the Bank for gold coin on demand and then melt down the coin and sell it, and likewise could take gold bullion

[1] Cf., Hollander, J. H., Editor, *David Ricardo on the Price of Gold, 1809—A Reprint of Economic Tracts;* Baltimore, Maryland, The Lord Baltimore Press, 1903.

to the Mint or to the Bank of England and obtain bank notes for it at the parity rate, or very close to it. Similar forces before the suspension of gold payments restricted foreign exchange fluctuations to the narrow range marked by the expenses incident to the shipment of gold. "This is therefore the natural limit to the fall of the exchange, it can never fall more below par than these expenses; nor can it ever rise more above par than the same amount." [1] According to Ricardo, "no efforts of the Bank could keep more than a certain quantity of notes in circulation, and if that quantity was exceeded, its effects on the price of gold always brought the excess back to the Bank for specie." [2] After the Restriction Act, "all checks to the over issue of notes were removed, excepting that which the Bank voluntarily placed on itself . . ." [3] He held that, so long as the banks were willing to lend, borrowers would want to borrow, and, as loans increased, bank-note issues would rise, with a resulting rise in the price of gold and with a like effect on the prices of provisions and on all other commodities. Under the same influences, foreign exchange rates would correspondingly decline. The extent to which the price of gold rose above parity, he maintained, roughly measured the degree to which bank notes had depreciated.

To the argument that a proof that bank notes had not depreciated was to be found in the fact that no shopkeeper would sell more goods for 20 guineas than for £21 in bank notes, he held: first, that this was not true, because secretly there was in practice a discrimination in favor of gold and against bank notes; and, second, that discrimination against bank notes was restrained by the fact that it "would expose the man who openly undertook it to so much obloquy and suspicion, that notwithstanding the profit, no one is hardy enough to encounter the risk, particularly as the law is very severe against melting the coin or exporting it." [4]

Ricardo's proposal for bringing the depreciated bank notes back to parity with gold was a vigorous contraction of the currency, which was to be enjoined upon the Bank by Parliament.[5]

> "If," he said, "our circulating medium has been augmented a fifth, till that fifth be withdrawn the prices of gold and commodities will remain as they are. Increase the quantity of notes, they will rise still

[1] *Ibid.*, p. 13.
[2] *Ibid.*, p. 10.
[3] *Ibid.*, p. 11.
[4] *Ibid.*, p. 11.
[5] *Ibid.*, pp. 14 and 18.

higher; but withdraw the same, as I earnestly recommend, and gold and every other commodity will find its just level. . . . Let the Bank be enjoined by Parliament gradually to withdraw to the amount of two or three millions of their notes from circulation, without obliging them, in the first instance, to pay in specie, and we should very soon find that the market price of gold would fall to its mint price of 3£ 17s. 10½d. that every commodity would experience a similar reduction; and that the exchange with foreign countries would be confined within the limits above mentioned."

Ricardo's proposal had been criticized by Mr. Cobbett on the ground that the withdrawal of the Bank of England notes from circulation would not contract the currency since country bank notes would be pushed into circulation to take their place as fast as they were withdrawn. Ricardo's reply was that all country bank notes were convertible into Bank of England notes on demand and that, therefore, a reduction in the supply of Bank of England notes would necessitate a corresponding reduction in the supply of the country bank notes for which these Bank of England notes served as the reserve.

Bullion Committee

Ricardo was not willing to let the matter drop with his *Chronicle* letters and his pamphlet on "The High Price of Bullion," especially since the currency situation at this time was getting worse instead of better. He obtained the support of his friend, Francis Horner, who was then a member of the House of Commons, and Horner in February, 1810 succeeded in having a Select Committee appointed by the House

"to enquire into the Cause of the High Price of Gold Bullion, and to take into consideration the State of the Circulating Medium, and of the Exchanges between Great Britain and Foreign Parts;—and to report the same, with their Observations thereupon, from time to time, to The House."

Horner, who was himself a capable economist, was made Chairman of the Committee. Most of the twenty-two members of the Committee were men well informed on monetary questions.[1]

[1] The Committee included such well-known names as Alexander Baring, W. Huskisson and Henry Thornton. The Committee took evidence over a period extending, with interruptions, from February 22 to May 25, and examined a large number of witnesses. The Hearings are reported in full in the Minutes of Evidence; and the Appendices of the Report contain much useful information. "Report together with Minutes of Evidence, and Accounts, from the Select Committee on the High Price of Gold Bullion. Ordered, by the House of Commons, to be printed, 8 June 1810." Hereafter cited as *Report*.

Conflicting Testimony. The witnesses before the Committee differed widely, both as to the facts themselves and as to their interpretation. Broadly speaking, there were two schools of thought and there were differences of detail among the witnesses adhering to each school. There were in addition a number of witnesses, mostly those testifying on special subjects, whom it is impossible to classify as belonging definitely to either school. The nature of the controversy can best be made clear by summarizing the two opposing schools of thought. The one school is perhaps best called "The Bank School," because its principal champions were officials and directors of the Bank of England; and the other school may be called "The Gold School," because it strongly favored the gold standard.

The Bank School. The position of this group was that the high price of gold bullion and the low exchange rates were not due to any excess in the issuance of bank notes, but rather to an increased demand for specie, particularly abroad, and to an unfavorable trade balance. The representatives of the Bank of England held that bank notes could not be issued to excess and could not depreciate so long as the Bank made loans only against high-grade, short-time bills, representing real commercial transactions; and they held, with occasional waverings, that the Bank's directors did not and should not consider the state of the exchanges or the price of bullion as factors of importance in determining their discount policy and the volume of their bank note issues.

John Whitmore, the Governor of the Bank of England, was asked if there was not reason to suspect that the present unfavorable state of the exchange might be due in part to the absence of that limitation upon the issuance of notes which used to be imposed by the Bank before the Restriction Act, on the occasion of the exchanges becoming unfavorable. He replied: [1]

> "My opinion is, I do not know whether it is that of the Bank, that the amount of our paper circulation has no reference at all to the state of the exchange." Q.—"Has that question ever been brought to a regular discussion and decision in the Court of Directors?" A.—"In the opinion of the Bank Directors, it had not sufficient bearing upon our concerns to make it more than a matter of conversation; it never was singly and separately a subject of discussion, though constantly in view with other circumstances."

[1] *Report*, p. 90.

With regard to this subject, Deputy-Governor Pearse testified: [1]

> " . . . I cannot see how the amount of Bank notes issued can operate upon the price of Bullion, or the state of the exchanges, and therefore I am individually of opinion that the price of Bullion, or the state of the exchanges, can never be a reason for lessening the amount of Bank notes to be issued, always understanding the control which I have already described."

Governor Whitmore concurred in this opinion, saying: [2]

> "I am so much of the same opinion, that I never think it necessary to advert to the price of Gold or the state of the exchange, on the days on which we make our advances. . . . I do not advert to it with a view to our general advances, conceiving it not to bear upon the question."

The representatives of the Bank of England applied this same principle in their interpretation of the issues of the country banks. Deputy-Governor Pearse said: [3]

> "If the country bankers regulated and limited their issues upon the same principle as uniformly governs the Bank of England, I do not see how any excess can arise in their circulating paper; but if any of their paper is issued otherwise than as representing securities arising out of real transactions and payable at fixed and not distinct [*sic*, distant] periods, I conceive such an excess may obtain . . ."

This same attitude was maintained by the representatives of the Bank when they were pressed as to its applicability under a régime of very low discount rates, as will be seen from the following excerpts from the testimony: [4]

> Q.—"State to the Committee what is the criterion which enables the Bank at all times to ascertain that the issue of Bank notes is kept precisely within the limits which the occasion of the public requires, and thereby to guard the circulation of this Country against the possibility of any excess; and in what manner the control necessary for maintaining uniformly an exact proportion between the occasions of the public and the issues of the Bank, is exercised and applied by the Court of Directors?" A. (Governor Whitmore)—"I have already stated that we never forced a Bank note into circulation, and the criterion by which I judge of the exact proportion to be maintained is, by avoiding as much as possible to discount what does not appear to be legitimate mercantile paper. The Bank notes would revert to us if there was a redundancy in circulation, as no one would pay interest for a bank note that he did not want to make use of." Mr. Pearse: "I agree in that opinion . . ."

[1] *Ibid.*, pp. 96 and 97.
[2] *Ibid.*, p. 97.
[3] *Ibid.*, p. 119.
[4] *Ibid.*, pp. 97 and 98.

Q.—"Then your measure of scarcity or abundance is by the greater or less application that is made to you for the discount of good paper?" A. (Governor Whitmore)—"Certainly." Q.—"Does not the circumstance, of individuals applying for advances, or not so applying, at 5 per cent. indicate rather a deficiency or a redundancy of the mercantile capital, than a superfluity or want of circulating medium?" A. (Mr. Pearse)—"I am not of opinion that the application for Bank notes is for any other purposes than as a circulating medium in the interchange of property." Q.—"Is it your opinion that the same security would exist against any excess in the issues of the Bank, if the rate of the discount were reduced from five to four per cent.?" A. (Governor Whitmore)—"The security against an excess of issue would be, I conceive, precisely the same." Mr. Pearse: "I concur in that answer." Q.—"If it were reduced to three per cent.?" A. (Governor Whitmore)—"I conceive there would be no difference, if our practice remained the same as now, of not forcing a note into circulation." Mr. Pearse: "I concur in that answer."

As to the influence of bank note issues upon exchange rates, Deputy-Governor Pearse testified that, in his opinion: [1]

"The amount of the Bank notes in circulation, controlled as it is by the occasions of the public for internal purposes, cannot influence the rate of the Hamburgh exchange, and the consequent export of Bullion. . . . From the manner in which the issue of Bank notes is controlled, the publick will never call for more than is absolutely necessary for their wants."

On the subject of the relationship between bank note issues and the commodity price level, the representatives of the Bank were somewhat halting and evasive in their answers. Deputy-Governor Pearse was asked: [2]

"Supposing the Bank paper to be diminished, as you suppose that it possibly might in the contemplation of the event of the opening of the Bank [namely, return to specie payments], do you not conceive that such diminution would tend in some degree to lower the general price of commodities?" A.—"As long as it only passes as a circulating medium, I think not." Q.—"Do you conceive that a very considerable reduction of the amount of the circulating medium, would not tend in any degree to increase its relative value compared with commodities, and that a considerable increase of it would have no tendency whatever to augment the price of commodities in exchange for such circulating medium?" A.—"It is a subject on which such a variety of opinions are entertained, I do not feel myself competent to give a decided answer."

Supporting the general position taken by Governor Whitmore and Deputy-Governor Pearse were five other witnesses, including

[1] *Report*, p. 112.

[2] *Ibid.*, p. 127.

Jeremiah Harman, a director of the Bank and J. L. Greffulhe, a prominent merchant "trading chiefly to the Continent."

The Gold School. It will not be necessary to discuss at this point the testimony of those witnesses who belonged to the Gold School and who disagreed fundamentally with the position taken by the officials of the Bank of England, for the reason that the Report of the Bullion Committee itself is an exposition of the opinions of this School. In summarizing that Report, therefore, the monetary philosophy of this School will be presented and the answers to the arguments advanced by the Banking School will be made evident. The three principal witnesses in this Gold School were Sir Francis Baring, the founder of the great banking house of Baring Brothers, Mr. Thomas Thompson, himself a member of the Bullion Committee, and a third man who testified under the name of "A Continental Merchant," and who is generally believed now to have been the great financier, N. M. Rothschild. These men attributed the high price of bullion and the low state of the exchanges chiefly to excessive issues of bank notes, the responsibility for which, in large part, they placed upon the Bank of England.[1]

The Bullion Committee Report. The Report, which was signed by all twenty-two members of the Committee and the text of which covered about thirty-three folio pages, was presented to the House of Commons and ordered printed June 8, 1810. It gave rise to a heated debate in periodicals and pamphlets, in which many eminent persons participated, including David Ricardo and Thomas R. Malthus.[2] Not until the following May did it come before the House of Commons for debate.

Briefly summarized, the argument of the Report is as follows:

High Price of Gold. The extraordinary rise in the market price of gold in recent years and the contemporaneous remarkable depression in the foreign exchanges are unusual phenomena that demand explanation. The argument of several witnesses that this is due to an unusual demand for gold on the Continent is fallacious, because there is no evidence of a rise in the *price* of gold abroad,[3]

[1] There were, as previously noted, seventeen other witnesses, most of whom testified on special problems, and none of whom took a clear stand on one side or the other of the fundamental questions in the controversy.

[2] For an account of this controversy and of the parliamentary history of the Report, cf., Cannan, *op. cit.*, pp. xxiv–xxviii. See also Ricardo, *Minor Papers on the Currency Question, 1809–1823*, edited by Jacob H. Hollander.

[3] That the world *value* of gold at about this time was rising the reader will see by referring to Column 6 of the Table on page 208, which shows that commodity prices

nor of an increase in its value at home in terms of commodities. Moreover, at previous times, when notes were convertible into specie on demand, extraordinary demands for gold abroad did not cause any such high prices for gold as the country has today. For many years prior to 1797 British gold coin, Bank of England notes and gold bullion were kept at approximate parity with each other. The greatest depreciation which could take place in the coin, when the Bank paid in gold, the Report said, was about 5½ per cent.; and accordingly it would be found, that, prior to 1797, the difference between the mint price and market price of gold never exceeded that limit.[1] Since the suspension in 1797, even if it should be admitted that gold were still our measure of value, which the Committee considers to be very doubtful,

> " . . . it has been exposed to a new cause of variation, from the possible excess of that paper which is not convertible into Gold at will; and the limit of this new variation is as indefinite as the excess to which that paper may be issued." [2]

Low State of the Exchanges. The Report took issue with the contention, that the fall in the exchanges was due wholly or chiefly to an unfavorable balance of trade or payments, and held that under the régime of convertibility unfavorable balances never caused such a depreciation, and that they would be automatically corrected through an outflow of gold, with the export point at the lower possible limit of exchange decline.

> "It appears to Your Committee," says the Report, "to have been long settled and understood as a principle, that the difference of Exchange resulting from the state of trade and payments between two countries is limited by the expense of conveying and insuring the precious metals from one country to the other; at least, that it cannot for any considerable length of time exceed that limit." [3]

In support of this conclusion, the Report earlier cited the testimony of "a very eminent Continental Merchant," (N. M. Rothschild), who conceived "that such fall of our Exchange as has exceeded that extent in the last 15 months, must certainly be referred

in the United States, a country then on a bimetallic basis, declined continually and substantially from 1805 to 1808.

[1] *Report*, p. 7.

[2] At this point the Report questions "whether we have any other standard of prices than that circulating medium, issued primarily by the Bank of England and in a secondary manner by the country banks . . ." *Ibid.*, p. 7.

[3] *Ibid.*, p. 11.

to the circumstance of our paper currency not being convertible into specie." [1]

Before suspension, declining exchange rates, and a slight rise in the price of bullion led to a withdrawal of gold from the Bank of England and from the country banks, and to its exportation. The gold was paid out by the banks against the presentation of bank notes, and the withdrawal from circulation of these bank notes contracted the currency. Such a withdrawal of gold brought pressure on the Bank to raise its discount rate and to curtail its loans. These automatic checks usually prevented the Bank from unduly extending its note issue.

Suspension of gold payments, however, took away these checks, and the Bank erroneously ceased to pay adequate attention in its discount policy to such important danger signals as falling exchange rates and a rising price of bullion. The Directors were wrong, the Committee maintained, in holding that, so long as the Bank's notes were issued only in the discounting of good commercial bills of short maturities and were not forced upon the public, they could not be issued in excessive amounts. This might be true, the Committee said, under a régime of convertibility, but it was not true when redemption in specie provided no check to note expansion. Notes issued against a discounted bill, to make one commercial payment, may continue in circulation for a long time and make many payments. Increasing note circulation tends to raise commodity prices, and the resulting higher price level necessitates the maintenance of the increased circulation. There is no limit to the possible expansion.

The situation was made worse by the usury law fixing the maximum rate of discount at 5 per cent. The making of discounts at rates below the real market rate encourages an expansion of the note circulation for speculative loans.

Country banks, after suspension, redeemed their notes to a large extent by drafts on the Bank of England and by the payment of Bank of England notes. The Bank of England notes formed an important part of their reserves, and, although in some districts near London Bank of England notes and country bank notes competed with each other in active circulation, taking the country as a whole an expansion in the Bank of England's note circulation was likely to be followed by an expansion in the circulation of the notes

[1] *Ibid.*, p. 8.

of the country banks, while a contraction in the circulation of Bank of England notes was likely to be followed by a contraction of the country bank circulation. In this respect, Bank of England notes served as the reserve of country banks and were performing to a considerable extent the function that the specie reserve of the country banks had performed before suspension. The Committee held: [1]

> " . . . that so long as the Cash payments of the Bank are suspended, the whole paper of the Country Bankers is a superstructure raised upon the foundation of the paper of the Bank of England. . . . If the Bank of England paper itself should at any time, during the suspension of Cash payments, be issued to excess, a corresponding excess may be issued of Country Bank paper which will not be checked; the foundation being enlarged, the superstructure admits of a proportionate extension."

This increase in the country bank note circulation, caused in large part by the mistaken policy of the Directors of the Bank of England in restricting their attention to the quality of the paper they were asked to discount and in ignoring the warnings given by declining exchange rates and a mounting premium on the price of bullion, explains in large part the unfortunate situation in which the country then found itself. Such was the opinion of the Bullion Committee.

The Committee based its conclusions upon what would be called today by most economists a form of the quantity theory of money, although it nowhere used that term.

> "An increase in the quantity of the local currency of a particular country," it says, "will raise prices in that country exactly in the same manner as an increase in the general supply of precious metals raises prices all over the world. By means of the increase of quantity, the value of a given portion of that circulating medium, in exchange for other commodities, is lowered; in other words, the money prices of all other commodities are raised, and that of Bullion with the rest. In this manner, an excess of the local currency of a particular country will occasion a rise of the market price of Gold above its Mint price. It is no less evident, that, in the event of the prices of commodities being raised in one country by an augmentation of its circulating medium, while no similar augmentation in the circulating medium of a neighbouring country has led to a similar rise of prices, the currencies of those two countries will no longer continue to bear the same relative value to each other as before. The intrinsic value of a given portion of the one currency being lessened, while that of the other remains unaltered, the

[1] *Report*, p. 28.

Exchange will be computed between those two countries to the disadvantage of the former.

"In this manner, a general rise of all prices, a rise in the market price of Gold, and a fall of the Foreign Exchanges, will be the effect of an excessive quantity of circulating medium in a country which has adopted a currency, not exportable to other countries, or not convertible at will into a Coin which is exportable." [1]

After making this general statement, the Committee qualified it by showing that in any statement of the relationship between the volume of money and the price level, such factors as the volume of trade, the velocity of monetary circulation, the extent of the use of bank checks, and confidence must be taken into account. In other words, it is a question of monetary demand as well as of monetary supply.

It is a "very important principle," the Committee said that: [2]

" . . . the mere numerical return of the amount of Bank notes out in circulation, cannot be considered as at all deciding the question, whether such paper is or is not excessive. It is necessary to have recourse to other tests. The same amount of paper may at one time be less than enough, and at another time more. The quantity of currency required will vary in some degree with the extent of trade; and the increase of our trade, which has taken place since the suspension, must have occasioned some increase in the quantity of our currency. But the quantity of currency bears no fixed proportion to the quantity of commodities . . . The effective currency of the Country depends upon the quickness of circulation, and the number of exchanges performed in a given time, as well as upon its numerical amount; and all the circumstances, which have a tendency to quicken or to retard the rate of circulation, render the same amount of currency more or less adequate to the wants of trade. A much smaller amount is required in a high state of public credit, than when alarms make individuals call in their advances, and provide against accidents by hoarding; and in a period of commercial security and private confidence, than when mutual distrust discourages pecuniary arrangements for any distant time. But, above all, the same amount of currency will be more or less adequate, in proportion to the skill which the great money-dealers possess in managing and economising the use of the circulating medium."

The Committee maintained that no adequate provision against excessive note issues could be found, except convertibility into specie on demand. It considered the existing depreciation of the bank notes and the instability of their value to be a great evil, which should be remedied at the earliest practicable moment.

[1] *Ibid.*, pp. 7 and 8.

[2] *Ibid.*, p. 26.

The remedy was a resumption of convertibility. It held that, if the bank notes should be permitted to continue for too long a time at this depreciated value, Parliament might decide that the gold content of the guinea should be reduced, so as to bring the value of the guinea down to the level of the bank notes. Such a debasement the Committee thought would be a "breach of public faith" and a "dereliction of a primary duty of Government." [1]

The Report recommended that the details of the plan for the resumption of cash payments should be left to the director of the Bank, but that the time of resumption should be fixed at a date two years in the future, and that resumption should become effective on that date, regardless of whether the war should continue until that time or not. The Committee said that domestic panic might possibly justify an extension of the date, but no such justification could be found in the state of the foreign exchanges.

Report Submitted to Parliament. The Report of the Bullion Committee did not come up for debate in Parliament until May 6, 1811, nearly a year after it was presented. The debate was opened by Horner in a speech presenting and defending at length the arguments of the Report and the policy it recommended, and concluding with the submission of a series of sixteen resolutions.[2]

Other members of the Bullion Committee made speeches supporting the Report; the speeches of Huskisson and Thornton were particularly able. The presentation of fundamental monetary principles by Thornton in his two speeches and the support of these principles by citations from the monetary history of Ireland, France, Russia, Sweden and the United States, are worthy of careful study by monetary students of today. In fact, many of the fallacies which Thornton so ably refuted are still held in high places. He stated effectively the principles of international price equilibrium, of foreign exchange fluctuations and of international specie movements. Without using the term, he clearly anticipated the "purchasing power parity" doctrine. He pointed out the difference between money interest and real interest, and set forth the theory which is now known under the term "depreciation, appreciation, and interest." He explained the theory underlying that we now call "Gresham's Law." The difficulty of liqui-

[1] *Report*, p. 31.

[2] The resolutions are given in Hansard's *Debates*, XIX, pp. 830 and 831. These Debates will be cited hereafter as Hansard.

dating wages and of bringing them back into equilibrium with prices in a period of currency appreciation, following a period of inflation, were discussed. He quoted David Hume's statement, that "it is only in the interval between the acquisition of money and rise of prices, that the increasing quantity of gold and silver is favourable to industry," [1] and added that his opponent would do well to remember that "it is only by the perpetual increase of paper that their object can be fully effected. They should also reflect, that, in proportion to this increase, the exchange will be prejudiced, and the standard of the country forsaken." If a long period of substantial depreciation has been permitted to exist in any country, say, eight, ten or twenty years, then, in his opinion, it may be considered unfair to restore the preëxisting value of the currency, for loans and other contracts would have been made under the expectation of a continuance of the existing depreciations.[2] If, however, the depreciation had lasted only two or three years, he believed, justice was on the side of returning to the antecedent metallic standard.

Thornton was at his best in discussing the balance of trade. It has appeared in the course of the present debates, he said, that "the chief circumstance which had led the Directors of the Bank to embrace the opinion that the quantity of their paper had no influence on the exchange, was the doctrine which they entertained respecting what is called the balance of trade." [3] Thornton did not use "balance of trade" in the present-day commodity sense, but included all the invisible items which today are included in the balance of payments.[4] According to the Directors, the state of the exchange was the unavoidable consequence of an unfavorable trade balance. To this contention he replied: [5]

> "Our ancestors, eager for the acquisition of the precious metals, exploring, as is well known, new continents, chiefly with a view to this article; and accustomed to consider trade as profitable or otherwise, in proportion as it brought in or took out gold and silver, were naturally led to denominate that part of our exports or imports which consisted of these metals, a balance. In truth, however, this was not a balance. Bullion was an article of commerce, rising or falling in value according to the

[1] Hansard, XX, pp. 86 and 87.
[2] *Ibid.*, XIX, p. 917.
[3] *Ibid.*, XX, p. 81.
[4] See article by Fetter, F. W., "The Term 'Favorable Balance of Trade,'" *The Quarterly Journal of Economics*, August, 1935, p. 621.
[5] *Ibid.*, pp. 81 and 82.

supply and the demand, exactly like any other, transporting itself in greater or less quantities according to the supply and the demand, exactly like any other, transporting itself in greater or less quantities according to the comparative state of the market for that and for other articles, and forming only an item on one side of the general account. Corn, or any other commodity might just as properly be said to pay the balance as gold or silver; but it would evidently be inaccurate to affirm that corn discharged it, because it would imply that the amount of all the articles except corn was fixed; and that these having first adjusted themselves with relation only to each other, a given quantity of corn was then added to pay the difference. It was, for the same reason, inaccurate to affirm, that gold or silver paid the difference."

Continuing this argument later, he said: [1]

"Suppose a fisherman on our southern coast, to collect a thousand guineas, and exchange them in the channel with some French fisherman for as much French brandy as should be deemed an equivalent, the gold, according to the doctrine in fashion, would have gone to pay the balance of trade. It would have been employed to discharge a previously existing national debt. It was always, according to these tenets, the brandy which forced out the gold, and not at all the gold which forced in the brandy. By the Frenchman's putting the brandy into his boat, the Englishman was compelled to put the gold into his. The brandy always went before; the gold always followed after. It was one of the peculiar properties of gold that it always served to pay a balance.

"The truth was, that our paper currency having become less valuable by nearly twenty per cent. than the gold contained in our coin, the coin could no longer circulate interchangeably for it, but went abroad, because there was a profit of nearly twenty per cent. on the transmission. This profit operated as effectually in withdrawing it from circulation, and causing that part of it which was not bought at a high price for manufacturing uses, to be exported, as if an actual bounty of twenty per cent. were given on the export of it; and as much prevented the importation of gold for the purpose of serving as currency—the only purpose for which large quantities of gold were usually imported—as if a tax of twenty per cent. were levied on the import of it. We deplored the loss of our gold coin; but by not limiting our Bank notes, we were thus, in substance, laying a tax on its importation, and giving a bounty on its exportation; and then, referring its absence to balance of trade, we imagined that we had no power of recalling it."

Following the argument, Thornton made some concessions to those who stress the influence of an unfavorable balance of trade on a country's currency caused by depression in business, a bad harvest, or large drafts for meeting the foreign expenditures of the Government. Under such circumstances, he conceded that the

[1] *Ibid.*, pp. 84 and 85.

country's manufactures, and other exportable commodities, might happen not to be in such demand abroad as to supply advantageously the whole of the remittance required. The precious metals might then be in greater demand than any other articles; and the transmission of a certain quantity of these might then prevent so low a selling price for commodities, in the foreign market, as might otherwise be necessary.[1]

Opposition to Bullion Committee's Report. The Bullion Committee's Report and the arguments advanced by the members of the Committee and their supporters in the debate were vigorously attacked in the House, the two principal assailants having been Mr. A. Rose and Mr. Nicholas Vansittart (Lord Bexley). In lengthy speeches these two men supported the position taken by the officials of the Bank of England. They denied that the bank notes were depreciating in terms of gold coin, and explained the high price of bullion and of commodities and the low state of the exchanges on such grounds as the increased demand for commodities, increased taxation, strong demand for gold on the Continent and unfavorable balance of trade. Their economic theory was often confused and usually unsound, and the historical incidents, which they martialed in its support, were frequently superficially interpreted. The modern student of economics will gain little by reading these long speeches, except a realization that the widely held popular monetary fallacies of this day are much the same as those of the early nineteenth century.

Vansittart countered Horner's sixteen resolutions by proposing seventeen of his own.[2] The third, sixteenth and seventeenth of his Resolutions will afford an adequate idea of his position. They were:

> 3. "That the promissory notes of the said Company [the Bank of England] have hitherto been, and are at this time, held in public estimation to be equivalent to the legal coin of the realm, and generally accepted as such in all pecuniary transactions to which such coin is lawfully applicable." [3]

> 16. "That it is highly important that the restriction on the payments in cash of the Bank of England, should be removed, whenever the

[1] Hansard, XX, p. 85.

[2] *Ibid.*, pp. 70–74.

[3] A large amount of evidence was given during the debate to show that this statement was false. See, for example, speech of Mr. Tierney, *ibid.*, pp. 151–154.

political and commercial relations of the country shall render it compatible with the public interest."

17. "That under the circumstances affecting the political and commercial relations of this kingdom with foreign countries, it would be highly inexpedient and dangerous, now to fix a definite period for the removal of the restriction of cash payments at the Bank of England, prior to the term already fixed by the act 44 Geo. 3. c. l. of six months after the conclusion of a definitive treaty of peace."

The final result of the long debate was, the adoption of the Vansittart Resolutions by a great majority, the vote on Resolution 3 having been 76 to 24.[1]

For many years the Bank of England continued to deny officially the doctrine of the Bullion Report, that the low foreign exchange rates, the high prices of gold and silver, and the rise in commodity prices had been due chiefly to excessive issues of Bank of England notes. As late as March 25, 1819, the Court of Directors passed a resolution denying this contention of the Bullion Report. In 1827 this resolution was rescinded on the motion of a director of the Bank. Five years later this director said: "the Bank should conduct itself, in its issues, with reference to the state of the foreign exchanges and the bullion market," and he did not "think there was one person in the Bank of England that denies it or is disposed to act in opposition to it."[2]

Shortly afterwards, the directors were willing to return to specie payments and believed themselves able to maintain them, but the Government was opposed. The nation was engaged in a great war and depended heavily upon the Bank for obtaining promptly emergency funds, and the Bank was not in position to refuse these government demands.

Bank of England Notes Made Legal Tender

At the time of the passage of the Vansittart Resolutions, Bank of England notes were not legal tender. Partly to protect his own financial interests and partly to test the claim of the opponents of the Bullion Committee Report, that the public accepted Bank of England notes as the equivalent of gold coin, Lord King, in the summer of 1811, demanded payment of the rents on all his lands

[1] Hansard, XX (May 15, 1811), p. 172.

[2] Quoted from Bank Charter Committee, *Evidence*, Vol. VI, of 1831–1832, by Cannan, p. xxxiv.

in specie, or its equivalent at the market price of gold bullion. After referring to the progressive depreciation of bank notes during the preceding twelve years and to the fact that "every hope and prospect of amelioration" had been destroyed by the recent Vansittart Resolutions, Lord King said [1] he had decided to take advantage of the privilege the law gave him of collecting the debts due him in specie or its equivalent, which he declared was not only his lawful privilege, but also was entirely equitable to those renting his land. The broad principle upon which he had acted, he said, was: [2]

> " . . . to require payment in a currency of the same intrinsic value which the currency possessed at the date of each respective agreement, and in order to ascertain this intrinsic value, I calculate the amount of gold which the stipulated rent was able to purchase at the date of the lease or agreement, and require the same weight of gold, or a sum in Bank notes sufficient to purchase that quantity of gold at the present time."

He sent out to each one of his renters a circular letter, demanding payment in this form and giving his reasons. Justifying these requirements on grounds of equity, he said: [3]

> "Where, may I ask, is the hardship of this demand? The price of the produce of land, the price of labour, the price of every great staple commodity, are all affected by the value of the currency which serves to circulate the wealth and industry of the country. In proportion as the currency is depreciated, the price of wheat, of cattle, of all the produce of the land, and of every commodity, is augmented." [4]

This action of Lord King seems to have given renewed strength to the movement to have Bank of England notes made a full legal tender at parity with specie in payment of debts, but not until twenty-one years later was an act to that effect passed by Parliament. [5]

[1] Hansard, XX, pp. 791 and 792.

[2] *Ibid.*, p. 792.

[3] *Ibid.*, p. 793.

[4] Lord King gives a full account of his plan, with a copy of one of the circulars he sent out, in a speech in the House of Lords, July 2, 1811. *Ibid.*, pp. 790–806.

[5] Horner, who believed the making of the bank notes a legal tender was a most dangerous step and who saw the influence which Lord King's notice was having, wrote an interesting letter on the subject to Lord Grenville on June 28, 1811; cf., *Memoirs and Correspondence of Francis Horner*, Vol. II, pp. 78–80.

FROM THE LEGAL-TENDER LAW TO RESUMPTION

This chapter is chiefly concerned with the controversy centering in the Report of the Bullion Committee. The subsequent history of the paper pound down to the resumption of gold payments in 1821 may, therefore, be passed over rapidly. The principal facts of the period, as regards government expenditures and government revenues, the significant items in the Bank of England's balance, the prices of gold and silver, and the conditions of the principal exchanges, are given in Tables II and III.[1]

With a slight interruption in 1814 and early 1815, during Napoleon's exile in Elba, Great Britain continued at war until after the Battle of Waterloo, June 18, 1815. Her annual expenditures increased every year but one from 1810 to 1815 under the stress of war, and in 1815 amounted to £173 million, as compared with £129 million in 1810.[2] The Government continued to borrow heavily and the public securities held by the Bank of England rose irregularly from £14.3 million in February, 1810 to a maximum of £35 million in August, 1814. If the Bank changed its policy as to discounts and note issue, under the influence of the criticisms of the Bullion Report, it made no announcement and no admission of such a change. A reference to the Table on pages 206 and 207 will show little change in the note issue of the Bank of England. Thereafter it advanced to a substantially higher level, which it maintained until the latter part of 1818. It then began a slow and interrupted decline continuing until the resumption of specie payments. Bullion reserves declined from 1811 to 1815, after which they rose for about three years and then moved irregularly until 1821. The premium on gold rose to a maximum of 36 per cent in 1813 and then declined to a level of between 2 per cent and 5 per cent, where it continued for most of the time until 1819, after which it slowly disappeared. The price of silver showed a similar movement; likewise, exchange rates on Paris and on Hamburg. Commodity prices reached their maximum in 1814 and then declined slowly.

The law provided that restriction should automatically cease six months after the conclusion of a treaty of peace. Such a treaty was signed May 30, 1814, but the Restriction Act was extended from time to time by legislative action for about six years.

[1] *Supra*, pp. 206, 207 and 208.

[2] Silberling, p. 215.

By the fall of 1816 the premium on gold for a short time reached a figure below 1 per cent, and the Bank's directors, in preparation for resumption of gold payments, slowly began to take positive action for increasing their stock of gold. In November they decided to experiment in order to find out how much gold the public would demand if specie payments were resumed, and, under authority of a provision in a law of 1797, they began to "feel their way" by offering to redeem on demand notes of small denominations. They gave notice that after December 2, 1816, they would redeem in gold on demand one and two pound notes bearing dates earlier than 1812. Few notes were presented for redemption, and in April they extended the offer to cover, after May 2, all such notes dated earlier than 1816. Again few notes were presented, while the Bank's gold reserve continued to grow. In September, 1817, although the premium on gold had risen considerably, they announced that, beginning October 1, they would redeem on demand in gold notes of all denominations bearing dates of issue before January 1, 1817. What happened is well described by Cannan:[1]

> "Their failure to 'advert to the price of bullion and the foreign exchanges' on this occasion had its natural effect. Melting and exportation being now profitable, large amounts of notes were sent in for redemption: the depletion was only gradual, presumably owing to the law against export preventing more than a dribble of coin and bullion outwards. Between August, 1817, and February, 1819, the treasure fell 7½ millions; we might expect to find the notes also reduced by that amount, and if they had been, the decrease of notes and the increase, outside the Bank, of gold might well have brought gold and notes to a parity in the market. But while repaying the pre-1817 dated notes, the Bank must have been counteracting the effect of that action by issuing additional new (and still inconvertible) notes, for while the treasure diminished by 7½ millions, the total of notes diminished by only 4½."

Early in the year 1819 both Houses of Parliament appointed secret committees to consider the question of resumption. These committees examined a number of witnesses and the weight of their testimony, even including that of the Governor, Deputy-Governor, and a number of Directors of the Bank of England, was in substantial agreement with the theories of the Bullion Committee Report. Both committees quickly sent in interim reports condemning the "partial resumption" with which the Bank had been experimenting and urging that it be stopped. The

[1] Cannan, pp. xxxi–xxxii.

two committees finally agreed in recommending that the Bank after February 1, 1820, should be required to redeem its notes in gold bullion on a specified scale of declining prices for gold, which would culminate in full cash payments not later than May 1, 1823. These recommendations were debated at some length in Parliament. One of the speakers was David Ricardo, who had been elected to Parliament in 1819. He was apparently largely responsible for this scheme of redemption in gold bullion on a scale of progressively improving rates. The final result was the Resumption Act of 1819.

The Act provided that:

(1) The restriction on cash payments by the Bank should terminate May 1, 1823.

(2) Trade in bullion and coin should be entirely free, and all restrictions upon the melting of coin and the exportation of coin and bullion should be removed; and

(3) The Bank of England's notes should be redeemed, at progressively improving rates, in gold bullion. From February 1 to October 1, 1820, the Bank was required to redeem all notes presented, in gold bullion at the rate of £4. 1s. per ounce. From October 1, 1820, to May 1, 1821, the rate was £3. 19s. 6d. From May 1, 1821, to May 1, 1823, the rate was to be the par rate of £3. 17s. 10½d. Thereafter, redemption was to be made in coin on demand.

This provision for redemption in gold bullion at graduated rates never came into effect. Before February, 1820 the gold premium had entirely disappeared and on May 1, 1821, cash payments were fully resumed. Thus, after a paper money régime of more than twenty-four years, the country found itself back upon a metallic money standard.

BIBLIOGRAPHY

Acworth, A. W., *Financial Reconstruction in England 1815–1822;* London, P. S. King & Son, 1925.

Andréadès, A., *History of the Bank of England;* London, P. S. King & Son, 1909.

Boyd, Walter, *A Letter to the Right Honourable William Pitt on the Influence of the Stoppage of Issues in Specie at the Bank of England on the Price of Provisions and Other Commodities;* London, J. Wright, 1801.

Bullion Committee, *Report together with Minutes of Evidence, and Accounts from the Select Committee on the High Price of Gold Bullion;* London, House of Commons, 1810.

Cannan, Edwin, *The Paper Pound of 1797–1821;* London, P. S. King & Son, 1919.

Digest of the Evidence of the Bank Charter taken before the Committee of 1832; London, James Ridgeway, 1833.

Feaveryear, A. E., *The Pound Sterling—A History of English Money;* Oxford, Clarendon Press, 1931.

Hansard, T. C., *The Parliamentary Debates;* Vols. XIX and XX; London, 1812.

Hawtrey, R. G., *Currency and Credit;* New York, Longmans, Green and Company, 1930.

Hollander, Jacob, "The Development of the Theory of Money from Adam Smith to David Ricardo," *Quarterly Journal of Economics*, Vol. XXV (May, 1911), pp. 429–470.

Horner, Francis, *Memoirs and Correspondence;* Leonard Hunter, Editor, 2 volumes; Boston, Little, Brown and Co., 1853.

King, Lord Peter, *Thoughts on the Effects of the Bank Restrictions;* Second Edition, Enlarged; Including Some Remarks on the Coinage; London, printed for Cadell & Davies, 1804.

Report from the Committee of Secrecy on Bank of England Charter with Minutes of Evidence, Appendix and Index; London, James and Luke G. Hansard & Sons, 1832.

Report, Minutes of Evidence and Appendix from the Committee on the Circulating Paper, the Specie, and the Current Coin of Ireland; and also, on the Exchange between that part of the United Kingdom and Great Britain; May and June, 1804; ordered by The House of Commons to be reprinted 26 May, 1826; Great Britain Parliamentary Papers, 1826.

Ricardo, David, *Works;* edited by J. R. McCulloch, New Edition; London, John Murray, 1888.

——, *On the Price of Gold—1809;* edited by Jacob H. Hollander; Baltimore, The Lord Baltimore Press, 1903.

——, *Minor Papers on the Currency Question, 1809–1823;* edited by Jacob H. Hollander; Baltimore, Johns Hopkins Press, 1932.

Silberling, Norman J., "British Prices and Business Cycles, 1779–1850," *The Review of Economic Statistics Supplement*, Vol. V, 1923.

——, "Financial and Monetary Policy of Great Britain during the Napoleonic Wars," *Quarterly Journal of Economics*, February and May, 1924.

CHAPTER XII

THE GREENBACKS

Since the beginning of European colonization in America, our country has had five extended experiences with inconvertible, legal-tender money; namely, the experiences (1) of the thirteen colonies, (2) of the states, between the Declaration of Independence and the adoption of the Federal Constitution, (3) of the Continental Congress, (4) of the National Government during the Civil War and the period of reconstruction, and (5) of the National Government beginning in early March, 1933 and extending to the present time.

The bibliography at the end of this chapter contains, in addition to the references to the greenbacks, a few references to these experiences, which will enable the reader easily to familiarize himself with them. A discussion of our recent experiences with inconvertible paper money will be given in Volume II. This chapter is concerned only with the fourth experience mentioned above, that of the so-called "Greenback Period," from 1862 to the end of 1878.

Monetary and Fiscal Situation Preceding Outbreak of Civil War

The year 1860, in which Abraham Lincoln was elected President of the United States and at the end of which South Carolina seceded from the Union, was a year of good crops and, until autumn when a financial crisis occurred, a year of business prosperity. For the National Government the ordinary receipts for the fiscal year 1860 had been $56 millions, which, when increased by postal revenues, had left a deficit for the year of $7 millions. This had to be met by borrowing. Of the total ordinary receipts, $53.2 millions came from customs duties and the tonnage tax, and $1.8 millions from the sale of public lands. At the time the National Government had no revenue from income or excise taxes.

The entire interest-bearing national debt on June 30, 1860, was only $65 millions—a sum almost exactly equivalent to the National Government's ordinary expenditures for that year. The credit of the Government was good.

In 1860 the currency of the country was on a metallic basis—legally the standard had been bimetallic since 1792. The currency at the outbreak of the War consisted chiefly of the following elements: (1) gold coin, (2) fractional silver coin,[1] (3) copper cents and (4) notes of state banks. In the autumn of 1861 the amount of specie in circulation in the loyal states was estimated by the Director of the Mint to be somewhere between $255 millions and $280 millions. The bank notes outstanding in the loyal states were estimated at something like $150 millions.[2] Although the coinage of fractional silver coins was less than $4 millions in the calendar year 1861, the coinage of gold was $83 millions—the largest coinage of gold of any year in the history of the mint down to that time—while the importation of foreign coin and bullion, the Director of the Mint reported, had been "unprecedentedly large." Bank notes were issued by state banks under widely different laws in the different states, and these notes were of varying degrees of goodness. When the Republicans took possession of the Government in 1861, all the banks of the country were either chartered or managed by the states. There were approximately 1,600 commercial banks in the country, having in circulation some 7,000 kinds of paper notes. It was estimated that at this time there were in circulation more than 5,000 varieties of counterfeit notes.

As a result of the financial crisis of late 1860, many banks failed and a considerable volume of the country's bank notes accordingly disappeared from circulation—a fact which caused much anxiety. This gap in the circulation, however, was made up, at least in part, by the issue of Treasury notes by the National Government under the Act of July 17, 1861. These notes were payable on demand, but were not legal tender. By October, 1861 their circulation amounted to about $33 millions.

Program of Secretary Chase for Financing the War

Salmon P. Chase, Lincoln's first Secretary of the Treasury, on assuming office, found the country confronted with war and the Treasury empty. In July, 1861, when Congress met in special ses-

[1] The mint ratio between silver and gold at this time undervalued silver dollars, and, since they were worth more as bullion than as money, they were rarely found in circulation. The silver coin of the country consisted of fractional coins, half-dollars, quarters, dimes, half-dimes and three-cent pieces.

[2] *Annual Report of the Secretary of the Treasury*, 1861, p. 17.

sion, he estimated the amount required for the fiscal year at approximately $319 millions. To provide this sum, the Secretary, in his Annual Report for 1861, proposed such modifications in the recently enacted tariff and

> "such internal taxes as would, in his judgment, produce the sum of eighty millions of dollars, and such loans, in various forms, not exceeding in their aggregate two hundred and fifty millions of dollars, as would yield the required residue."

Chase, like most people in 1861, expected the War to be a short one.

With reference to his recommendation that part of the proposed borrowing be made in the form of short-time treasury notes of low denominations and bearing a low rate of interest, to meet immediate treasury needs, he held that great care would be necessary to prevent such issues from degenerating into an irredeemable paper currency, "than which no more certainly fatal expedient for impoverishing the masses and discrediting the government of any country can well be devised."

Congress approved only part of the Secretary's rather weak tax program, but responded fully to his recommendations for loans. In the summer of 1861, it passed laws authorizing the Secretary to borrow up to $250 millions in 7.3 per cent three-year Treasury notes—this is two cents a day interest on $100—or in long-time government bonds. Also, in place of part of the above loan, the Secretary was empowered to pay out for salaries and other obligations of the United States, and to exchange for coin either small denomination Treasury notes bearing interest at 3.65 per cent, that is, one cent a day on each $100, and fundable into one-year Treasury notes of large denominations, or Treasury notes of denominations of less than $50 and not less than $5, "payable on demand and receivable for all public dues." These were the so-called "demand notes." A limit of $50 millions was placed on the two issues combined.

Pursuant to this authority, Chase undertook to borrow $150 millions by the issue of 7.3 per cent three-year Treasury notes. To this end he called a conference of representatives of banks of New York, Boston and Philadelphia, and these bankers agreed to coöperate with the Government in the flotation of the loan. They were to take and, as conditions would permit, sell to the public an immediate installment of $50 millions and two subsequent installments of $50 millions each.

There had already been considerable withdrawal of specie from circulation and from the banks, partly because of the declining confidence resulting from the War and from the numerous bank failures that took place late in the year 1860, and partly because of the competition of the Government's demand notes with specie as bank reserve and media of exchange. The banks, to protect their specie reserves, wanted Chase to leave with them on deposit the proceeds of these loans and to check them out only as the Government should need funds. Such a practice, which previously would have been in conflict with our Independent Treasury Law of 1846, had been legalized by a recent act of Congress (August 5, 1861) that suspended the provision of the Independent Treasury Act,

> "so far as to allow the Secretary of the Treasury to deposit any of the money obtained on any of the loans now authorized by law, to the credit of the Treasurer of the United States, in such solvent specie-paying banks as he may select; and the said moneys, so deposited, may be withdrawn from such deposit for deposit with the regular authorized depositories, or for the payment of public dues, or paid in redemption of the notes authorized to be issued under this act or the act to which this is supplementary, payable on demand, as may seem expedient to, or be directed by, the Secretary of the Treasury."

Despite the broad authority here given and in the face of the vigorous protests of the banking community, Chase insisted upon withdrawing from the banks in specie the proceeds of the loan as soon as they were made available.[1] This policy increased enor-

[1] Congressman E. G. Spaulding of the Ways and Means Committee later said that the primary object of Mr. Appleton and himself in preparing the abovementioned section of the law of August 5, 1861, "was to relax the rigid requirements of the sub-treasury act, in regard to the receipt and disbursement of coin, and instead of paying solely from *coin deposits* in the treasury, to allow all the money obtained on these loans to be deposited in solvent banks; the United States Treasurer to draw his checks directly on such deposit banks in payment of war expenses, which checks would be paid in state bank notes then redeemable on demand in gold, or in the ordinary course of business, to a large extent, they would pass through the New York clearing house, and the clearing houses of other cities, and be settled and cancelled by offset, without drawing large amounts of specie. This mode of payment would have enabled the Secretary more easily to effect such loans and make his large disbursements, without materially disturbing the coin reserves held by the banks, which were then well protected by these reserves in their vaults. Referring to Chase's failure to maintain such deposits, Spaulding said: "The first material mistake in the management of the finances, occurred when Secretary Chase discarded the use of the bank check, and the clearing house, in the fall of 1861. The Secretary of War might, with the same propriety, have rejected the railroad, the locomotive, and the telegraph. The modern invention of the bank check and the clearing house for the transaction of large financial operations with facility,

mously and needlessly the pressure on the banks for specie. Confidence was further shocked in December, 1861 by the Trent affair, which, for a time, threatened to cause war between the United States and England.

The Secretary, in his annual report to Congress, of December, 1861, was required to revise his previous estimates. Taxes he found would give less than he had previously expected and appropriations would be larger by something like $214 millions. Notwithstanding this great increase in anticipated expenditures, Chase had little to recommend in the line of increased taxes, and said: "It will be seen at a glance that the amount to be derived from taxation forms but a small portion of the sums required for the expenses of the war. For the rest, the reliance must be placed on loans."

The Secretary's failure to present in his annual report of 1861 a plan for a comprehensive and vigorous tax policy was a great disappointment to the public, who were patriotically in favor of strongly aggressive measures, and who were "praying to be taxed."

This combination of unfortunate developments proved to be too much for the banks, and, at the end of December, 1861, there was a general suspension of specie payments by the banks of the country and by the Government—a suspension that lasted for seventeen years.

In his 1861 Report, Chase recommended a new currency, to be uniform throughout the United States, which would be prepared by the National Government and delivered under government direction to existing banks, and which would be secured as to prompt convertibility into coin by the pledge of United States bonds and by other needful regulations. The old bank-note currency was to be gradually taxed out of existence. The new currency, the Secretary maintained, would be well secured, uniform throughout the country, and, by increasing the market for United States bonds, would be profitable to the Government. These were only a few of the many advantages which Chase claimed for his plan of bond-secured bank notes.[1]

are quite as useful as are railroads and telegraphs in carrying on military operations with success." Spaulding, E. G., *History of the Legal Tender Paper Money Issued during the Great Rebellion*, Second Edition, pp. 1–2.

[1] Cf., *Finance Report*, 1861, pp. 17–20, and Schuckers, J. W., *The Life and Public Services of Salmon Portland Chase*, Chaps. 31 and 32.

Origin of the Greenbacks

The various recommendations contained in Chase's Report of 1861 were referred to the House Committee on Ways and Means, and by it to a sub-committee of which Spaulding was chairman. At first, in accordance with Chase's recommendation, Spaulding undertook to frame a bill for a bond-secured bank note system; but he was soon brought to realize that such a system at best could not be gotten into operation in time to give the Treasury the immediate relief it required. This decision led the sub-committee to shift its ground in favor of an issue of $100 million of legal-tender notes which could be made available for the immediate needs of the Government. After obtaining unofficially from the Attorney-General a favorable opinion as to the constitutionality of such an issue of legal-tender notes, Spaulding introduced in the House this legal-tender section as a separate bill. Into the details of the legislative history of this legal-tender bill through Congress we cannot go. It is well narrated by Barrett.[1]

On January 11, 1862, we find the Secretary of the Treasury and the Finance Committees of both houses of Congress in conference, on the matter of ways and means for meeting the Government's urgent financial needs, with a group of ten bankers from New York, Philadelphia and Boston. The bankers submitted a plan which provided that there should be: (1) a more vigorous policy of taxation, (2) no new issues of demand notes, (3) the issuance of $100 millions of two-year interest-bearing Treasury notes, (4) the issuance of 6 per cent bonds, without any limit as to price, and (5) the granting to the banks of the privilege of becoming depositories of the proceeds of all Government loans, with the understanding that the deposits would be drawn against by checks as needed by the Government.

This plan was rejected both by Chase and by the Committees of Congress, apparently on the ground that it did not give the Government adequate control over the currency. Concerning the objections raised to the bankers' plan, the *New York Tribune* of January 13, 1862, said:

> "The Sub-committee of Ways and Means, through Mr. Spaulding, objected to any and every form of 'shinning' by Government through Wall or State streets to begin with; objected to the knocking down of Govern-

[1] *Op. cit.*, pp. 16–19.

ment stocks to seventy-five or sixty cents on the dollar, the inevitable result of throwing a new and large loan on the market, *without limitation as to price.*"

Another objection to the bankers' plan was that it did not include any provision for the national bank-note currency which was so dear to Secretary Chase.

According to Spaulding,[1] the delegates of the banks and others continued their consultations with Secretary Chase through two or three days and finally arrived at an agreement with the Secretary alone, which was given to the press January 15. The Committees of the Senate and the House never gave their assent to this agreement.[2]

In the meantime, the legal-tender bill, after having been considerably revised, was submitted to Chase by the sub-committee for his opinion. He returned the bill January 22, only one week after the above-mentioned agreement with the bankers' representatives, accompanied by a letter,[3] giving a qualified approval of the bill. This letter was not satisfactory to all the members of the committee. Accordingly, a resolution was passed, requesting Chase's opinion concerning the desirability of the immediate passage of the bill. His reply, which was given January 29, is as follows: [4]

> "It is not unknown to the committee that I have felt, nor do I wish to conceal that I now feel, a great aversion to making anything but coin a legal tender in payment of debts. It has been my anxious wish to avoid the necessity of such legislation. It is, however, at present impossible, in consequence of the large expenditures entailed by the war and the suspension of the banks, to procure sufficient coin for disbursements; and it has, therefore, become indispensably necessary that we should resort to the issue of United States notes. The making them a legal tender might, however, still be avoided if the willingness manifested by the people generally, by railroad companies, and by many of the banking institutions to receive them and pay them as money in all transactions were absolutely or practically universal; but, unfortunately, there are some persons and some institutions which refuse to receive and pay them, and whose action tends not merely to the unnecessary depreciation of the notes, but to establish discriminations in business against those who, in this matter, give a cordial support to the government,

[1] *Op. cit.*, p. 21.
[2] *Op. cit.*, p. 22.
[3] The letter is given in full by Spaulding, p. 27.
[4] The letter is quoted by James Ford Rhodes in his *History of the United States*, First Edition, Vol. III, p. 564.

and in favor of those who do not. Such discriminations should, if possible, be prevented; and the provision making the notes a legal tender, in a great measure at least, prevents it, by putting all citizens, in this respect, on the same level, both of rights and duties."

After receiving the above reply from Chase, the Committee approved the bill and reported it to the House on the same day. The bill as originally submitted underwent a number of important changes in the House and in the Senate, and finally became law February 25, 1862.

The First Legal-Tender Act

The main provisions of this first legal-tender paper money act may be briefly summarized as follows:

(1) The Secretary of the Treasury was authorized to issue $150 millions of United States notes, in denominations of not less than $5. These notes were to bear no interest and were nominally "payable to bearer on demand." Fifty millions of the above amount were to be used to replace the demand notes previously issued.

(2) The new notes were made receivable in payment of all taxes, debts and other obligations of any kind due to the United States, except duties on imports, which were payable only in coin and demand notes, and were likewise made receivable in payment of all claims and demands against the United States, except those for interest upon bonds and notes, which were to be paid in coin.

(3) The new notes were declared to be "lawful money and a legal tender in payment of all debts public and private, within the United States, except duties on imports and interest as aforesaid."

(4) Any holder of these United States notes might deposit them in sums of $50 or multiples thereof in the United States Treasury and receive in exchange for them certificates of deposit which were made convertible on demand at par into United States 5–20 six per cent bonds.

(5) With the approval of the Secretary of the Treasury the notes were to be receivable by the Treasury on deposit, in sums of not less than $100, and to an aggregate amount which at no time should exceed $25 millions—a figure that was later increased to $50 millions and then to $100 millions. These deposits were to be evidenced by certificates of deposit which should bear interest

at the rate of 5 per cent per annum. The deposits were withdrawable at any time on ten days' notice.

(6) The notes were to be reissued from time to time, as the interests of the public service might require.

The Debate over the Legal-Tender Bill

The legal-tender bill while in Congress was the subject of vigorous debate, and concerning its advisability there were wide differences of opinion, in Congress, in President Lincoln's Cabinet, and among bankers, business men and the general public throughout the country. The question of the necessity or of the wisdom of this enactment is one upon which economists and historians still differ. It will be useful here to review briefly the principal arguments advanced on both sides of this debate.

Arguments in Favor of the Greenbacks

The most important argument advanced for issuing legal-tender notes was the so-called "argument of necessity." It usually ran somewhat as follows: The Government needed large sums of money for financing the War and needed them promptly. It would have taken a long time to create new taxes and organize the administrative machinery for their collection on a sufficient scale to yield the necessary revenues. It was doubtful how far a public suffering from the strains of the War would stand for increased taxes. Lincoln had been chosen President on a very narrow margin. Moreover, if the War was to be short, as most people at that time expected, why labor to set up an elaborate tax system which might well become obsolete before it had come into full operation? The other alternative was borrowing, but the Government was having difficulty in floating its bonds, except at rates of interest that appeared to many to be excessive. The disappearance of specie from circulation and the deplorable condition of a large proportion of the notes issued by the state banks, it was argued, had left the public with an insufficient supply of money for current business and for the purchase of Government bonds. Treasury notes without the legal-tender quality, it was claimed, would be refused by many people. Hence, the proponents of the measure concluded, a temporary issue of legal-tender notes to a limited amount was absolutely necessary for meeting the immediate needs of the Government.

On February 3, 1862, Chase wrote to Spaulding: [1]

"The Treasury is nearly empty. I have been obliged to draw for the last installment of the [bankers'] November loan; so soon as it is paid, I fear the banks generally will refuse to receive" the demand notes. Two days later, he wrote: "It is very important the bill should go through to-day, and through the Senate this week. The public exigencies do not admit of delay." [2]

Senator John Sherman declared: [3]

"If you strike out the tender clause you do so with a knowledge that these notes will fall dead upon the money market of the world."

Representative Kellogg, in the House Debate of February 6, 1862, said:

"I am pained when I sit in my place in the House and hear members talk about the sacredness of capital; that the interests of money must not be touched. Yes, sir, they will vote six hundred thousand of the flower of the American youth for the Army, to be sacrificed, without a blush; but the great interests of capital, of currency, must not be touched."

Senator Charles Sumner said: [4]

"Surely we must all be against paper money—we must all insist upon maintaining the integrity of the government—and we must all set our faces against any proposition like the present, except as a temporary expedient, rendered imperative by the exigency of the hour." Again, on February 13, he said: "Whatever may be the national resources, they are not now within reach, except by summary process. Reluctantly, painfully, I consent that the process should issue. And yet I cannot give such a vote without warning the Government against the danger from such an experiment." [5]

This last statement of Sumner's is fairly typical of the position taken by most advocates of the bill both in the House and in the Senate. They were frank in saying that they did not like the idea of legal-tender paper, but held that a limited and temporary issue of such paper convertible on demand into Government bonds seemed to be "the best way out," the "choice of evils." Senator William P. Fessenden, Chairman of the Finance Committee of the Senate, was not far from the truth when he said: [6]

1 Spaulding, *op. cit.*, pp. 59 and 60.
2 Sherman, *Recollections*, I, p. 273.
3 *Congressional Globe*, Feb. 13, 1862, p. 791.
4 *Ibid.*, Feb. 13, 1862, p. 799.
5 *Ibid.*, Feb. 13, 1862, p. 800.
6 *Ibid.*, Feb. 12, 1862, p. 763.

" . . . Everybody who has spoken on this question, I believe, without an exception—there may have been one or two—but all the opinions that I have heard expressed agree in this: that only with extreme reluctance, only with fear and trembling as to the consequences can we have recourse to a measure like this of making our paper a legal tender in the payment of debts."

Although this statement was approximately true, there were then, as always when paper money propositions are under consideration, some who not only had no misgivings concerning the proposed legal tenders but who were actually advocates of such paper money as a matter of monetary policy. Concerning them Senator T. O. Howe of Wisconsin said: [1]

"There is no probability that a currency based upon the resources of a great nation, the whole of which will be demanded once in each year for payment of dues to the Government, and which may be used any time in payment of private dues so long as any private dues exist, and may be loaned to the nation upon interest, even after every individual in the nation has ceased to borrow, will depreciate fifty per cent. or even five per cent. No such paper ever did depreciate, and none such, I venture to predict, ever will."

Financial Program of Those Opposing the Greenbacks

Before considering the arguments advanced against the legal-tender acts, a brief statement is desirable of the financial measures which the opposition in Congress recommended as the alternative to the greenbacks. These recommendations are found in the report of the minority of the Ways and Means Committee—actually half of the Committee—and were briefly as follows:

(1) The issuance of $100 millions in Treasury notes with interest at 3.65 per cent, payable to bearer in two years. These notes were to be in denominations not less than $5 and were made receivable for all public dues, except duties on imports. They were to be convertible into 7–30 coin bonds and were reissuable.

(2) The issuance of $500 millions of 10- and 20-year bonds, the former bearing interest at the rate of 7.3 per cent and the latter at the rate of 6 per cent. These bonds were to be sold for lawful money of the United States or for Treasury notes.

(3) A continuation in circulation of the $50 millions of demand notes which had been authorized by the act of July 17, 1861, was contemplated by the minority report.

[1] *Congressional Globe*, Feb. 12, 1862, Appendix, p. 55.

(4) The receipt by the Government from the public of temporary deposits of money without limit as to amount at 5.4 per cent interest.

Such deposits, in the form of United States notes, were, in fact, authorized by section 4 of the legal-tender act, though the total amount was at first limited to $25 millions, a limit later increased to $50 millions, and then to $100 millions. They were to be made for a period of not less than 30 days, to be in sums not less than $100, to bear interest at 5 per cent, to be evidenced by certificates of deposit and to be withdrawable at any time after 10 days' notice. They proved to be a much more important source of funds to the National Government than was originally anticipated.[1]

Under the minority plan, it was recognized that a policy of vigorous taxation would be necessary, but events soon proved that such a policy was also necessary even with the greenbacks.

Chase's plan of providing a national currency and strengthening the borrowing power of the Government by provision for the issuance of bank notes throughout the country, secured by United States bonds, was applicable to both the majority and the minority plan, and in both cases it was important that, if Chase's plan were to be adopted, it should be adopted promptly.

Arguments against the Issue of the Greenbacks

The opponents of the greenbacks challenged the argument of fiscal necessity and stressed the dangers of a legal-tender "fiat money."

One of the strongest opponents of the legal-tender act was Representative Justin S. Morrill of Vermont, himself a member of the Ways and Means Committee. He said the bill was [2] "a measure not blessed by one sound precedent, and damned by all!" He condemned it as "immoral" and "a breach of the public faith." He prophesied that it would raise prices, increase manyfold the cost of the War, drive all specie from circulation, cripple American labor, and at last throw larger wealth into the hands of the rich. He insisted "that there was no necessity calling for such a desperate remedy." In a speech February 19, 1862, he said [3] that he did not believe the patient was in such great danger

[1] Barrett, *op. cit.*, pp. 27–33, and *Annual Report of the Secretary of the Treasury*, 1863, pp. 15 and 16.

[2] *Congressional Globe*, Feb. 4, 1862, pp. 629–633.

[3] *Ibid.*, Feb. 19, 1862, pp. 886–887.

as to justify the calling in of "quack doctors" and called the measure "but quack medicine to relieve a patient that is in no need of any medicine at all." He declared:

"I believe that if we could stand up here in the vigor of a nation not yet taxed a single dollar for the cost of this war, and mature a proper policy by which we can negotiate a loan standing on the credit of the country, standing on the proposed taxation of the country, standing on our hitherto untarnished honor, that there could be no need whatever of a resort to such a desperate scheme as the one now under consideration."

Representative Roscoe Conkling of New York said in a speech in the House February 4, 1862: [1]

"What does this plea of necessity mean . . .? The arguments must be two-fold: First, that the people will be better ready at some other time than the present to pay what, in the end, they must pay, with interest; and second, that necessary and legitimate taxation will be unpopular, and bring denunciation upon those who vote it. Sir, I take issue upon both propositions. I say the country is rich and ready. Money is abundant—very abundant. . . . The whole country is full of wealth. . . . We are able to pay now, and we never can pay better than now."

Speaking of the "moral imperfections" of the bill, he said:

"It will, of course, proclaim throughout the country a saturnalia of fraud—a carnival for rogues. Every agent, attorney, treasurer, trustee, guardian, executor, administrator, consignee, commission merchant, and every debtor of a fiduciary character who has received for others money, hard money, worth a hundred cents in the dollar, will forever release himself from liability by buying up for that knavish purpose, at its depreciated value, the spurious currency which we shall have put afloat . . . Think of savings banks entrusted with enormous aggregates of the pittances of the poor, the hungry, and the homeless, the stranger, . . ."

It was denied that it was necessary to give the legal-tender quality to these Treasury notes—for that is what they were, despite the new and high sounding name of "United States notes"—in order to make them circulate as money, if they were made acceptable for Government dues, like the demand notes, and were convertible on demand into interest-bearing bonds. Non-legal-tender demand notes and non-legal-tender notes of state banks were widely accepted by the public. The public had to have

[1] *Congressional Globe*, Feb. 4, 1862, pp. 633–635.

money and what else could it use, now that specie, except on the Pacific Coast, had been driven from circulation? [1]

Representative Crisfield of Maryland called attention to the enormous extent of existing debts, national, state, municipal, corporate and private, and the great volume of our bank deposits, all contracted on a gold and silver basis and now, by this bill, made payable in a paper money that was certain to depreciate. He called the bill a plan of "gigantic confiscation," [2] and said that it would destroy private credit and make the value of the monetary unit depend upon the vicissitudes of war and of politics. He declared that the legal-tender quality was not necessary and advocated greatly increased taxation. Senator Fessenden, who later very reluctantly voted for the bill on the ground of necessity, said, in answer to the question, "What shall we do?" [3] "We must tax speedily, strongly, vigorously. We have the ability to meet it. The people can bear it, and will bear it with cheerfulness and hope."

Congressional Debate over Constitutionality of Legal-Tender Notes

The question of the constitutionality of the issuance of legal-tender notes was frequently discussed in the debate. There was no express power given by the Constitution to the National Government either to issue bills of credit or to make bills of credit a legal tender. The question of the desirability of giving to the National Government the power to issue bills of credit was debated in the Constitutional Convention, and, although the power was neither expressly given nor expressly denied, the debate left a doubt as to whether or not the framers of the Constitution intended that the National Government should possess this power, a power which the Constitution expressly denied to the states.[4] In the debate over the adoption of the Constitution by the states, Alexander Hamilton had said:

> "The emitting of paper money by the authority of government is wisely prohibited to the individual States by the National Constitution; and the spirit of that prohibition ought not to be disregarded by the Govern-

[1] The inconvertible and depreciated Bank of England notes were accepted everywhere throughout England from 1797 to 1820, although Bank of England notes were not made legal tender until 1833.

[2] *Congressional Globe*, Feb. 5, 1862, Appendix, pp. 47–50.

[3] *Ibid.*, Feb. 12, 1862, p. 766.

[4] Cf., Dewey, pp. 67–70.

ment of the United States. The wisdom of the Government will be shown in never trusting itself with the use of so seducive and dangerous an expedient."

During the discussions over the issue of the greenbacks in January and February, 1862, those who opposed the issue on constitutional grounds maintained that the Government had no express power to make bills of credit a legal tender, and that this power could not reasonably be implied in any of the granted powers; while the proponents of the constitutionality of the legal-tender issues found the power implied in such granted powers as those "to borrow money on the credit of the United States," "to coin money, regulate the value thereof," and "to regulate commerce . . . among the several states." The subsequent attitude of the United States Supreme Court on this question will be considered later.[1]

Although the need of a uniform national currency to replace the heterogeneous collection of state bank notes then in circulation was later the chief argument advanced in support of the creation of a national banking system, with the bond-secured bank-note issue, this argument was distinctly secondary to the fiscal necessity argument in the discussion over the greenbacks.

Further Issues of Greenbacks

Notwithstanding the fact, that it was expected and declared by many advocates of the first issue of greenbacks, including Chase himself, that this first emergency issue would be the only one, it was quickly followed, as is usually the case with such issues, by other issues, despite depreciation and despite the protests of the opposition.

In June, 1862, Chase recommended a second issue of $150 millions of greenbacks and his recommendation was enacted into law July 11. Here again the argument of fiscal necessity was the principal one for the proposal. Many who opposed this argument favored the issuance of government bonds at whatever price they would bring in the market, and Representative Sheffield declared that

> "it would be far better for the people of the country to sell bonds at a large discount than to further disturb the relations between price and value by a further issue of these notes." [2]

[1] *Infra*, pp. 260 *et seq.*

[2] *Congressional Globe*, June 23, 1862, p. 2888.

By the end of the year, we find Chase again in serious straits for funds and again playing, though very reluctantly and hesitatingly this time, with the idea of another issue of legal-tender notes. Referring to a balance of disbursement of about $277 millions, to be provided for by the end of the fiscal year 1863, he said that the easiest method of providing this money would doubtless be an issue of the required amount of greenbacks, but he added: [1]

> "The addition of so vast a volume to the existing circulation would convert a currency, of which the benefits have thus far greatly outweighed the inconveniences, into a positive calamity. Its consequences would be inflation of prices, increase of expenditures, augmentation of debt, and, ultimately, disastrous defeat of the very purposes sought to be attained by it."

He then weakened by saying:

> "To a certain extent, however, and under certain circumstances, a limited additional issue of United States notes may perhaps be safely and advantageously made."

No increase in taxation was suggested by him at this time, but he again urged further borrowing and the adoption of his national bank-note system plan.

In this report Chase advances the specious argument that there had been no great excess in the aggregate currency of the country, that any excess that existed was not due to issues of United States notes, and that the depreciation of the greenbacks in terms of gold had been due to increased demand for gold and to speculation.

Congress responded by authorizing on January 17, 1863, a third issue of $100 millions of greenbacks, a sum which was increased to $150 millions on March 3, all of which might be in denominations of one dollar or over. These newly authorized notes might be reissued when received by the Government. Unlike the previous issues, they were not made convertible into bonds, and the act of March 3 removed after July 1, 1863, the right to convert the previously issued United States notes into Government bonds on demand. This was done on Chase's recommendation in order to strengthen the market for contemplated new issues of bonds. It proved to be one of the greatest mistakes the Government made in connection with the greenback issues, for it discontinued a provision which, in a few years' time—namely, shortly after the War,

[1] *Annual Report of the Secretary of the Treasury*, Dec. 4, 1862, pp. 12–13.

when the Government's credit would be improved and the prices of its bonds would be advancing—would have automatically retired the greenbacks from circulation and have brought the currency back to par within a comparatively short time. It is not fair to claim, however, as some writers have done, that the withdrawal of this privilege was a breach of faith on the part of the Government, for the public, after the enactment of the law, were given nearly four months' time in which to convert their greenbacks into bonds before July 1, 1863, when the privilege was to expire.

By Act of June 30, 1864, the total amount of United States notes, issued or to be issued was limited to $400 millions and an additional temporary issue not to exceed $50 millions. This law was maintained, with the result that the maximum volume of greenbacks actually outstanding at any time was, in round numbers, $431 millions, which was the amount in circulation June 30, 1864.

Fractional Money

When the greenbacks depreciated so far that the fractional silver coins were worth more as bullion than as money, these coins were driven out of circulation, and, finally, the depreciation of the greenbacks went so far as to drive out of circulation, likewise, nickel and copper coins. To meet the resulting need for fractional money, the government issued legal tender, fractional notes in denominations less than one dollar, which were popularly called "shinplasters." The smallest of these notes was for three cents. The total amount of "shinplasters" has been roughly estimated at more than $15 millions.[1]

Fluctuations in the Value of the Greenbacks

The story of the depreciation of the greenbacks and of their subsequent appreciation to gold parity during the years 1862 to 1879, as expressed in terms of gold, wholesale prices, retail prices, the cost of living and wages, is told in detail by Wesley C. Mitchell, in his valuable studies: *A History of the Greenbacks*, and *Gold, Prices and Wages under the Greenback Standard.* The figures shown in the following chart are taken from the latter book.[2] For all index numbers the year 1860 is used as 100.

[1] Carothers, *Fractional Money*, p. 169.

[2] P. 279.

PRICES AND WAGES IN TERMS OF GREENBACKS, 1860–1880
Mitchell's Index Numbers

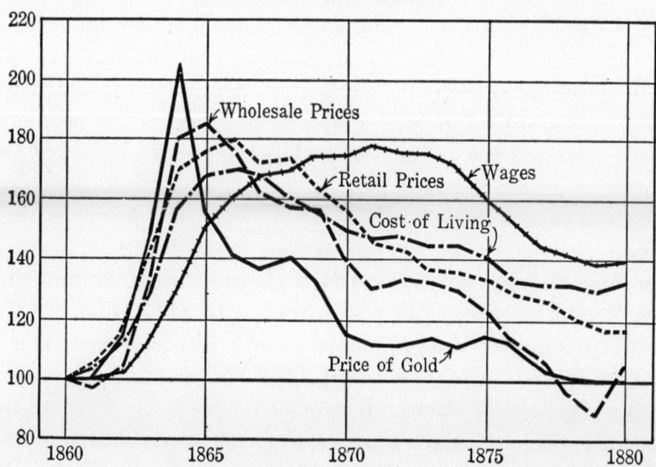

During the entire period of inconvertibility, gold was bought and sold as a commodity. It was needed by the public for the payment of customs duties, for making certain settlements abroad, and for merchandise purposes. It continued during the entire period to circulate as money on the Pacific Coast. The National Government needed substantial quantities for paying interest on a large part of its public debt.

As soon as gold went to a premium, regular dealings in gold began on the New York Stock Exchange. A second market later developed into an exchange known as "The Gold Room." Speculation in gold at times was very active, reaching a climax in the so-called Black Friday, September 23, 1869, when an attempt of a group of speculators to corner the gold market collapsed.

First let us consider the fluctuations in the price of gold as compared with wholesale prices of commodities.[1] The price of gold rose rapidly after the suspension of specie payments in December, 1861, reaching its annual maximum in 1864, and its actual maximum on July 11, 1864, when it required 2.85 greenback dollars to buy a gold dollar, which meant that the greenback dollar at its lowest point had a gold value of 35 cents. The greenback price of

[1] The figures for the price of gold are the annual averages of the greenback price of $100 of gold coin. The figures for wholesale prices of commodities are averages of the quarterly medians for each year of 92 commodities. Mitchell, pp. 279 and 19 *et seq.*

gold then dropped sharply and with frequent and often wide fluctuations it slowly and haltingly worked its way back to parity by the end of 1878.[1]

While the wholesale prices of different classes of commodities and of different commodities in each class responded differently to the inflationary forces, practically all wholesale prices rose rapidly during the war, and then declined irregularly until 1879. Both on the advance and on the decline, wholesale commodity prices lagged behind the price of gold. The wholesale price index number reached its annual maximum of 185 in 1865, while the price of gold reached its annual maximum of 203 the year before. Wholesale prices, moreover, continued a substantial rate of decline after the price of gold had become relatively stable within a few points of parity.

The market for gold was more speculative than that for most, if not all, commodities, and operations in the gold market were made on a much smaller margin of profit. England at this time was on the gold standard, and, if we measure the value of gold itself by its purchasing power over commodities at wholesale in England, we find that gold was comparatively stable in value from 1860 to 1870, and fell substantially from 1870 to 1873. It then rose rapidly from 1873 to 1879, so that during its latter years the greenback dollar was straining itself to catch a gold dollar that was running away from it, and prices would have been falling in the United States at this time, even had we been on a gold standard.

Next let us consider the relationship between the annual movements of the index number of wholesale prices and those of the index number of retail prices [2] and of the cost of living. In the index number of the cost of living, data for house rent are added to those for retail prices, and 35 individual items are weighted as nearly as possible in accordance with their respective relative importance in the cost of living of a representative family.[3]

It will be observed that, while wholesale prices reached their maximum of 185 in the year 1865, retail prices and the cost of living did not reach their maxima of 180 and 170, respectively,

[1] For daily figures showing the greenback price of gold and the gold price of greenbacks for the entire period see Mitchell, pp. 287–338.

[2] The figures for retail prices are the medians for 34 commodities. See Mitchell, *Gold*, pp. 66–69, 87 and 279.

[3] *Ibid.*, pp. 83–90 and 279.

until a year later. Retail prices and the cost of living, likewise, lagged behind wholesale prices on the decline after the War and at the time of resumption of specie payments were relatively much higher than wholesale prices.

On the rise the cost of living lagged somewhat behind the wholesale prices, as it did also during most of the period of the decline, and it stood at 130 in 1879, as compared with 88 for wholesale prices. Goods at retail were sold in smaller quantities than goods at wholesale and on larger percentage profits, and price competition was less keen. Conventional prices and limited markets played a much more important rôle in retail trade than in wholesale. Prices, therefore, were more rigid and less responsive to inflationary forces. House rents in general were even less responsive than retail commodity prices and this is one of the principal reasons why the cost of living index lagged behind the retail price index during most of the greenback period. While urban rents generally lagged behind retail prices both on the advance and on the decline, this situation did not exist to anything like the same extent with farm rents. Of these Barrett says:[1]

> "It is safe to conclude, judging from the best evidence attainable, that three-quarters of rented farms were let in those days, not for a fixed money payment, but for a payment in kind. In the case of this large proportion of rural landlords no great injury was inflicted by depreciated greenbacks."

The next relationship to consider is that between the movements of the cost of living and of wages.[2] Just as retail prices and the cost of living in general lagged behind wholesale prices during both the period of rising prices and that of falling prices, so did wages in general lag behind the cost of living during both periods. While the cost of living reached its maximum of 170 in 1866, wages did not reach their maximum of 179 until five years later. Then, on the decline, the cost of living stood at 132 in 1878, as compared with a wage figure for that year of 141.

Labor was more fully employed during the War than during the previous years; the army itself and other activities incident to the War absorbed millions of men. After the War, there was much unemployment and many labor troubles, especially in the

[1] *Op. cit.*, p. 121.

[2] The wage figures are Mitchell's averages of the January and July medians of relative rates of wages. *Ibid.*, pp. 226–248 and 279.

year 1867 and the depression period 1873–1877. Since the cost of living rose faster than money wages down to 1867, real wages declined and the laborers suffered.

> " . . . The ability to lay by for a rainy day was threatened, and . . . labor came to regard itself as aggrieved; it assumed an attitude of hostility toward employers and took concerted measures in self-defense. . . . The winter of 1863–1864 and the ensuing months were accordingly a time of unusual industrial unrest, which increased in severity as the discrepancy between wages and prices continued." [1]

After 1867, the index numbers for money wages were most of the time much higher than those for the cost of living, but many of the benefits that would normally have accrued to labor from such a situation were lost by reason of the large amount of unemployment occurring during the business depression of 1873 to 1877—a depression that was caused in no small degree by the deflation itself.

Extravagance

The period in which the greenbacks were depreciating most rapidly and when, as a result, people saw the value of their savings continually fading away was favorable to the philosophy, "what you save you lose and what you spend you have." Partly as a result of this philosophy, partly as a recourse for relief against the strains and sorrows of the War, and partly because war-time speculation turned an unusually large percentage of the national income into the hands of the new and vulgar rich, this period, like the period of the Assignats in France,[2] was one of widespread extravagance. According to the *London Times:* [3]

> "The indulgence in every variety of pleasure, luxury, and extravagance is simply shocking. The jewelers' shops in all these cities have doubled or trebled their trade; the love of fine dresses and ornaments on the part of the women amounts to madness. They have the money, well or ill gotten, and must enjoy it."

Speaking of this same extravagance the *New York Independent* said: [4]

> "Go into Broadway, and we will show you what is meant by the word 'extravagance.' Ask Stewart about the demand for camel's-hair shawls, and he will say 'monstrous.' Ask Tiffany what kind of diamonds and

[1] Fite, pp. 183–184.
[2] *Supra*, p. 194.
[3] November 3, 1863.
[4] June 25, 1864.

pearls are called for. He will answer 'the prodigious,' 'as near hen's-egg size as possible,' 'price no object.' . . . And as for horses the medium-priced five-hundred-dollar kind are all out of the market. A good pair of 'fast ones,' 'all right,' will go for a thousand dollars sooner than a basket of strawberries will sell for four cents."

Events in Post-War History of Greenbacks

We may now retrace our steps somewhat and review the post-war history of the greenbacks.

When the War formally ended in the summer of 1865, the money stock of the United States, aside from the gold coin and most of the subsidiary silver, which did not circulate to any appreciable extent except on the Pacific Coast, and aside from the notes of the Confederate States which had become worthless, consisted chiefly of about $431 millions of greenbacks, $15 millions of United States Government fractional notes, $146 millions of national bank notes—the national banking system recommended by Secretary Chase had been established by laws of 1863 and 1864—and $143 millions of notes of state banks, and a small amount of minor coins. This money all circulated at parity with the greenbacks. The great currency problem before the country at the close of the war was to get this money back to parity with gold and silver.

The Movement for an Early Return to a Specie Basis

The Secretary of the Treasury, Hugh McCulloch, in his annual report of December 5, 1865, referred to the legal-tender acts as war measures and said that

> "They ought not to remain in force one day longer than shall be necessary to enable the people to prepare for a return to the constitutional currency. It is not supposed that it was the intention of Congress, by these acts, to introduce a standard of value, in times of peace, lower than the coin standard, much less to perpetuate the discredit which must attach to a great nation which dishonors its own obligations by unnecessarily keeping in circulation an irredeemable paper currency."

He held that this currency was inelastic, and that, if continued, its issue would be likely to be governed by the fiscal needs of the Treasury or the interests of political parties, rather than by the demands of trade, and that this fact would keep the currency constantly before the public as a political issue, than which few things would be more injurious to business. In defending a vigorous policy of currency contraction, he took issue with those who held that contraction by reducing prices would be injurious to trade, be likely to bring on a financial crisis, would reduce government revenues, endanger the public credit by preventing funding, and would compel both the government and the people, who are in debt, to pay their debts in a dearer currency than that which the debtor received when the debts were contracted.[1]

He recommended to Congress: (1) the removal of the legal-tender quality from the compound interest notes from the date of their maturity; and (2) the giving to the Secretary of the Treasury of authority to issue bonds for the purpose of retiring not only compound interest notes, but also the greenbacks.

He held, in this connection, that the process of contracting the currency could not be injuriously rapid; and that there was no necessity of retiring more than $100 millions or, at most, $200 millions of greenbacks, in addition to the compound notes, before the desired result would be attained. He said, however, that neither the amount of the reduction, nor the time required to bring up the currency to gold parity could then be estimated with any degree of accuracy. In his judgment, the first step was to decide upon the policy of contraction.[2]

With this view both the public and Congress seemed to be in sympathy. On December 18, 1865, the House, by a vote of 144 to 6 adopted a resolution of cordial concurrence,

> "In the view of the Secretary of the Treasury in relation to the necessity of the contraction of the currency with a view to as early a resumption of specie payments as the business interests of the country will permit,"

and it pledged its coöperation to that end.[3]

In its issue of September 23, 1865, the *Commercial and Financial Chronicle* took the position that the actual and prospective evils of inflation and of an unstable currency were leading to a growing public conviction that the time had arrived when a permanent contraction in the volume of the country's redundant paper money should be undertaken. A week later the same publication said that the fundamental cause of the premium on specie was not the traffic in the precious metals, nor in the foreign exchanges, nor even in the activities of speculators, but the redundancy of

[1] *Annual Report of the Secretary of the Treasury*, 1865, pp. 4, 11 and 12.
[2] *Ibid.*, p. 14.
[3] *Congressional Globe*, 39th Congress, 1st Session, p. 75.

the currency, the fact that our paper money had been issued to excess. The *Boston Advertiser*, then under the editorship of Professor Charles F. Dunbar, is quoted by Barrett [1] as expressing the belief that at that time nine men out of ten in the country desired an early resumption of specie payments.

But enthusiasm for contraction was short-lived, and after the early beginning progress was exceedingly slow. Every forward step met strong opposition, and, more than once, the forces of inflation temporarily triumphed.

Various Schools of Monetary Reform

Gradually there grew up a number of different schools of monetary reform, each of which at one time or another during the succeeding fourteen years, was a powerful factor in determining our monetary policy. Five such schools of thought may be distinguished, although the lines that separate them are often rather hazy.[2] They are:

(1) The school that advocated a prompt return to a specie basis without waiting for contraction of the currency or legislative action. The slogan of this school, which was apparently first used by Chase in 1866,[3] was: "The way to resume is to resume." This slogan, however, was also later used by other groups.

(2) The second school consisted of those who favored the accumulation of a gold reserve by borrowing and otherwise, and the use of this reserve for establishing the convertibility of the greenbacks at an early date.

(3) The third school, the one to which Secretary McCulloch belonged and the one dominating the situation immediately after the War, was the "contraction" school, which advocated a return to specie payments, largely through a continual contraction of the currency. The withdrawal of the greenbacks through the sale of government bonds was the plan generally advocated by this school. The extremists of this school advocated the so-called "cremation process," concerning which David A. Wells said: [4]

"I would have it enjoined upon the Secretary of the Treasury to destroy by burning on a given day of every week, commencing at the earliest

[1] *Op. cit.*, p. 131.

[2] A description of these five schools or "theories of resumption" is given by Dewey, *Financial History of the United States*, pp. 335–338.

[3] Barrett, pp. 129 and 130.

[4] Quoted by Dewey, p. 336.

practical moment, a certain amount of the legal tender notes, fixing the minimum at not less than $500,000 per week, or at the rate of $26 millions per annum. This process once entered upon and continued, the gradual appreciation of the greenback to par with gold, and the ultimate equalization of the two, would not be a question of fact but simply of time. What specific amount of contraction of the legal tender would be necessary no one can tell with certainty."

(4) The fourth school consisted of those who believed in "growing up to specie payments," something as India later did between 1893 and 1899.[1] They believed that, if the currency supply were kept limited, the specie value of the greenbacks would continually rise, toward parity, under the influence of increasing population and trade, and therefore of a growing demand for money.

(5) The fifth school was what would be called today the "paper money" school. It was the school that later developed into the National Greenback Party, which figured in our elections from 1876 to 1884. This school favored the permanent retention of the greenbacks and an expansion of their circulation. They wanted cheap money and plenty of it.

The Opposition to Currency Contraction

In opposition to the contraction of the currency practically all the arguments against currency deflation which are familiar to the student of monetary problems today were advanced. Contraction would prove burdensome and unjust to the debtor classes, including the National Government itself, would depress business, cause unemployment by bringing about continually declining prices and decrease government revenues. The difficulties of a speedy contraction were well summarized shortly after the War by a leading financial journal.[2] After speaking of the artificial stimulus to commerce and industry which had been given by the previous inflation and of the resulting benefits to debtors and harm to creditors, the article said:

"But how different is the work of recovery and contraction! It is next to impossible to get back to a specie basis without disaster and monetary spasms; for now the pressure falls on the debtor, while his creditor has the advantage. And since the debtor class is always more weak, more numerous, and less able to bear losses, there is a much greater amount of individual injury than when it was the creditors who were suffering."

[1] Cf., *supra*, pp. 26–29.

[2] *Commercial and Financial Chronicle*, Oct. 21, 1865, p. 514.

The article claimed that an appreciating dollar would cause trade to stagnate, break down credit, depress wages and yield an increasing crop of bankruptcies. These evils would be the more severe in proportion as the transition were abrupt and spasmodic. It was accordingly urged that the process of returning to a specie basis should be a gradual one. In this way only, the article said, could the national industry escape violent shock, and the people be spared the disastrous revulsions, which would occur if the currency were contracted too suddenly and too violently.

The Question of Paying Government Bonds in Greenbacks

In the post-war history of the greenbacks, one subject which became a matter of great controversy was the question as to whether the government's bonds must be paid in specie or could be paid in legal-tender notes. This question was apparently not seriously considered in the early days of the War, because it was expected at that time that the War would be brief and that the régime of depreciated paper money would last but a short time, terminating long before there would be any appreciable payments on the principal of the war bonds.

Bonds floated prior to the War would presumably be paid in specie as they matured because the Government had received specie for them from the public when they were sold. On January 1, 1863, a debt of the Government contracted in 1842 for eight million dollars became due and Chase paid it in gold.

The law of February 25, 1862, authorizing the first issue of greenbacks made them legal tender in payment of all debts, public and private, except duties on imports and "of all claims and demands against the United States of every kind whatsoever, except for interest upon bonds and notes, which shall be paid in coin." While the laws authorizing some of these bond issues expressly provided that the bonds should be payable, principal and interest, in coin, some of the laws were silent as to the money in which the principal should be paid. When the bonds were issued, it seems to have been the general understanding—although this claim has been emphatically denied by some—that the principal, as well as the interest, would be paid in specie. This belief undoubtedly made it possible for the Government to borrow on much better terms than it would have received, had the expectation been that payment would be made in paper money. Secretary McCulloch, in his report of November 30, 1867, said: [1]

> "Did any member of the House or of the Senate, prior to 1864, in the discussions of these bills, ever intimate that the bonds to be issued in accordance with their provisions might be paid, when redeemable, in a depreciated currency? Was there a single subscriber to the five-twenty bonds or to the seven and three-tenths notes, which by their terms were convertible into bonds, who did not believe, and who was not given to understand by the agents of the government, that both the principal and interest of these bonds were payable in coin? Does any one suppose that the people of the United States, self-sacrificing as they were in the support of the government, would have sold their stocks, their lands, the products of their farms, of their factories and their shops, and invested the proceeds in . . . [these government obligations] if they had understood that the bonds were to be redeemed after five years from their respective dates in a currency of the value of which they could form no reliable estimate? . . . Would the Secretary of the Treasury, or would Congress, when the fate of the nation was trembling in the balance, and when a failure to raise money for the support of the federal army would have been success to the rebellion and ruin to the Union cause, have dared to attempt the experiment of raising money on bonds redeemable at the pleasure of the government after five years in a currency the convertible value of which might not depend upon the solvency of the government, but upon the amount in circulation? No such understanding existed, and fortunately no such experiment was tried. The bonds were negotiated with the definite understanding that they were payable in coin. . . . The contracts were made in good faith on both sides, a part of them when the government was in imminent peril and needed money to preserve its existence, the balance when its necessities were scarcely less urgent. . . . Good faith and public honor, which to a nation are of priceless worth, require that these contracts should be complied with in the spirit in which they were made."

James A. Garfield, speaking to the House in 1868 with reference to the original five-twenty bond bill when it was before the House in 1862 said that all who referred to the subject stated that the principal of these bonds was payable in gold, and coin payment was the understanding of every member of the Committee on Ways and Means. It was only because of an occasional doubt then expressed that it was considered necessary "from abundant caution" to make a definite promise in the ten-forty act of 1863.[2]

On the other hand, in selling these bonds the government received depreciated paper money at par, and such bonds as were not made by law specifically payable in coin—and that meant most of

[1] Pp. xxiii–xxiv.

[2] Cited by Dewey, p. 346.

the bonds—were presumably *legally* payable in greenbacks, which the Government had expressly made legal tender for all debts, public as well as private, except those specifically mentioned in the law.

About 1868 there began a vigorous movement for the payment in legal-tender money of the principal of all bonds which were not by law made specifically payable in coin. One of the leaders in this movement was Thaddeus Stevens, who, referring to the suggestion that certain Government bonds were payable in gold, said:[1]

> "After they fall due they are payable in money, . . . just as we all understood it when we passed the law authorizing that loan . . . I want to say that if I knew that any party in this country would go for paying in coin that which is payable in money, thus enhancing it one-half; if I knew there was such a platform and such a determination this day on the part of any party, I would vote for the other side . . . I would vote for no such swindle on the taxpayers of this country; I would vote for no such speculation in favor of the large bondholders, the millionaires who took advantage of our folly in granting them coin payment of interest."

It was urged that the money of the plough-holders should be good enough for the bondholders.

President Johnson, in his message of December, 1868, advocated a form of repudiation of part of the public debt, saying that there was gold in interest and principal for the owners of a 5–20 bond, but only depreciated paper in pension money for the wounded soldier and in salaries for men engaged in government service. In reply to these declarations, the Senate by a vote of 43 to 6 passed a resolution saying that "properly cherishing and upholding the good faith of the nation [we do hereby] utterly disapprove of and condemn the sentiments and propositions contained in . . . the late message of the President." A similar resolution was passed by the House by a vote of 155 to 6. President Grant, in his inaugural address of March 4, 1869, said: "To protect the national honor, every dollar of government indebtedness should be paid in gold unless otherwise expressly stipulated in the contract." This continued to be the policy of the National Government until the problem disappeared with the resumption of specie payments.

The Resumption Act

The law providing for a definite return to specie payments on January 1, 1879, known as the Resumption Act, was passed

[1] *Congressional Globe*, July 17, 1868, p. 4178.

January 14, 1875, by what later would have been called "a lame duck" Republican Congress, after the Republican Party had suffered disastrous defeat at the polls in the Congressional election of 1874. The bill in its essentials was drafted by a sub-committee of the Senate, among the members of which were Senators Sherman and Edmunds. It was apparently drafted by Edmunds and was introduced in the Senate by Sherman, as Chairman of the Senate Finance Committee. It later became Sherman's lot to administer the law as Secretary of the Treasury. At this time the inflationist sentiment in the United States was strong and was growing luxuriantly in the fertile soil of discontent created by the depression which began in 1873. The public, moreover, did not take the Resumption Act very seriously, because the date set for resumption was four years off and there was widespread doubt as to whether the plan could ever be carried through.

The Act covered a variety of provisions, but, from the standpoint of the greenbacks, the principal ones were five in number, as follows:

(1) Provision for the minting and issue of fractional silver coins to be used for the redemption and withdrawal from circulation of all fractional paper money.

(2) The granting of greater freedom in the establishment of national banks and the removal of restrictions provided for the sectional apportionment of national bank note issues.

(3) Imposing upon the Secretary of the Treasury the duty of redeeming greenbacks outstanding in excess of $300 millions to the amount of 80 per cent of the new issues of national bank notes. Inasmuch as the national bank law of that time required national banks in the principal cities to maintain a reserve of 25 per cent of lawful money against their national bank notes, and required the banks in other cities to maintain a reserve of 15 per cent, it was reasoned that the above-mentioned 80 per cent limit would keep the net circulation of greenbacks and national bank notes combined about where it was.

(4) Provision that on and after January 1, 1879 the Secretary of the Treasury should "redeem, in coin, the United States legal-tender notes then outstanding on their presentation for redemption, at the office of the Assistant Treasurer of the United States in the City of New York, in sums of not less than fifty dollars."

(5) In order to provide funds for the redemption of the greenbacks, the Secretary was authorized "to use any surplus revenues, from time to time, in the Treasury . . . and to issue . . . at not less than par, in coin" certain kinds of United States bonds which had been authorized by previous legislation.

Within the broad limits of these powers, the Secretary of the Treasury was to work out his own plan for bringing about resumption on the scheduled date. His responsibility was large and his powers were commensurately large.

One serious handicap, however, placed upon the Secretary was the absence of any authority to redeem the greenbacks directly in United States bonds, a privilege which, it will be recalled, had been given the Secretary by the original greenback law and had been removed in 1863. The only form of specie in which redemption could be made was gold, since silver dollars had not circulated in the United States for more than a generation and had had their legal-tender quality removed in 1873. There was comparatively little gold coin in the country and a good share of that was circulating on the Pacific Coast. To obtain gold, therefore, the Secretary was forced to sell bonds abroad—a policy which brought upon him an avalanche of criticism not only from the radical Greenback Party, but from many more conservative people. For a time Benjamin H. Bristow, Secretary of the Treasury, did not take any action for accumulating a gold reserve, in the hope that he could obtain from Congress authority to redeem the notes directly in bonds; but when, in March, 1877, John Sherman became Secretary of the Treasury under President Hayes, he initiated a vigorous policy of accumulating a reserve, and of making the other preparations necessary for carrying through the resumption program.

Briefly summarized, the facts of the next few years were as follows:

> "In January, 1875, the volume of bank-notes in circulation was $352 millions, and of greenbacks $382 millions. By April 1, 1878, $43 millions of new bank-notes had been issued, while $74 millions of earlier bank-note issues had been retired, leaving a net reduction of $31 millions. Meanwhile the United States notes had been redeemed to the extent of $35 millions, thus making for the period a total contraction, as to these elements of the currency, of approximately $66 millions." [1]

The enemies of resumption attacked the act and insisted that the country needed more money, not less money. Opposition to resumption grew and soon became so strong that concessions to inflationist sentiments became politically necessary. Congress

[1] Barrett, pp. 189 and 190.

accordingly passed a measure on May 31, 1878, prohibiting further contraction of greenbacks, and requiring the Treasury to reissue those which it received in the ordinary course of business. This act gave the country a permanent greenback currency. At that time the amount of greenbacks stood at $346,681,016 and it has stood at this figure ever since.[1] Thereafter, notes presented for redemption were not retired but were reissued and kept in circulation.

Sherman believed that the lowest gold reserve consistent with safety, with which the country would be able to resume specie payments was 40 per cent, or about $138 millions. By January 1, 1879, he had accumulated $133 millions, about two-thirds of which came from the sale of bonds and one-third from surplus revenue. Under his strong policy, the gold value of the greenbacks slowly but surely advanced, and two weeks before January 1, 1879, greenbacks were quoted at par.

A factor retarding the rise of the greenbacks to the gold parity between 1875 and 1879 was the fact that during these years gold itself was rising in value. The purchasing power over commodities at wholesale, for example, of England's gold standard currency rose during those four years over 15 per cent.

Thus after a period of 17 years of depreciated paper money, a period that it was thought would last but a few months when it was begun, the country again returned to a gold basis, a basis which it maintained (with a minor qualification during the World War), but often against great difficulties, until early in the year 1933.

Legal-Tender Cases

From the time of the first suggestion of legal-tender notes in January, 1862, as we have previously noted, the question of the constitutional power of Congress to issue such notes was debated. Naturally, this question was soon taken to the courts and in due time appeared before the United States Supreme Court. The various cases in which different phases of this problem were decided are known as the "legal-tender cases," the more important of which we shall briefly summarize.

[1] The Act of May 12, 1933, authorized the President to increase the issue of greenbacks up to an aggregate of $3 billion; but up to the present time the President has not exercised this authority.

Contracts Specifically Payable in Specie

The principal case covering this subject is Bronson vs. Rodes, (1868).[1] Metz in 1851 borrowed from Bronson $1,400, giving his bond and mortgage for repayment in 1857, with interest, "in gold and silver coin, lawful money of the United States." Payment was not made nor demanded at maturity, but interest was paid until January, 1864. A year later Rodes, who had become owner of the mortgaged property tendered full payment of principal and interest in greenbacks at a time when a greenback dollar was worth 44½ cents gold. This tender was refused, and the case came before the United States Supreme Court in 1868. As fate would have it, Salmon P. Chase, who had been Secretary of the Treasury when the greenbacks were issued, now, as Chief Justice of the Supreme Court, was called upon to render this as well as other legal-tender decisions. The question was: Was Bronson bound by law to accept these legal-tender notes in full payment of the debt?

The Court first asked: What was the intent of the parties to the contract? It found that at the time the contract was made gold and silver coin were in circulation and were legal tender for debts, that the notes of the various state banks which constituted the bulk of the money of the country were of unequal value and that many of them were depreciated and unsafe. This situation gave rise to contracts containing the specific coin clause. The Court said:

> "A contract to pay a certain number of dollars in gold or silver coin is, in legal import, nothing else than an agreement to deliver a certain weight of standard gold, to be ascertained by a count of coins, each of which is certified to contain a definite proportion of that weight."

This was the intent of both parties to the contract and this intent was lawful.

The next question was: Can such a contract to pay coin be satisfied by a tender of legal-tender notes? The answer was, that gold and silver coins are still minted and still legal tender and that if there is no express provision in law to the contrary, "it is a just, if not a necessary inference, from the fact that both descriptions of money were issued by the same government, that contracts paid in either were equally sanctioned by law."

[1] 7 Wallace, 229.

The Court then went on to show that a contrary interpretation would lead to absurd results. For example, according to law, duties on imports must be paid in coin and likewise interest on the public debt. How could importers get gold for paying their duties if all contracts to pay gold were actually payable in legal-tender notes, and equally how could the United States Government get gold within the country for paying its interest?

The Court's conclusion was that "express contracts to pay coined dollars can only be satisfied by the payment of coined dollars. They are not 'debts' which may be satisfied by the tender of United States notes."

Following this decision, there was a tremendous growth of indebtedness in the United States "payable in gold coin of the United States of the present standard of weight and fineness." These debts, down to early 1933, covered most federal, state and county bond issues, most of the bonds of railroads and public utilities whose rate structures are regulated by law, and a large proportion of the bonds of industrial corporations, the mortgages of farmers and of city home-builders and of a great many other obligations. On June 5, 1933, all such specific gold contracts were rendered ineffective by a joint resolution of Congress. Up to the present time (April 24, 1934), the United States Supreme Court has not rendered any decision as to the constitutionality of this action.

In the decision of Lane County vs. Oregon,[1] rendered by the United States Supreme Court in 1868, it was decided that taxes imposed by a state government were not debts within the meaning of the legal-tender acts, and that states could therefore collect their taxes in any medium they deemed proper.

The principal controversy centering in the Legal-Tender Cases related to the three questions: (1) Are the legal-tender acts constitutional when applied to contracts made before their passage? (2) Are they constitutional as applied to debts contracted after their enactment? (3) Are legal-tender notes issued in time of peace constitutional?

The first of these questions was first answered by the United States Supreme Court in 1870 in the case of Hepburn vs. Griswold.[2] In 1860 a Mrs. Hepburn made a promissory note to a Mr. Griswold for $11,250, payable February 20, 1862, five days before the first legal-tender act was passed. The note was not paid

[1] 7 Wallace, 71. [2] 8 Wallace, 603.

at maturity. Later in 1864 Mrs. Hepburn tendered greenbacks in payment of the note, principal and interest, and the tender was refused. The case came to the United States Supreme Court on appeal, and Chief Justice Chase delivered the opinion.

Briefly summarized, the argument was as follows: It is an established rule of interpretation that the terms employed in a law are not to be interpreted so as to conflict with the principle of justice if they are open to an interpretation that favors justice. It is clearly unjust to a creditor to oblige him to accept greatly depreciated paper money in settlement of a debt contracted when the currency of the country was on a specie basis, and such an interpretation of the law "is not to be admitted if any other can be reconciled with the manifest intent of the legislature."

What then was the intention of Congress? To this the answer is that in all the debates in Congress "no suggestion was ever made that the legal-tender clause did not apply as fully to contracts made before as to contracts made after its passage."

If this was the intent of Congress, did Congress possess the constitutional power "to make notes . . . a legal tender in payment of debts, which, when contracted, were payable by law in gold and silver coin?" The Government of the United States is one of limited powers, and no department of the National Government possesses any authority not granted by the Constitution either expressly or by implication. There is no express grant of authority in the Constitution of legislative power to make any description of credit currency a legal tender in payment of debts. Is such a power implied in any of the powers expressly granted? The Court then reviews the powers that might be interpreted as carrying this right by implication, such as the power to coin money, to declare war, to regulate commerce and to borrow money on the credit of the United States; and in each case the Court answers the question in the negative. With reference to the admitted power of borrowing money through the issuance of notes to circulate as currency, the Court maintains that this power is entirely distinct from the power to make such notes a legal tender. The Congress of the Confederation could emit bills of credit, but could not make them legal tender. The useful purposes of the notes, the Court held, would have been fully answered without making them legal tender for preëxisting debts. This quality added very little to their value.

Is the making of such notes a legal tender for preëxisting debts consistent with the spirit of the Constitution? Among the cardinal principles of the Constitution is the establishment of justice. The spirit of the Constitution is seen in the provision that "no state shall pass any law impairing the obligation of contracts."

> "We cannot doubt," says the Court, "that a law not made in pursuance of an express power, which necessarily and in its direct operation impairs the obligation of contracts, is inconsistent with the spirit of the Constitution." The conclusion was "that an act making mere promises to pay dollars a legal tender in payment of debts previously contracted, is not a means appropriate, plainly adapted, really calculated to carry into effect any express power vested in Congress; that such an act is inconsistent with the spirit of the Constitution; that it is prohibited by the Constitution."

The decision was rendered by a divided Court, the vote being four to three, one Associate Justice not voting. It was received by the country at large with a storm of protest. Gold at the time stood at about 120 and people feared that they would have to pay a large part of their debts in gold. The debtor classes everywhere protested, and especially large corporations with maturing pre-war bonds to pay. A railroad president wrote Chase: [1]

> "How do you suppose the railroads of the country are to pay their interest in gold and receive only a depreciated currency for their revenues, limited as they are by their charters to a fixed price? Wouldn't we have a nice time in making passengers pay their fares in gold?"

Another correspondent wrote: [2]

> "Your decision in regard to legal tenders, if not reversed, is likely to cause the greatest possible distress and ruin among the classes of people already in debt; among the rest, very many widows and orphans owing money on mortgage of real estate of a long date back."

There was a widespread popular feeling that this four to three decision would soon be reversed. Shortly after it was made, the number of judges was increased from eight to nine, and two new appointments were made. The charge was frequently made that the new appointees were pledged in advance to vote for a reversal of this decision at the first opportunity, but there seems to be no evidence to support this charge.[3]

The public, the administration and the Supreme Court itself all seemed anxious for another test case at an early date on the

[1] Hart, *op. cit.*, p. 397. [2] *Ibid.*, pp. 397–398. [3] Cf., *ibid.*, pp. 399–403.

question of the constitutionality of the greenbacks. In the following year an opportunity for reconsidering the question presented itself in the cases of Knox vs. Lee and Parker vs. Davis.[1] In these cases the controlling questions were: (1) Were the legal-tender acts constitutional when applied to contracts made before their passage? And (2) were they constitutional when applied to debts contracted since their enactment? Briefly summarized, the Court's position was as follows:

Consideration must be given to the circumstances under which the legal tenders were issued. Seasons of exigencies may justify acts which at other times would be inappropriate. When the greenbacks were authorized, a civil war was raging which seriously threatened the overthrow of the government. The nation required military equipment and support for the army and the navy. Money was needed by the government to an extent beyond the capacity of all ordinary sources of supply. The public treasury was nearly empty and the credit of the government was nearly exhausted. Taxation was altogether inadequate and it was impossible to await the income of new taxes.

> "The entire amount of coin in the country . . . was insufficient to supply the need of the government three months, . . . had it all been poured into the treasury. . . . We say nothing of the overhanging paralysis of trade and of business generally, which threatened loss of confidence in the ability of the government to maintain its continued existence . . ."

Having drawn this dismal picture, the Court proceeded with the *post hoc, propter hoc* argument:

> "Something revived the drooping faith of the people; something brought immediately to the government's aid the resources of the nation, and something enabled the successful prosecution of the war, and the preservation of the national life. What was it if not the legal tender enactments?"

The Court did not believe that any other possible measure could have met the situation; but, at any rate, it held that the degree of necessity of the greenback issues and the relative degree of their appropriateness were matters for Congress to decide.

It was not enough, the Court maintained, for the government to issue notes that circulated as money. It had to make these notes a legal tender for debt, as

[1] 12 Wallace, 457.

"no one could be compelled to take common treasury notes in payment of debts, and as the prospect of ultimate redemption was remote and contingent. . . . Making the notes legal tender gave them a new use, and it needs no argument to show that the value of things is in proportion to the uses to which they may be applied."

The conclusion was, therefore, that the notes were not an inappropriate means for carrying into execution the legitimate powers of the government.

Next the Court asked the question: Was such a legal-tender provision forbidden by the letter of the Constitution—a question which it answered in the negative. It then asked: Was it contrary to the spirit of the fifth amendment to the Constitution which forbids taking property for public use without just compensation or due process of law? Its reply was that this provision was always understood to apply only to direct appropriation by the government, and not to property losses or destruction of contracts that should result from public acts, such as tariffs, wars and embargoes. The argument of those who maintained that the legal-tender acts were contrary to the spirit of the Constitution, the Court held, assumed that (1) they impaired the obligation of contracts and that (2) Congress was prohibited from taking action which might indirectly have that effect. Both of these assumptions the Court denied. The legal-tender laws compelled a creditor to accept depreciated greenbacks in payment of debts, "but whether the obligation of the contract is thereby weakened can be determined only after considering what was the contract obligation." This obligation, the Court held, was not an obligation to pay gold or silver or the particular kind of money recognized by law when the contract was made, but rather to pay whatever kind of money should be recognized by law when payment should be made.

Furthermore, the Court held that it could not be "truly asserted that Congress may not, by its action, indirectly impair the obligation of contracts, if by the expression be meant rendering contracts fruitless or partially fruitless," for Congress does this very thing whenever it enacts bankruptcy law, declares war or lays embargoes on trade.

The Court's decision was that the legal-tender acts were constitutional as applied to contracts made either before or after their passage, and it accordingly overruled so much of the Hepburn vs. Griswold case as ruled these acts to be unconstitutional so far as they applied to contracts made before their enactment.

Chief Justice Chase and three other justices dissented.

In the cases of Knox vs. Lee and Parker vs. Davis, the issue of the legal tenders was justified as constitutional as a means to meet a great national emergency, that would not be constitutional in normal times. In the next important legal-tender case, that of Juilliard vs. Greenman,[1] decided in 1884, the question was "whether notes of the United States issued in time of war . . . and afterwards in time of peace redeemed and paid in gold coin at the Treasury and then reissued . . . can under the Constitution . . . be legal tender" in payment of debts.

The Court invoked the doctrine of a liberal interpretation of expressed powers, with particular reference to the powers granted to the National Government, of levying taxes, coining money and regulating the value thereof, and of borrowing money on the credit of the United States, and to the general clause of the Constitution authorizing Congress "to make all laws which shall be necessary and proper for carrying into execution" the specified powers. The Court's case was built chiefly on the power to borrow money which, it held, meant the power to raise money for public use by the pledge of the public credit, and might be employed to meet either present or anticipated expenses and obligations of the government. This power to borrow money, the Court held, included

> "the power to issue, in return for the money borrowed, the obligations of the United States, in any appropriate form, of stocks, bonds, bills or notes . . . Congress has authority to issue these obligations in a form adapted to circulate. . . . In order to promote and facilitate such circulation, to adapt these to use as currency, and to make them more current in the market, it may provide for their redemption . . . and may make them receivable for debts to the government."

From the power to borrow and to issue bills as a form of borrowing, the Court continued, it logically followed that Congress might impress upon such bills the qualities of being usable as currency for the purchase of merchandise and for the payment of debts, in accordance with the usages of sovereign governments. The power of making notes a legal tender, the Court said, as incident to the power of borrowing was usually understood to belong to sover-

[1] 110 United States, 421.

eignty in Europe and America when the Constitution was adopted, and had been exercised by the American colonies, and later by the thirteen states prior to the adoption of the Constitution.

The decision was, therefore:

> "We are irresistibly impelled to the conclusion that the impressing upon the treasury notes of the United States the quality of being a legal tender in payment of private debts is an appropriate measure, conducive and plainly adapted to the execution of the undoubted powers of Congress and therefore, within the meaning of that instrument necessary and proper for carrying into execution the powers vested by this Constitution in the government of the United States."

The question as to whether at any particular time, either time of war or time of peace, the exigency is such as to justify the issue and circulation of legal-tender notes was held a political question to be determined by Congress and the President and not by the Courts.

The greenbacks are still with us. The legal limitation of their issue to $346 millions, which was imposed by the law of 1878, continued in force until the Agricultural Adjustment Act of May 12, 1933. In the meantime, our total monetary circulation had grown from $819 millions in 1879 to over $5.5 billions at the end of February, 1935. The greenbacks today, therefore, represent a very small and declining percentage of our total currency. Their history after the resumption of specie payments in 1879 is of comparatively little importance except for a brief period in the last decade of the century and for the provision of the law of May 12, 1933, authorizing the President to increase their issue up to $3 billions—an authority fortunately not yet exercised by the President. These matters will be discussed in Volume II. It is sufficient here to say that the Gold Standard Act of 1900 created a special gold reserve which was to be used for the redemption on demand of greenbacks and other kinds of United States paper money as required, and that the law imposed upon the Secretary of the Treasury the duty of maintaining this reserve and of redeeming the greenbacks, not "in coin" as was the obligation before, but specifically in gold coin of the standard then fixed by law. This was the law and the practice until the enactment of the Emergency Banking Act of March 9, 1933, when the convertibility of the greenbacks as well as of all other kinds of United States money was suspended.

BIBLIOGRAPHY

Barrett, Don C., *The Greenbacks and Resumption of Specie Payments, 1862–1879;* Cambridge, Mass., Harvard University Press, 1931.

Bayley, Rafael A., *National Loans of the United States from July 4, 1776 to June 30, 1880;* Washington, Government Printing Office, 1882.

Carothers, Neil, *Fractional Money;* New York, John Wiley & Sons, 1930.

Dewey, Davis Rich, *Financial History of the United States*, Tenth Edition; New York, Longmans, Green and Company, 1928.

Finance Reports, The Annual Reports of the Secretary of the Treasury; *passim;* Washington, Government Printing Office.

Fite, Emerson David, *Social and Industrial Conditions in the North during the Civil War;* New York, The Macmillan Company, 1910.

Hart, Albert Bushnell, *Salmon Portland Chase;* Boston, Houghton Mifflin Company, 1899.

Hepburn, A. Barton, *A History of Currency in the United States;* New York, The Macmillan Company, 1915.

Kemmerer, Edwin Walter, *Kemmerer on Money*, Second Edition; Philadelphia, The John C. Winston Company, 1934.

de Knight, William F., *History of the Currency of the Country and of the Loans of the United States;* Washington, Government Printing Office, 1900.

McCulloch, Hugh, *Men and Measures of Half a Century;* New York, Charles Scribner's Sons, 1888.

Mitchell, Wesley Clair, *Gold, Prices and Wages under the Greenback Standard;* Berkeley, Calif., The University Press, 1908.

——, *A History of the Greenbacks;* Chicago, University of Chicago Press, 1903.

Moses, Bernard, "Legal Tender Notes in California," *Quarterly Journal of Economics*, Vol. VII, 1893.

Noyes, Alexander Dana, *Forty Years of American Finance;* New York, G. P. Putnam's Sons, 1909.

Oberholtzer, Ellis Paxon, *Jay Cooke, Financier of the Civil War*, 2 volumes; Philadelphia, George W. Jacobs & Company, 1907.

Schuckers, J. W., *The Life and Public Services of Salmon Portland Chase;* New York, D. Appleton & Company, 1874.

Sherman, John, *Recollections of Forty Years in the House, Senate and Cabinet—An Autobiography*, 2 volumes; Chicago, The Werner Company, 1895.

Spaulding, E. G., *History of the Legal Tender Paper Money Issued during the Great Rebellion;* Buffalo, N. Y., Express Printing Company, 1869.

Stilwell, Silas Moore, *Notes Explanatory of Mr. Chase's Plan of National Finance;* Washington, Government Printing Office, 1861.

U. S. Government, *The Range of Prices of Staple Articles in the New York Markets at the Beginning of Each Month in Each Year from 1825 to 1863;* Executive Documents Nos. 2 and 3, 38th Congress, 1st Session, Vol. 6, 1863–1864.

——, *Specie Resumption and Refunding of the National Debt;* House Executive Documents, 46th Congress, 2d Session, Vol. VII, No. 9; Washington, Government Printing Office, 1880.

——, "Statement Exhibiting the Amount of Coin and Bullion Imported and

Exported Annually from 1821 to 1863," also "Gross Value of Exports and Imports of Merchandise, 1790–1863," *Report on Finances;* Executive Documents Nos. 2 and 3, 38th Congress, 1st Session, Vol. 6, 1863–1864.

Wells, Gideon, *The Diary of Gideon Wells*, 3 volumes; Boston, Houghton Mifflin Company, 1911.

White, Horace, *Money and Banking*, Fifth Edition; Boston, Ginn & Company, 1911.

Wildman, Murray Shipley, *Money Inflation in the United States;* New York, G. P. Putnam's Sons, 1905.

Woodburn, James Albert, *The Life of Thaddeus Stevens;* Indianapolis, Indiana, The Bobbs-Merrill Company, 1913.

CHAPTER XIII

GERMANY'S EXPERIENCE WITH INFLATION, 1914–1923

To the student of money the monetary experiences of the belligerent countries during the World War and the half dozen years immediately following are particularly illuminating. What was done was done on a large scale and the experiences are written in capital letters. Within the short period of twelve years, more than a half dozen of the most advanced nations of the world, to say nothing of many less advanced ones, ran through the whole gamut of paper money experiences known to history, and then returned gladly—albeit in many cases but temporarily—to the gold standard. In their broad outlines, the monetary experiences of these countries during the twelve years ending about 1926 were strikingly similar, both in the methods adopted and in the results attained, although in their details they were often very different. In a book like this one space will not permit a treatment sufficiently comprehensive to be of much value of more than one of these World War monetary experiences. The one chosen is that of Germany, an experience which has the double advantage of appealing to a widespread interest and of offering to the student an exceptionally large amount of readily available data. Here, moreover, is a case of extreme inflation as contrasted with the two instances of comparatively mild paper money inflation described in the preceding two chapters.

Germany's Pre-War Currency

When the War broke out in 1914, Germany had been on the gold standard for over forty years, her organic gold standard laws having been enacted during the period 1870–1875. The monetary unit, the gold mark, which was not coined in any denomination less than ten marks, contained .398 gram of gold .900 fine and was, therefore, equivalent in its gold content to 23.8 cents United States gold coin. There was free coinage of gold, and gold coins in denominations of 10 and 20 marks circulated freely. By reason of the limitations placed upon their issue, of the privileges of convertibility into gold offered by the Reichsbank and of their acceptability by the Government at par in payment of taxes, the paper money of Germany and the fiduciary coins of silver, nickel and copper always circulated at a parity with the gold coin. At approximately the time of the outbreak of the War, Germany had about four billion gold marks, of which over two-thirds were reliably estimated to be in circulation and one-third to be in the vaults of the Reichsbank. Her note circulation consisted of three kinds; namely, (1) Reichsbank notes of about M2,593,000,000, of which between two-thirds and three-fourths were normally covered mark for mark by gold, and the balance by high-grade discounted bills of not more than three months' maturity; (2) about M160,000,000 of notes of four local note-issuing banks, whose issues were being gradually taken over by the Reichsbank; (3) Reichskassenscheine, to the amount of M149,000,000, which were issues of government paper money of small denominations. The total note circulation was, therefore, about M2,902,000,000.[1]

Adding to this paper money the 2,750,000,000 gold marks in circulation, the M750,000,000 of silver coin, and the minor coins of nickel and copper, we arrive at a total monetary circulation for Germany, at the outbreak of the War, of 6½ billion marks, or approximately 96 marks per capita.

The history of German inflation may for convenience be divided into three periods; viz.: (1) the war period, extending from the outbreak of the War to the Armistice of November 11, 1918; (2) the early post-war period, extending from the Armistice to the fixing of Germany's total reparations indebtedness by the Reparations Commission Decision of April 27, 1921; (3) the later post-war period, extending from the aforementioned decision of the Reparations Commission to the stabilization which became effective about the end of 1923.[2]

The War Period

Emergency Measures to Protect the Currency. Immediately upon the outbreak of the War, the Government took vigorous measures

[1] Cf., League of Nations, *Memorandum on Currency and Central Banks, 1913–1924,* Vol. I, p. 120; and Young, John Parke, *European Currency and Finance,* Vol. I, pp. 387–390.

[2] Inasmuch as the demarcations of these periods do not coincide with the beginnings and endings of either calendar or fiscal years, and as much of the statistical material used is available only on a yearly basis, the divisions into periods cannot be followed rigidly in the discussion. There will always be a certain amount of overlapping, and, for the convenience of the readers, the figures for the overlapping years will be repeated, wherever comparable, in the tables that follow.

to protect the currency and to liquefy the assets of the Reichsbank. The convertibility of bank notes into gold was suspended. The exportation of gold was prohibited and the use of gold in the arts was narrowly restricted. By a decree of September 28, 1914, the Bundesrat declared invalid all transactions calling for payment in actual gold, and by a decree of November 23 it imposed heavy penalties upon anyone selling German gold coin at a premium. Through appeals to national patriotism and in other ways, strenuous efforts were made to bring into the vaults of the Reichsbank as much of the country's gold coin and bullion as possible. People who would patriotically give up their gold ornaments to the Government were given a memorial medal, bearing the legend:

> "Gold I gave to defend my country,
> Iron I took for a badge of honour."

In the place of three-name bills (occasionally two-name) of 90 days or less as cover for the Reichsbank's note issue, the Reichsbank was authorized to substitute Government Treasury notes and bills with maturities not exceeding three months. The 5 per cent tax previously imposed on uncovered notes issued in excess of the normal Kontingent was repealed, while the cash reserve requirement against Reichsbank notes which since 1909 had been limited to gold was now "liberalized," so as to include two forms of paper money issued by the Government; namely, the Reichskassenscheine previously mentioned, and a new form authorized to meet the war emergency and known as "Darlehnskassenscheine" (Loan Bureau Notes). The Darlehnskassen or Loan Bureaus were affiliated with the Reichsbank and under its administrative control. They were particularly concerned with the granting of credit to the smaller financial and business concerns and to individuals of moderate means. Their notes, the Darlehnskassenscheine, were issued against the pledge of produce, merchandise, securities and other things of value. No gold cover was required for them. A legal authorization given to the Reichsbank to hold them like Reichskassenscheine as part of the cover for Reichsbank notes greatly facilitated the expansion of the note circulation.

With the beginning of the War, the gold standard in Germany ceased to exist in fact, although for years it was retained in name and in the publicly expressed legal concepts of the Government.

Henceforth, for approximately ten years, Germany was on a fiduciary paper money standard.

The Motive for Inflation Chiefly a Fiscal One. The principal reason for the initiation of this inflation policy and for its continuation during this long period was the fiscal one, the need of the Government to obtain the vast revenues required for financing the War and for meeting the extraordinary government expenses of the early post-war years with a minimum of resistance on the part of the German public. It was an application of the principle, which a great French statesman applied to taxation when he said: "The gentle art of taxation is to pluck the maximum amount of feathers from the goose with the minimum amount of squawking." It was the old story of exploiting the monetary function of government—that is, the function of providing the public with a good medium of exchange—for the benefit of the fiscal function of providing the Government with an adequate revenue.

The German authorities believed that the War would be short and they expected to saddle their war expenses ultimately upon a defeated enemy. It is usually difficult greatly to increase tax revenues in the early days of a war, when the normal economic machinery of the country is being thrown out of order and large numbers of men are being withdrawn from their usual economic activities to enter the nation's fighting forces. Heavy taxes at such a time tend to dampen war enthusiasm. Recourse to foreign borrowing upon an extensive scale was impossible, for the magnitude of the War greatly weakened Germany's foreign credit. Domestic borrowing was the most promising immediate recourse for large sums. The extent of the revenues demanded and demanded quickly, however, was so great that dependence upon domestic borrowing to obtain them required an enormous expansion of circulating credit for the discount of Treasury bills at the Reichsbank. The expansion took place largely in the form of increased issues of Reichsbank notes and of giro or transfer credits at the Reichsbank. As a substitute for gold in the Reichsbank's reserves against these increased issues, the Reichsbank was authorized to use the newly created Treasury bills and notes previously mentioned.

With reference to this situation Hjalmar Schacht, President of the Reichsbank, said: [1]

[1] Schacht, *The Stabilization of the Mark*, pp. 14–15, 33–34.

"The English people was prepared for financial as well as personal sacrifice. The German people, on the other hand, was given no such call to sacrifice by its officials. . . . Secretary of State Helfferich built up his entire system of war finance on the shifting sand of a personal belief in the rapid victory of Germany." And again: "The German war finance consisted mainly in the Reich satisfying its needs as they arose by the discount of Treasury bills and bonds at the Reichsbank, the floating debt thus incurred being funded (so far as possible) twice a year by the public issue of long-term loans. . . . What the public at large, and all but a very few of the country's economic leaders, failed adequately to appreciate was the fact that inflation on a heavy scale was the concomitant of the whole of this form of war finance."

The Fiscal Situation. The situation as regards national expenditures, borrowing and paper currency issues during this period is shown in the following table:

TABLE I. EXPENDITURES, TAX REVENUES, BORROWINGS AND PAPER CURRENCY ISSUES OF REICH, WAR PERIOD
(Billions of Marks)

Fiscal Year Beginning April 1	Expenditures—Ordinary and Extraordinary [a]	Amount of Treasury Bills Discounted at End of Fiscal Year [b]	Total Debt at End of Fiscal Year [a]	Tax Revenues [a] Including Customs	Total Circulation of Paper Currency (Other than Emergency Money) at End of Fiscal Year [c]
1914	9.6	7.2	17.0	1.6	6.6
1915	26.7	8.6	39.9	1.1	8.6
1916	28.8	18.7	69.2	1.4	12.9
1917	53.3	33.4	105.3	3.1	19.5
1918	48.1	63.8	156.5	6.1	37.1 [d]
1919	63.0	91.6	182.9	13.6	59.5

[a] Statistisches Reichsamt, *Statistisches Jahrbuch für das deutsche Reich, passim.*

[b] German Government, *Material for a Study of Germany's Economy, Currency and Finance,* 1924, p. 63.

[c] Statistisches Reichsamt, *Zahlen zur Geldentwertung in Deutschland 1914 bis 1923,* pp. 45 and 46.

[d] At this time the paper money circulation consisted of M25,491 million Reichsbank notes, M11,028 million Darlehnskassenscheine, M353 million Reichskassenscheine, and M279 million private bank notes, *Zahlen zur Geldentwertung in Deutschland 1914 bis 1923,* p. 46.

During the five years covered by the table, the Government's expenditures increased 556 per cent and its total debt 2,910 per cent.

Expansion of Currency and Bank Credit. For this war period the amount of paper money in circulation (exclusive of emergency money) increased 1,274 per cent. In the interpretation of the figures here given the fact should be borne in mind that, at a time like this one of pronounced inflation and rapidly rising prices, the velocities at which money and bank deposits circulate are greatly increased, so that a given volume of money or of bank deposits does more money work than in periods when the monetary unit is not depreciating.[1]

From the end of June, 1914, just prior to the outbreak of the War, to the end of November, 1918, immediately after the Armistice, the amount of Government Treasury and commercial bills discounted and of advances made by the Reichsbank increased (in round numbers) from M1,300,000,000 to M22,100,000,000, and demand deposits of the Reichsbank increased from M858,-000,000 to M10,683,000,000.[2] The gold reserves of the Reichsbank and Darlehnskassen increased from M1,253,000,000 to M2,308,-000,000.[3]

Shortly after the outbreak of the War, there was experienced a shortage of small coin and notes, particularly in connection with the needs of the army. This was met by the issue of an emergency currency, known as "Notgeld," which was continued in increasing volume until long after the close of the War. The notes were covered by a blocked credit for their full amount at the Reichsbank. They were issued in small denominations varying from 5 pfennig to 3 marks, and were put into circulation by a great variety of bodies, over 2,200 in number, including municipalities, districts, banks, Chambers of Commerce and many industrial companies. They soon largely took the place of the fractional coins of silver, nickel and copper, which were early forced out of circulation.[4]

Depreciation of Mark. To what extent did the mark depreciate during the war period? Because of the absence of any free market for gold and of the non-existence of any *de facto* gold standard currency in the world during most of the period, and because of the extent to which prices were controlled in Germany and to which international trade and financial movements were restricted, it is impossible to obtain anything more than a very rough estimate of the fluctuations in the value of the mark.

First, we may consider the value of the mark as measured by

[1] Cf., *infra*, pp. 289, 293.
[2] Young, J. P., *European Currency and Finance*, Vol. I, pp. 526–527.
[3] Statistisches Reichsamt, *Zahlen zur Geldentwertung in Deutschland 1914 bis 1923*, pp. 49 and 51.
[4] Cf., Schacht, *The Stabilization of the Mark*, pp. 24–25.

its purchasing power in the countries adjoining Germany that departed the least from the gold standard during these years.

TABLE II. FLUCTUATIONS IN VALUE OF GERMAN PAPER MARK DURING WAR PERIOD

Calendar Year	(a) Average Value of a "Gold Mark" Abroad in Terms of Paper Marks in Germany [a]		(b) Value of Dutch Guilder as Measured by Its Purchasing Power over Commodities at Wholesale in Holland [b]	(c) Average Price in Paper Marks in Germany of What a Gold Mark Would Have Bought Abroad in 1914 [c]	(d) Wholesale Prices in Germany 1914 = 100 [d]
	(1) Certain European Countries Jan.–July 1914 = 1.00	(2) United States 1914 = 1.00			
1914	1.00	1.00	1.00	1.00	100
1915	1.15	1.14	0.73	1.58	134
1916	1.36	1.29	0.47	2.89	144
1917	1.68	1.54	0.38	4.41	169
1918	1.62	1.41	0.27	6.15	206

[a] Figures represent monthly averages. Those for European countries in Column (a) (1) have been obtained for the year 1914 by taking as a basis the mark exchange in Stockholm, and for 1915 to 1918 the mark exchanges in Zurich and Amsterdam. Computed from monthly figures given in *Material for a Study of Germany's Economy, Currency and Finance*, prepared by the German Government, p. 60. Those for the United States have been adjusted to a 1914 base and are computed from figures given in *Zahlen zur Geldentwertung in Deutschland 1914 bis 1923*, Statistisches Reichsamt, p. 5.

[b] The value of the Dutch guilder as given in this column has been computed from the official index number of wholesale prices in Holland as given in the *Memorandum on Currency and Central Banks*, 1913–1924, Vol. 1, p. 198 (League of Nations).

[c] Inasmuch as the figures given in Column (a) (1) are partly based on Amsterdam exchange and partly on Zurich exchange, it would have been better, were the data available, to compute the figures in Columns (b) and (c) on the same bases of Zurich and Amsterdam, but data were not available for such a computation, so that the figures used are based upon the price indices of Holland alone. The discrepancy is probably not important in a rough estimate like the present one, since throughout the period covered by the table exchange between Switzerland and Amsterdam showed no wide variations. Cf., *Federal Reserve Bulletin*, June, 1919, p. 552.

[d] These index numbers cover 38 commodities. The official figures which are on the 1913 base have been adjusted to the 1914 base. Cf., Young, I, p. 530.

Column (a) shows the value in terms of German paper marks of the amount of gold contained in a gold mark (1) in Holland and Switzerland, and (2) in the United States, on the assumption that the currencies of these three countries were at an approximate parity with gold. Column (b) shows the rate of depreciation in the purchasing power of the Dutch guilder in Holland. And Column (c), on the basis of the figures contained in Columns (a) (1) and (b), shows the average price in terms of paper marks in Germany of the quantity of goods that the gold in a gold mark would have bought in Holland in the year 1914. The figures show a continual depreciation in the external value of the paper mark during the war period, whether that value is measured in terms of gold or in terms of purchasing power abroad. Its purchasing power in Holland in 1918 was approximately one-sixth of what it was in 1914.

Turning from the external value of the paper mark to the internal value, as measured by the movements of the wholesale prices of the 38 commodities covered by the German Government's index number, we find a rise in the price level from 100 to 206, registering a depreciation in the internal value of the paper mark of a little over one-half. During the war period, therefore, the mark maintained its value at home much better than abroad—a situation that will be found to apply during most of the subsequent history of inflation, and which existed in other countries with inflated currencies during the War and the early post-war years.[1]

Retail Prices, Rents and Wages. Little information of a quantitative character can be given concerning the movements of retail prices, rents and wages during the war period; but there is considerable useful information concerning these movements for the latter years of the inflation. Although there do not exist any comprehensive index numbers for retail prices [2] or rents in Germany for the war years, it is clear that the movements in these items, which became pronounced when inflation later assumed extreme forms, had their beginnings in the war years of moderate inflation and in the main were different from the later movements more in degree than in kind.

The table on page 279, showing the movements of real wages—that is, wages in terms of purchasing power over the cost of living—for a few groups of laborers and government officials during the war period will give a rough suggestion of what probably happened to the earnings of other groups of working people.

It will be noted that every class of labor suffered heavily in its earnings during this period. Each class had received substantial increases in money wages, but for no class was the increase sufficient to compensate for the rise in the cost of living.

[1] For valuable discussions of this subject, and of the concept of "purchasing power parity" which is involved, see, Young, J. P., *European Currency and Finance*, Vol. I, pp. 36–39, 411–417; and Graham, Frank D., *Exchange, Prices, and Production in Hyper-Inflation: Germany, 1920–1923*, Chaps. 4, 5 and 6.

[2] The average retail price of rye bread in Berlin rose 69 per cent from 1914 to 1918, and that of shoulder of beef rose 146 per cent. Statistisches Reichsamt, *Zahlen zur Geldentwertung in Deutschland 1914 bis 1923*, p. 34.

TABLE III. MOVEMENTS OF REAL WAGES OF CERTAIN CLASSES OF LABOR DURING WAR PERIOD[1]

1913 = 100

Calendar Year	Industrial Laborers in Gov't Railway Service		Miners and Mine Helpers in Ruhr Region	Printers	Officials of Nat'l Gov't—(Married)		
	Skilled	Unskilled			High Class	Middle Class	Subordinate Class
1913	100	100	100	100	100	100	100
1914	97	97	93	97	97	97	97
1915	80	81	81	77	77	77	77
1916	69	74	74	61	59	59	59
1917	64	74	63	49	43	49	54
1918	83	100	64	54	47	55	70

The drafting of men into military service and the feverish demand for war supplies increased the demand for labor and reduced the volume of unemployment; but inflation cut deeply into the earnings of the laboring classes. Skilled labor was in relatively less demand than unskilled and its real wages fell more rapidly. The real wages of government officials showed a great decline, and the higher the class of the officials, the greater was the rate of decline.

Government Control of Prices and Rents. The lag in the rise of retail prices and rents as compared with wholesale prices under wartime inflation was in part due to the Government's efforts to restrain advances in the cost of living—efforts which are described by Dr. Schacht as follows: [2]

> "On August 4, 1914, the first legislation was passed for the control of prices, the Government being empowered to fix maximum prices in the case of certain commodities, notably food and fodder stuffs, raw materials and heating and lighting materials, with penalties for exceeding the limits fixed. This measure was followed by a number of others giving the Government the right to commandeer for its own purposes stocks of every kind, with the inevitable result that commodities were held back and concealed as much as possible, making new measures of compulsion necessary. The control and the penalties had continually to be made more severe. Smuggling became more and more prevalent and necessitated fresh counter-measures."

Not only were the prices of many articles fixed officially during the War at rates far below what they otherwise would have been in

[1] These figures (which are given to the nearest percentage) represent the purchasing power of the money wages paid, calculated on the basis of a rough cost of living index. Statistisches Reichsamt, *Zahlen zur Geldentwertung in Deutschland 1914 bis 1923*, pp. 40, 41 and 43.

[2] Schacht, *The Stabilization of the Mark*, p. 20.

a free market, but the supplies of the goods themselves were rationed to the public.[1] House rents were controlled and tenants were protected from eviction if they paid the rents that were fixed by governmental authorities, rents that were raised slowly as inflation progressed, but which always lagged far behind the rate at which the mark had depreciated.

The Early Post-War Period

The second, or early post-war, period of Germany's inflation history may be passed over briefly. According to the division we have made of the period covered by German inflation, this second period extended from the Armistice until April 27, 1921, when the Reparations Commission gave the people of Germany a terrific shock by fixing the amount of Germany's indebtedness at the staggering sum of 132 billion gold marks. Shortly after the spring of 1921, the mark entered upon a rapidly accelerating rate of depreciation.

This was a period of small crops, great economic and political disorganization, and of business depression. The political events in Germany for these two and a half years were of greater significance than the economic. They included the signing of the Treaty of Versailles on June 28, 1919, which, among the many penalties it imposed, deprived Germany of all her colonies and of about 10 per cent of her European territory and 13 per cent of her population in Europe. It called upon Germany to pay to the Allies damages to an amount subsequently to be determined by a Reparations Commission, and provided that "in order to enable the allied and associated Powers to proceed at once to the restoration of their industrial and economic life, pending the full determination of their claims, Germany shall pay . . . during 1919, 1920, and the first four months of 1921, the equivalent of 20,000,000,000 gold marks." This period also covered the establishment of the German Republic, the adoption of the Weimar Constitution, the First Brussels Conference, the Spa Conference, the dispute between Germany and the Allies over the coal deliveries demanded of Germany and over the alleged failure of Germany to meet other payments which were required by the Treaty, with the accompanying threat of "sanctions," including that of occupying further German territory.

[1] The principal foodstuffs would doubtless have been rationed even had there been no inflation, for during this period there was an actual shortage due in large part to causes other than inflation.

Volume of Fiscal Operations of the Government and Paper Money Issues. Table IV which follows shows for these early post-war years the volume of government expenditures, government debt and paper money circulation. The figures are comparable with those given in Table I (p. 275) for the war period.

TABLE IV. EXPENDITURES, TAX REVENUES, BORROWINGS AND PAPER CURRENCY ISSUES OF REICH, 1919–1921
(Billions of Marks)

Fiscal Year Beginning April 1	Expenditures—Ordinary and Extraordinary [a]	Amount of Treasury Bills Discounted at End of Fiscal Year [b]	Total Debt at End of Fiscal Year [a]	Tax Revenues [a] Including Customs	Total Circulation of Paper Currency (Other than Emergency Money) at End of Fiscal Year [c]
1919	63	92	183	13.6	59
1920	145	166	249	39.6	80
1921	299	272	338	80.2	140

[a] Statistisches Reichsamt, *Statistisches Jahrbuch für das deutsche Reich, passim.*
[b] German Government, *Material for Study of Germany's Economy, Currency and Finance,* 1924, p. 63.
[c] Statistisches Reichsamt, *Zahlen zur Geldentwertung in Deutschland 1914 bis 1923,* p. 46.

A reference to the table will show that discounts of Treasury bills at the Reichsbank and other public debt flotations continued the strong upward movement that characterized the war period, and that the same was true of the paper money circulation. While the figures showing these increases appeared large at the time, they seem very small as we view them today in comparison with the astronomical figures required to express in terms of paper money the fiscal operations of the next period.

Although the Government during these early post-war years continued to depend for its income to a large extent on borrowing, it placed much more reliance upon taxes than during the war period. The new Republican Government from the beginning enacted measures for increasing tax revenues. While it continued and even increased many of the excise taxes on consumption that had been imposed during the latter years of the War, it now paid particular attention to direct taxes. A Federal Tax Administration under the new Constitution was provided for in 1919. In July of that year customs duties were placed on a gold basis, an extraordinary tax levy had been imposed on corporations and a heavy tax had been laid on war profits. During the year a turnover tax and a special capital levy had been decreed. Under Finance Minister Erzberger the tax system was thoroughly revised early in 1920, rates were increased, and the control of taxation was largely taken from the States and given to the Federal Government. Calculated on the cost of living index, 36 per cent of the government revenues for the fiscal year 1920–1921 were received in the form of taxes.[1]

The following table covers material similar to that given for the war period in Table II (p. 277). It shows the movements in the value of the paper mark during the early post-war period as they are expressed in the mark prices in Germany of gold in the United States, in the mark prices in Germany of goods in the American market and in the mark prices of goods in Germany. In other words, it shows the changes in the "external" and the "internal" value of the mark, as they are expressed through price movements in Germany and the United States and exchange rates between Berlin and New York.

Table V. Fluctuations in Value of German Paper Mark During Early Post-War Period, 1918–1921

	(a)	(b)	(c) External Value of Mark		(d) Internal Value of Mark	
			1	2	3	4
Calendar Year	Average Value of Gold Content of Mark in U. S. in Terms of Paper Marks in Germany[a] 1914 = 1.00	Average Value of Gold Content of Mark in U. S. as Measured by Purchasing Power of Gold Dollar over Commodities at Wholesale[b] 1914 = 1.00	Average Price in Paper Marks of What Gold Content of a Mark Would Have Bought at Wholesale in U. S. in 1914 1914 = 1.00	Relative Value of Paper Mark (Reciprocal of Preceding Column)	Wholesale Prices in Germany 1914 = 1.00	Relative Value of Paper Mark in Germany (Reciprocal of Preceding Column)
1918	1.407	.520	2.7	.37	2.1	.48
1919	4.725	.492	9.4	.11	3.9	.25
1920	14.760	.445	33.2	.03	31.6	.032
1921	24.500	.701	35.0	.029	33.3	.03

[a] Cf., Statistisches Reichsamt, *Zahlen zur Geldentwertung in Deutschland 1914 bis 1923*, p. 5.
[b] Based on Bureau of Labor Statistics Index Number of Wholesale Prices.

Starting with the Armistice year 1918, we find that the price of gold in the United States in terms of German paper marks rose continually through these four years and was over 17 times as

[1] German Government, *Material for a Study of Germany's Economy, Currency and Finance*, p. 30.

high in 1921 as in 1918; and that, while the mark price of gold was thus rising rapidly, the value of gold itself (as measured by its purchasing power over commodities in the United States) was itself continually changing, having declined moderately from 1918 to 1920, and then advanced substantially in 1921. If one considers the value of the gold mark in 1914 (as measured by its purchasing power) as 100 pfennig, both in the United States and in Germany, its relative values in terms of the pfennig of 1914, during the years 1918 to 1921, respectively, would be for the external market, as shown in Column (c) (2) and for the German internal market as shown in Column (d) (2). Abroad the paper mark was worth 37 pfennig in 1918 and 2.9 pfennig in 1921, and at home it was worth 48 pfennig in 1918 and 3 pfennig in 1921. Its depreciation abroad was always greater during this period than at home, although the difference was slight during the last two years.

The Cost of Living. As during the war period, retail prices in general, rent and most other items entering directly into the cost of living lagged behind wholesale prices on the rise. Index numbers covering these items are not available for the years 1918 and 1919; but they are available for a number of them for eleven months of the year 1920 and for all the year 1921. In the following table the more important of the available figures are summarized and brought into comparison with the wholesale price figures for the same period.

TABLE VI. CHANGES IN COST OF LIVING IN GERMANY [1]
1913–1914 = 1.00

Calendar Year	Food, Heat, Light, Clothing and House Rent	Food	Clothing	Rent	Cost of Living (Exclusive of Rent)	Wholesale Prices
1920 Feb.–Dec.	10.4	12.3	18.8	1.8	13.1	15.1
1921	13.4	16.0	22.3	2.1	16.8	19.1

It will be noted that the cost of living in general (Column 1) increased from 1914 to 1921 over thirteen-fold, but that the item of house rent only slightly more than doubled. Clothing, for which raw materials like cotton and wool were imported, in general rose considerably faster than food. The slow rates of advance for rents

[1] Computed from figures given in Statistisches Reichsamt, *Zahlen zur Geldentwertung in Deutschland 1914 bis 1923*, pp. 5 and 33.

and food are to be explained largely by the continuation of the policy of governmental control of rents and of the prices of some of the more important classes of food which was inaugurated during the War.[1]

Wages. Money wages during this period continued to advance rapidly, but in different classes of labor very unequally and irregularly, while the cost of living likewise, as we have seen, moved strongly upward. The results, as regards real wages in the few wage groups for which figures are available, are shown in the following table, in which the data covered by Table III (p. 279) are extended through 1921.

TABLE VII. MOVEMENTS OF REAL WAGES OF CERTAIN CLASSES OF LABOR DURING EARLY POST-WAR PERIOD[2]

1913 = 100

Calendar Year	Industrial Laborers in Gov't Railway Service		Miners and Mine Helpers in Ruhr Region	Printers	Officials of Nat'l Gov't—(Married)		
	Skilled	Unskilled			High Class	Middle Class	Subordinate Class
1918	83.3	99.8	63.7	54.1	46.8	55.0	69.6
1919	92.2	119.8	82.4	72.3	40.2	54.8	89.3
1920	66.7	89.1	77.6	60.8	31.7	43.9	71.3
1921	74.5	100.0	89.1	68.9	39.3	52.2	98.8

The practically continuous decline in real wages that characterized the war period came to an abrupt halt with the end of the War. In every wage group mentioned the year 1918 showed a rise, and in all but the groups of high- and middle-class government officials the year 1919 showed a very substantial further rise. The real wages for every group declined sharply in 1920 and then rose again in 1921. Every group except the unskilled laborers in the railway service and the lowest grade of government officials was substantially worse off in 1921 than it was at the beginning of the War and the group that suffered by far the most was that of the highest class of government officials.

Unemployment. Labor during this period was on the whole about as fully employed as it was immediately preceding the War,

[1] Compare *supra*, pp. 279–280. From 1913 to November 1921 street car fares in Berlin increased ten-fold, third-class railway passenger fares in Germany six-and-a-half-fold, railway freight rates in general nearly fifteen-fold, and postage six-fold. Statistisches Reichsamt, *Zahlen zur Geldentwertung in Deutschland 1914 bis 1923*, pp. 36 and 37.

[2] This table is a continuation of Table III (p. 279) and the sources of the data there cited were used here.

according to the statistics of unemployment furnished by the trade unions. Of the 1920 situation the International Labour Office at Geneva said:

> " . . . as the relief granted to unemployed during that same year was considerably higher than before the war, the effects of unemployment on the aggregate income of the industrial population must have been much the same in these two periods. In 1921 the percentage of unemployment was practically the same as that recorded before the war." [1]

While the year 1920 in Germany was on the whole a year of disorganization, the country suffered no such economic collapse as did the United States, England and France under the influence of the great post-war deflation of that year.

The Latter Post-War Period of Inflation

We now come to the last period of German inflation. It began in the spring of 1921 with the fixing of German reparations at 132 billion gold marks and ended with the rentenmark stabilization which became effective about the end of 1923. In contrast with the preceding two periods in which the inflation was more or less orderly and controlled, inflation during the greater part of this period was wild and it finally assumed proportions never before known in the world's monetary history. This was a period in which the economic and financial life of Germany was dominated by the pressure of her erstwhile enemies, to exact from her a preposterous amount of reparations, a pressure which reached its extreme form in the occupation of the Ruhr by French and Belgian troops in January, 1923. This period witnessed the Second and Third London Conferences, the unfavorable Report to the Reparations Commission of the Committee of foreign experts and bankers to consider a foreign loan to Germany, and the Report of the Committee of foreign private experts called by Germany to make recommendations on the stabilization of the mark. The end of the period saw the making of the definitive arrangements for the Dawes Committee and the McKenna Committee of foreign experts, to study and report on the subjects of the balancing of the German budget and the stabilization of the currency, and to investigate the amount of German capital exported and possible methods of bringing it back.

[1] International Labour Office, *The Workers Standard of Life in Countries with Depreciated Currency*, pp. 20–22.

This period is so short and during it inflation progressed so rapidly that, in so far as the figures are available, the quantitative data concerning it are better presented by months than by years.

Volume of Government's Fiscal Operations. First, we may examine the movement of government expenditures, government indebtedness and tax revenues, extending through 1923 the annual figures given for the years 1914–1921 in Tables I and IV.[1]

TABLE VIII. EXPENDITURES, TAX REVENUES AND BORROWINGS OF REICH, FISCAL YEARS 1921–1923
(Billions of Marks)

Fiscal Year Beginning April 1	Expenditures —Ordinary and Extraordinary [a]	Amount of Treasury Bills Discounted by Reichsbank at End of Fiscal Year [b]	Total Debt End of Fiscal Year [a]	Tax Revenues Including Customs [c]
1921	299	272	338	80
1922	8,294	6,601	6,661	913
1923	48,725,711	191,580,465,422 [d]	2,630,000,000,000 [e]	5,057

[a] *Statistisches Jahrbuch*, 1923, pp. 356–357.
[b] German Government, *Material for a Study of Germany's Economy, Currency and Finance*, p. 63.
[c] *Statistisches Jahrbuch*, 1923, pp. 351–352.
[d] This figure is for November 15, 1923, the latest date in the fiscal year 1923 for which these data are available in terms of the old marks.
[e] This is the debt as of the end of the fiscal year 1923 (March 31, 1924), expressed in terms of the old marks at the official rate of conversion of a trillion to one.

The stupendous growth of Germany's expenditures during this period from approximately 300 billion paper marks in 1921 to nearly 49 quadrillion marks in 1923 was, to a large extent, due to the expense of financing "passive resistance" in the Ruhr and to the reparations payments Germany was required to make under the Treaty of Versailles. The payments were made by the Government mostly in gold, foreign currency credit and goods.

The gold itself and the bank notes and other bank credit used for buying foreign currency, for buying other gold and for buying the goods were obtained largely from the Reichsbank by means of loans. The gold withdrawn directly from the Reichsbank reduced its gold reserves, and the balance of the loans obtained by the Government from the Reichsbank took the form chiefly of Reichsbank note issues. Broadly speaking, the more the Government borrowed, the larger the note issues, and the larger the note issues, the higher the price of the gold, of the foreign currencies and of

[1] *Supra*, pp. 275 and 281. The figures for circulation of paper currency given in these preceding tables are not included here, but are given in greater detail in Table IX, p. 288.

the goods the Government was required to deliver to the Allies; while the higher the prices of these means of making reparations payments, the more the Government needed to borrow and the larger the volume of Reichsbank notes issued. Although undoubtedly Germany would have inflated her currency substantially during these years, even had there been no heavy reparation charges—economic rehabilitation in the unsettled economic and political conditions of the time would have forced it—there is no question but that the enormous proportions which the inflation of these years assumed were, to a large extent, due to the demands for reparations payments.

Paper Money Circulation and Gold Reserves. The increase in the volume of the paper money circulation and the changes in its gold value, together with the changes in the gold reserves, are shown in the table on page 288.

These figures will be considered primarily with reference to their relationship to the contemporary movements of prices and wages shown in the next table (Table X), and the interpretation of them will, therefore, be postponed largely until later. In passing, however, a few significant facts may be noted.

The volume of the circulation did not run away wildly until about the time of the Ruhr occupation at the beginning of 1923, when Germany became desperate. The trillion magnitude was reached in December, 1922, the quadrillion in September, 1923 and the quintillion in October.

From February, 1921 to November, 1922, the gold value of the total amount of paper money in circulation, as measured by exchange rates in Berlin on New York, or by the purchasing power parity with the United States, fell almost continually. After November, 1922, it moved irregularly, but by December, 1923, when the volume of the circulation was at its maximum of 496.6 quintillion marks, the gold value stood at next to the lowest figure of any month for the three years. Here we see the phenomenon of so-called "hyper-inflation"—a phenomenon frequently found in other countries that have had heavy inflation [1]—where the value of the total volume of paper money in circulation becomes less and less as the volume increases. As measured by Berlin-

[1] For another interesting case of hyper-inflation, see the account of the Russian war-time experience given by S. S. Katzenellenbaum in his *Russian Currency and Banking, 1914–1924*, pp. 94–97.

Table IX. Volume of Paper Money in Circulation, Its Total Gold Value, and Gold Reserves
Calendar Years 1921–1923

Month	[a] Paper-Money Circulation (Billions of Marks)	[b] Average Exchange Rates Berlin–New York (Cents per Mark)	[c] Gold Value of Circulation on Basis of Exchange Rates ($000)	[d] Gold Value of Paper Money Circulation on Basis of Purchasing Power Parities [g] ($000)	[e] Gold Reserves of Reichsbank and Darlehnskassen Gold Marks ($000)
1921					
Jan.	78.5	1.60	1,256,000	2,206,000	1,091.6
Feb.	79.7	1.64	1,307,000	2,201,000	1,091.6
March	80.1	1.60	1,281,500	2,211,000	1,091.6
April	80.9	1.57	1,270,000	2,146,000	1,091.6
May	81.4	1.63	1,327,000	2,151,000	1,091.6
June	84.6	1.44	1,218,000	2,089,500	1,091.6
July	86.3	1.30	1,122,000	2,028,000	1,091.6
Aug.	88.4	1.19	1,052,000	1,557,000	1,023.7
Sept.	94.5	0.96	906,400	1,531,000	1,023.7
Oct.	99.4	0.68	676,000	1,362,000	993.6
Nov.	108.8	0.39	424,300	1,067,000	993.7
Dec.	122.5	0.53	649,200	1,176,000	995.4
1922					
Jan.	123.9	0.52	644,200	1,120,000	995.7
Feb.	128.5	0.48	617,400	1,058,000	996.4
March	140.0	0.36	504,000	866,000	996.9
April	150.2	0.35	526,150	813,000	1,000.9
May	162.0	0.34	550,800	891,000	1,002.9
June	180.2	0.32	576,600	919,000	1,003.9
July	202.6	0.20	405,200	730,000	1,004.9
Aug.	252.2	0.10	252,200	479,000	1,004.9
Sept.	331.9	0.07	232,350	431,000	1,004.9
Oct.	484.7	0.03	145,400	291,000	1,004.9
Nov.	769.5	0.01	76,950	246,000	1,004.8
Dec.	1,295.2	0.01	129,520	324,000	1,004.8
1923					
Jan.	T [f] 1,999.6	0.007	140,000	264,900	1,004.8
Feb.	T 3,536.3	0.004	141,400	235,100	1,004.8
March	T 5,542.9	0.005	277,300	427,200	1,004.8
April	T 6,581.2	0.004	263,300	475,600	910.0
May	T 8,609.7	0.002	172,200	389,400	757.9
June	T 17,340.5	0.001	173,400	325,000	716.9
July	T 43,813.5	0.000,300	131,400	209,700	596.4
Aug.	T 668,702.6	0.000,033,900	226,700	253,200	510.5
Sept.	Q [f] 28,244,405.8	0.000,001,880	531,400	432,400	443.9
Oct.	Quin. [f] 2,504,955,700.0	0.000,000,068	170,300	128,300	467.0
Nov.	" 400,338,326,400.0	0.000,000,000,143	172,100	199,700	467.0
Dec.	" 496,585,345,900.0	0.000,000,000,023	114,200	141,600	467.0 [h]

[a] These figures are taken from Statistisches Reichsamt, *Zahlen zur Geldentwertung in Deutschland 1914 bis 1923*, pp. 45–47. They include Reichsbank notes, Darlehnskassenscheine, Reichskassenscheine, and the notes of private banks, about 8/9 of the total consisting of Reichsbank notes in 1921. After that year the proportion of the above-mentioned notes other than Reichsbank notes was negligible. The figures do not include Notgeld or any of the so-called "stable currencies."

[b] Young, *European Currency and Finance*, I, pp. 537–538.

[c] This column gives in terms of U. S. dollars the value of the total paper mark circulation shown in Column (1), converted at the average exchange rate given in Column (2).

[d] This column has been calculated by raising the figures under the caption given by Young which cover only Reichsbank note circulation by the percentage which the paper money circulation referred to in the first column exceeds the Reichsbank note circulation. The difference is negligible after 1922.

[e] Statistisches Reichsamt, *Zahlen zur Geldentwertung in Deutschland 1914 bis 1923*, p. 53.

[f] The *T* is for trillion, *Q* for quadrillion, and *Quin.* for quintillion, the letters designating the magnitude of the highest digits; thus the volume of paper money circulation for October, 1923 is 2 quintillion, 504 quadrillion, etc.

[g] "Purchasing power parities" here express the ratio of the price level in the United States to the price level in Germany, related to a given base year, and expressed in terms of the gold par of exchange between the mark and the dollar; thus, $\frac{\text{Index Number, U.S.A.} \times \$0.2382}{\text{Index Number, Germany}}$.

[h] Figure is for November 15.

New York exchange rates, for example, the 79.7 billion paper marks in circulation in February, 1921 were worth 1,307 million dollars, while the 496.6 quintillion paper marks in circulation in December, 1923 were worth less than one-eleventh as much—namely, 114.2 million dollars.

This extreme rate of depreciation is explainable largely by the increasing velocity of circulation. The money supply of a country, as previously explained (pp. 32 and 51–62), is a question not only of the number of units in circulation, but also of the rates or velocities at which the money circulates. When the mark began to depreciate rapidly because the public lost faith in it, the velocity of circulation was sped up. Everyone wanted to convert his money into goods and services as soon as possible, because its value rapidly faded away while he held it. Dr. Hjalmar Schacht describes this situation, as it existed in 1922, as follows:

> "The rush to get rid of cash as soon as possible further led to an extraordinary increase in the rapidity of the circulation of money. Everyone who had payments to make, endeavoured to make them as quickly as possible, before he could be caught by the depreciation. . . . Clearing (Giro) transactions were immensely extended at the expense of cash transactions, which were too slow. . . . The one idea was to dispose of them [the bank balances] as speedily as possible. Thus the State, the entrepreneur, and the private individual were all engaged in the struggle, each for himself, to escape the terrors of the inflation . . ." [1]

An investigation made at the Reichsbank showed that, at the end of 1922, assuming 40 days as the approximate average tenure of bills discounted at the Reichsbank, the proceeds of such bills were used on an average during that 40-day period for 75 payments.[2] Compare this with the average *annual* velocity of circulation of demand deposits of 141 leading cities in the United States for the year 1922 of 46.

Another fact worthy of mention here is, that, although the gold reserve of the Reichsbank and the Darlehnskassen tended downward during practically the entire three years and was less than half as much at the end of the period as at the beginning, the gold reserve in October and November, 1923 had a gold value between two and three times the gold value of all the paper money in circulation which it was supposed to support. In November, 1922 this ratio had reached a peak of 13 to 1.

[1] Schacht, *The Stabilization of the Mark*, pp. 68–69.
[2] *Ibid.*, p. 75.

Prices, Rents and Wages. We now turn to an examination of the effects of the extreme inflation during this period on prices, rents and wages. In a broad and general way, these effects are shown in the following chart [1] and table.

INFLATION IN GERMANY

EXCHANGE RATE OF THE MARK, WHOLESALE PRICES AND VOLUME OF CIRCULATING MEDIUM, JAN., 1914–DEC., 1923

Index Numbers, 1913 = 1

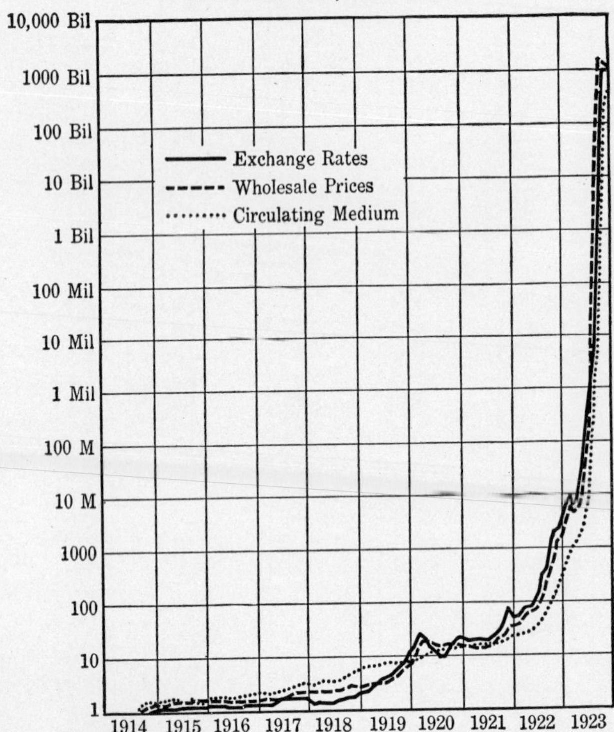

For the entire period up to September, 1923, the wholesale price index number lagged behind the mark price of dollar exchange on the rise. In other words, for these thirty months, the mark depreciated more rapidly abroad in terms of gold than at home

[1] The chart, it will be observed, is drawn on a ratio scale, in which an equal vertical space is always given to the same percentage movement. For example, a 10 per cent rise from 10 to 11 covers an equal space with a 10 per cent rise from ten billion to eleven billion. Were the scale plotted on an arithmetic instead of a ratio scale, with the vertical distance from 1 to 10 that is used, the chart would have to be 560 thousand miles high to carry the figures for December, 1923.

TABLE X. MOVEMENTS OF PRICES, COST OF LIVING AND WAGES IN GERMANY DURING PERIOD OF GREATEST INFLATION, 1921–1923 [1]

Month	Wholesale Prices 1913 = 1	Cost of Living 1913 = 1	Wages: Government Industrial Laborers: Skilled 1913 = 1	Wages: Government Industrial Laborers: Unskilled 1913 = 1	Wages: Higher Government Officials	Prices of Stocks 1913 = 1
1921						
Jan.	14.4	11.8	8.5	11.4	4.3	2.8
Feb.	13.8	11.5	8.5	11.4	4.3	2.6
March	13.4	11.4	8.5	11.4	4.3	2.6
April	13.3	11.3	8.5	11.4	4.3	2.7
May	13.1	11.2	8.5	11.4	4.3	2.8
June	13.7	11.7	8.5	11.4	4.3	3.0
July	14.3	12.5	8.5	11.4	4.3	3.4
Aug.	19.2	13.3	9.9	13.4	4.9	3.9
Sept.	20.7	13.7	9.9	13.4	4.9	4.9
Oct.	24.6	15.0	14.0	18.8	8.1	6.4
Nov.	34.2	17.7	14.0	18.8	8.1	9.4
Dec.	34.9	19.3	14.0	18.8	8.1	7.3
1922						
Jan.	36.6	20.4	15.1	20.3	8.3	7.4
Feb.	41.1	24.5	15.1	20.3	8.3	8.4
March	54.3	29.0	15.1	20.3	8.3	9.9
April	63.5	34.4	21.8	29.9	10.2	10.2
May	64.6	38.0	28.3	38.4	13.1	8.7
June	70.3	41.5	33.9	46.2	16.0	8.2
July	100.6	53.9	41.8	56.9	20.1	9.0
Aug.	192.0	77.6	62.1	85.3	30.6	11.6
Sept.	287.0	133.2	117.7	161.4	58.4	12.6
Oct.	566.0	220.7	138.3	190.6	80.0	20.6
Nov.	1,151.0	446.1	241.7	333.2	137.7	50.7
Dec.	1,474.8	685.1	400.0	553.9	227.8	89.8
1923						
Jan.	2,785	1,120	643.8	890.1	372.6	224
Feb.	5,585	2,643	1,343.1	1,857.2	783.2	452
March	4,888	2,854	1,678.8	2,321.5	979.1	336
April	5,212	2,954	1,678.8	2,321.5	979.1	502
May	8,170	3,816	2,283.7	3,152.9	1,365.2	951
June	19,385	7,650	6,002.4	8,293.2	3,421.1	3,520
July	74,787	37,651	24,870	34,492	14,227	13,493
Aug.	944,041	586,045	577,836	799,156	285,576	124,743
	Millions	Millions	Millions	Millions	Millions	Millions
Sept.	23.9	15.0	12.0	16.6	6.9	5.3
	Billions	Billions	Billions	Billions	Billions	Billions
Oct.	7.1	3.7	5.7	7.8	1.6	1.7
Nov.	725.7	657.0	315.0	402.2	162.6	236.8
Dec.	1,261.6	1,247.0	694.4	789.9	509.0	268.9

[1] The figures given in this table are taken from Statistisches Reichsamt, *Zahlen zur Geldentwertung in Deutschland 1914 bis 1923*, p. 5.

in terms of commodities. During this period, except the early months of 1921, the value of gold was fairly stable in the gold markets of the world and the purchasing power parity of the mark was continually above the mark's foreign exchange value.[1] The last four months of 1923, however, showed a more rapid depreciation of the mark at home than abroad. Foreigners at this time apparently had more confidence in the mark than the Germans themselves had.

The rates at which wholesale prices rose for different groups of commodities, e.g., agricultural products, minerals and manufactured products, varied widely, as likewise did the rates of different commodities within the respective groups. This is a large subject, however, and the limits of space will not permit a further discussion of it here.[2]

The cost of living index, covering food, house rent, heat, light and clothing, continually lagged behind wholesale prices as the mark depreciated, and the extent of the lag which was modest at the beginning became large in the latter part of 1921 and continued large until approximately the time of the rentenmark stabilization of 1923, when it quickly disappeared. During the last year and a half of this period of "runaway inflation," house rents, which continued to be held down and rigidly controlled by governmental authority, became negligible in the working man's budget. It is doubtful, however, if working men gained much by this practical elimination from their budget of an item which normally constituted 10 to 15 per cent of their expenditures. The reason is that wage scales at the time were pressing strongly on the minimum of subsistence—an exemplification of the old "iron law of wages"—with the result that "as the cost of housing was gradually reduced, the part of wages intended to cover this expenditure similarly disappeared."[3]

Velocities of Circulation. As the cost of living rose, or, in other words, as the mark depreciated, at phenomenal rates, the public madly rushed to spend their money as rapidly as possible, in order to avoid seeing the little value it still had fade away in their hands. A friend of mine who lived in Berlin during the latter years of the

[1] Cf., Young, J. P., I, pp. 534–535.

[2] For detailed figures on this subject, cf., Statistisches Reichsamt, *Zahlen zur Geldentwertung in Deutschland 1914 bis 1923*, pp. 23–32.

[3] International Labour Office, *The Workers Standard of Life in Countries with Depreciated Currency*, Geneva, 1925, p. 36.

inflation told of the following personal experience in buying a pair of shoes. The price quoted by the dealer at half-past nine in the morning was M3,250,000 a pair. About noon the dealer asked M7,000,000, and half an hour later M14,000,000; but after a rather vigorous protest he sold for M7,000,000. At times when the mark was depreciating most rapidly, people in their desperate efforts "to save something from the wreck" often bought goods they did not need. Such goods were at least safer to hold than money, and it frequently happened that people could not buy the things they really wanted quickly enough to save themselves. Commenting on a similar situation at about this time in Austria, while the crown was depreciating precipitately, de Bordes says:

> "On days when there was a sharp rise in prices there would be a run on the shops. Prices would then increase from hour to hour, and the public were content to buy whatever they could lay their hands on. On such days one could witness 'those ludicrous scenes in which some old bachelor would be seen buying swaddling clothes, because the local shop had no other wares left for sale, or another would invest in four dozen toothbrushes simply to get rid of his money by some means or other.' "[1]

It was this speeding up of the velocities of the circulation of money and of deposits at the banks that explains the rather unusual situation discussed by Graham; that is, the general tendency up to the last few months of the post-war inflation for wholesale prices to advance more rapidly than the volume of the circulating medium itself.[2]

As we have seen, money depreciates when the supply of money and deposit currency increases relatively to the demand; and the supply varies not only with the number of units of the medium of exchange in circulation, but also with the velocities at which these units circulate. When, as a result of excessive issues, people once lose faith in their money, they "drop it" at progressively increasing rates or velocities, with the result that prices rise faster than the increase in the volume of the circulating medium itself. The public in anticipating further rises in prices virtually discounts in advance prospectively increased issues of paper money and circulating bank credit, and this discounting is expressed in increased velocities. Speaking of this situation in Germany, as it existed after the summer of 1921, Graham says:[3]

[1] de Bordes, J. van Walré, *The Austrian Crown*, p. 163.

[2] Compare Graham, *op. cit.*, pp. 146–173.

[3] *Ibid.*, pp. 163 and 115.

"The volume of circulating medium again caught up with internal prices in mid-1921 but thereafter lagged far in the rear. The acceleration in the rate of monetary turnover increased prices relative to the volume of circulating medium, the rising prices gave a further fillip to the rate of monetary turnover, this again affected prices, and so on. . . . [None the less] while the cause and effect relationship of rate of monetary turnover and prices is one of interaction, and while prices therefore do not respond in nice symmetry with the volume of circulating medium, there can be no doubt that the ultimate causal sequence runs from volume of money to prices."

Wages. Unfortunately, the wage statistics available for this period are very meager and offer at best an opportunity for "sampling." The figures cover wages for skilled and unskilled labor in the employment of the Imperial Government, and the salaries of the higher administrative officials of the Reich.

The salaries of the higher government officials throughout the entire period lagged far behind the cost of living on the rise, and their "real wages" for the last four months of 1923 varied roughly between one-fourth and one-half of what they were in 1913. The wages of skilled labor lagged substantially behind the cost of living until August, 1923, when they nearly caught up. At the end of 1923 the real wages of this group were only a little over half what they were in 1913. As for the previous period, the evidence is, that unskilled labor fared much better than skilled labor. Wages of unskilled labor and the cost of living advanced something like *paripassu* throughout the years 1921 and 1922. During the first five months of 1923, the wages of this group lagged moderately behind the cost of living, while during the last seven months of the year the wage index number was higher than the cost of living index number in four months and lower in three. By and large, therefore, it may be said, that, from the standpoint of wages alone, unskilled labor probably did not suffer during the last three years of the inflation. This favorable position of unskilled labor, however, as compared with skilled labor, was in part one of the social effects of the Revolution itself.

Germany suffered no such catastrophic decline in business during the latter half of 1920 and the first half of 1921 as did the United States under the influence of the great post-war gold standard deflation of these months, and labor in Germany, therefore, did not suffer at that time from unemployment to anything like the extent that it did in the United States. Unemployment, however, became much greater beginning about October, 1923.

The International Labour Office of the League of Nations, after citing figures for yearly averages of percentages of unemployment among trade unions for the years 1912–1924, says:

> " . . . during the period 1920–1922 the intensity of unemployment was not widely different from that which existed before the war. . . . In 1923 unemployment assumed much greater proportions. During the first half of the year the percentage of totally unemployed among trade unionists was not very high as yet, but for several months those partially unemployed represented about one-quarter of the membership. It was in the autumn that the crisis developed with full intensity, a quarter of the members being totally unemployed, and more than a third and sometimes even one-half on short time." [1]

One important reason why wages lagged behind prices to such an extent on the rise was the fact that the wage scales for a large percentage of laborers in Germany were fixed for definite periods of time, by agreements between employees and employers that were made at varying intervals.[2] The tendency, therefore, was for wages to remain fixed during the period covered by the wage agreement, while during that period prices were continually rising. To meet this difficulty, laborers demanded a progressive shortening of the period to be covered by wage agreements, and these demands were met, although with considerable resistance on the part of employers. The shorter the period, however, the more frequent were the disputes over wage agreements, the larger the number of strikes and lockouts, and the greater the uncertainty of entrepreneurs over labor costs. When inflation was at its worst, prices rose so rapidly that the depreciation of wages was greater even over these short periods than it had previously been over the longer ones.

[1] International Labour Office, *The Workers Standard of Life in Countries with Depreciated Currency*, pp. 21 and 22.

[2] "In the early post-war years the development of a system of regulation of the relations between employer and employed had brought the great majority of workers within the scope of agreements set up by collective bargaining between the organizations of employer and employee. The Minister of Labor might at any time declare such agreements compulsory upon the whole industry to which they applied. The progressive depreciation of the currency required constant revision of the wage clauses of these agreements and led to elaboration of the machinery of adjustment along certain well-defined lines.

"The sections of the agreements dealing exclusively with wages were gradually made subject to revision without affecting the operation of other sections . . ." Graham, *op. cit.*, p. 90.

Another sort of loss to the laborers consisted in the fact, that wages earned in any given week would ordinarily be spent for the most part during the following week. As the rate of depreciation increased, however, it became more and more common for laborers to spend the greater part of their pay on the day on which they received it. They literally rushed to the stores to spend their money before its value faded away in their hands. This practice of buying in bulk to cover the needs of a week or more of time obviously could not be extended very far to cover perishable foods, and the situation was even worse "in the case of articles involving rather large expenditures (e.g., clothing, furniture), for which workers were in the habit of putting aside part of their weekly wage for some length of time." [1] Because of the necessary delays between the time wages were received and the time they were spent, "the employer paid more wages than the workman really received." [2]

Devices to Protect the Worker from Undue Losses Arising from Inflation. Various other devices were employed to protect the worker from undue losses resulting from the rapid depreciation of the mark, among which may be mentioned cost of living allowances, sliding wage scales, so-called "family allowances," and the payment of "stable money wages." Some of the measures of this type taken in the interest of the poorer classes, however, were in part, at least, economic results of the Revolution itself, and probably would have been taken even had there been no inflation.

The cost of living allowance or bonus was extensively used during the War, and its use was continued in varying degrees throughout the period of the post-war inflation. The cost of living bonus, which was always looked upon as a temporary measure, was preferred by employers to increases in the regular wage rates, because the bonuses would be less likely to become permanent. They would decline as the cost of living went down. Furthermore, they provided a method of automatically adjusting wages and therefore offered a means of avoiding "the lengthy and delicate negotiations involved in establishing new wage scales." [3] The bonuses were based upon an officially constructed cost of living index number calculated on a theoretical budget of a supposedly typical working-class family consisting of father, mother and three children. There

[1] International Labour Office, *op. cit.*, p. 57. [2] *Ibid.*, p. 57. [3] *Ibid.*, p. 48.

were continual disputes over the fairness of the cost of living index number.

It was the usual practice to supplement the basic wage agreed upon for the particular wage group by a general cost of living bonus, and frequently there were local supplements to the general cost of living bonus, representing adjustments to cost of living conditions peculiar to different localities.

As inflation became more pronounced, the idea of a basic wage supplemented by a cost of living bonus developed into the practice of using sliding wage scales calculated according to various index numbers including those for cost of living, wholesale prices, dollar exchange rates and "the economic conditions" in the respective industries concerned. Each plan had its advocates and its opponents. Employers, in general, were opposed to basing wages entirely upon any such sliding scale. They argued that it would increase their cost of production and their risks, would weaken their power to compete with other countries in the world's export markets and would accelerate the depreciation of the mark. An agreement, involving a compromise, was reached in the summer of 1923, according to which basic wages were to be fixed regularly at short intervals, with regard not only to the cost of living, but also to the general economic situation of the industry concerned.

The idea of "family allowances," namely, of granting higher compensation, in each particular labor group, for married men than for single men, and of making an additional allowance for children in a family, is an old one, but it was endowed with new interest by the inflation situation and by the social philosophy of the Revolution. The reduction of national income and the laggardly adjustment of wages to the rising cost of living under the influence of inflation were driving many kinds of laborers to the subsistence minimum. To protect those with dependents, who were thus being forced over the margin, such family allowances were advocated. Cost of living bonuses were sometimes proportionate to the number of dependents, and in some cases the basic wage itself was made larger for married workers than for single ones. One result of this latter practice was a tendency for employers to replace married men by bachelors. In general, the system was not popular among the workers and, although found to some extent in the majority of industries, it was not widely adopted and the scale of extra allowances to persons with dependents was usually low.

The next device mentioned above, namely, the payment of wages on a so-called "stable money basis," marks the beginning of the end of the inflation. It was in reality a long forward step toward stabilization. The custom had prevailed for some time among business houses doing extensive business abroad of keeping their accounts in some "stable" foreign currency, such as the Swiss franc, the Dutch guilder or the United States dollar, and of making and receiving payments largely in paper marks at the current rate of exchange of the day the payment was made. Insurance companies had received the legal authority to keep all their accounts on a gold basis. Retailers, however, were prohibited by law under heavy penalty from quoting their prices in anything but paper marks. Many of them, however, during the last five or six months of 1923 kept their accounts with some "stable" foreign money unit and varied the prices in paper marks at which they sold the merchandise at frequent intervals with the fluctuations in mark exchange with this "stable" foreign unit. During October and November such price changes were often made several times a day. Wage payments on such a gold basis became common during the latter part of 1923. The arrangement often consisted in making wage agreements in terms of some "stable" monetary unit and then of paying the wages themselves either in paper marks at the current rate of exchange of the "stable" unit chosen or partly in paper marks and partly in the "stable" unit itself. As the International Labour Office says, this involved

> "the acceptance in principle of the dissociation of the two functions of money, as a standard of value and as a medium of exchange. Owing to its remarkably rapid depreciation, the paper mark was incapable of fulfilling the first-named function, which was therefore conferred on another monetary unit. The paper mark was retained as a medium of exchange. . . ." [1]

Even before the establishment of the rentenmark, there appeared in Germany certain forms of "stable" money currency that were used to some extent for the payment of wages. The Government itself had issued a loan on a gold value basis, and part of the bonds representing this loan were put out in small denominations,

[1] International Labour Office, *op. cit.*, p. 74.

running as low as one-tenth of a dollar. Authority was given to use these obligations as a medium of exchange.

> "Afterwards, the provinces, towns, chambers of commerce and large industrial concerns were allowed to issue emergency gold mark notes. This emergency money had to be covered by the issuing parties by depositing gold loan bonds of high denomination. Later on, gold loan bonds being scarce, permission was given to cover the issues by 6 per cent. Reich Treasury bills made out in gold." [1]

Other issues of stable emergency currencies based on gold were made by the German railways, by certain banks and by some eight German provinces. All of these various kinds of "currencies," some of them bearing interest, were used in the latter part of 1923 to some extent in making wage payments.

Inflation and Debts. One of the outstanding effects of the inflation was the extent to which it wiped out the debts of the German Government, German corporations and the German people in general. All debts (until near the end of the inflation) were payable, principal and interest, in the depreciated mark. The extent of the loss to the creditor and of the gain to the debtor in each case, of course, depended upon the rate at which the mark depreciated between the date on which a loan was made and the date upon which it was paid. In the case of long-time bonds, notes and similar obligations issued before the War and becoming payable in 1923 at the time of greatest inflation, the loss to the creditor was the greatest, for the value of the principal of the loans paid at maturity was negligible, while the value of the regular interest payments preceding final settlement had declined as the mark depreciated. In the cases of loans with short maturities, the losses of the creditors were not proportionately so great, although even here creditors often lost nearly everything on loans that were made and repaid during the latter months of the inflation period.[2]

The total funded debt of the Reich immediately before the

[1] German Government, *Material for a Study of Germany's Economy, Currency and Finance*, p. 68.

[2] In the summer of 1925 there was enacted a complicated revalorization law (Aufwertungsgesetz), which provided for the restoration in gold values of certain small percentages of different kinds of long-time obligations, such as bonds, debentures, mortgages, savings bank deposits and insurance policies, the values of which had been destroyed by the inflation. This law was put into effect with widely varying degrees of success among different classes of obligations. The story of how it worked does not fall within the scope of this study. *Vide* Viscount d'Abernon, "German Currency—Its Collapse and Recovery, 1920–6," *Journal of Royal Statistical Society*, January, 1927, pp. 38 and 39.

War was about five billion marks, or, say, approximately 1,250 million dollars. This amount of indebtedness could be paid in full the latter part of 1923 by the number of paper marks that one could buy with one-eighth of one cent United States currency. The entire mortgage indebtedness of the German people, which was estimated to amount to approximately 40 billion marks in 1913, could have been paid off in November, 1923 with one American cent.

As the mark depreciated, the creditor classes were naturally less and less willing to lend, while the debtor classes, or, more correctly, practically all classes, were more and more desirous of borrowing.[1] This pushed up interest rates, which often reached very high figures, but, when inflation was at its worst, the highest interest rates charged rarely compensated the creditor for the loss of the real value of the principal. Many merchants and manufacturers, and particularly the so-called large industrialists of which the leader was Hugo Stinnes, made it a practice to borrow to the limit of their ability during the latter years of the inflation, making the maturities of their loans as long as possible and continually making repayments in less valuable marks than they borrowed. Farmers and urban home owners paid off their mortgages at the cost of a few days' labor or a few bushels of grain. But what the debtor gained, the creditor lost, and the creditors were often the most worthy classes in the community, as, for example, the small investors who had put their life savings in government bonds or in the bonds of the large corporations, the middle-class clerk or artisan with a savings bank account, the owner of a life insurance policy upon which premiums had been paid for many years,[2] or the widow or orphan living upon the income from trust funds invested in bonds and mortgages. The

[1] During the year 1923, when the public began to believe that there were some prospects of an early stabilization with a possible increase in the value of the mark, the statement made a century and a half before by John Witherspoon concerning the American continental currency was said to have applied in Germany: "Creditors were seen running away from debtors and debtors pursuing them in triumph and paying them without mercy."

[2] The revalorization plan of 1925 provided for the revaluation of the claims of holders of life insurance policies. The assets of the different life insurance companies were to be handed over to a trustee. They were to constitute for each company a revalorization fund (Aufwertungsstock). The revaluation of the policies was to be made in proportion to the available funds of the Augwertungsstock. According to a statement of the governmental office which controlled private life insurance, the policies of different companies were revalued at rates varying from 12 to 16½ per cent. *Magazin der Wirtschaft*, Feb. 9, 1928, p. 215.

savings of these people were practically wiped out, as well as those of the wealthier classes. This was not a destruction of wealth, but a change in ownership, a blind and ruthless robbing of one class of people in Germany for the benefit of another class, without any regard to the merits of the persons concerned. Most of the debts thus wiped out were debts of Germans to Germans and their practical cancellation, therefore, did not change the total wealth of Germany. A few of the debts, however, represented loans to Germans made by foreigners. Many represented speculative purchases by foreigners of German paper money. In these latter cases the foreigners lost and the Germans gained.

The virtual cancellation of the internal debts of German governmental units reduced the taxes which Germans had to pay for the support of the Government, but it likewise reduced the ability of thousands of Germans to pay taxes because it destroyed the value of their investments in government securities.

Bond Prices. Short-time government paper, which was held in large volume by the Reichsbank as security for Reichsbank notes, was maintained at practical parity throughout the inflation. Long-time bonds of the National Government declined somewhat but the decline was not great. German Government 4 per cents, for example, stood at 87 in January, 1922, taking the 1913 price as 100. They then advanced to parity by September. At the end of the year 1922, however, rumors became common that in case of stabilization the Government was likely to show special consideration to the holders of these bonds. A strong demand for them developed both in Germany and abroad—at the rates of exchange then prevailing an American dollar would buy an enormous volume of these bonds—and for a few months the prices soared to extravagant figures. The rumor proved to be false and the prices later collapsed. In general, high-grade bonds in Germany, corporate as well as governmental, maintained their prices fairly well during the inflation in terms of marks, but the value of the mark in which they were payable faded into nothingness. The owner of the bonds kept the bottles, but the wine rapidly leaked out. The prices of these bonds in general did not greatly decline, but the prices of everything else rose and rose astronomically, leaving them far behind.[1]

[1] Information concerning bond prices will be found in Statistisches Reichsamt, *Wirtschaft und Statistick, passim.*

Inflation and the Corporation Stockholder. While, generally speaking, creditors suffered heavy losses and debtors realized large gains from the inflation, even after full allowance is made for the adjustments under the revalorization law of 1925,[1] there were wide differences in the extent of the losses and gains ultimately realized by different classes of creditors and debtors. In this connection, the experiences of one large class of debtors were of a character somewhat different than would ordinarily be expected. I refer to the stockholders of the large industrial corporations. Most of these corporations had obtained their capital through the sale of both bonds and stocks. The bonds represented debts of the corporation and the stocks were certificates of ownership. The stockholders, as owners of the corporation, subject to the lien of the bonds, were the debtors and the bondholders were the creditors. As the mark depreciated, the prices of the products or services sold by the corporation rose rapidly, but the service of a given amount of bonded indebtedness continued to be paid by the same number of marks as before. Although the prices of a corporation's products might have risen a thousand- or a million-fold, it required no more paper marks than it had previously required of gold marks to pay the principal and interest of, say, five million marks of bonded indebtedness floated before the inflation. The stockholders therefore gained what the bondholders lost. Inflation canceled to a very large extent the stockholders' debts. This being the case, one would expect a great shift from bonds to stocks in the public's purchase of securities in the investment and speculative markets; in other words, an increasing preference for corporate equities in contrast with corporate debts, a preference which would push up the prices of stocks but leave the prices of high-grade bonds practically unchanged.[2]

This, in fact, happened. The last column in Table X (p. 291) shows the rise in the index number covering a selected group of corporation stocks during the last period of the inflation. In these index numbers allowance has been made for stock dividends.

[1] Cf., *supra*, p. 299, note 2.

[2] As the income of corporations increased with the rise in the prices of their products, their financial positions naturally became stronger and bankruptcies became less and less frequent. This pushed the prices of lower grade bonds up toward parity with those of the higher grade bonds; but, after this point was reached, their prices did not advance much further. The risk of non-payment was practically eliminated in the case of all bonds, while the risk of payment in a continually cheapening mark applied equally to all bonds.

It is a striking fact, that the rate of increase in the prices of stocks even before 1921 had lagged far behind the rate of increase not only of the price of gold, wholesale prices and the cost of living, but also even far behind the rates of increase in the wages of both classes of labor for which figures are available and of the salaries of government officials. This disparity, in general, increased during 1922 and early 1923, but decreased during the months of extreme hyper-inflation in the latter part of 1923. Even at the end of that year, however, prices of stocks had risen only a little over one-fifth as much as wholesale prices in general or the cost of living, and only slightly more than half as much as the salaries of the higher government officials, on the basis of 1913 figures. While, obviously, the man who invested in stocks, generally speaking, during the early post-war years fared infinitely better than the man who invested in bonds, the slow rate of the advance in the prices of stocks as compared with commodity prices and wages is surprising. What is the explanation?

This question is a complicated one and there is much difference of opinion as to the answer. Briefly summarized, however, the explanation is probably something as follows:

(1) The profits were often not so great as they appeared. Between the time an order for merchandise was accepted at an agreed price and the time payment was made there was often a great decline in the value of the mark. During the latter two years of the inflation, manufacturers and merchants found themselves much of the time in a position where they were selling their merchandise at prices lower than the costs of replacement.

(2) It took time for a corporation to distribute profits through dividend payments, and, in the process of doing so, the profits often faded away through the depreciation of the mark. One result of this was that dividends were usually kept low and the profits were increasingly ploughed into the business.

(3) A third reason for the surprising lag in the advance in the prices of stocks during the years 1922 and 1923 was the comparatively small amount of funds available to the public for stock speculation.

> "The mounting commodity prices absorbed so large a proportion of the monetary supply that relatively little was left for the working of the financial markets, and the banks were not inclined to put credits at the disposal of stock speculators." [1]

[1] Graham, *ibid.*, p. 181.

(4) A further reason for the failure of stocks to rise more rapidly was the high real rate of interest which the inflation caused, particularly during the years 1922 and 1923. As is well known, rising prices stimulate the demand for capital and tend to push up real interest rates. It was at such high interest rates that the profits of the corporations, actual and prospective, were capitalized, at least during part of this period, thus making the prices of the stocks low in comparison to their income yield.

(5) Finally, although this reason does not apply to the particular stock index numbers here under consideration,[1] the shift in the demand of investors and speculators from bonds to stocks accompanied by an inflation-stimulated business activity and by expectations of extraordinary profits led to large increases in the capitalization of industries. Enormous quantities of new stock were issued, and the values of the shares of many corporations became progressively diluted.

Effect of Inflation on Germany's Industrial Plant and Equipment

The extraordinary nominal profits resulting from the inflation were used during the inflation period chiefly for extending plant and improving equipment, and many of these capital expenditures subsequently proved to be unwise. They were made hastily in order to avoid losses from the depreciation of the mark. Inflation stimulated Germany's export trade and gave her manufacturers an artificial protection against imports from abroad. Her manufacturers enjoyed a sheltered market for their products at home comparatively free from foreign competition. In this sheltered position they knew little and cared little about the new inventions and mechanical improvements that were being introduced in the corresponding industries abroad. Moreover, the real wages of many kinds of labor had become so low, with the depreciation of the mark, that there was less incentive than usual for introducing labor-saving machinery. The result was, that the extraordinary profits arising from the inflation were often employed in comparatively useless extensions of plant and in providing equipment of types that had already become antiquated abroad, and that proved to be of little value after the German currency became

[1] The index numbers given in the table on p. 291 include the necessary adjustments for new stock issues and stock dividends.

stabilized. Concerning this situation the International Labour Office of the League of Nations said:

> "During the period of inflation an enormous amount of capital had been invested in extensions and improvements of factories; apart from foreign investments this was the only means of avoiding depreciation of profits; but all this new plant stood unused and simply increased interest charges and the cost of upkeep. . . . The relatively easy conditions induced by inflation often led to less economical management, waste of raw material, and cessation of technical improvements." [1]

With reference to the same situation, Graham says:

> "Much of the apparatus installed in the years 1920 to 1923 was therefore scrapped in the reconstruction of industry which, under the name of 'rationalization,' has been something of a fetish to the post-inflation German economy." [2]

Concerns That Were Both Debtor and Creditor

In speaking of the gains of debtors and the losses of creditors due to the inflation, it should be noticed, that many individuals and most corporations were both debtor and creditor, and that the same person or corporation would be gaining as a debtor and losing as a creditor. There were, moreover, certain types of corporations in which debits and credits were so balanced that "one hand washed the other." Banks, for example, received the depreciated mark at par from their debtors and paid out the same marks at par to their depositors. A similar situation existed among life insurance companies. It is true that the bank depositor in the one case and the policy holder in the other may have lost in terms of purchasing power value practically everything due him. The corporation itself, however, in each case remained solvent and usually prospered, but often lost a part of its capital.

Influence of Inflation on Germany's Trade

Germany's domestic industry and trade and her export trade during the years 1921, 1922 and the fore part of 1923 were feverishly stimulated by inflation. Let us briefly consider, first, the country's domestic business and then its foreign business.

Domestic Industry and Trade. The evidence is strong that Germany's economic activity increased throughout the years 1921, 1922 and the fore part of 1923, and that, unlike most of the rest of

[1] *The Workers Standard of Life in Countries with Depreciated Currency*, pp. 7 and 8.
[2] Graham, *op. cit.*, p. 323.

Europe and the United States, Germany suffered no industrial collapse in the latter part of 1920 and the fore part of 1921. The indices of the per capita physical volume of industrial production and of the production of agricultural products for various countries covered in the *Bulletin de la Statistique Générale de la France* show that, on the basis of the year 1913 as 100, Germany's production stood for the four years 1920 to 1923 as follows:

Year	Agricultural Production	Industrial Production
1920	62	61
1921	63	77
1922	69	86
1923	69	54

As we have previously seen,[1] the amount of unemployment during the years 1921, 1922 and the fore part of 1923 was exceptionally small, and the same is true of the number of bankruptcies, the low figure here continuing throughout the year 1923. Industrial production, however, suffered a great slump with the currency collapse of the latter months of 1923, and at that time unemployment increased enormously and there was a large increase in the number of persons receiving public relief benefits. Inflation prosperity had ended in an inflation collapse. An organism that functions under the influence of continually increasing doses of a powerful stimulant will suffer a strong reaction when that stimulant is suddenly discontinued.

Foreign Trade. Germany's foreign trade was hit hard by the War and had only recovered moderately by 1922. In terms of 1913 gold values, the foreign trade of Germany (exclusive of treasure and of deliveries under the Treaty of Versailles) was as follows for the years under review: [2]

Table XI. Germany's Foreign Trade

Year	Imports		Exports	
	M000,000	Index No.	M000,000	Index No.
1913	10,769.7	100	10,097.2	100
1922	6,290.4	58.4	6,186.8	56.3
1923	4,808.2	44.7	5,338.1	48.6

It will be noted that by the year 1923 the percentage decline in imports was greater than in exports, and that for the three years

[1] *Supra*, pp. 294 and 295.

[2] Statistisches Reichsamt, *Statistisches Jahrbuch*, 1924–1925, p. 141.

mentioned that year of extreme inflation alone showed an excess of exports.

During the War foreign trade and operations in foreign exchange had been rigidly controlled by the Government, the purpose of the control having been four-fold: (1) to prevent operations that would be useful to the enemy; (2) to restrict imports to the commodities most needed for the conduct of the War and to prevent the country from exporting goods needed at home for war purposes; (3) to protect the mark from undue depreciation and undue fluctuations in value that might otherwise arise from excessive speculations in exchange; and (4) to prevent a flight of capital from Germany.

Immediately after the War these trade restrictions and foreign exchange regulations were largely abandoned, partly because the war-time reasons for their imposition had to a great extent passed, and partly because the Allied occupation permitted goods to pour through the "Hole in the West," despite any efforts the German Government could make to prevent it. Within about a year after the Armistice, however, new control measures began to be imposed, and soon an elaborate system of foreign trade and exchange control was again in operation, a system in the enforcement of which that part of the business public interested in foreign trade coöperated with the Government. In a comprehensive discussion of this subject, Graham [1] cites five different motives for this control as regards export trade:

"(i) *Assurance for the home population of a sufficient supply of necessaries.* Foodstuff exports were unconditionally prohibited, a certain latitude was given in the case of raw materials, while manufactured goods were, in the main, freely exportable.

"(ii) *Assurance of reasonable prices.* Since domestic prices consistently lagged far behind the upward surge of exchange rates there was a constant tendency for such German exporters as were basing their quotations on domestic market conditions to sell their goods at extremely low prices when measured in stable-value currencies. The foreign exchange proceeds of exports tended therefore to provide for but a very limited volume of imports. . . . In order to prevent a 'selling-out' of the country at bargain-counter rates exporters were forbidden to dispose of their goods below certain minimum prices officially established for every transaction . . .

"(iii) *Assurance that the foreign exchange proceeds would be brought back to Germany.* In order to avoid the loss of purchasing power which was

[1] Graham, *op. cit.*, Chaps. 3 and 8.

involved in holding mark balances there was a strong disposition on the part of exporters to leave abroad the foreign exchange proceeds of their exports rather than convert them into marks. The supplies of foreign exchange requisite for imports and reparations were thus not forthcoming and, to combat this situation, the permit to export was made conditional on the delivery to the authorities of a smaller or larger share of the foreign exchange proceeds according as the raw materials required for the manufacture of the commodity in question were or were not of foreign origin.

"(iv) *The participation of the Reich in the gains on the export trade.* Since the minimum prices on goods sold abroad were ordinarily much above those currently prevailing in the domestic markets exporters were in a highly advantageous position as compared with producers of goods for home consumption. There was no reason for permitting the price differential officially established to accrue to one favored class. Duties were therefore imposed on exports." [1]

For the enforcement of these regulations an elaborate bureaucratic organization was created under a Federal Commissar for Import and Export Permits. At one time there were some 170 different boards of control, employing between four and five thousand persons engaged in this work.

These measures of control over foreign trade were accompanied by equally minute restrictions on dealings in foreign exchange. An official publication of the German Government lists 44 different measures adopted by the Reich between February, 1922 and the end of 1923 for the control of foreign exchange.[2] These measures related to the purchase of foreign moneys, the sale of German currency abroad and to the purchase and sale of foreign exchange. They provided for the fixing by governmental authority of exchange rates, required the licensing of all foreign exchange operations, and limited such operations to a few especially authorized banks, and even then only on notification to the Minister of Finance. A Presidential Decree of September 7, 1923, which set aside certain fundamental provisions of the Constitution, gave to a Special Commission for the Requisition of Foreign Currency power among other things

"to lay hands on all foreign payment media and/or negotiable instruments in foreign currency, as well as upon foreign securities and precious metals, . . . [to] demand any information, . . . [to] examine into anyone's affairs, search anyone; summon anyone before him to make decla-

[1] Graham, *op. cit.*, pp. 81 and 82.

[2] German Government, *Material for a Study of Germany's Economy, Currency and Finance*, p. 71.

rations and require anyone to make solemn affirmation as to the correctness and completeness of his declarations. He may seize in favour of the Reich without any compensation all foreign payment media acquired illegitimately or retained contrary to his orders." [1]

On the whole, the regulations of foreign trade and of foreign exchange, despite the severity of the penalties imposed for their infraction, were far from being effective. There was widespread evasion of the law.

The fact that during the last inflation period prior to the autumn of 1923 foreign exchange rates in terms of marks with "stable-money countries" rose much more rapidly than the price level in Germany; or, in other words, that foreign money like the dollar and the Swiss franc would buy at the prevailing foreign exchange rates very much more in Germany than they would at home, stimulated not only the purchase by the people of these countries of German merchandise but also heavy investments by them in German real estate and German securities. Many foreigners obtained valuable properties in Germany at a song, but foreign purchasers of German securities usually lost heavily. Foreign tourists flooded Germany and lived luxuriously at costs in their own currencies that were ridiculously small. At one time in 1923 a good room with private bath and electric lights in the best of Berlin hotels cost less than the equivalent of 15 cents United States currency a day. On the other hand, foreign speculators, in the hope of realizing large profits from a subsequent rise in the gold value of the German paper mark, built up in Germany enormous bank balances and bought large amounts of German paper money. The McKenna Committee estimated that Germany had profited from the sale of mark credits to persons living abroad by an amount equal to something like 1,750,000,000 to 2,000,000,000 dollars and that an additional profit of something like 150 to 175 million dollars had been realized by her from sales of paper marks in foreign countries.

Inflation and Tax Revenues

One of the evil consequences of the inflation was the reduction of tax revenues and, more particularly, of the revenues from direct taxes such as various forms of income taxes. Germany financed the War largely through loans, paper money issues and the sale of

[1] *Ibid.*, p. 70.

her gold and foreign securities. Her modest tax revenues of the war period came largely from various kinds of excise taxes. In early 1920, under the leadership of Finance Minister Erzberger, the tax system was thoroughly reorganized, and an increasing resort was made to direct taxes. The inflation, however, soon forced a return, in a continually increasing degree, to borrowing, and, so far as tax revenues were concerned, to a larger and larger dependence upon indirect taxes.

As the mark depreciated, no finance minister could even roughly estimate in advance what the Government's expenditures would be nor how much revenue a given tax would yield. The principal recourse of the Finance Minister, therefore, was to borrow funds from the Reichsbank as they were needed. Calculated upon a cost of living index, the Reich received 44 per cent of its revenue in 1921 from taxes, 35 per cent in 1922, 11 per cent in the first nine months of 1923 and a negligible percentage during the last three months of 1923.[1]

The difficulty with most kinds of direct taxes was that their value faded away in the process of levy and collection. It took time to make a tax levy and, except in some cases of collection at source, it took further time to collect the tax after it had been levied. But, during the inflation, time was the essence of value, and the longer the delay, the less in real value was the tax. Taxpayers naturally postponed payment as long as possible, and watched their taxes fade away as they delayed. Despite frequent advances in rates and serious efforts to speed up collection, the depreciation of the mark continued to eat up the revenues.[2]

A striking example of this type of difficulty was reported from Russia after the War when the ruble was depreciating rapidly. As prices rose it became necessary for the Government to make frequent advances in postage rates and in that connection to "scale up" the denominations of postage stamps. It required considerable

[1] Cf., German Government, *Materials for a Study of Germany's Economy, Currency and Finance*, p. 30.

[2] "According to the Act of December 23, 1922 the income of a married man with two children, such as was at that date equivalent to $1020, was subject to a tax the equivalent of $230 and, on the larger incomes, the ratio was much higher. But the levy and payment were both in paper marks. If this tax had been paid in full as early as the end of June 1923 (and some such interval must elapse to give time for assessment and collection) it would then have been worth slightly over $10, at the end of July about $1.50, at the end of August about 15¢, at the end of September a fraction of a cent, while, at the end of October, it would have been in that twilight zone where infinitesimals fade into nothingness." Graham, *op. cit.*, p. 44.

time, however, for the Government to issue new denomination stamps. By reason of this delay and of the rapid increase in postage rates, at one time in Moscow the highest denomination stamp one could buy was 10,000 rubles, but this stamp would not carry its own weight on a letter. It followed that the more stamps one put on a letter, the greater the deficiency of the postage.

Inflation and the Distribution of Wealth

The inflation proved to be in Germany, as it has proven to be, in every other country in which it has been practiced on a large scale, a gigantic engine of wealth redistribution, an engine that worked night and day and worked blindly, taking wealth here and giving it out there, robbing one economic group or one social class for the benefit of another, and doing it all without rhyme or reason and with no regard whatever to the merits or demerits of those benefited and those despoiled.

While inflation in Germany undoubtedly affected the tempo and the direction in which economic production moved, its greatest and most enduring influence was clearly in the field of distribution. Viewed from the angle of economic groups, the inflation, on net balance, probably benefited the great industrialists and the great merchants, who through it got possession of Germany's enormous industries and stores by means of continual borrowing and subsequent repayments in continually depreciating marks. It probably benefited unskilled laborers up to the autumn of 1923, by giving them more regular employment at a fairly normal real wage than they presumably would have had without the agio in business activity due to the inflation. As a class it benefited farmers, who in general enjoyed good markets for their crops throughout the inflation period and who were able to pay off their mortgage indebtedness at a very small expense in terms of farm produce. On the other hand, inflation despoiled practically every other class of labor, the skilled artisan in every trade, clerks and other so-called "white-collar" workers, professional men of all classes, particularly those receiving their pay in the form of salaries as contrasted with fees; and it likewise despoiled public officials of every grade, those of the higher grades suffering most. Of course, the institution and individual whose income came in the form of interest on investments in bonds and mortgages lost heavily, and the value of life insurance, the premiums on which had often been paid by great sacrifices over long periods of years, was reduced to pitifully small figures.[1]

Viewed from the standpoint of social classes, the lowest class suffered least, while the great middle class, which was the backbone of pre-war Germany, suffered most. Concerning this class, Angell well says:[2]

> "Composed largely of people with small fixed incomes, such as salaried officials and clerks, recipients of pensions, and little investors living on interest and rent—of whom the latter group were hit especially hard by the government control of city rentals—they were precisely the group most exposed to the evil consequences of currency depreciation, while they lacked both the knowledge and the opportunity to combat it. Their savings disappeared, their pensions and annuities melted away, and the sons who might have supported them had all too commonly been killed in the war. Hundreds of thousands of educated men and women, too old or feeble or untrained to earn their own living, were abruptly faced with starvation. Many died. The others, passing from day to day without hope, survived only by the sacrifice of treasured books, furniture, jewelry, and all their salable possessions, and at the end by domestic and foreign charity. Their history is one of the most genuinely pitiful chapters in all the war and post-war tragedy."

Measures for Combating the Evils of Runaway Inflation

As we have seen, the inflation got completely out of control and ran away in the latter part of 1923. The inflation "horse," already nervous and excitable, had been finally lashed into desperation by the extravagant expenditures by the Government of funds borrowed from the Reichsbank for maintaining "passive resistance" in the Ruhr.

The currency and credit situation toward the end of 1923 was a fantastic one. Only about $\frac{1}{1000}$ of the expenditures of the National Government were being covered by tax revenues. By November the Reichsbank's note circulation amounted to the astronomical figure of approximately 400 quintillion marks, which in terms of gold value were equal to only 400 million of the marks of 1913, or to $\frac{1}{15}$ of Germany's monetary circulation when the War broke out in August, 1914. Wholesale prices were over 1,400,000,000,000 times as high as they were in 1913; while, on November 15, the volume of Treasury bills discounted by the

[1] Cf., *supra*, p. 300, note 2.

[2] Angell, James W., *The Recovery of Germany*, pp. 38–39.

Reichsbank, practically all of which were held by the Bank itself, amounted to over 191 quintillion marks.

Of course, long before the situation reached this pass, there had been many proposals for stabilization and some abortive attempts. The great difficulty with all proposals had been that the progressively increasing outpouring of Reichsbank notes could not be stopped. The Government "needed the money" and saw no other politically feasible method of getting it.

As we have seen, while the paper mark was thus depreciating, various plans were adopted to escape the evils of inflation. Many commodity prices were adjusted to the daily variations of Berlin's exchange rate with stable-money countries. Wages were adjusted in part to a cost of living index, and debts of various kinds were made in terms of dollars or of French francs or of the cost of living index and then paid in paper marks at the current rate of exchange, or at their index number value on maturity date. Furthermore, there were placed in circulation along with the unstable paper currency various kinds of so-called "stable currencies," and the Reich itself, as well as 30 states, the railways and a few banks, in the latter part of 1923 issued various kinds of paper on a gold basis, paper that circulated to some extent as money, although much of it was interest-bearing. By the beginning of 1924 the amount of such paper in circulation (aside from the rentenmark, to be described presently) amounted to something like a billion gold marks.[1]

The "Rye Mark." Of the various devices employed for the purpose of effecting business operations on a stable money basis the one that proved to be the parent of the stabilization plan finally adopted was the so-called "roggenmark" or "rye mark" currency. The story of the origin of this currency and of how it developed into the rentenmark is told in an interesting way by Dr. Hjalmar Schacht, President of the Reichsbank, one of the active participants in carrying through Germany's currency stabilization plan.[2]

Rye was the principal grain crop of Germany, just as wheat is in the United States and rice is in China. After pointing out that even in everyday business prices in Germany in 1923 were

[1] A tabular statement of these issues will be found in the *Report of the First Committee of Experts* (The Dawes Committee), Annex No. 7.

[2] *The Stabilization of the Mark*, pp. 76–89.

frequently quoted in terms of specific commodity quantities, Dr. Schacht says:

"In agricultural transactions in particular, lease agreements and prices of agricultural products were being based on the value of the pound of rye. The States of Oldenburg and of Mecklenburg-Schwerin issued loans denominated in values of rye at the end of 1922. . . . In the period which followed numerous other rye loans were issued by the most various bodies . . . There were [also] coke loans, coal loans, potash loans, lignite loans, and even kilowatt loans. The principle of basing values on prices of commodities was extended to mortgage transactions, and mortgages in rye, potash, etc., were admitted to register in addition to mortgages in fine gold." [1]

In the summer of 1923 Karl Helfferich, who was Minister of Finance for some time during the War, submitted to the Government a plan for currency stabilization based upon a "rye mark." Briefly summarized, the plan was as follows:

1. "The various economic units of Germany (agriculture, industry, trade, transportation, and banking) were to establish" an independent currency bank, the statutes of which were to be approved by the Imperial Chancellor.

2. "The original capital was to be raised by a 5 per cent. first charge [a sort of capital levy] in the form of mortgages or bonds on the economic units described, one-half of the total [placed at four billion marks] . . . being raised by agriculture and the other half by the other units. Against these mortgages or bonds interest-bearing Rentenbriefe [income notes] . . . were to be issued."

3. "These Rentenbriefe were to serve as cover for the notes which were to be issued by the bank, denominated in 'rye marks.' "

4. "The rye mark notes were to be exchangeable on demand at any time for interest-bearing Rentenbriefe."

5. "The rye note was to become legal tender on a date fixed by the Government, and a fixed legal ratio of conversion was to be laid down as between rye notes and paper marks."

6. "The discount of Government bills at the Reichsbank was to cease. The existing debt of the Reich was to be amortized by the new bank placing 300 million rye marks at the disposal of the Reich in return for remission of the taxation . . . imposed on business in August 1923. With this 300 million rye marks the Reichsbank was to redeem its own notes and thereby stabilize the paper mark."

7. "The new bank was to be empowered to give credit to the Reich up to the extent of half its original capital and original reserve." [2]

[1] *Ibid.*, pp. 77 and 78.

[2] *Ibid.*, pp. 80 and 81.

The Rentenmark. After an extended debate in which there was much difference of opinion, the plan was adopted with three important changes: (1) the bank, instead of becoming an essentially independent organization was to become in fact, if not in name, practically a division of the Reichsbank; (2) the notes were to be expressed in gold values and not in rye values; (3) the notes were not to be legal tender.

The law incorporating this plan was passed October 15, 1923. The new bank which was called the Rentenbank was opened for business the following month.

The Rentenbank law fixed the capital of the Bank at 3,200,000,000 rentenmarks, and this capital was to be provided by a compulsory levy upon owners of agricultural land and upon industrial, commercial and banking institutions. The amount of the levy was 4 per cent of the value of the property. The levy was stated in terms of gold marks and the liens thus imposed took precedence over all other domestic debts of the owners of the property. The obligations ran for a minimum of five years and bore interest at 6 per cent. Against these mortgages the Rentenbank issued mortgage bonds, known as *Rentenbriefe,* which were to serve as 100 per cent cover for the circulating Rentenbank notes which the Bank was authorized to issue up to an amount not exceeding its capital and surplus. The Rentenbank's notes were made redeemable on demand in sums of 500 rentenmarks in the 5 per cent Rentenbriefe. While the authorized capital and the authorized note issue were both fixed at 3,200,000,000 rentenmarks, 800,000,000 rentenmarks of this sum were to represent liens on property in the occupied territories which could not be made effective for some time, so that the original amounts were fixed at 2,400,000,000 rentenmarks. Half of the notes could be issued to the public, while the other half was to go to the Government, and of this latter half 300,000,000 rentenmarks were to be without interest. With the proceeds of the loan the Government was expected to redeem all Treasury bills which it had discounted at the Reichsbank and to cover the deficits expected in the National budget during the next two years. All discounting of Treasury bills at the Reichsbank was to cease. Although the rentenmarks were not made legal tender, they were made receivable by the Government in payment of all government obligations. This Rentenbank currency was not looked upon as a permanent currency, but as an intermediate step toward the return to the gold standard.

At the end of November the Government officially valorized the outstanding paper marks at the rate of one trillion of the old marks to one rentenmark. This rate was looked upon as, roughly speaking, equivalent to the market rate at the time, although on this subject there was considerable difference of opinion. The rate adopted was, therefore, looked upon as a recognition of the *status quo*. The old depreciated mark became acceptable in payment of government dues and interchangeable at the Reichsbank at this rate of a trillion to one, and, inasmuch as no rentenmarks were issued in denominations below one mark, the old marks at this trillion to one rate became the fractional money for the time being of the country. The writer in January, 1924, in purchasing a cigar in Berlin, worth 12 cents United States currency, paid a rentenmark and received for his change M500,000,000,000, which was the equivalent of 12 cents. These five hundred billion marks, like the one rentenmark, were in the form of one small bank note.

To the surprise of many students of the problem, both in Germany and abroad, the scheme proved a success. Exchange with gold standard countries was soon stabilized at approximately 4,200,000,000,000 marks to the dollar, and the trillion to one rate in Germany became effective.

The all-important reasons for the success of the plan were, that government borrowing at the Reichsbank (except to the limited extent authorized by the Rentenbank law) was stopped, a strict limitation upon further note issues was imposed, and the public had faith that the terms of the law would be lived up to. In other words, public confidence in the currency was restored, and the extravagant velocities at which the old money had been circulating, as the public anticipated ever increasing issues, were cut down. Money and bank credit again circulated at normal velocities. This reduction of velocities was so great at the start that it resulted in an actual scarcity of money and the authorities were compelled to increase the volume of paper money somewhat at the beginning in order to maintain the approximate price level prevailing at the time of the rentenmark stabilization.[1]

The rentenmark stabilization worked out, as planned, to be the stepping stone to a complete gold standard. The pre-war gold

[1] Compare, *supra*, pp. 61–62.

value of the mark that was reëstablished with the opening of the Rentenbank was continued under the legislation of 1924, which, in carrying out the currency and banking recommendations of the Dawes Committee, brought Germany back to a full-fledged gold standard. But that is another story and does not fall within the scope of this chapter, which is concerned only with Germany's experiences with an inflated paper currency.

BIBLIOGRAPHY

d'Abernon, Viscount, "German Currency: Its Collapse and Recovery 1920–6," *Journal of the Royal Statistical Society*, XC, January, 1927.

Angell, James W., *The Recovery of Germany;* New Haven, Conn., Yale University Press, 1929.

Bente, Hermann, *Die deutsche Währungspolitik von 1914 bis 1924;* Weltwirtschaftliches Archiv, January, 1926, pp. 117–191. Contains a chronology and a bibliography.

Bergmann, Carl, *The History of Reparations;* Boston, Houghton Mifflin Company, 1927.

de Bordes, J. van Walré, *The Austrian Crown: Its Depreciation and Stabilization;* London, P. S. King & Son, 1924.

Dulles, Eleanor Lansing, *The French Franc 1914–1928: The Facts and Their Interpretation;* New York, The Macmillan Company, 1929.

Feilen, Josef F., *Die Umlaufsgeschwindigkeit des Geldes;* Berlin, W. de Gruyter & Co., 1923.

German Government, *Material for a Study of Germany's Economy, Currency and Finance;* Berlin, 1924.

Graham, Frank D., *Exchange, Prices, and Production in Hyper-Inflation: Germany, 1920–1923;* Princeton, N. J., Princeton University Press, 1930. Contains a comprehensive bibliography.

International Labour Office, *The Workers Standard of Life in Countries with Depreciated Currency;* Geneva, 1925.

Katzenellenbaum, S. S., *Russian Currency and Banking 1914–1924;* London, P. S. King & Son, 1925.

League of Nations, *Memorandum on Currency and Central Banks 1913–1924*, Vol. I; Geneva, 1925.

Reichsbank, *Verwaltungsbericht der Reichsbank.* Annual, 1913–1925; Berlin, Reichsdruckerei.

Reparation Commission, *Report of the First Committee of Experts;* Paris, 1924.

——, *Report of the Second Committee of Experts;* Paris, 1924.

——, *Text of the Bank Laws;* Annex 2122 e, g, h of the Reparation Commission.

Rogers, James Harvey, *The Process of Inflation in France 1914–1927;* New York, Columbia University Press, 1929.

Schacht, Hjalmar, *The Stabilization of the Mark;* London, George Allen & Unwin, Ltd., 1927.

Statistisches Reichsamt, *Deutschlands Wirtschaftslage unter den Nachwirkungen des Weltkrieges;* Berlin, Zentralverlag, G.m.b.H., 1923.

Statistisches Reichsamt, *Statistisches Jahrbuch für das Deutsche Reich;* 1919 to 1924–25; Berlin, Verlag für Politik und Wirtschaft.

——, *Zahlen zur Geldenwertung in Deutschland 1914 bis 1923;* Berlin, Verlag von Reimar Hobbing, 1925. (In Wirtschaft und Statistik, 5. Jahrgang, Sonderheft 1, 1925.)

United States Department of Commerce, *The Reparation Problem 1918–1924;* Trade Information Bulletin No. 278; Washington, Government Printing Office, 1924.

Young, John Parke, *European Currency and Finance,* 2 volumes; Commission of Gold and Silver Inquiry, United States Senate; Washington, Government Printing Office, 1925.

CHAPTER XIV

FRENCH AND AMERICAN BIMETALLISM

The theory of bimetallism has previously been explained.[1] This chapter describes how bimetallism worked contemporaneously in France and the United States over a period of something like three-fourths of a century. During most of this time France, from an economic point of view, was a more important country than the United States, and she gave bimetallism the longest and probably the fairest trial which it ever had. In view of these facts and of the fact that much of the ammunition of both sides of the bimetallic controversy which was so hotly waged throughout Europe and America during the last third of the nineteenth century was drawn from this experience of France, it will be useful to study the experience in some detail.

FRENCH BIMETALLISM

The French Monetary Law of 1803

When France in 1796 returned to a specie basis after her inflation orgy with the Assignats and the Mandats,[2] her money consisted chiefly of gold and silver coins. These coins circulated under a dual or parallel standard at the ratio of 15½ to 1, which had been established by Calonne in 1785.

Napoleon placed France upon a bimetallic basis soon after he came into power. In 1803, through his Minister Gaudin, he put through a new monetary law, which, although not mentioning bimetallism, created an effective bimetallic standard. The law contained three divisions: (1) a general disposition providing that "five grams of silver, 9/10 fine, constitute the monetary unit, which retains the name of franc"; (2) Title I dealing with the fabrication of coins. This Title provided for the coinage of full weight coins of both silver and gold. All coins were to be 9/10 fine and of proportionate weights. Although the nominal ratio of gold to silver established by this law was 15½ to 1, the actual ratio was slightly

[1] *Supra*, Chap. VI.

[2] *Supra*, Chap. X.

different because of the different coinage charges applying to the coinage of gold and silver. Since there was free coinage of both gold and silver and since coins of both metals stood on an exact equality before the law, the monetary system which the law created was, in fact, bimetallic, although it declared the silver franc to be the monetary unit.[1]

Ratio and Coinage

During the years 1803 to 1835 the French mints coined both gold and silver every year, and both kinds of money always circulated. The mint ratio, which was actually 15.69 to 1 although nominally 15½ to 1, was above the commercial ratio and therefore favorable to gold in twelve of the eighteen years from 1803 to 1820, inclusive; and it was below the commercial ratio and therefore favorable to silver in six of these years. In the twelve years during which the ratio was favorable to gold, the French mints coined 6,011 million francs of gold and 5,913 million francs of silver; and in the six years in which the ratio was favorable to silver they coined 2,744 million francs of gold and 5,114 million francs of silver.

In 1835 the mint charges for coinage were changed, with the result that the actual mint ratio was reduced from 15.69 to 1 to 15.626 to 1; and in 1850 a further change was made, reducing it to 15.586 to 1.

During the years from 1821 to 1850 the mint ratio was below the market ratio in every year but two (when it was practically the same as the market ratio). During this whole period, therefore, there was an overvaluation of silver by the mint, and during those years there were coined at the mint 31,909 million francs of silver as against only 4,634 million francs of gold.

From 1851 to 1872, inclusive, chiefly as a result of the enormous increase in the world's production of gold following the Californian and Australian gold discoveries, the mint ratio was above the market ratio every year, the mint ratio (allowing for coinage charges) having been 15.586 to 1 for the years 1851 to 1853, and 15.583 to 1 from 1854 to the virtual discontinuance of bimetallism in 1874. Under the compensatory principle, the overvaluation of gold and undervaluation of silver should have led to a great preponderance of gold over silver in the coinage at the mints. This is

[1] An English translation of the law with a synoptical table of French coins which it authorized is given in the *Report of the International Monetary Conference of 1878*, pp. 155–157.

exactly what happened. In every one of these years except one (1872) more gold was coined than silver, and in that one year no gold was coined at all, and only 400,000 francs of silver. During these twenty-two years 6,586 million francs of gold were coined and only 533 million francs of silver, or over twelve times as much gold as silver.

By 1873 the tide had turned in the other direction. The market ratio in that year rose above the mint ratio and continued above it until the mints of France (and of the other nations of the Latin Union, mentioned below) were closed to the free and unlimited coinage of silver on January 31, 1874. In 1873 no gold was coined by France, while the silver coinage amounted to 154.6 million francs. In 1874 24.3 million francs of gold were coined and 60.0 million francs of silver.

The Latin Union

During the latter years of her experience with bimetallism, France had associated with her certain other states in what is known as the Latin Union. According to a treaty effective August 1, 1866, France entered into a monetary union with Belgium, Switzerland and Italy, for a uniform regulation of the currency.[1] The French currency of 1803, as subsequently modified, was to serve as the model for the other states of the Latin Union, except that silver coins below five francs were to be fiduciary money, coined only on government account and with limited legal tender.[2] The weights, finenesses, dimensions and denominations respectively of the gold and silver coins of the different countries in the Latin Union were to be the same. While the coins in one country were not made legal tender in the other countries, they were made receivable by the government treasuries in the respective countries, and, to a limited extent, by the public banks. A per capita limit of six francs (subject to some qualifications) was

[1] Greece and Roumania joined the Union in 1867. The following year Spain, without joining the Union, began regulating her coinage on the same basis as that of the Union.

For the text of the Treaty constituting the Latin Union and an official account of the Union's origin written by the French Minister of Finance, see the *Report* of the International Monetary Conference Held in Paris, in August, 1878, pp. 781–794.

[2] The system of a limited circulation of fiduciary coins with limited legal tenders was first introduced in France on a small scale by the law of May 25, 1864, where it was applied only to pieces of fifty and twenty centimes. Later it was extended to pieces of larger denominations. *Ibid.*, p. 782.

placed upon the amount of fiduciary silver pieces below the denomination of five francs that each country could issue.

According to the eminent American bimetallist, Francis A. Walker,[1] French bimetallism was not greatly strengthened by the coöperation of the other states of the Latin Union.

Significant Facts in the Experience of France with Bimetallism

In studying the experience of France with bimetallism for the period 1803 to 1874, the following facts deserve emphasis:

(1) Both gold and silver coins were minted under free coinage in every year of the entire period but two (1872 and 1873), and both kinds of coins were continually in circulation.

(2) Although these years of French bimetallism witnessed revolutionary changes in the proportions of gold and silver produced in the world—changes varying from 50.3 ounces of silver to 1 ounce of gold for the ten-year period ending in 1810 to 4.5 ounces of silver to one ounce of gold for the ten-year period ending 1860—variations in the average annual commercial ratio of the value of gold to the value of silver were small. The extreme range for the entire seventy-two years was only from 15.04 to 16.25.

(3) This comparative stability of the commercial ratio in the neighborhood of the mint ratio was brought about chiefly through the application by France and, latterly, by all of the states of the Latin Union, of the compensatory principle. Whenever the market ratio rose appreciably above the effective mint ratio, evidencing an undervaluation of gold and an overvaluation of silver at the mints, as in the years 1842 to 1847, for example, France drew into her circulation large amounts of silver and used less and less gold, throwing large quantities of the yellow metal onto the world's markets, and thereby forcing the market ratio down toward the mint ratio. When, on the other hand, the market ratio fell appreciably below the mint ratio, evidencing an overvaluation of gold and an undervaluation of silver at the mints, as, for example, during the years immediately following the Californian and Australian gold discoveries, France again acted as a buffer, drawing into her circulation great quantities of gold and throwing out on the world's markets great quantities of silver, thereby forcing the market ratio back toward the mint ratio.

[1] *International Bimetallism*, p. 132.

Discontinuance of Bimetallism

Bimetallism in France and the other states of the Latin Union was given up early in 1874. Among the more important reasons for this action, concerning which there has been much controversy, the following may be mentioned:

(1) The comparative scarcity of silver coin that had existed during the years 1851 to 1872, a period during which, as we have seen, France coined over twelve times as much gold money as silver money, had made gold coins familiar and popular.

On the other hand, the problem of retaining silver coins in circulation, against the pressure of Gresham's Law, had been a serious one for many years, and had only lately been partly solved by France through making her smaller silver coins fiduciary coins with limited legal tender.[1] Because of such difficulties, the question of the desirability of substituting the single gold standard for the bimetallic standard had received much attention in France before 1870. France before the War "had completed long and exhaustive enquiries into the problem of the standard, and she tended quite definitely in favor of the gold standard." [2] In 1865, when the Latin Union was organized, Belgium, Switzerland and Italy had all favored a single gold standard in preference to a continuation of bimetallism. They yielded, however, to the French preference for a continuation of bimetallism for the time being. At the International Monetary Conference held in Paris in 1867, which was concerned chiefly with the seeking of greater uniformity in the world's coinage systems, the tendency had been strongly in the direction of obtaining uniformity through a gold standard. In fact, at this conference at which there were approximately a dozen and a half states represented, France appeared to have been the only strong advocate of bimetallism.[3]

(2) A second reason was the decision of Germany, at the time of the formation of the German Empire in 1871, to adopt an imperial gold standard in place of the silver standards that then prevailed in most of the German States. For some time previous to the War there had been much sentiment in these Silver Union German States in favor of the gold standard. England had been

[1] *Supra*, p. 321, note 2.

[2] Helfferich, pp. 153–154.

[3] Cf., "Proceedings of the International Monetary Conference in 1867," published in *Report of the International Monetary Conference of 1878*, pp. 803–878; also Russell, *International Monetary Conferences*, Chap. 2.

on the gold standard for about half a century and her monetary demand had been exerted chiefly on gold; on the other side of France, the German States had exerted their monetary demand mostly on silver; France had been the monetary buffer between England and the German States. Disastrously defeated in the Franco-Prussian War, in serious straits both economically and financially, and with the obligation of paying Germany an indemnity of five billion francs, France naturally viewed with anxiety the effect upon her monetary system of the heavy drain of gold to Germany which these conditions would be likely to cause and of the counter-flow into the world's markets and into her own of the great quantities of monetary silver which were known to have been accumulated in Germany, and which the adoption of the gold standard by the new German Empire was likely to release.

(3) A third factor, although probably a minor one, was that about 1866 the world's silver production began to increase considerably, largely as a result of the outpouring of the newly discovered silver mines of Nevada. The world's silver production increased from 35 million ounces in 1865 to 63 million ounces in 1871, while the world's production of gold declined during the same period from 5.9 million ounces to 5.6 million ounces. In 1867 the commercial ratio for the first time since 1852 averaged above the nominal mint ratio of France of 15½ to 1, being 15.57 to 1, and it continued above 15½ to 1 every year down to the closing of the mints of the Latin Union to the free coinage of silver. It was not, however, until 1873 that the market ratio rose above the actual mint ratio (that is, the ratio which allows for coinage charges) of 15.583 to 1. Many feared that silver coins of the larger denominations would come back into circulation in increasing quantities and would drive out of circulation the gold which had been supplied in such large quantities since 1850 by California and Australia and which had now become very popular.

(4) Then there was a natural pride on the part of some in favor of using the dearer metal as a standard, and of "not being outdistanced by Germany and England in monetary progress."

Regardless of the reasons, however, the important facts are that bimetallism ceased in France and the other states of the Latin Union at this time through the closing of the mints to the free coinage of silver and that since January, 1874 true bimetallism has nowhere existed in the world.

AMERICAN BIMETALLISM

Movement for a National Coinage

Efforts looking toward the establishment of a national coinage began long before the adoption of the American Constitution. As early as January 7, 1782, the Congress of the Confederation had instructed Robert Morris, then Superintendent of Finance, "to prepare and report to Congress a table of rates, at which the different species of foreign coins most likely to circulate within the United States, shall be received at the Treasury thereof." Eight days afterwards, Morris submitted to Congress a lengthy report proposing a comprehensive coinage scheme for the Confederation, and justifying his submission of a more ambitious report than that called for in the resolution of Congress on the ground that "as we are now shaking off the inconveniences of a depreciating medium, the present moment seems to be that, in which a general currency can best be established. . . ."

Currency System Recommended by Robert Morris

After considering the relative merits of a gold standard, a silver standard and a bimetallic standard, Morris decided in favor of a silver standard. He said:

> "Gold is more valuable than silver, and so far must have the preference, but it is from that very circumstance the more exposed to fraudulent practices. Its value rendering it more portable is an advantage, but it is an advantage which paper possesses in a much greater degree, and of consequence the commercial nation of England has had recourse to paper for the purposes of its trade; although the mass of circulating coin is gold. It will always be in our power to carry a paper circulation to every proper extent. There can be no doubt therefore, that our money standard ought to be affixed to silver."

Inasmuch, however, as he found silver, like everything else, variable in value, Morris favored a substantial coinage charge on the coinage of silver bullion in order to protect the coins from exportation and from the melting pot. He advocated the decimal system for the new coinage because of its simplicity, adding "whenever such things required labor, time and reflection, the greater number who do not know, are made the dupes of the lesser number who do."

The coin coming nearest to a general standard he found to be the

Spanish dollar, and he thought that the new money in order to be perfectly intelligible to the whole people "must have some affinity to the former currency." He found that at the time Spanish dollars, as a result of the various state ratings, passed

> "in Georgia at five shillings, in North Carolina and New York, at eight shillings, in Virginia and the four Eastern States, at six shillings, in all the other States except South Carolina at seven shillings and sixpence, and in South Carolina at thirty-two shillings and sixpence. The money unit of a new coin to agree without a fraction with all these different values of a dollar except the last, will be the fourteen hundred and fortieth part of a dollar. . . ."

This would be equal to about ¼ of a grain of fine silver. No coin of this size would need to be coined, he said, because it was sufficient that the value of the unit should be precisely known. Morris favored the immediate establishment of a mint, and the rating of foreign coins at so many dollars per ounce.

Following Morris's recommendation, Congress on February 21, 1782, approved the establishment of a mint, and directed Morris to prepare and report to Congress a plan for conducting the same. Morris expended about $2,000 for the establishment of "The Mint of North America," which manufactured a few dies for copper coinage, and struck a few copper coins.

Currency Plan of Thomas Jefferson

Thomas Jefferson left some undated notes on "The establishment of a money unit and of a coinage for the United States" which were apparently written in 1782 or 1783. He favored making the Spanish milled dollar the monetary unit, and dividing it into tenths and hundredths according to the decimal system. The unit suggested by Morris he opposed as being altogether too small, requiring cumbersomely large figures to express the values of ordinary commodities, and as being neither equal nor near to any of the known coins in value. He favored the coinage of gold along with that of silver at a ratio near the market ratio of the principal countries.

> "Perhaps," he added, "we might with safety lean to a proportion somewhat above par for gold, considering our neighborhood and commerce with the sources of the coins and the tendency which the high price of gold in Spain has to draw thither all that of their mines, leaving silver principally for our and other markets."

Currency Plan of Grand Committee of Congress

A Grand Committee on the Money Unit of the Continental Congress made a report in 1785. This Committee opposed the recommendation of Robert Morris that the monetary unit be 1/1440 of a Spanish milled dollar, and favored making this dollar itself the unit. Although favoring the coinage of gold at a ratio of not more than 15 to 1, the Committee declared that

> "sundry advantages would arise to us from a system by which silver might become the prevailing money. This would operate as a bounty to draw it from our neighbors by whom it is not sufficiently esteemed. Silver is not exported so easily as gold and it is a more useful metal."

The Committee favored the decimal system for the coins, and a substantial brassage charge so as to protect the coins from being unduly melted or exported.

On July 6, 1785, the Congress of the Confederation took under consideration the Grand Committee's report and voted unanimously "that the money unit of the United States of America be one dollar," "that the smallest coin be of copper, of which 200 shall pass for one dollar," and "that the several pieces shall increase in a decimal ratio."

Currency Plans of the Board of Treasury

Nine months later (April 8, 1786) the Board of Treasury, consisting of Samuel Osgood and Walter Livingston, recommended to the consideration of Congress three different coinage plans, the differences consisting chiefly in the sizes of the coins and the coinage ratio between silver and gold. All three of the plans recommended the silver dollar as the monetary unit, the decimal notation, and the coinage of gold along with silver. Congress passed a resolution on August 8, 1786, in response to the recommendations of the Board of Treasury, providing for the coinage of gold, silver and copper coins, with the respective denominations arranged in decimal ratios.

First Mint Ordinance

On October 16, 1786, Congress passed an ordinance "for the establishment of the Mint of the United States of America, and for regulating the value and alloy of coin." The mint ratio thus established, when allowance is made for coinage charges, was about 15.22 to 1.

Before any considerable progress was made in carrying out these plans, the Government of the Confederation ceased to exist, and the new National Government, under the Constitution, came into being. The above developments were therefore the background for the coinage legislation of the national period.

The National Period

With the ratification of the Constitution, the National Government was given the power "to coin money, regulate the value thereof, and of foreign coin and fix the standard of weights and measures" (Art. 1, sec. 8, par. 5); and this power was made exclusive by the provision (Art. 1, sec. 10) that "no state shall . . . coin money; emit bills of credit; make anything but gold and silver coin a tender in payment of debts."

The records of the Constitutional Convention and of the debates over the adoption of the Constitution show that there was practically no controversy over the provisions of the Constitution relating to coinage. They were everywhere taken for granted.

On April 15, 1790, the House of Representatives passed a resolution ordering "that it be an instruction to the Secretary of the Treasury to prepare and report to this House a proper plan or plans for the establishment of a national mint."

Hamilton's Report on the Mint

Pursuant to this resolution, Hamilton submitted to the House on April 28, 1791, his Report on the Mint—a report which shows a remarkable understanding of the principles of monetary science.[1]

The Report gives a broad discussion of the question of a proper coinage policy for the new nation. It then undertakes to answer the following six questions, the first two of which are by far the most important:

(1) "What ought to be the nature of the money unit of the United States?"

(2) "What the proportion between gold and silver, if coins of both metals are to be established?"

(3) "What the proportion and composition of alloy in each kind?"

[1] The Report will be found in the *Annals* of Congress, 1st Congress, II, pp. 1582 *et seq.;* also in the *Report of the International Monetary Conference of 1878*, pp. 454–484.

(4) "Whether the expense of coinage shall be defrayed by the government, or out of the material itself?"

(5) "What shall be the number, denominations, sizes, and devices of the coins?"

(6) "Whether foreign coins shall be permitted to be current or not; if the former, at what rate, and for what period?"

The Money Unit of the United States in 1791

Before answering the question of what ought to be the money unit, Hamilton undertook to answer the question, what is the money unit; on the theory that the new unit ought, if practicable, to have a value very close to that of the existing one, so as to avoid disturbances in prices and wages, and in the relations between debtors and creditors. He concluded that, although the pound was the unit in the money of account of all the states, the dollar was best entitled to be considered as the unit in the coins. The argument in favor of the dollar, however, he found lost much of its weight from the following considerations:

"That species of coin has never had any settled or standard value, according to weight or fineness, but has been permitted to circulate by tale, without regard to either, very much as a mere money of convenience, while gold has had a fixed price by weight and with an eye to its fineness. This greater stability of value of the gold coins, is an argument of force for regarding the money unit as having been hitherto virtually attached to gold, rather than to silver.

"Twenty-four grains and six-eighths of a grain of fine gold, have corresponded with the nominal value of the dollar in the several states, without regard to the successive diminutions of its intrinsic worth.

"But, if the dollar should, notwithstanding, be supposed to have the best title to being considered as the present unit in the coins, it would remain to determine what kind of dollar ought to be understood; or, in other words, what precise quantity of fine silver."

After considering the fine silver contents of the Spanish dollars of different coinages and concluding that the more ancient and more valuable dollars were not then to be met with at all in circulation and "that the mass of those generally current is composed of the newest and most inferior kinds," he found that the present unit was somewhere between a dollar of about 368 grains of fine silver and one of about 374 grains.

Approaching the problem from another angle, he found the market ratio of gold to silver to be approximately 15 to 1, and multiplying the fine gold equivalent of the dollar, namely, 24¾ grains by 15, he arrived at 371¼ grains of silver for the dollar—almost exactly the average of the fine silver weights of Spanish dollars of the two more recent issues.

Approaching the problem, then, either from the standpoint of assays of the silver dollars picked from the kinds then most widely circulating at the time, or from the standpoint of the amount of silver the dollar should contain in the light of the gold equivalent of the dollar in circulation and the market ratio between the value of gold and silver, he arrived at a fine silver content of 371 to 372 grains of fine silver.

Hamilton Favors Bimetallism

The next question considered by Hamilton was whether the new coinage system should be silver monometallism, gold monometallism or bimetallism. Up to that time, he said, the suggestions and proceedings had had for their object the annexing of the future money unit "emphatically to the silver dollar." Despite these prevailing ideas, however, he declared himself as "upon the whole, strongly inclined to the opinion, that a preference ought to be given to neither of the metals for the money unit," and that, "perhaps, if either were to be preferred, it ought to be gold rather than silver." "Gold," he said, "may, perhaps, in certain services, be said to have greater stability than silver; as, being of superior value, less liberties have been taken with it, in the regulations of different countries." The value of gold he thought was less likely than that of silver to be influenced by circumstances of commercial demand, and the revolutions which might take place in the comparative values of gold and silver in the future he thought would be more likely to be due to changes in the value of silver than of gold. However, these advantages of gold over silver he did not consider sufficient to justify the use of gold alone as a standard metal and he concluded that

> "upon the whole, it seems to be most advisable . . . not to attach the unit exclusively to either of the metals; because this cannot be done effectually, without destroying the office and character of one of them as money, and reducing it to the situation of a mere merchandise. . . . To annul the use of either of the metals, as money, is to abridge the quantity of circulating medium; and is liable to all the objections which arise from a comparison of the benefits of a full, with the evils of a scanty circulation."

The use of the two metals as standard money he thought would also be of an advantage in the development of the country's foreign trade since "it is often, in the course of trade, as desirable to possess the kind of money, as the kind of commodities best adapted to a foreign market."

The Ratio Question

Hamilton then took up a study of what should be the proper mint ratio between gold and silver, recognizing that the mint ratio should conform as nearly as possible to the market ratio in the leading markets of the world, and that if a mint ratio materially different from this market ratio should be established, the over-valued metal would drive the undervalued metal out of circulation. After a lengthy discussion of the ratio question, he concluded with some hesitation that, all things considered, the best ratio to adopt would be 15 to 1.

Summary of Hamilton's Recommendations

On this basis he concluded "that the unit, in the coins of the United States, ought to correspond with 24 grains and ¾ of a grain of pure gold, and with 371 grains and ¼ of a grain of pure silver, each answering to a dollar in the money of account." Following the British practice, he favored making both gold and silver coins $^{11}/_{12}$ fine. He recommended the decimal system of notation. Six denominations of coins were recommended to begin with; namely, gold pieces of ten dollars and of one dollar, silver pieces of one dollar and of ten cents and copper pieces of one cent and of a half cent. He did not expect many dollar gold pieces to be coined, saying that "the chief inducement to the establishment of the small gold piece, is to have a sensible object in that metal, as well as in silver, to express the unit." Hamilton recommended weights for the copper coins such that the value of the coins would "about correspond with the value of the copper and the expense of coinage." The question of whether the mint should impose a charge for the coining of gold and silver brought to it he discussed, with the conclusion that

> "under an impression that a *small* difference between the value of the coin and the mint price of bullion, is the least exceptionable expedient for restraining the melting down, or exportation of the former, and not

perceiving that, if it be a very moderate one, it can be hurtful in other respects—the Secretary is inclined to an experiment of one half per cent. on each of the metals."

As to foreign coins, Hamilton said the discontinuance of their circulation was a necessary part of the system contemplated for the new national coinage. He recommended, however, that the foreign coins should be "suffered to circulate, precisely upon their present footing, for one year after the mint shall have commenced its operations" and that thereafter their demonetization should be gradually extended over a period of two years.

Mint Act of 1792

On April 2, 1792, after a debate which was concerned chiefly with the question whether a representation of President Washington should be stamped on the new gold coins or an emblem of Liberty with the word Liberty, the Senate standing for the former and the House for the latter, the House won, and the mint bill became law.[1] In all important respects, save two, the mint act followed the recommendations of Hamilton's report. These two were: (1) the denominations of the coins to be minted; and (2) the fineness of the silver coins.

As to the former, the act provided for all the denominations recommended by Hamilton except the gold dollar, but added gold pieces of $5 and $2.50 and silver pieces of 50¢, 25¢ and 5¢, thereby departing from the almost strictly decimal system of denominations recommended by Hamilton. The coins were therefore to be of the following metals and denominations:

Gold: $10, $5 and $2.50, dubbed, respectively, by the law "eagles," "half eagles" and "quarter eagles."

[1] During the debate in Congress over the emblems to be used on the silver dollars, an amusing incident occurred, which is described as follows by Evans in his *History of the United States Mint at Philadelphia*, p. 15:

"A member of the House from the South bitterly opposed the choice of the eagle, on the ground of its being the 'king of birds,' and hence neither proper nor suitable to represent a nation whose institutions and interests were wholly inimical to monarchical forms of government. Judge Thatcher playfully, in reply, suggested that perhaps a goose might suit the gentleman, as it was a rather humble and republican bird, and would also be serviceable in other respects, as the goslings would answer to place upon the dimes. This answer created considerable merriment, and the irate Southerner, conceiving the humorous rejoinder as an insult, sent a challenge to the Judge, who promptly declined it. The bearer, rather astonished, asked, 'Will you be branded as a coward?' 'Certainly, if he pleases,' replied Thatcher; 'I always was one and he knew it, or he would never have risked a challenge.'"

Silver: $1, 50¢, 25¢, 10¢ and 5¢, dubbed, respectively, "dollars or units," "half dollars," "quarter dollars," "dismes" and "half dismes."

Copper: "cents" and "half cents."

Both gold and silver coins were all to be made 11/12 fine (equivalent to a decimal fineness of .91667) according to Hamilton's recommendation. Congress, however, for all the silver coins substituted a fineness of .89240. The object of this departure from Hamilton's recommendation was to make the amount of alloy in the silver dollar such, that when added to the 371¼ grains of pure silver in the dollar it would give the coin a gross weight of 416 grains—the estimated approximate weight of the Spanish milled dollar then in circulation.

A ratio of 15 to 1 was adopted, the fine silver content of a silver dollar, 371¼ grains, being made exactly 15 times the fine gold content of a dollar gold, 24¾ grains.

No coinage charge was to be imposed if the person bringing the bullion to the mint would wait for his coin until the bullion could be minted; but, if he took his coin at once, a charge of ½ of 1 per cent was to be imposed.

Silver coins of all denominations were to be made of the same fineness and of weights proportionate to their respective values.

All gold and silver coins were made unlimited legal tender.

The copper coins authorized by the mint act and the subsequent act of May 8, 1792, carried practically their full value in their copper content.

Debasement of coins or embezzlement of metal by officers or employees of the mint was declared to be a felony and was punishable by death.

The disposition of the foreign coins in circulation was not covered by the mint act but was left for later legislation.

How did the system of bimetallism established by this act work?

American Bimetallism in Practice

The United States was legally upon a bimetallic standard from the Mint Act of 1792 to the Coinage Act of 1873, although within that time, for two periods, viz., 1814–1817 and 1862–1878, most of the country was actually on a fiduciary paper money standard.

America's experience with actual bimetallism may be conveniently divided into two periods: (1) the period of the 15 to 1 ratio from the Mint Act of 1792 to the Coinage Act of June 28, 1834; and (2) the period of ratios of approximately 16 to 1 from the Act of 1834 to the suspension of specie payments December 30, 1861. During the first of these periods the mint ratio overvalued silver and during the second it overvalued gold.

The Period of Overvalued Silver

On July 31, 1792, the cornerstone was laid of a building in Philadelphia to be used as a mint—the first building to be erected by the new National Government for public purposes. The work of coinage began in October, 1792, with the minting of a small amount of silver. Copper coins were first minted in 1792 and gold coins in 1795.

At first the affairs of the mint were assigned to the Department of State of which Jefferson was Secretary, but in 1795, in response to a letter to Washington written by Hamilton the day he resigned from the Cabinet, they were transferred to the Treasury Department, under which they have been ever since.

The Director of the Mint Fails to Follow Legal Ratio

In considering the operation of the coinage system established under the Mint Act of 1792, the first fact to note is that the legal ratio of 15 to 1 established by the act was not followed during the first three years of our national coinage system.[1] The first Director of the Mint, David Rittenhouse, objected to the decimal fineness of .8924 established by the law for silver coins, on the grounds that it was a clumsy fraction to operate with in the work of coinage, and that it gave such a large percentage of alloy as to make the silver coins "too black." Relying on the belief that Congress would promptly follow his recommendation and change the fineness to .900 for all silver coins, he proceeded to mint all silver coins on a basis of .900 fine. This would have done little damage had he made the change by reducing the amount of the alloy, leaving the fine silver content at 371¼ grains, but in order to realize the fineness of .900 he raised the fine silver content of a dollar of silver money to 374¾ grains—an increase of nearly

[1] The use of a mint ratio different from that provided by law was said many years later to have been sanctioned by both Secretary of State Jefferson and the Secretary of the Treasury. See, letter of Representative Campbell P. White to the Director of the Mint, Dr. Samuel Moore, under date of April 25, 1832. *Report of Committee*, 23d Congress, 1st Sess., Vol. II, No. 278, pp. 74–75.

1 per cent. This made the actual ratio approximately 15.14 to 1, instead of the legal ratio of 15 to 1. Congress did not make the change in ratio Rittenhouse expected, and accordingly until this illegal practice was stopped in November, 1795, persons bringing silver to the mint received approximately 1 per cent less dollars for their silver than they were entitled to receive under the law.[1]

Foreign Coins

It has been noted that the Mint Act of 1792 made no reference to foreign coins. The proper treatment of these coins presented to the new Government a difficult problem, which led to considerable legislation over a period of many years, and was not finally solved until 1857. Into the details of this history we cannot go, although occasional references to it will be made later, and here a few of the high spots will be noted.

An Act of February 9, 1793, declared that "from and after the first day of July next, foreign gold and silver coins shall pass current as money . . . and be a legal tender for the payment of all debts and demands" at certain rates in United States money specified for designated foreign coins; gold coins to be taken according to their weights and silver coins at specified values provided the coins did not fall below the minimum weights mentioned in the law. The Act further provided that at the expiration of three years after the time when the coinage of gold and silver "shall commence at the mint of the United States, (which time shall be announced by the proclamation of the President of the United States,) all foreign gold coins, and all foreign silver coins, except Spanish milled dollars and parts of such dollars, shall cease to be a legal tender . . . "

President Adams, on July 22, 1797, issued a proclamation pursuant to the above law removing the legal-tender quality from all foreign gold coins after July 31, 1797, and from all foreign silver coins, except Spanish milled dollars and parts of such dollars, after October 15, 1797.[2] In consequence of the inconveniences

[1] For an account of the use of this illegal ratio, see Carothers, *Fractional Money*, pp. 69–71.

[2] About four months after the issuance of this proclamation, a treasury circular was sent to collectors of customs and supervisors of the revenue, referring to the proclamation and saying that since the Bank of the United States had consented to receive foreign silver coins at the rates at which they had previously been legal tender, they would be received as before by the government in payment of taxes and other government dues. *Finance Report*, I, p. 503.

resulting from the withdrawal of the legal-tender quality from this foreign money, Congress reinstated foreign coins as legal-tender money for a period of about three years by an Act of February 1, 1798. The legal-tender quality of these coins expired by limitation in 1802, but was again restored by Congress in 1806 for another period of three years. In December, 1810, a committee of the House of Representatives recommended that the legal circulation of these foreign coins should be restored because there was not sufficient coin in circulation without them.[1] This recommendation, however, was not followed, and foreign coins, except Spanish dollars and their fractions, ceased to be legal tender in the United States in 1809. This, however, did not prevent them from continuing to circulate in substantial quantities.

United States Gold Coins, 1792–1834

There has been considerable dispute as to whether the ratio of 15 to 1 recommended by Hamilton and followed by the mint act was at the time in conformity with the market ratio in the leading markets of the world or not, and it was later claimed by Thomas Benton and others that Hamilton deliberately undervalued gold with the idea that it would thereby be driven out of circulation and thus would create a vacuum in the circulation into which the bank notes of the first United States Bank might readily flow. There is very little evidence, however, in support of this claim, and the verdict of history seems to be that Hamilton conscientiously tried to recommend a mint ratio that was in conformity with the market ratio at the time. He apparently succeeded, but the market ratio soon changed and for many years thereafter ruled substantially higher than 15 to 1.[2] This conclusion will be borne out by a reference to the chart opposite page 336 which shows the average annual ratios for this period in the Hamburg market, then the dominant silver market of the world.

For not a single year of the period 1792 to 1834 did the average market ratio fall below 15 to 1, and for only three years of the entire period did it fall below 15.17 to 1. The average ratio for the entire forty-three years was 15.61 to 1. From the establish-

[1] *Finance Report*, II, pp. 456–457.

[2] See annual ratio figures computed by Adolf Soetbeer and given in his *Edelmetall-Produktion*, pp. 130–131.

ment of the mint to 1834, therefore, the American mint ratio overvalued silver and undervalued gold,[1] thereby encouraging the flow of silver to the mint and discouraging the flow of gold and also encouraging the melting down of any new gold coins

COINAGE OF GOLD AND SILVER AT THE UNITED STATES MINT 1793–1833

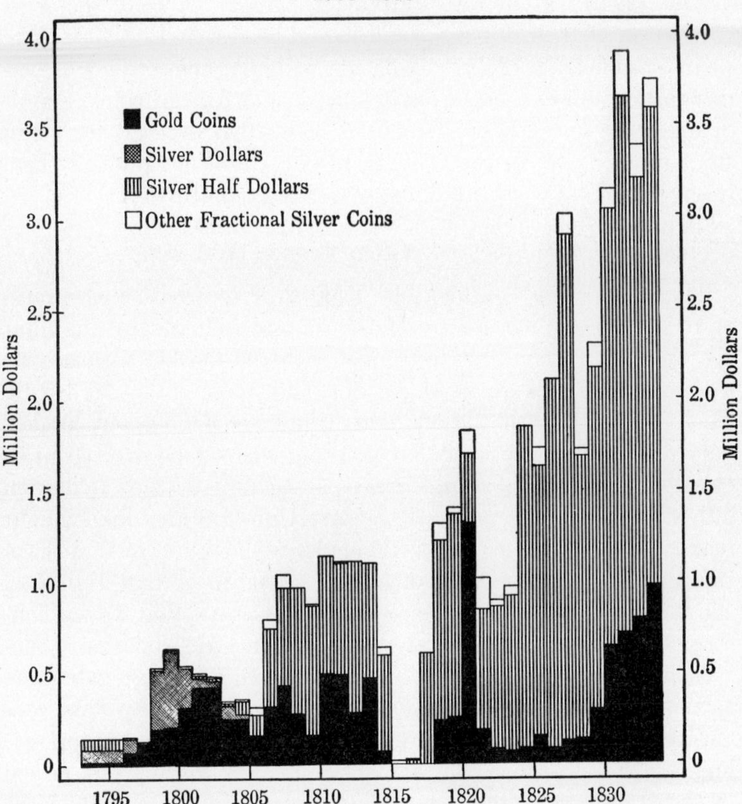

that were minted. Furthermore, as we have seen,[2] France, under her monetary law of 1803, opened her mints to the coinage of gold and silver at an effective ratio of 15.69 to 1, so that France, with probably the largest coin circulation at the time of any country in the world, was attracting gold from this country for coinage

[1] For one year, 1793, when the market ratio averaged 15.00 to 1, the mint ratio overvalued gold and undervalued silver.

[2] *Supra*, pp. 319 and 320.

purposes. Flying in the face of the bullion market, and of the mint ratio of France, we could not have reasonably expected to get much gold at our mint, nor to keep in circulation much of what we coined. When one considers the extent to which we undervalued gold at our mint during this period, it is surprising that we got so much gold as we did.

The chart on the preceding page shows the coinage of gold and silver by years from 1793 to 1833.[1] During that entire period we coined only $11.8 million of gold coins; while France coined $200 million, or over 17 times as much.

Gold Disappears from Active Circulation

There has been some dispute as to when gold coins began to leave the United States in substantial quantities. Laughlin [2] supports by some evidence his claim that "gold began to disappear as early as 1810, if not before, and that little of it was in circulation by 1818." The evidence, however, seems to be stronger for the claim that gold did not leave the country in any considerable quantities until about the time of the great increase in the foreign demand for gold accompanying England's return to specie payments.[3]

A report of the House Committee on the Currency made February 2, 1821, declared that:

> "It is ascertained, in one of our principal commercial cities, quite in the vicinity of the mint, that the gold coin, in an office of discount and deposit of the Bank of the United States, there located, in November 1819, amounted to $165,000, and the silver coin to $118,000. That since that time, the silver coin has increased to $700,000, while the gold coin has diminished to the sum of $1,200, $100 only of which is American. And it is then stated, that the vaults of the state banks, in the same city, having a capital, in the aggregate, as is believed, of nearly $8,000,000. exhibits a similar result. It is scarcely to be doubted, that on examination in the other commercial cities similar additional proof would be furnished."

Samuel Moore, Director of the Mint, wrote to the Secretary of the Treasury, S. D. Ingham, September 30, 1829: "I find no trace

[1] The coinage figures on which the chart is based are given in the United States Treasury Department *Circular* No. 52 of July 1, 1912, pp. 52 and 53.

[2] Laughlin, J. Laurence, *History of Bimetallism in the United States*, pp. 28–30.

[3] Of course, there was little specie, either gold or silver, in active circulation during the period of the suspension of specie payments from the summer of 1814 to the spring of 1817—in fact, until some months later—for specie payments were far from being completely resumed in the spring of 1817.

of a premium on gold, in this city, Philadelphia, before 1821, for the purpose of export and remittance, in preference to bills of exchange." John White, Cashier of the Baltimore Branch of the United States Bank, wrote Secretary Ingham, November 16, 1829:

> " . . . The *disappearance* of our gold coin is altogether attributable to the reformation in the currency of England, which created an *unprecedented* demand, probably not less in amount than *twenty millions of pounds sterling*, and the great change thus unavoidably produced in the *denomination* of our specie basis, (gold having been so abundant previously, that I was enabled to transmit to the Parent Bank, from this office, between November, 1819, and June, 1820, upwards of $240,000,) has excited public attention . . ."

In its Report of February 22, 1831, on coins the C. P. White Committee of the House of Representatives said: "It does not appear that there was any export of gold from the United States, of consequence, from 1792 till 1821 . . ."

Regardless of the exact time when the gold went out, there was apparently little gold in circulation between 1821 and 1833. During those years the market ratio between gold and silver ruled high, and the low mint ratio of 15 to 1 in the United States was especially unfavorable to gold.

The coinage of eagles was discontinued in 1804 and from that time until 1833 the great bulk of the gold coins minted were half eagles.

Silver Coins

A reference to the chart on page 337 will show that during the period 1793–1833 the coinage of silver was much larger than that of gold, although the preponderance of silver coinage was not pronounced until after 1820. From 1793 to 1820, inclusive, the total coinage of silver was in round numbers $11.0 million as compared with $7.4 million for gold; but for the entire period 1793–1833, inclusive, the silver coinage was, in round numbers, $36.3 millions, while the gold coinage was only $11.8 millions.

Coinage of Silver Dollars Discontinued

The life of the new American silver dollars during this first period of our national coinage history was brief. Although these dollars contained less silver than unworn Spanish milled dollars of the more recent dates, they contained more silver than the clipped, bored and sweated pieces usually found in circulation. The new dollars were quickly picked up by dealers who sent them through trade channels to the West Indies, where, on account of their brightness, they made a strong appeal to the native population, and were readily exchanged for the heavier Spanish dollars which were in circulation there. These Spanish dollars were then brought to the United States and put in circulation after some of the silver had been abstracted from them by clipping, sweating or boring.

The transaction was a profitable one to the coin and bullion dealers, but rendered the coining of new dollars by the mint of no advantage to the country. To meet the situation President Madison wrote the Director of the Mint, November 1, 1806:

> " . . . In consequence of a representation from the director of the Bank of the United States, that considerable purchases have been made of dollars coined at the mint for the purpose of exporting them, and as it is probable further purchases and exportations will be made, the President directs that all silver to be coined at the mint shall be of small denominations, so that the value of the largest pieces shall not exceed half a dollar."

The coinage of silver dollars was accordingly discontinued, and was not resumed until 1836. From the opening of the mint to 1805, when the last silver dollars were coined, their total coinage was only $1,435,517.

Importance of the Half Dollar

The most striking fact of the coinage of 1793 to 1833—a fact overlooked by most writers on American monetary history—was the great preponderance of half dollars. How pronounced this was will be seen when it is noted that of a total silver coinage for this period amounting in round numbers to $36.3 millions, $33.0 millions or 90.9 per cent consisted of half dollars. Silver dollars comprised 4.0 per cent of the total and fractional silver of the denominations below 50 cents (i.e., 25¢, 10¢ and 5¢) amounted to $1.9 million, or 5.1 per cent (see chart on page 337).[1]

[1] Annual coinage figures by denominations are given in U. S. Treasury Department *Circular* No. 52 of July 1, 1912, "Information Respecting United States Bonds, Paper Currency, Coin, Production of Precious Metals, etc.," pp. 52 and 53.

Chief among the reasons for the relatively large coinage of half dollars were the following:[1]

(1) After the disappearance from circulation of the American silver dollar, the half dollar was the only American coin between the 25-cent piece and the gold quarter eagle. It was therefore called upon to fill a very large gap—one that grew larger as the gold coins were driven out of circulation. With the disappearance of gold, moreover, the half dollar became the most convenient coin for purposes of bank reserves.

(2) Dollar for dollar the 50-cent piece was cheaper to coin than the smaller silver coins. The time and expense required for coining a dime or half dime were almost as great as were required for coining a 50-cent piece. From the beginning of its history the mint had been under criticism because of its expensiveness and repeated efforts had been made to have it closed. Naturally, therefore, the mint authorities in coining the bullion brought to them showed preference for the half dollar—the denomination that could be coined most cheaply.

(3) Persons bringing bullion to the mint for coinage were required either to pay a brassage charge of one-half of 1 per cent, or wait for their money until the bullion could be coined. The delay was longer when the bullion was coined into the smaller denominations.

Although the coinage of silver half dollars was substantial, it must not be thought that these coins played a very important rôle in hand to hand circulation. Apparently the bulk of those remaining in the country were held in bank reserves. Some of them, moreover, were exported to India, China and the West Indies. Their exportation, however, was not as profitable as that of the silver dollar, for twice as many coins had to be collected for the same money value, and the half dollars were, on the whole, more abraded than the dollars. None the less, just as the new overvalued silver coins tended to drive out of circulation the undervalued gold coins, so likewise did the worn and clipped foreign silver coins tend to drive out the new American silver coins, while the excessive issues of bank notes, many of them running down to fractional denominations, were continually exerting an influence, under Gresham's Law, toward driving out of circulation all coins having a large bullion content in proportion to their money value.

[1] Cf., Carothers, *op. cit.*, pp. 76–78.

Disappearance of United States Silver Coins from Circulation

As early as 1799 the Director of the Mint reported that the practice of melting down the coin of the United States by workmen in gold and silver was becoming "too common to the manifest loss of the United States." [1] From a valuable report on "The State of the Current Coins" submitted to the Senate by Senator Sanford from a Select Committee, January 11, 1830,[2] the following estimates are taken:

The coins of all kinds in the United States amounted to about $23 million in 1830. Of this amount about $14 million consisted of American coins—practically all silver [3]—about $5 million consisted of Spanish dollars and their parts; and about $4 million of various other foreign coins. In the opinion of the Committee,[4] more than one-third of our American coined silver, amounting to not less than $11 million, had departed from circulation. Almost all the early silver coins of our mint, the Committee held, had disappeared, making the greater portion of the American silver coins then current those that had been coined within the previous ten years.

Foreign Silver Coins

The Spanish coins in circulation were said to have averaged about 7 per cent below their legal weights, and about 6 per cent below the weights of corresponding American coins. The great bulk of the Spanish coins, however, were of denominations below a half dollar, and these were the coins that had been most mutilated and abraded. For the various denominations of Spanish coins the estimated average diminutions of weights were as follows:

[1] *Finance Report*, I, p. 616.

[2] *Senate Doc.*, 21st Congress, 1st Sess., No. 19.

[3] The C. P. White Select Committee's Report to the House, of February 22, 1831, estimated the total national silver coins then in circulation as not likely to exceed seven to eight million dollars. *House Report* No. 278, 23d Congress, 1st Sess., Vol. I, p. 67.

[4] The Director of the Mint in a letter sent to the White Committee of the House, and cited in its Report of Feb. 22, 1831, said: "The specie of the United States Bank is now nearly eleven millions, and of this amount they have less than two millions in our coin—a sum which does not exceed the amount delivered that bank from the mint within the present year." *Ibid.*, p. 72.

Dollar	about	1%
Half dollar	"	3%
Quarter dollar	"	6%
Eighth dollar	"	11%
Sixteenth dollar	"	19%[1]

Light-weight foreign coins, however, had the same purchasing power in current trade as heavy American coins (or as heavy foreign coins). On this subject the C. P. White Committee of the House in its Report of June 30, 1832, said:[2]

"The small change in use was long exclusively, and is yet partially, Spanish coins, greatly debased by wear; yet, until recently that the banks have made some objections to receive *large amounts of quarter dollars* by tale, these small coins have circulated without the slightest inconvenience or disadvantage, though the coins of 25 cents are believed to be defective about 4 per cent.; 12½ cent pieces from 10 to 12 per cent.; and those of 6¼ cents from 15 to 20 per cent.; and it may be noticed, as a striking illustration of the effect of a limited supply, that these small defective coins are as readily received and disbursed by retailers as our own recent issues of perfect coin, of twenty-five, ten and five cents each."

Hence, under the influence of Gresham's Law, there was a tendency for a progressive deterioration of the currency, the poorer coins always tending to drive out the better ones. The better coins were worth more as bullion, or as money abroad than as money in the United States, and they simply moved to the best market.

In the early thirties of the last century, therefore, our supply of coins in the United States was very meager, and their condition was far from satisfactory. There were few gold coins in circulation, and no silver dollars. A large proportion of the fractional silver coins consisted of clipped and worn foreign coins of small denominations. The half dollar was the principal American coin.

Agitation for Monometallism

About 1830 there were many influential people in the country who believed that bimetallism was fundamentally unsound, and that the United States should adopt a single standard. A good example of this position is found in the letters and reports of S. D. Ingham, who was Secretary of the Treasury from the spring

[1] *Sanford Committee Report*, Senate Document, 21st Congress, 1st Sess., No. 19, p. 9.

[2] *Report Committee*, 23d Congress, 1st Sess., II, No. 278, p. 16.

of 1829 to the summer of 1831. Ingham was one of the most active defenders of monometallism in American public life at that time. In a report to the Senate, dated May 4, 1830, he said: [1]

> "The proposition that there can be but one standard in fact is self-evident. The option of Governments charged with this duty is therefore between having property measured sometimes by gold and sometimes by silver, and selecting that metal which is best adapted to the purpose for the only standard. . . . All agree that measures of weight and capacity should be based on a unit, determinable by some fixed law of nature; and none will pretend that this measure could be perfected by referring to two or more variable laws, having no connection or equalizing principle to correct their aberrations.[2] Yet such is the theory of two standard measures of property. It may, indeed, be alleged that the supply and demand, or value of either gold or silver, is not governed by an invariable law; but this will not prove that the value of both is less variable than that of either, and still less that the variations of the one will counteract those of the other."

And again he said: [3]

> "The values of gold and silver, compared with each other . . . are liable to fluctuations, resulting from the operations of human enterprise, the political convulsions of nations, and from the laws of nature, which can neither be anticipated, controlled, nor averted. And even if all other causes which affect the supply and demand of the precious metals were uniform, every new mint regulation, changing the legal relative values with a view to conforming them more nearly to the true values, must produce a change in the true value of the metals, by creating an increased demand for that which is raised, the extent or effect of which cannot be calculated; and hence a new fluctuation is caused by the measure designed to correct an existing error. . . . A simple and certain remedy is within the reach of all. This remedy is to be found in the establishment of one standard measure of property only."

Gold Monometallism vs. Silver Monometallism

Although there were many advocates of the single standard at that time, there was a difference of opinion as to which of the two precious metals should be adopted as the standard. Secretary Ingham himself favored the silver standard. The standard measure of property he thought should be made of "a metal sufficiently abundant to enter into general circulation, determining values in

[1] See *International Monetary Conference Report of 1878*, p. 578.

[2] The claim that there is such an equalizing principle is the basis of the present-day theory of bimetallism. *Supra*, pp. 84–91.

[3] *Ibid.*, p. 577.

small as well as large transactions."[1] In a country like the United States where the great bulk of the transactions of any size were performed by means of paper money, he thought the absence of gold coin from circulation would not be a serious inconvenience. He pointed out that we had had long experience with a currency without gold, but very little with a currency without silver. The inconvenience of the former, he held, had been slight, but the inconvenience of the latter he thought would be serious. If any event should drain off our silver coins, their place, he said, would be "supplied, not by gold, but by small bank notes and paper tokens, which are the most obnoxious of all the various materials for currency."[2] The Director of the Mint, Samuel Moore, also favored silver monometallism.[3]

At this time Jackson was having his fight with the United States Bank and there was a tendency for the pro-bank people to advocate either the silver standard or a low bimetallic ratio favorable to silver, because either of these plans would be favorable to a large circulation of bank notes. It was with gold rather than with silver that bank notes competed to be the money of hand to hand circulation. For the opposite reason, anti-bank people were inclined to favor either the gold standard or a high bimetallic ratio favorable to gold.

Advocates of the gold standard claimed that gold was preferable to silver as the standard money metal, because it was more stable in value—a contention that silver standard advocates denied. They held that, under a gold standard, silver could be kept in circulation in sufficient quantities to meet all needs, by the expedient of limiting the coinage of silver and making it fiduciary money, with limited legal tender. They pointed to the success of the gold standard in England, with its fiduciary silver coinage, and to the desirability of our having a standard conforming to that of the country with which we had our largest trade relations. The gold standard was believed to be preferable to the silver standard also because a given amount of money was cheaper to coin in the form of gold coins than of silver coins; the expense, for example, of coining one gold eagle being much less than that of coining ten silver dollars.

[1] Cf., *International Monetary Conference Report of 1878*, p. 578.
[2] *Ibid.*, p. 576.
[3] See White *Report*, No. 278, p. 78.

The hands of gold monometallists were strengthened by the fact that at about that time some gold discoveries were made in Georgia and North Carolina which fired the imagination of many people and created special and local interests favorable to legislation that would give preference to gold.

Arguments for Continuing Bimetallism

Nonetheless, the majority of thinking people apparently still favored bimetallism, which they saw succeeding in France, and which they did not think had been given a fair trial in the United States. One of the strongest advocates of the continuance of bimetallism was Albert Gallatin who had been Secretary of the Treasury from 1801 to 1813. In a letter to Secretary Ingham, dated December 31, 1829, Gallatin strongly declared himself in favor of the continuance of bimetallism.[1] He supported his position by pointing to what he claimed to be the success of bimetallism in France, where he had been United States Minister from 1816 to 1823. The inconveniences arising from the simultaneous use of gold and silver as standard metals consisted wholly, he said, in the fact that when the market ratio varied from the mint ratio the debtor would pay in the cheaper metal. This disadvantage was not a serious one, he held, because in all those instances when the cheaper metal remained the more stable in value, a single standard based upon the metal that was dearer would be more unjust. But the stronger answer he found [2] in the fact that the fluctuations in the relative values of gold and silver were usually very slight, "less in amount than the fluctuations, either in the value of the precious metals, as compared with that of all other commodities, or in the relative value of bullion to coin, and even than the differences between coins . . ." So small were these fluctuations in the relative values of the two kinds of coin, that, as regards relations between debtor and creditor, he thought they might be ignored.

The New Mint Ratio and the Overvaluation of Gold

The new coinage system had not been in operation many years before it was realized that the 15 to 1 ratio was out of harmony with the market ratio and with the mint ratio of France. Agitation in favor of raising our mint ratio to approximately the mint ratio

[1] *International Monetary Conference Report of 1878*, p. 595.
[2] *Ibid.*, p. 595.

of France became increasingly strong after about 1820. A Select Committee of the House of Representatives on the subject of the relative values of gold and silver coins of the United States, made a report to the House on February 2, 1821, favoring an increase of our mint ratio to about 15.6 to 1. The Committee said that:[1]

> " . . . on inquiry, they find that gold coins, both foreign and of the United States, have, in a great measure, disappeared; and, from the best calculation that can be made, there is reason to apprehend they will be wholly banished from circulation. . . . There remains no longer any doubt that the gold coins of the United States are, by our laws, rated at a value lower than in almost any other country in comparison with that of silver."

Secretary of the Treasury Ingham made a long report to the Senate, May 4, 1830, on the question of the desirability of changing the ratio.[2] He said that, if bimetallism were to be continued and an effort made to restore gold to the circulation, probably the best ratio to adopt would be 15.625 to 1. Albert Gallatin a few months before had maintained that the French ratio of approximately 15.69 to 1 was apparently very close to the true market ratio because the French mint had been abundantly supplied with gold and silver for the last twenty-five years.[3] He favored a ratio for the United States of about 15.6069 to 1.[4] The C. P. White Committee of the House in one of its reports (that of February 22, 1831), although it preferred a single silver standard and desired gold coins if placed in circulation at all to be treated as subsidiary money "restricted to small payments," favored the ratio of 15.625 to 1. Again in its report of June 30, 1832, the Committee endorsed this ratio. The Director of the Mint, Samuel Moore, favored the single silver standard, but said that, if both gold and silver were to be coined, the ratio of 15.62 to 1 recommended by the Committee did not appear likely to produce any disturbance in the currency.[5] In 1832 the White Committee introduced a bill for coinage reform providing for the ratio of 15.625 to 1; and two years later, after much deliberation, introduced a new bill February 19, 1834, also providing a ratio of 15.625 to 1; although imposing coinage charges that would

[1] *Finance Report*, III, pp. 660–661.
[2] *International Monetary Conference Report of 1878*, pp. 558–672.
[3] *Ibid.*, p. 591.
[4] *Ibid.*, p. 594.
[5] C. P. White *Report*, No. 278, p. 78.

have made the effective ratio about 15.7 to 1. At a later date, Thomas H. Benton who became a leader in Congress on monetary questions said that the ratio of 15.62 to 1 in 1834 was the "ratio of nearly all who were best calculated, from their pursuits, to understand the subject." [1]

Coinage Acts of 1834 and 1837

Despite all the reasons favorable to a ratio conforming closely to the French ratio and the market ratio and despite the White Committee's having favored such a ratio (if bimetallism were to be continued) in at least three congressional reports and in an even larger number of bills which it had reported favorably to Congress, the ratio in the final bill was suddenly changed without explanation from 15.625 to 1 to 16.002 to 1, and the bill was hurriedly forced through Congress, becoming law June 28, 1834.

The motives for this sudden change in the ratio have never been satisfactorily explained. The two motives most commonly given, however, are: (1) that it was designed to help the gold industry then developing in the Southern slopes of the Alleghenies,[2] and (2) that it would help drive out of circulation the notes of the Second United States Bank—an institution which at that time was receiving sledge-hammer blows from President Jackson.

The Act of 1834 left all the silver coins unchanged as to weight and fineness. It reduced the gross weight of a dollar of gold coin (whether in the form of eagles, half eagles or quarter eagles) from 27 grains to 25.8 grains, and the pure gold content from 24.75 grains to 23.2 grains. The new gold coins therefore were given gold contents of about 6.7 per cent less than the corresponding coins under the old law. The new gold coins had a decimal fineness of .8992—an odd decimal fineness involving a repeating fraction—that proved unsatisfactory for the mint to work with, and which was accordingly raised to .900 by an Act of January 18, 1837, that raised the gold content of a dollar of gold coin from 23.2 grains to 23.22 grains—the content of all our gold coins down to 1933 when the coinage of gold was discontinued. The Coinage Act of 1834 also decreased the amount of alloy in the silver coins, reducing the gross weight of a dollar of silver coins from 416 grains to 412½

[1] *International Monetary Conference Report of 1878,* p. 685.

[2] Cf., *House Executive Doc.*, 33d Congress, 2d Sess., Vol. II, No. 3, p. 279.

grains, but leaving the fine silver content unchanged at 371¼ grains to the dollar. Since the Act of 1837 all of our gold and silver coins (except the 3-cent silver piece for a brief period) have been .900 fine. The change in the gold coins made by the Act of 1837 reduced the value ratio of gold and silver at the mint from 16.002 to 1, established by the Act of 1834, to 15.9884 to 1.

The Act of 1834 made the old gold coins receivable in all payments at the rate of 94.8 cents per penny-weight, which was their bullion value in terms of the new gold coin.

A reduction of 6.7 per cent in the weight of the pure gold in United States gold coins at most later periods in our history would have been a serious debasement of our currency. Such was not the case, however, in 1834, because practically no United States gold coins had circulated for over a decade, during which time United States gold coins had borne a premium. Persons contracting debts during that period contemplated their payment in United States silver coins, or Spanish silver coins or their equivalents in bank notes, and the Act of 1834 did not affect the silver content of these coins. Nonetheless, as we shall see later, there was a slight debasement, because the new gold coins proved to be worth slightly less, dollar for dollar, than the American silver coins then in circulation and therefore they slowly drove the latter out of circulation, thereby making the gold dollar the actual monetary unit in place of the dollar of fractional silver coins.

The Act of 1837 discontinued all coinage charges. To enable the mint more promptly to pay persons bringing bullion to it for coinage, the Act (Sec. 31) declared that:

> " . . . It shall be the duty of the Secretary of the Treasury to keep in the said Mint, when the state of the Treasury will admit thereof, a deposit of such amount of public money, or of bullion procured for the purpose, as he shall judge convenient and necessary, not exceeding one million of dollars, out of which those who bring bullion to the Mint may be paid the value thereof, as soon as practicable, after this value has been ascertained . . ."

In paying for bullion the Director of the Mint was required to give priority according to priority of deposit only, and in the denominations of coin delivered, the Treasurer was required to "comply with the wishes of the depositor, unless where impracticable or inconvenient to do so"; in which case the denominations of coins were to be designated by the Director. These provisions were intended to eliminate evils that had previously grown up in connection with the administration of the mint.[1]

How Did the New Ratio Work?

The accompanying chart shows the average annual commercial value ratio of silver to gold from 1790 to 1934.[2] In not a single year from the Coinage Act of 1833 to the discontinuance of legal bimetallism by the Act of 1873 did this ratio reach the new mint ratio. Furthermore, during the greater part of the two decades 1850–1870, when the gold discoveries of California and Australia were pouring their new floods of gold into the world's markets, the ratio ruled below 15½ to 1. In only six different months of the 39-year period from the Act of 1834 to the Act of 1873 was the minimum market price of silver in London below $58\frac{15}{16}$ pence per ounce of British standard silver—the price corresponding to our mint ratio of approximately 16 to 1. The minimum price of silver during the whole period gave a ratio of less than 1 per cent above our mint ratio.

Commercial Value Ratio of Silver to Gold
Annual Average, 1790–1934

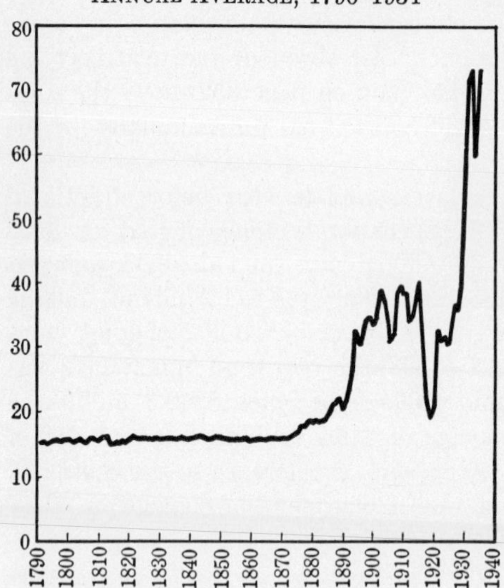

France had changed her coinage charges three times during this period, making her actual mint ratios as follows:[3]

1834–1835	15.69 to 1
1835–1850	15.626 to 1
1850–1854	15.586 to 1
1854–1874	15.583 to 1

[1] *Supra*, p. 341.

[2] The Annual Reports of the Director of the Mint of the United States give for each year since 1790 the average commercial ratio of silver to gold.

[3] The changes were all made after the beginning of the year so that in each transitional year each rate was employed part of the time.

Our American mint ratio was therefore during the whole period (except a few days) not only above the London market ratio, but it was also continually far above the mint ratio of France—the country then using the largest amount of gold and silver money of any country in the world.

With such an overvaluation of gold at our mints and undervaluation of silver, it was inevitable that gold coinage should heavily predominate over silver coinage, and that gold should tend strongly to drive silver out of circulation—particularly the larger silver coins which were the ones least abraded, and relatively the least expensive to collect. The chart on page 352 shows the coinage of standard gold and silver coins at our mint annually for the period 1830 to 1873.[1]

From 1834 to 1852 (the last complete year before fractional silver coins were made fiduciary) the total coinage of gold was $225 million, and that of full-weight silver coins (i.e., all silver coins except the 3-cent pieces of 1851 and 1852) was $41.2 million, making the gold coinage approximately $5.50 to each dollar of silver coinage. Extending the figures to 1873, the year legal bimetallism was discontinued, the total gold coinage becomes $840.3 million as compared with a silver coinage of $46.7 million, or about $18 of gold coin to one dollar of silver coin. A reference to the chart will show that, although there was a considerable coinage of silver nearly every year from 1834 to 1850, after 1850 the coinage of full-weight silver coins was negligible—so small as not to be portrayable on a chart of the dimensions of this one.

The great bulk of the silver coins minted during the years 1834 to 1852 were half dollars (as it had been prior to 1834), while the coinage of silver dollars was almost negligible, having amounted to

[1] Fractional fiduciary silver coins minted on government account after the Act of 1853 not being standard coins are not included in the chart.

The mint figures are not given in such a form as to make it possible to tell what amounts of gold and silver coins were coined in 1834 before July 31 when the new weights for gold coins went into effect; nor to tell what amount of the silver coinage minted in 1853, the year when all fractional silver coins were made fiduciary coins after June 1, was full weight coins and what amount was fiduciary coins; nor do they make it possible to tell the amount of gold coinage in 1873 up to the time of the passing of the Act of February 12, 1873, which discontinued the coinage of standard silver dollars. As a result it is impossible to give exactly comparable figures as to gold and silver coinage for these three transitional years in which there was important coinage legislation. The figures given in the chart for 1834 cover the total gold and silver coinage of that year; those for 1853 assume that all fractional silver coins minted that year were fiduciary coins, and the figures for 1873 cover the total gold coinage and the total coinage of standard silver dollars for the whole year.

only $1,067,000 out of the total standard silver coinage of $41.2 million. The coinage of quarters, dimes and half dimes was much larger than during the preceding period. During most of the years prior to 1850 the value ratio of gold to silver was not sufficiently below 16 to 1 to give a very large premium on silver coins—the

COINAGE OF GOLD AND SILVER AT THE UNITED STATES MINT
1830–1873

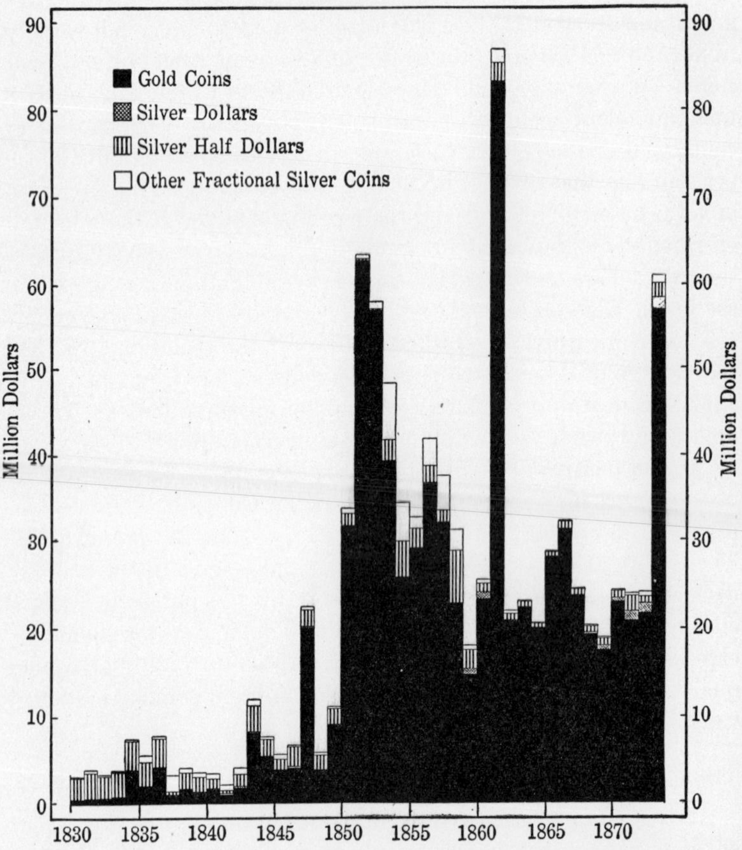

premium having ruled in most of the years in the neighborhood of 1 per cent. While this premium led to the rapid disappearance from circulation of the few silver dollars that were minted and of some of the half dollars and smaller fractions, it was not sufficient to cover the cost of collecting and shipping fractional coins of lower denominations than 50 cents on any considerable scale and yield a fair profit on the transaction. Down to about 1850 therefore the supply of fractional silver money, though often not adequate, was still not sufficiently deficient to cause serious inconvenience. Much of the fractional money, however, during those years was in a bad condition.

Under the influence of the great flood of gold poured on the world's markets from the newly discovered gold fields in California and Australia, the value ratio of gold to silver fell rapidly from 1848 to 1859 and this meant an increasing premium on silver coins. For example, while the ratio of 15.85 to 1 prevailing in 1848 was equivalent to a premium of .8 per cent on American silver coins, that of 1850, 15.70 to 1, was equivalent to a premium of 1.8 per cent and that of 1853, 15.33 to 1, was equivalent to a premium of 4.3 per cent. Not only did the receipts of silver at the mint fall off rapidly, but the silver in circulation began to disappear, at first the half dollars and then the smaller denominations. Everywhere the public were protesting against the scarcity of small change.

Various measures were adopted to meet the situation. In 1849 the Government began to coin gold dollars, and from then until 1862 it coined approximately $19 million of these pieces. Three-dollar gold pieces began to be minted in 1854, and the coinage of $2.50 gold pieces was greatly increased after 1849. Large amounts of bank notes for fractional parts of a dollar were put in circulation, also bank notes for odd amounts such as $1.25, $1.50 and $1.75. There were also privately issued notes and coins. In the country districts there was an increasing resort by the public to "sharp change" or "cut money," namely Spanish dollars cut into quarters, eighths and sixteenths. Bank notes were also torn into halves and quarters and these fractional parts of notes were popularly dubbed "rags."

The Three-Cent Piece Our First Fiduciary Silver Coin

At this time there was introduced into circulation the 3-cent silver piece, a coin of considerable historical significance because it was the first American fiduciary silver coin. It was authorized by the Act of March 3, 1851, which reduced the rate of letter postage in the United States from 5 cents to 3 cents. This 3-cent piece was to weigh 12⅜ grains gross and to be .750 fine—all of our other gold and silver coins were .900 fine. This gave 33⅓ 3-cent pieces the same gross weight as a silver dollar but a pure silver content of only 309⅜, as compared with a pure silver content of 371¼ grains to the dollar for all of our other American silver coins. This gave the 3-cent piece a deficiency in its silver content of 16⅔ per cent as compared with our other silver coins. The difference was ample to protect the 3-cent piece from the melting pot and from exportation. Its legal-tender quality was limited to 3 cents, and it was therefore the first American silver coin to have its legal-tender quality limited. England had made her silver coins fiduciary with limited legal tender in 1816, and the matter of the desirability of our reducing the silver content of our fractional silver coins and treating them as subsidiary money had been discussed in official circles from time to time for at least a generation, and a number of bills containing carefully worked out plans for making our fractional silver coins fiduciary had been from time to time introduced in Congress. It was with the small beginning represented by this 3-cent piece, however, in 1851, motivated in part by a desire to have a coin of a denomination convenient for the purchase of postage stamps at the new letter rate, that fiduciary silver coinage was inaugurated in the United States. Originally even our American copper coins had carried with them practically their full money value in the value of their copper content. These 3-cent pieces were coined in large quantities during the years 1851 to 1853, inclusive, their total issue during these years having been $1,086,907.

Fiduciary Coinage Act of 1853

By 1853 the inconveniences to the public arising from the scarcity of fractional money had become so great that Congress was forced to act. Its remedy was the law of February 21, 1853, which closed the mints to the free coinage of silver in fractional denominations, reduced the weight of all fractional silver coins (except the 3-cent piece) and limited the legal-tender quality of these coins to five dollars. The new fractional silver coins were given a gross weight of 384 grains to the dollar, or exactly 80 per cent of an ounce troy, and, since their fineness was to continue unchanged at .900, they were to contain 345.6 grains of fine silver to the dollar. These fractional coins were to be coined on Government account and to be paid out at the mint, only in exchange for gold coins at par, in sums not less than $100. Ten days later Congress passed a law providing that "hereafter the three-cent coin now authorized by law shall be made of the weight of three fiftieths of the weight of the half dollar . . . and of the same standard of fineness," thus bringing all of our fractional silver coins into conformity as to weight and fineness. During the next eight years the coinage of fractional silver coins was large, and their reduced weights gave them adequate protection from the melting pot; although for a brief period in 1854 and again in 1859 the high price of silver seemed to threaten them. For a few years after 1853, largely as a result of administrative practices which were contrary to the law of 1853 and practically amounted to giving free coinage to fractional money, the mint coined excessive quantities of fractional coins—a practice which led to a redundancy in their circulation.

Foreign Coins

During all this time Spanish dollars and their fractional parts had continued in circulation. Although the circulation of Spanish (and Mexican) dollars was at this time small, the circulation of Spanish fractional coins (namely, the two-*real* or 25-cent piece, the one-*real* or 12½-cent piece and the half-*real* or 6¼-cent piece) was still large, and the problem of getting rid of them was a difficult one for the Government. As previously noted,[1] these coins, although greatly underweight by reason of long use and of fraudulent practices, circulated at par with the newer and heavier American coins. These coins in small trade passed at par with United States coins. They contained much less silver, however, than the corresponding American coins, and the Government would have suffered a substantial loss (uncertain in amount) if it had redeemed them at par in United States coins and reminted them. In the past it had actually done this on a considerable scale only to see its own new coins disappear from circulation and other worn Spanish coins come into the country to take their place. The redemption of these foreign coins at rates materially below par was impossible, for obviously the public would not sell them to the Government below par when they were worth par in the retail purchase of goods.

When Senator Dickinson in 1850 first introduced his bill providing for the coinage of a fiduciary 3-cent piece to be coined on Government account and to be limited legal tender, he provided in the bill that this 3-cent piece should be placed in circulation only in exchange for foreign fractional coins, at the rate of 6 cents

[1] *Supra*, pp. 342 and 343.

for the 6¼-cent piece, 12 cents for the 12½-cent piece, and 24 cents for the 25-cent piece. It will be noted that the 3-cent piece was not a decimal denomination that fitted well into our system of coins, but was a denomination well adapted to be exchanged for foreign coins of denominations of 6¼, 12½ and 25 cents. Moreover, the fact that the alloy was to be 25 per cent instead of the 10 per cent used in other coins would have yielded the Government a substantial seigniorage profit on the coinage. This profit would probably have been more than sufficient to cover the losses incidental to receiving the foreign coins in exchange for them at near par. The bill, however, failed in its original form, although the 3-cent piece it provided for appeared in the postal legislation of the following year.

The difficulty was met by the Act of February 21, 1857, which removed the legal-tender quality from all foreign coins that still possessed it,[1] and provided new methods for the withdrawal of these coins from circulation. One of these methods was redemption at par, for a period of two years, of Spanish silver coins below the denominations of four *reales* (50 cents) in new American copper cents which were authorized by the Act and of which the copper content was made sufficiently small to yield the Government a substantial seigniorage profit on their coinage. The Act also provided that the foreign coins should be receivable, other than in exchange for these copper cents, at the Treasury of the United States and at the post offices and land offices at the following rates: two *reales* or 25-cent pieces at 20 cents, one *real* or 12½-cent pieces at ten cents, one-half *real* or 6¼-cent pieces at five cents.

This Act, coming at a time when our new fiduciary fractional coins were being provided in abundance soon resulted in driving the foreign coins into the United States Treasury, by which they were sent to the mint for recoinage into American money. This happy result, however, had not been accomplished until 65 years had elapsed from the Mint Act of 1792.

In the latter fifties we had in the United States a generous supply of gold coins. We had got rid of our foreign coins and were well provided with fractional silver. At this juncture, however, the country found itself in the cataclysm of a Civil War. The banks suspended specie payments December 30, 1861, government legal-

[1] Cf., *supra*, pp. 335 and 336.

tender issues were soon resorted to, and both gold and silver coins were driven out of circulation except in a few parts of the extreme West, notably California and Oregon. Not until January 1, 1879, did the country return to a specie basis, and shortly before it did so, it was surprised to find out that during the paper money period a codification of our coinage laws had changed our legal monetary standard from bimetallism to gold monometallism. How this was done will be described in the following chapter.

American bimetallism was not a great success. Neither was it an entire failure. We never gave bimetallism a fair chance. Throughout most of its history in the United States bimetallism was handicapped by three forces: (1) Excessive issues of paper money by the banks prior to the Civil War, and by the banks and the Government thereafter—issues which exerted a strong force, under Gresham's Law, toward driving out of circulation gold coins and the larger denomination silver coins. This would have been an obstacle to successful monometallism as well as to bimetallism. (2) The large quantities of worn and mutilated foreign coins which we tolerated and many of which we made legal tender throughout the greater part of our bimetallic period. This likewise would have been an almost equally serious handicap to a monometallic standard; and (3) the unwise mint ratios which we attempted to maintain, involving a competition with France in the maintenance of bimetallism rather than coöperation.

BIBLIOGRAPHY

Carothers, Neil, *Fractional Money—A History of the Small Coins and Fractional Paper Currency of the United States;* New York, John Wiley & Sons, 1930.

Darwin, Leonard, *Bimetallism;* New York, D. Appleton & Company, 1898.

Director of the Mint of the United States, *Annual Reports, passim;* Washington, Government Printing Office.

Evans, George G., *History of the United States Mint at Philadelphia;* Philadelphia, George G. Evans, 1885.

Helfferich, Karl, *Money.* Translated from the German by Louis Infield; 2 volumes; London, Ernest Benn, Ltd., 1927.

International Monetary Conference Held in Paris, in August, 1878; Washington, Government Printing Office, 1879. Contains also Proceedings of the International Monetary Conference of 1867.

International Monetary Conference Held at Brussels in 1892; Washington, Government Printing Office, 1893.

Jevons, W. Stanley, *Investigations in Currency and Finance;* London, Macmillan and Company, Ltd., 1909.

Johnson, Joseph French, *Money and Currency;* Boston, Ginn & Company, 1905.

Laughlin, J. Laurence, *The History of Bimetallism in the United States;* New York, D. Appleton & Company.

de Laveleye, Emil, *La Monnaie et Bimetallisme International;* Paris, Felix Alcan, 1891.

Nicholson, J. Shield, *A Treatise on Money,* Third Edition; London, Adam and Charles Black, 1895.

Reports of the Silver Commission of 1876; Washington, Government Printing Office, 1887.

Russell, Henry B., *International Monetary Conferences;* New York, Harper and Brothers, 1898.

Soetbeer, Adolf, *Edelmetall-Produktion und Werthverhältniss zwischen Gold und Silber seit der Entdeckung Amerika's bis zur Gegenwart;* Gotha, Justus Perthes, 1879.

Walker, Francis A., *International Bimetallism;* New York, Henry Holt and Company, 1897.

Willis, Henry Parker, *A History of the Latin Monetary Union;* Chicago, University of Chicago Press, 1901.

CHAPTER XV

THE SILVER CONTROVERSY IN THE UNITED STATES, 1873–1900

When the states of the Latin Union closed their mints to the free coinage of silver and thereby gave up bimetallism, the great bimetallic controversy, which was to rage on three continents for about two and a half decades, was in its incipiency. Let us now consider briefly the chief facts in this controversy which culminated in the defeat of bimetallism in the closing years of the nineteenth century.

Between 1873 and the early 90's, there were two striking monetary developments of world-wide importance. The first was a great and unprecedented rise in the ratio between the value of gold and the value of silver; and the second was a great decline in commodity prices in all gold standard countries.

A reference to the chart on page 365 will show that the ratio between gold and silver from 1687 to 1872 had been remarkably stable. The lowest average annual ratio recorded during these 186 years was 14.14 to 1 (1760), and the highest was 16.25 to 1 (1813)—a range of only 15 per cent in nearly two centuries. In 1873 the ratio began to shoot upwards, reaching 22 to 1 by 1888, and 35 to 1 by 1898. Here was a variation between the years 1873 and 1898—26 years—of about 120 per cent, as contrasted with one of only 15 per cent during the preceding 186 years.

Fall in Prices

A second economic phenomenon that played an important rôle in the bimetallic controversy was the great decline in commodity prices that took place in all gold standard countries during the years 1873 to 1896. The following table of price index numbers (adjusted to the basis of 100 for the year 1873), covering seven countries, will afford a rough idea of the progress and extent of this price decline.

COMMODITY PRICES IN GOLD STANDARD COUNTRIES, 1873–1896

YEAR	UNITED STATES [a]	ENGLAND [b]	FRANCE [c]	GERMANY [d]	BELGIUM [e]	AUSTRALIA [f]	NEW ZEALAND [g]
1873	100.0	100.0	100.0	100.0	100.0	100.0	100.0
1874	97.9	91.0	92.5	92.3	99.7	95.6	98.2
1875	93.0	86.5	89.9	86.5	104.4	92.1	90.2
1876	85.9	85.6	90.6	84.4	99.7	93.0	85.4
1877	85.6	84.7	91.2	84.7	94.8	90.3	87.8
1878	81.8	78.4	83.7	78.1	90.6	83.8	82.3
1879	79.2	74.8	81.8	71.3	88.2	83.4	77.4
1880	87.6	79.3	83.7	78.9	92.2	76.4	79.3
1881	86.6	76.6	81.8	77.2	90.1	77.2	76.2
1882	88.9	75.7	79.9	75.2	78.3	88.8	75.0
1883	86.9	73.9	76.7	73.5	78.9	81.5	71.9
1884	81.5	68.5	70.4	70.4	76.2	78.0	70.1
1885	76.2	64.9	69.2	65.6	72.8	76.1	67.7
1886	75.3	62.2	66.7	62.2	71.6	75.0	65.8
1887	75.9	61.3	64.1	64.3	70.2	72.7	62.8
1888	77.2	63.1	67.3	67.9	69.6	74.0	62.8
1889	77.2	64.9	69.8	71.3	65.8	80.7	67.7
1890	75.7	64.9	69.8	76.0	64.5	72.6	65.2
1891	75.6	64.9	68.6	74.0	64.4	65.1	65.8
1892	71.8	61.3	66.7	67.4	61.2	63.3	63.4
1893	71.5	61.3	65.4	65.1	59.3	58.6	61.0
1894	65.0	56.8	60.4	59.2	54.3	51.6	59.7
1895	63.3	55.9	59.1	59.0	56.6	52.4	56.7
1896	61.1	55.0	57.2	59.3	56.2	63.5	58.5

[a] Falkner Index, gold basis, based on 223 commodities.
[b] Sauerbeck Index, based on 45 commodities.
[c] *Annuaire Statistique de France*, Index, based on 43–45 commodities.
[d] Otto Schmitz Index, based on 24–29 commodities.
[e] Denis Index, based on 50 commodities.
[f] Knibbs Index, based on 80–92 commodities.
[g] McIlraith Index, based on 33–45 commodities.

The table shows, broadly speaking, a world-wide decrease in wholesale prices in gold standard countries between the years 1873 and 1896 averaging approximately 41 per cent.

DID SILVER DEPRECIATE OR DID GOLD APPRECIATE?

A heated controversy arose concerning the causes of this rise in the gold-silver ratio and this fall in commodity prices.

The change in the ratio, it may be said here parenthetically, was believed by many to have been due chiefly to the depreciation of silver—a depreciation which, it was claimed, resulted largely from the great increase in the world's production of silver in that period. By five-year periods from 1861 to 1895, the world's average annual production of silver in millions of fine ounces was as follows:

1861–1865	35.4
1866–1870	43.0
1871–1875	61.5
1876–1880	70.6
1881–1885	85.6
1886–1890	108.9
1891–1895	157.6

This was a substantial increase, the average annual production of 1866 to 1870 having practically doubled by the quinquennium ending in 1885, and more than tripled by 1891–1895.

For the year 1873 the average gold value of the silver bullion in an American silver dollar was 100.4 cents, and for the year 1895 it was 50.6 cents. This decline in the gold price of silver was generally spoken of in gold standard countries as the depreciation of silver; and the American silver dollar, viewed from the standpoint of its bullion content, was frequently dubbed "a 50-cent dollar." However, to people in silver standard countries of that time, like Mexico, Japan and China, the situation looked very differently. They thought in terms of a silver monetary unit. To their minds, silver had remained constant and gold had appreciated. In China, for example, they spoke of the American dollar as a "two-dollar dollar." It took approximately twice as many Mexican dollars in 1895 and 1896 to buy an American gold dollar or a British sovereign as it took in 1873. If an American gold dollar which in 1873 was worth approximately a Mexican silver dollar came to be worth two Mexican silver dollars in 1896, was it because the Mexican dollar was only half as valuable as it was in 1873, or was it because the American dollar had become twice as valuable?

Obviously, these questions could be answered only by comparing each of these dollars with other commodities. If the gold dollar stayed with commodities in general, while the silver dollar departed from them, the presumption would be that silver had depreciated. On the other hand, if the silver dollar stayed with commodities in general and the gold dollar departed from them, the presumption would be that gold had appreciated.

The problem can be examined in two closely related ways: (1) By inquiring concerning the movement of prices in gold standard countries and in silver standard countries and finding out in which group of countries prices were the more stable; and (2) by converting prices in gold standard countries to a silver basis through expressing them in terms of silver dollars, according to the current market price of silver in terms of gold; in other words, expressing prices in a representative gold standard country in terms of silver standard monetary unit.

The following chart [1] shows the movements of the values of gold and silver during the 21 years 1873 to 1893, inclusive. The value of

RELATIVE VALUES OF GOLD AND SILVER AS EXPRESSED IN PURCHASING POWER OVER COMMODITIES
1873–1893

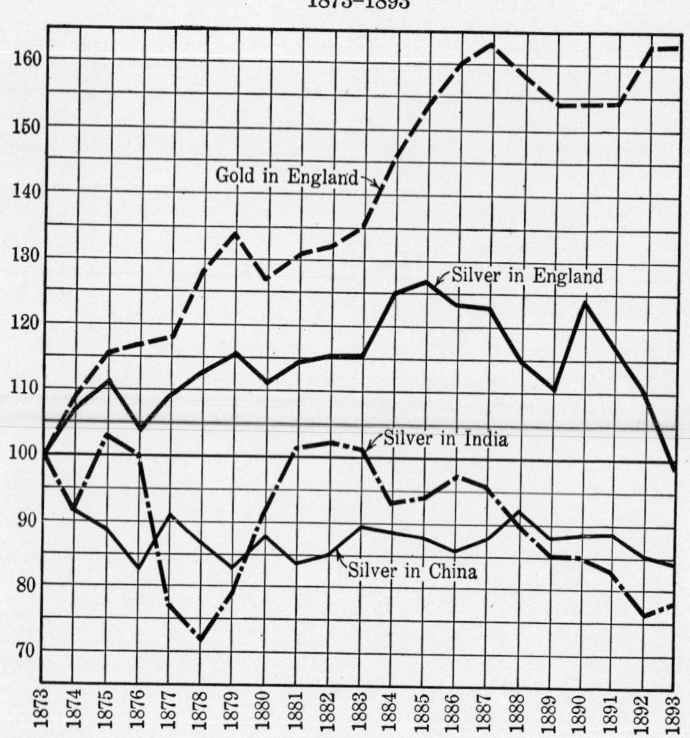

gold is expressed by the reciprocals of the Sauerbeck index numbers of wholesale prices in the United Kingdom, while the value of silver is expressed in three different ways: (1) by the purchasing power of the Indian silver standard rupee, as shown by the reciprocals of the Atkinson index numbers of Indian wholesale prices;

[1] The chart has been reproduced from the author's *Modern Currency Reforms*, p. 20.

(2) by the purchasing power of silver in China, as shown by the reciprocals of wholesale price index numbers for Shanghai; and (3) by the purchasing power of silver bullion over commodities in England, computed on the basis of the Sauerbeck index numbers and the market price of silver in London.

Of the four curves, that representing the value of gold was clearly the most unstable, while that representing the value of silver in

VARIATIONS IN THE PRICES OF COMMODITIES AND OF SILVER 1873–1893

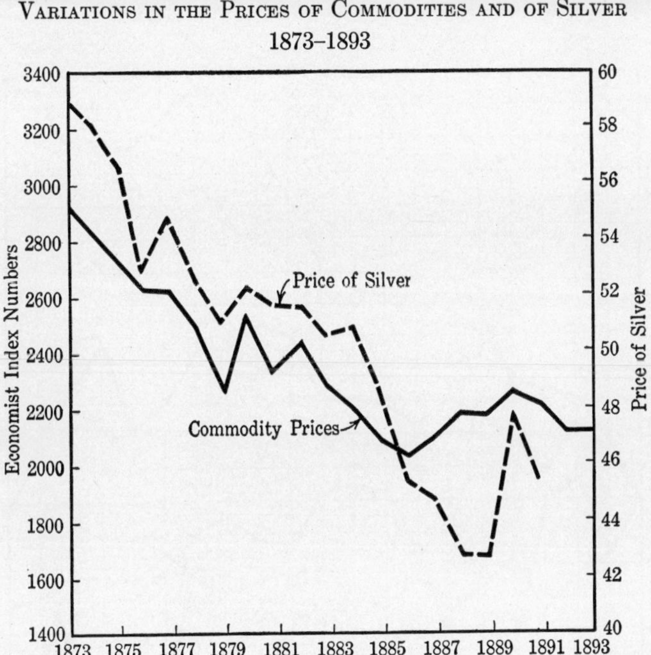

Shanghai was the most stable. In India the value of the silver standard rupee varied much less widely than that of the pound sterling in England—and this is particularly true if one eliminates, as it seems reasonable he should, the heavy drop in the value of the rupee (i.e., rise in rupee prices) of the years 1877 to 1879, which was due largely to the rise of food prices caused by the great Indian famine of that period.[1]

[1] Professor George R. Davies has computed the coefficients of average deviation and of standard deviation for the purchasing power of gold and of silver in the United States, based on wholesale prices, for the years 1873 to 1892, inclusive, using the continuous series of index numbers of wholesale prices 1860–1892 computed by

By the above tests, therefore, the conclusion seems justifiable that, regardless of causes and regardless of subsequent events, for the period 1873–1893 the decline in the gold price of silver was chiefly an expression of an appreciation of gold, not of a depreciation of silver. It was, therefore, more nearly correct to say that the gold dollar of 1873 had become a two-dollar dollar in 1893 than it was to say that the silver dollar of 1873 had become a 50-cent dollar.[1]

The close parallelism between the price movements of silver and of commodities in general during this period is shown by the chart on the preceding page.

Changes in Annual Production of Gold and Silver Affect Value Ratio Very Slowly

If the remarkable change in the ratio between the values of gold and silver that took place between 1873 and the early 90's was due chiefly to the appreciation of gold rather than to any depreciation of silver, and if the value of silver remained fairly constant during the greater part of this period as the evidence above cited shows, the claim so widely made that the change in the ratio was due largely to the increased production of silver must be discarded.

The world's annual production of a highly durable commodity like gold or silver is such a small percentage of the supply on the market, that it requires a long time for moderate changes in the proportion of the two metals produced to have any considerable effect upon their value ratio. Prior to the discontinuance of bimetallism enormous changes in the relative production of the two metals, such as occurred at the time of the great silver discoveries in South America and Mexico during the latter part of the eighteenth century, and at the time of the Californian and Australian gold discoveries about the middle of the nineteenth century, had little effect on the ratio. This is shown in the following chart covering the period from 1687 to 1930.

the Bureau of Labor Statistics and published in its *Bulletin* No. 181, p. 266. The coefficient of average deviation is .122 for gold and .047 for silver; and the coefficient of standard deviation is .138 for gold and .056 for silver.

[1] For the pound sterling the extreme range of the index numbers was 63 points (namely, from 100 to 163); while for the rupee it was but 31 points (namely, from 103 to 72); and for silver in Shanghai only 17 points (namely, from 100 to 83). For silver in England it was 29 points (namely, from 127 to 98).

For example, for the 20-year period 1741–1760 the world produced about 22 ounces of silver to each ounce of gold and the average value ratio was 14.64 to 1. During the next three 20-year periods, respectively, the number of ounces of silver produced to

WORLD PRODUCTION AND COMMERCIAL VALUE RATIOS OF GOLD AND SILVER, 1687–1930

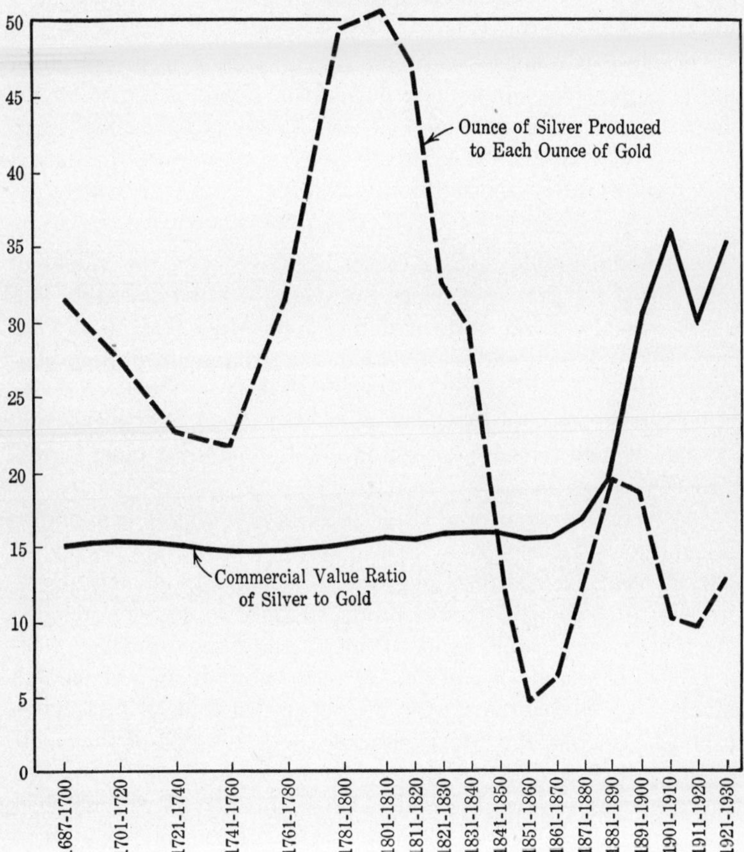

each ounce of gold was 31, 50 and 49; but the average value ratios for these three periods, respectively, were only raised to 14.73: 1, 15.09: 1 and 15.50: 1. The production ratio dropped during the period 1820–1840 to 30 to 1, and during the period 1841–1860 to 6 to 1 but the value ratios for these two periods, respectively, were only slightly changed; namely, to 15.83 to 1 for the former period and to 15.60 to 1 for the latter. In the light of these facts, it seems extremely improbable that changes in the production ratio so slight as those for the periods 1861–1880 and 1881–1900—that is, from 6 to 1 for the period 1841–1860 to 9 to 1 for the period 1861–1880, and to 12 to 1 for the period 1881–1900—should cause a change in the value ratio from 15.60 to 1 to 25.08 to 1, a change eight times as great as the extreme range for the average 20-year ratios of the 160 years ending 1860. Whatever effect the increased production of silver may have had on the change in the ratio must have been small.

The same statement and reasoning will apply to the influence on the ratio of the declining production of gold, the figures for which follow:

World's Average Annual Production of Gold by Five-Year Periods, 1851–1895[1]

Period	Number of Fine Ounces 000
1851–1855	6,410
1856–1860	6,486
1861–1865	5,950
1866–1870	6,270
1871–1875	5,591
1876–1880	5,543
1881–1885	4,795
1886–1890	5,461
1891–1895	7,883

If changes in the relative production of the two metals cannot adequately explain the phenomenal changes in the value ratio that took place during the quarter century following the demonetization of silver in 1873, one must look to changes in the relative demands for the two metals for an explanation. Inasmuch as there is no evidence of any great increase in the demand for gold relative to that for silver in the industrial uses at this time, one is led to look for possible changes in the monetary demand.

Changes in Monetary Demand for Gold and Silver

Here we find the chief explanation for the appreciation of gold in terms of silver and for the increase in the value of gold in terms of commodities. With the discontinuance of bimetallism, the unlimited markets for silver at fixed prices at the mints of all bimetallic countries ceased to exist. These mints no longer purchased

[1] *Report* of the United States Director of the Mint, 1920, p. 294.

all of the silver brought to them at a fixed price. The discontinuance of bimetallism, itself, would probably have depressed the value of silver within a short time, had it not been for the temporary buoyant effect on the value of silver exerted by the heavy silver purchases by the United States Government under the Bland-Allison Act of 1878 [1] and the Sherman Purchase Act of 1890.[2] Under the former act the United States Government, largely in response to the agitation of silver-producing interests, bought approximately two million dollars' worth of silver bullion a month for the period 1878 to the summer of 1890, paying for it by new issues of silver dollars; and under the latter, the Secretary of the Treasury bought 4,500,000 ounces of silver a month from the summer of 1890 to November, 1893, paying for it in new issues of circulating Treasury notes.

Accompanying the closing of the mints of many countries to the free coinage of silver was a shift of the world's demand for standard commodity money increasingly to gold—a shift which greatly enhanced the demand for gold and therefore increased its value. Germany demonetized silver and adopted the gold standard in 1871, Holland in 1873, the Latin Union in 1873 and 1874, the United States (nominally) in 1873,[3] Spain in 1874 and Sweden, Norway and Denmark in 1875. Other countries followed in rapid succession. The fundamental cause for the change in ratio and for the fall in prices from 1873 to 1893 was, therefore, the increased demand for gold resulting from the discontinuance of bimetallism throughout the world and the discontinuance of silver monometallism in many countries, with the consequent shifting of the world's monetary demand more heavily to gold.

Evil Effects of Falling Commodity Prices

Falling prices in gold standard countries carried with them many evil consequences, among which the following may be mentioned.

Increased Burden on Debtor Classes. They imposed a heavy and unjust burden upon persons having long-time debts, notably farmers with mortgages on their farms, city and town home buyers with mortgages on their homes and corporations with heavy bonded indebtedness. The dollar in which these debts were expressed and payable—principal and interest—was almost continually increasing in value, but this fact did not reduce one iota

[1] *Infra*, pp. 375–382. [2] *Infra*, pp. 382–388. [3] *Supra*, p. 259.

the number of dollars covered by a debt. It did mean, however, that for the paying of a given amount of a debt—principal or interest—the farmer had to give an ever increasing number of bushels of wheat, corn or potatoes; many city dwellers had to give an ever increasing number of days' labor [1] and the corporation an ever increasing number of units of its products. If one called the United States gold dollar of 1873 a 100 per cent dollar in its purchasing power over goods at wholesale, the dollar of 1883 would have been a 115 per cent dollar, that of 1893 a 140 per cent dollar and that of 1896 a 164 per cent dollar.

From 1873 to 1896 the average gold price of middling cotton in New York fell from 17.7 cents a pound to 7.9 cents; that of wheat (No. 2 red winter and spring wheat averaged) from $1.34 a bushel to 64 cents a bushel; that of choice beeves from $5.83 a hundredweight to $4.96. A farmer giving a mortgage for $2,000 with interest at 6 per cent in 1873 could have bought for $2,000 1,492½ bushels of wheat in 1873 and could have bought for $120 (his annual interest charge) 89½ bushels. If he paid off the entire principal of the mortgage in 1896, together with the one year's interest then due, the payment of the principal would have required the equivalent of 3,125 bushels of wheat, and that of the interest the equivalent of 187½ bushels. What the debtor lost in such transactions, the creditor gained, with the qualification that falling prices tended somewhat to depress the interest rate on new contracts. According to the United States census figures, over 9½ million mortgages were made between 1880 and 1889, representing over $12 billion, and nearly every year of that period showed an increase in the number and in the amount of mortgages made, as compared with the preceding year, the amount made in 1889 being $1,753 million as against $711 million in 1880. Of course, this increase in debt burden forced many farmers and home buyers into bankruptcy. Many of them lost their properties, while many creditors suffered heavily because of inability to collect from overburdened debtors.

It was but natural that those who were burdened with long-time debts, particularly the agricultural classes, should be aroused over the evils of a rapidly appreciating dollar.

[1] Average wages advanced slightly during the period 1873 to 1896, but the wages of many kinds of labor fell, and there was a large amount of unemployment during the period. Cf., *Bulletin* of Department of Labor, No. 18, September, 1898.

Depressing Effect of Falling Prices on Business. Another evil of falling prices was the depressing effect they had on most kinds of business. Falling prices throw a wet blanket over industry. When the prospects are strong for a period of declining prices, consumers postpone purchases, retailers and wholesalers let their supplies run down, manufacturers "play safe" both in running their plants and in purchasing raw materials. New buildings and other new capital equipment are postponed for the day of lower prices. Under such conditions there is much unemployment with all its resulting hardships.

Effect of Discontinuance of Bimetallism on Foreign Trade

The discontinuance of bimetallism had given rise to another evil—one not connected with falling prices. It had broken down the so-called fixed par of exchange between countries on different metallic money standards. So long as French bimetallism existed, the value ratio between gold and silver was fairly constant, especially over short periods of time. In other words, the fluctuations were very slight in the gold price of silver in gold standard countries, and in the silver price of gold in silver standard countries, and in the price of both gold and silver in bimetallic countries. Foreign exchange rates therefore among countries on these different standards were very stable. With the discontinuance of bimetallism all this was changed. The *nexus* between gold and silver was broken, and each metal went its own way. There was no longer any limit to the possible variations in exchange rates between a gold standard country and a silver standard country. This brought an element of risk and speculation in foreign trade between countries on different standards. It was an obstacle to the ordinary development of trade between gold and silver standard countries, likewise to the flow of funds for investment between such countries.[1]

Argument for Restoration of Bimetallism

It was from conditions like these that bimetallists throughout the world drew their arguments for the restoration of bimetallism. Although by 1894 the value ratio between gold and silver had risen above 32 to 1, most advocates of bimetallism favored a mint ratio

[1] Cf., *supra*, pp. 142–146.

in the neighborhood of $15\frac{1}{2}$ or 16 to 1, if bimetallism were to be restored. They reasoned that such a ratio had stood the test of centuries prior to the demonetization of silver in 1873, that the appreciation of gold leading to the rise in the ratio had been due chiefly to the giving up of bimetallism, and that with the return to bimetallism the time-honored ratio would again assert itself.

Bimetallists further argued that with the restoration of silver to its coequal position with gold as a standard money metal the monetary scarcity, which was chiefly responsible for the fall in prices beginning in 1873, would be relieved, because henceforward silver as well as gold could furnish standard money for the leading countries of the world. They pointed out that gold and silver were produced under very different conditions, and that as a matter of history the periods of heavy production of one metal were frequently periods of small production of the other, so that there was an equalizing process that made for the stability of a standard based upon the two metals.

The two chief advantages claimed for bimetallism then were: (1) It would provide a more stable monetary unit and therefore greatly lessen the evils of falling and fluctuating prices; and (2) it would restore the fixed par of exchange between countries on different metallic standards.

Let us now consider briefly a few of the more important arguments against bimetallism and the difficulties in the way of its restoration.

Arguments against Bimetallism

One argument against bimetallism is the inconvenience that would result from the extensive use of a bulky metal like silver as standard money in advanced countries. Silver dollars are clumsy and inconvenient as media of exchange. At as low a ratio as 16 to 1, they would be dollar for dollar 16 times as heavy as gold coin; while at the ratio of about 32 to 1 prevailing in the market in 1894 they would be 32 times as heavy. The average market ratio in 1932 was over 59.06 to 1. A small value in these dollars occupies a large space in vaults and tills, and the weight of silver makes it more expensive than gold to ship in making international payments. Because of their bulk, silver dollars were unpopular in most sections of the country and it was impossible to keep many of them in circulation.

According to the compensatory principle of bimetallism previously described,[1] the weight of the monetary demand would shift from time to time from one metal to the other, always exerting itself more heavily on the cheaper metal. For this reason the bulk of the metallic money (aside from fractional money) would at one time be gold and at another time silver—a shifting process which, it was argued, would be very inconvenient for banks and merchants from the standpoint of the adaptability of their money vaults and tills.

These arguments, bimetallists replied, might have considerable weight in countries where the great bulk of the transactions were performed by means of metallic money. In the United States, however, and most other advanced countries, only a small percentage of the total volume of trade was effected by means of coins. When the bimetallic controversy in this country was at its height, approximately 75 per cent of the total business of the United States was performed by paper money. Neither silver dollars nor gold coins were popular in most parts of the country, and few of them were seen in active hand to hand circulation, except in a few limited sections. American gold circulated in the form of gold certificates and our silver dollars in the form of silver certificates. A ten-dollar silver certificate was no larger and weighed no more than a ten-dollar gold certificate.

It is true that silver would be more bulky than gold for international payments, and more expensive to ship, handle and otherwise take care of. A successful international bimetallic league, however, would almost certainly have devised a plan whereby international payments could be made to a considerable extent by the transfer of gold and silver certificates issued against gold and silver deposited in some international settlement fund.

A strong argument against bimetallism, at a 16 to 1 ratio, or perhaps more correctly against its reëstablishment, after it had been given up for a period of years, was that whatever may have been the evils that demonetization of silver had caused, they could not be remedied by the reëstablishment of bimetallism after a lapse of many years. Many debtors who had suffered from an appreciating unit of value had paid off their debts, and some had since become creditors. The successful establishment of international bimetallism at a ratio of 16 to 1 in the 80's and early

[1] *Supra*, pp. 84–91.

90's of the last century would have turned falling prices into rising ones, would have made silver dearer and gold cheaper, and would have brought their values closer together, giving a bimetallic unit with a value somewhere between the values of the two metals as they stood when the bimetallic league was established. This would have meant a short period of rapidly rising prices in the gold standard countries that adopted bimetallism, and in those that continued on the gold standard; and, on the contrary, would have meant a short period of rapidly falling prices in the former silver standard countries that adopted bimetallism and in those that continued on the silver standard. This would have caused further injustice in the relations between debtors and creditors and further business disturbances. It would have benefited some and harmed others, but there would have been no assurance at all that those persons who would have benefited by the remonetization of silver would have been the same persons who would have suffered by its demonetization, and vice versa.

Moreover, a strong confidence in the future is an essential of business prosperity. A large percentage of the country's leading business men and financiers did not believe that international bimetallism was economically sound. These men thought that any attempt to put it into operation would result in economic disaster. With so many men of influence in that state of mind, the economic disturbances otherwise necessary for such a period of transition from monometallism to bimetallism would have been increased.

The argument was well stated by Professor J. Shields Nicholson, himself a bimetallist, as follows: [1]

> "Now it is one thing to maintain that, if the status quo had been preserved, and still more if, in 1873, international bimetallism had been adopted, the world would have been saved from great financial and monetary disturbances, but it is quite another thing to suppose that the evil can be undone and the future guaranteed by the simple expedient of doing now what might have been done before these disturbances occurred . . . In the language of our forefathers, it may be a case of *Humpty Dumpty.*"

Efforts to Obtain International Bimetallism

The most serious obstacle to bimetallism was the difficulty of obtaining an international agreement for a bimetallic league on the part of a sufficient number of strong countries to assure its

[1] *Principles of Political Economy*, Vol. II, p. 8.

success. There were powerful groups favorable to international bimetallism in all the leading countries, in the early 90's. In France, India and the United States probably the weight of intelligent public opinion was favorable to international bimetallism. While England was generally opposed, there was a strong favorable element even in England. In the United States in 1892 the Republican Party, the Democratic Party and the Peoples Party, all declared for bimetallism in their national platforms. Again in 1896 both the great parties declared for bimetallism, but in this instance the Democratic Party took the extreme position of favoring national bimetallism by the United States alone in case an international bimetallic agreement could not be obtained. Up to this time the term "bimetallism" in the political platforms had always meant international bimetallism. The Republican platform in 1896 declared:

> " . . . We are . . . opposed to the free coinage of silver except by international agreement with the leading commercial nations of the world, which we pledge ourselves to promote, and until such agreement can be obtained the existing gold standard must be preserved . . ."

The Republicans won the 1896 Presidential campaign and the Walcott Commission was appointed by President McKinley in April, 1897, to go to Europe and carry on negotiations with the governments of London, Berlin and Paris, looking toward another international monetary conference whose object would be an agreement for international bimetallism. Three international monetary conferences had previously been held which dealt with the subject of international bimetallism, one in Paris in 1878, another there in 1881 and one in Brussels in 1892. These efforts had been supplemented by a number of special missions, but all had been to no avail.[1] For reasons which we need not here discuss, the Walcott mission also accomplished nothing.

South African Gold Discoveries Put an End to Bimetallic Controversy

The failure of the Walcott Commission in 1897 practically marked the end of the active bimetallic controversy. The chief reason for this was a fundamental change in the world's monetary situation. The great impetus to bimetallism had been given by a world-wide fall in prices caused by the inadequacy of the world's

[1] Cf., Russell, Henry B., *International Monetary Conferences*, pp. 459–463.

production of gold to meet the increased demands for the yellow metal which had resulted from the demonetization of silver. Bimetallists wanted more money in circulation primarily for the purpose of putting a stop to falling prices. Beginning about 1896, a great increase in the world's production of gold began to produce this very result. The extent of this increase will be seen from the following table:

Average Annual Gold Production, 1886–1915, by Quinquennial Periods
(Thousands of Fine Ounces)

Period	Africa	Rest of the World	Total
1886–1890	229	5,232	5,461
1891–1895	1,448	6,435	7,883
1896–1900	2,620	9,827	12,447
1901–1905	3,090	12,517	15,607
1906–1910	7,806	13,189	20,995
1911–1915	10,000	12,204	22,204

This enormous increase in the world's production of gold, accompanied by a rapid development in the use of bank credit, as media of exchange, greatly increased the world's supply of circulating media, turned falling prices to rapidly rising prices, and changed the world's great monetary problem from one of the appreciation of gold and the resulting injustice to debtor classes to one of the depreciation of gold, the rising cost of living and of resulting injustice to the creditor classes. Since the early nineties, silver though more constant in its annual production than gold has been even more unstable in its value than gold,[1] as the following chart will show.

For a long period from 1896 to 1920, the value of silver, like that of gold, tended strongly downward, so that a bimetallic system functioning successfully during these years would presumably have given an even less stable monetary unit than the gold standard did.

Aside from a slight revival of interest in bimetallism in 1919, when the value ratio of gold and silver in the market temporarily stood in the neighborhood of the time-honored figure of 16 to 1, there was little discussion of bimetallism during the first three decades of the twentieth century. The world economic depression beginning in 1929 caused another small revival of interest in the subject, a revival that was limited almost entirely to a small part

[1] *Supra*, pp. 364–366, and chart on p. 375.

of the United States and was due chiefly to the political agitation of representatives of a half a dozen silver-producing states.

Although the advocates of the free and unlimited coinage of silver under a bimetallic system were defeated in the bimetallic controversy of the last quarter of the nineteenth century, the

VALUES OF GOLD AND SILVER AS MEASURED BY THEIR RESPECTIVE PURCHASING POWERS OVER COMMODITIES AT WHOLESALE, 1818–1933
1867–1877 = 100

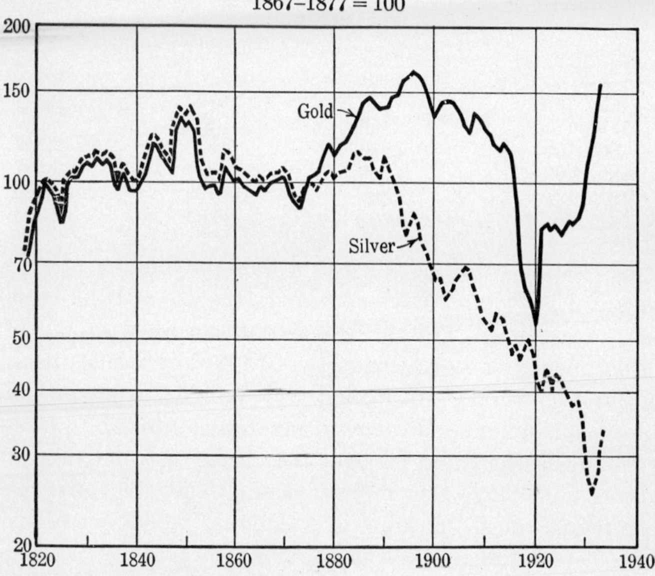

protagonists of silver succeeded by way of compromise in obtaining two pieces of legislation that increased the monetary demand for the white metal and retarded, at least for a time, the depreciation of its gold value. These laws were the Bland-Allison Act of 1878 and the Sherman Purchase Act of 1890.

THE BLAND-ALLISON ACT

The Bland-Allison Act had its inception in a bill providing for the free and unlimited coinage of silver and for making the silver dollar unlimited legal tender in payment of debts. This bill was introduced in the House of Representatives July 25, 1876, by Richard P. Bland of Missouri, familiarly known, by reason of his activities in the interests of silver, as "Silver Dick." After much debate, this free coinage bill was passed by the House November 5, 1877, by the large majority of 163 to 34. The bill reached the Senate December 6, 1877, where it was placed in the hands of William B. Allison of Iowa, Chairman of the Committee on Finance. After prolonged debate in the Senate, the bill was adopted with two important amendments, one substituting for the free coinage provision of the House bill a provision for the coining of not less than two million dollars' worth of silver a month, nor more than four million dollars' worth; and the other providing for the issuance of silver certificates "backed" dollar for dollar by silver dollars. As thus amended, the bill was passed by the Senate February 15, 1878, by a vote of 48 to 21. The substitution of limited coinage for free coinage was very unpopular among the members of the silver group in the House, but they decided that it was the best they could get at the time, and, accordingly, with disappointment and with determination to continue the fight for the free coinage of silver in the future, they decided to vote for the bill. The final vote in the House was 203 to 72. The bill, therefore, had the support of a large majority in both houses. It was immediately sent to President Hayes, who vetoed it February 28, accompanying his veto by a vigorous message giving his objections to the bill.

In this veto message, which is a state paper of high rank, President Hayes said:

> "The bill provides for the coinage of silver dollars of the weight of 412½ grains each, of standard silver, to be a legal tender at their nominal value for all debts and dues, public and private, except where otherwise expressly stipulated in the contract. . . . The silver dollar authorized by this bill is worth 8 to 10 per cent less than it purports to be worth, and is made a legal tender for debts contracted when the law did not recognize such coins as lawful money."

He pointed out that there were at that time outstanding over eleven hundred million dollars of United States bonds issued prior to February, 1873, at times when the silver dollar was unknown in the circulation of the country. He showed that nearly six hundred million dollars of the nation's funded debt had been issued after February, 1873, when gold alone was the coin in which both parties to the contract understood that the bonds would be paid. He then based his veto squarely upon the moral obligation of the Government to meet its contracts.

> "The standard of value," he said, "should not be changed without the consent of both parties to the contract. National promises should be

kept with unflinching fidelity. There is no power to compel a nation to pay its just debts. Its credit depends on its honor. The nation owes what it has led or allowed its creditors to expect. I can not approve a bill which in my judgment authorizes the violation of sacred obligations. The obligation of the public faith transcends all questions of profit or public advantage."

This message aroused the ire of both houses, and on the very day it was received, they passed the bill over the President's veto. The vote in the House was 196 to 73 and that in the Senate 46 to 19. Thus the Bland-Allison silver bill became law February 28, 1878. The supporters of the bill came chiefly from the West and South, while the opponents came principally from the East. The cheap money interests, including those formerly affiliated with the Greenback Party and most of the opponents of the Resumption Act, were nearly all supporters of the bill.

The Act contained three important provisions; viz.: (1) It authorized the resumption of the coinage of silver dollars of the weight and fineness provided for in the Act of 1837 [1] (i.e., 412½ grains, .900 fine), but limited this coinage to the amount of dollars that could be minted out of the silver bullion that the Secretary of the Treasury could buy at the market price of silver each month by the expenditure of not less than $2 million nor more than $4 million. Under this provision, the lower the price of silver, the greater the number of dollars that could be minted.

(2) It made these silver dollars unlimited legal tender for all debts and dues public and private, except where otherwise expressly stipulated in the contract; and

(3) It authorized holders of the new silver dollars to deposit them in the Treasury in sums of not less than $10 and to receive in exchange silver certificates which the Treasury was authorized to issue in denominations of not less than $10.[2] The coin so deposited was to be retained in the Treasury for the payment of the silver certificates on demand.

While the Bland-Allison bill was being pushed through Congress, Senator Matthews of Ohio introduced a concurrent resolution, which was debated along with the Bland-Allison bill itself. The Matthews Resolution, after the usual "whereases," declared: [3]

[1] Cf., *supra*, p. 349.

[2] The Act of August 4, 1886, authorized the issue of silver certificates also in denominations of $1, $2 and $5.

[3] For the history of this resolution, see Laughlin, pp. 201–213.

"That all the bonds of the United States issued, or authorized to be issued, under the said acts of Congress hereinbefore recited, are payable, principal and interest, at the option of the Government of the United States, in silver dollars of the coinage of the United States containing 412½ grains each of standard silver; and that to restore to its coinage such silver coins as a legal tender in payment of said bonds, principal and interest, is not in violation of the public faith, nor in derogation of the rights of the public creditor."

The Resolution was passed by the House January 25 and by the Senate three days later; in both cases by large majorities. As Laughlin points out, there was no doubt as to the legal right of the United States to pay interest and principal of its public debt in silver if it should so choose; the real question was not one of law but of moral and public policy.

Before the passage of either the Matthews Resolution or the Bland-Allison Act, there were many dire prophesies from high financial quarters as to the effects the passage of these measures would have on our national credit. Typical of them is the following, quoted from a letter written November 7, 1877, by August Belmont to John Sherman, then Secretary of the Treasury:[1]

"I fear that the threatening position of the silver question will check completely any demand for the four per cent. bonds here and in Europe. The damage which the passage of this measure will do to our public credit abroad *cannot be over estimated.* To remonetize silver upon the old standard, and make it a legal tender for all private and public debts, will be considered by the whole civilized world as an act of repudiation on the part of the federal government, and cast a stain upon our national credit, which has hitherto stood as high and bright as that of any government in the world. . . . To do such a thing now as is contemplated by the Bland silver bill, when the federal finances are in a flourishing condition, when the premium of gold has been reduced two and a half to three per cent., and when our funded debt sells equal to that of any other public security in the world, is actually as if a man of wealth and position, who had by a life-long course of strict honesty acquired the well-earned confidence and respect of his fellow-citizens and of the outer world, should in the midst of his affluence, and without any palliating excuse of any temptation of want or necessity, commit open theft.

"I am sure I do not over estimate the damaging effect which the passage of the bill must have upon American credit. All my letters from abroad, and conversations with persons familiar with the English and continental money markets, confirm my convictions on that point."

[1] John Sherman's *Recollections of Forty Years in the House, Senate and Cabinet—An Autobiography*, Vol. II, pp. 604 and 605.

How the Bland-Allison Act Worked

The Bland-Allison Act was in operation from 1878 until 1890, and during these twelve years each succeeding Secretary of the Treasury, in the exercise of his option to buy not less than $2,000,000 nor more than $4,000,000 worth of silver, kept close to the minimum figure. During this period, however, despite the artificial demand for silver created by these purchases, the gold price of silver declined almost continually,[1] the average price for fine silver in New York for the year 1877 having been $1.19 an ounce and for 1889, 93.6 cents an ounce. As the price declined, dollars bought increasing amounts of silver bullion and therefore resulted in the pumping into circulation of a continually increasing volume of silver dollars and silver certificates. For the years 1878 to 1889 the coinage of silver dollars under the Bland-Allison Act was as follows: [2]

	$000,000
1878	22.5
1879	27.6
1880	27.4
1881	27.9
1882	27.6
1883	28.5
1884	28.1
1885	28.7
1886	31.4
1887	33.6
1888	32.0
1889	34.7
Total [3]	344.9

These silver dollars, however, were not popular in most parts of the country. The public found them cumbersome and inconvenient. They piled up in the banks, and the public returned them in large quantities to the Government in the payment of taxes and other Government dues. Their circulation, "by proxy," was greatly facilitated by the use of silver certificates, and particularly by certificates of the lower denominations which were authorized by the law of 1886. Throughout the period 1878 to 1890 a large and generally increasing proportion of the issues under the Bland-

[1] Cf., *supra*, pp. 360–364.

[2] Cf., U. S. Treasury *Circular* No. 52, July 1, 1912, pp. 54 and 55.

[3] In computing the total, complete figures have been used.

Allison Act was in the form of silver certificates. By July 1, 1890, the circulation of silver dollars was only $56 million, while that of silver certificates was $298 million.

Throughout his first Administration, President Cleveland used his influence for the repeal of the Bland-Allison Act. In his message of December 6, 1886, after pointing out that silver had just declined to the lowest price in its history, he said:

> "Every fair and legal effort has been made by the Treasury Department to distribute this currency among the people. The withdrawal of United States Treasury notes of small denominations and the issuing of small silver certificates have been resorted to in the endeavor to accomplish this result, in obedience to the will and statement of the representatives of the people in the Congress."

He then showed that these efforts had been of little avail, and called attention to Congress to the fact that the Director of the Mint "again urges the necessity of more vault room for the purpose of storing these silver dollars which are not needed for circulation by the people."

The extent to which the country could absorb these monthly outpourings of new silver money without disturbance depended in large part upon the volume of the country's business activity. In prosperous years, when business was active and the demand for money was large, as in the years 1886 and 1887, this new money was readily absorbed, while in periods of business depression, as in the years 1883 and 1884, it became a drug on the market and, under the principle of Gresham's Law, tended to drive gold out of circulation and out of the country. The absorption of the silver certificates into the circulation during these years was aided by the fact that our bond-secured national bank-note circulation was declining at this time as a result of the rapid rise in the price of United States government bonds.[1]

In November, 1878, when the New York Sub-Treasury was admitted to the New York Clearing House, the Clearing House passed a resolution prohibiting the payment of balances at the Clearing House in silver certificates or silver dollars. This action in a short time aroused in Congress vigorous criticism of the Eastern bankers who were alleged to be trying "to discredit the country's silver currency." In July, 1882, when the twenty-year charters of the national banks came up for renewal by the Government,

[1] Cf., Kemmerer, *The A B C of the Federal Reserve System*, p. 15.

Congress prescribed that "no national banking association shall be a member of any clearing-house in which [silver] certificates shall not be received in settlement of clearing-house balances." The Clearing House was accordingly forced to rescind its resolution.

In his Annual Report for 1880, Secretary Sherman declared that it was impossible to keep in circulation more than 35 per cent of these newly coined silver dollars, and in a personal letter to James A. Garfield under date of July 19, 1880, he said that "the silver law threatens to produce within a year or so a single silver standard . . . I could at any moment, by issuing silver freely, bring on a crisis." [1]

Grover Cleveland, after his first election but before his inauguration, came out vigorously and fearlessly for the repeal of the Bland-Allison Act in the face of an overwhelming majority in Congress favorable to the Act. In a letter to Representative A. J. Warner, made public February 24, 1885,[2] he said that this act had resulted in the heaping up in the Treasury vaults of large quantities of 85-cent silver dollars, and that the fact that these dollars were being received in increasing quantities by the Treasury in payment of government dues was diminishing the flow of gold into the National Treasury. He said:

> "Silver and silver certificates have displaced and are now displacing the gold in the Federal treasury now available for the gold obligations of the United States and for the redemption of the United States notes called 'greenbacks.' If not already encroached upon, it is perilously near such encroachment. . . .
>
> "These being the facts of our present condition, our danger, and our duty to avert that danger, would seem to be plain. I hope that you concur with me and with the great majority of our fellow-citizens, in deeming it most desirable at the present juncture to maintain and continue in use the mass of our gold coin, as well as the mass of silver already coined. This is possible by a present suspension of the purchase and coinage of silver. I am not aware that by any other method it is possible."

Two days later the House defeated the amendment for suspending silver coinage by a large majority, the opposition consisting of 118 Democrats and 52 Republicans, while the proponents of repeal were 54 Democrats and 64 Republicans. Thus, says Nevins: [3]

[1] Quoted by Noyes, p. 74.
[2] McElroy, *Grover Cleveland*, Vol. I, pp. 107–109.
[3] *Grover Cleveland*, p. 204.

> "The first Democratic President in a quarter century had been slapped in the face by his own party before he took his seat. Nevertheless, the letter was a statesmanlike piece of initiative. It served notice that Cleveland, following in the footsteps of Seymour and Tilden, would turn a face of granite against all inflationist schemes. By its very vigor it put heart into frightened bankers and restored confidence."

Exports of gold, which had been very heavy in 1884, became negligible in 1885, and under the prosperous conditions prevailing during most of the next four years the new issues of silver certificates were fairly well absorbed and resulted in driving very little gold out of the country, except for the year 1889.[1]

This brings us to the second silver-purchase measure, the so-called Sherman Silver Purchase Act of 1890.

The Sherman Purchase Act

During the latter eighties interest in the silver purchases under the Bland-Allison Act was quiescent, since the new silver certificates that were being forced into the circulation were, for a time, readily absorbed thanks to the business prosperity and to a declining national bank-note circulation. However, Mr. William Windom, President Harrison's first Secretary of the Treasury, unexpectedly pushed the subject of silver prominently into public attention by recommending in his first Annual Report to the President a new silver coinage plan supplementing the Bland-Allison Act, which he wished to have continued. Among other things this plan called for the issuance of Treasury notes against the deposit of silver bullion at the market price of silver at the time when the bullion was deposited. The Treasury notes were to be redeemable in gold, or in silver bullion at the market value at the time of redemption. Concerning the plan President Harrison said that he had been able to give it "only a hasty examination . . . owing to the fact that it had been so recently formulated." Although this plan was never adopted, it became the basis of the Silver Purchase Act of 1890, which was approved by the President July 14, 1890, and which replaced the Bland-Allison Act of 1878. This Act was a compromise between the demands of the extreme bimetallists and those of the gold monometallists. The compromise character of the law explains in part why, although the Democratic

[1] Cf., chart showing United States Notes and Treasury Notes Redeemed in Gold, and Exports of Gold, 1879–1897, *Indianapolis Monetary Commission Reports*, p. 434.

Party was much more favorable to silver than the Republican Party, not a single Republican member of either house voted against the bill, and not a single Democratic member voted in favor of it.

The political situations underlying the passage of the Sherman Act were described by Senator John Sherman a few years later. He said: [1]

> "The authorship of this law has been generally credited to me, and it was commonly called the 'Sherman silver law,' though I took but little part in framing the legislation until the bill got into conference. The situation at that time was critical. A large majority of the Senate favored free silver, and it was feared that the small majority against it in the other House might yield and agree to it. The silence of the President on the matter gave rise to an apprehension that if a free coinage bill should pass both Houses he would not feel at liberty to veto it. Some action had to be taken to prevent a return to free silver coinage, and the measure evolved was the best obtainable. I voted for it, but the day it became a law I was ready to repeal it, if repeal could be had without substituting in its place absolute free coinage."

The principal provisions of the Act were as follows:

(1) The Secretary of the Treasury was required to purchase silver bullion to the amount of 4,500,000 ounces each month, or such a part of that sum as might be offered at a price not greater than a dollar for the amount of silver contained in a silver dollar; that is, about 77 per cent of an ounce; and to pay for the silver so bought by the issuance of a new kind of money called Treasury notes. It will be noted that when the price of silver declined the volume of Treasury notes issued also declined, and when it rose the volume of Treasury notes increased; whereas, under the Bland-Allison Act, which required the monthly purchase of not less than $2 million worth of silver or more than $4 million worth, when the price of silver declined the amount of silver purchased for coinage into silver dollars rose, and when the price rose the volume purchased declined.

(2) The Treasury notes were made "redeemable on demand, in coin," and the law provided that when so redeemed, they "may be reissued." The redemption provision of the law is noteworthy in the light of subsequent developments. It was:

[1] John Sherman's *Recollections of Forty Years in the House, Senate and Cabinet*, Vol. II, pp. 1069–1070.

"That upon demand of the holder of any of the Treasury notes herein provided for the Secretary of the Treasury shall, under such regulations as he may prescribe, redeem such notes in gold or silver coin, at his discretion, it being the established policy of the United States to maintain the two metals on a parity with each other upon the present legal ratio, or such ratio as may be provided by law."

(3) Unlike the silver certificates of the Bland-Allison Act, the Treasury notes were made unlimited legal tender.

(4) The Secretary of the Treasury was required to coin monthly until July 1, 1891, two million ounces of the silver bullion purchased, and thereafter so much as should be necessary for the redemption of the Treasury notes. Since the public in presenting Treasury notes for redemption almost invariably asked for gold instead of silver dollars, this latter provision of the law was of little importance.

Issues of Treasury Notes of 1890

During approximately three and a quarter years in which silver bullion purchases were made under the Act of July 14, 1890, the Government bought (in round numbers) 169 million fine ounces of silver in payment for which it issued $156 million in Treasury notes. The volume of these notes in circulation at the end of each of the years during which they were issued for the purchase of silver was as follows:

	$000,000
1891	40.3
1892	98.3
1893	140.9
1894	134.7

On June 30, 1893, they constituted about 9 per cent of the nation's total monetary circulation.

These four years were years of business depression throughout most of Europe and, also, except for the year 1892, in the United States. It was not a time in which the country could readily absorb substantial increases in the monetary circulation. Since many people were skeptical about the soundness of these new Treasury notes, "backed" as they were by silver which had been depreciating for years in terms of gold, the public early began to discriminate against the Treasury notes and in favor of gold coin and gold certificates. In other words, in accordance with the principle of Gresham's Law, they held back the better money and passed on to others the poorer money. Furthermore, as money became relatively redundant and, in consequence, exchange rates went to the gold-export point, gold, which had a ready foreign market, went abroad, while the fiduciary money, including the increasing volume of these Treasury notes, stayed at home.

According to Dewey: [1]

> "Before the passage of the Sherman Act nine-tenths or more of the customs receipts at the New York customhouse were paid in gold and gold certificates; in the summer of 1891 the proportion of gold and gold certificates fell as low as 12 per cent., and in September, 1892, to less than 4 per cent. The use of United States notes and treasury notes of 1890 correspondingly increased."

The Sherman Purchase Act, it will be recalled, required the Secretary of the Treasury to redeem the Treasury notes "in gold or silver coin at his discretion." The Secretary, however, had always redeemed the Treasury notes, as he was legally obliged to redeem the United States notes, on demand in gold. Beginning with the summer of 1892, demands for redemption of both kinds of notes began to increase rapidly. They fell off, however, with the crop moving demand for paper money in the fall, but increased enormously in December. For the first four months of 1893 redemptions amounted to over $50 million, as compared with less than $2¼ million in the corresponding months of the year 1892.[2] By April, 1893, the net gold in the Treasury had fallen below the conventional $100 million limit.[3] The excess of gold exports over imports for the fiscal years 1890 to 1893 inclusive were:

	$000,000
1890	4.3
1891	68.1
1892	0.5
1893	87.6 [4]

[1] Dewey, Davis R., *Financial History of the United States*, pp. 443 and 444.

[2] *Finance Report*, 1897, p. 139.

[3] While there was no statutory provision for a gold reserve of $100 million, the public for some years had been accustomed to expect the reserve to be maintained at a figure not lower than this sum. There were two reasons for this tradition: (1) under the Resumption Act of 1875 no part of the face value of the bonds sold for providing the funds for redemption purposes, amounting to about $96,000,000, could be used for fiscal purposes; and (2) the Act of 1882 in authorizing the issue of gold certificates provided that the Secretary of the Treasury should suspend their issue whenever the amount of gold in the Treasury "reserved for the redemption of United States notes falls below one hundred millions of dollars."

[4] *Finance Report*, 1897, p. 140.

The Philadelphia & Reading Railway Company went into bankruptcy February 20, with a capital of $40 million and a debt of more than $125 million. In early May

> " . . . the National Cordage Company, with twenty millions capital and ten millions liabilities, followed suit. . . . In January, National Cordage stock had advanced twelve per cent. on the New York market, selling at 147. Sixteen weeks later, it fell below ten dollars per share, and with it, during the opening week of May, the whole stock market collapsed." [1]

The number of commercial failures in the country increased 50 per cent in 1893 over the preceding year and the total liabilities were three times as large as they were in 1892. Pig iron production, which was considered to be one of the best indices of industrial production at that time, declined 24 per cent in 1893.

Moreover, just at the time when our circulation was being glutted with Treasury notes as a result of the large silver purchases and when the public were becoming increasingly fearful that the country would be driven from the gold standard to a silver standard, India, whose silver standard currency for many years had been providing an unlimited market for the purchase of silver, closed her mints to the free coinage of silver (June 26, 1893) and thereby gave a severe blow to the value of the white metal. Since this action by the Indian Government had been expected, anticipation of it had been depressing the gold price of silver for a considerable period. The average prices for an ounce of silver in New York for the years 1891 to 1894 inclusive were:

1891	$0.99
1892	0.88
1893	0.78
1894	0.64

The situation became so bad that the business men of the country began to urge strongly the calling of a special session of Congress for the purpose of repealing the Sherman Purchase Act. The Commercial Club of St. Louis, for example, on May 20 passed a resolution declaring that the Sherman Act was

> "only productive of evil in our monetary system and disturbance to the national credit, and that the prosperity of the whole country, agricultural, manufacturing and commercial will be in a great degree promoted by its early and unconditional repeal." [2]

[1] Noyes, pp. 188–189.

[2] Quoted by Barnes, James A., *John G. Carlisle—Financial Statesman*, p. 259.

The following month the banking house of Harvey Fisk and Sons in New York issued a circular which, after describing the growing distrust throughout the country resulting from the Sherman Act, said:

> "Still this great American nation is obliged to calmly face inevitable ruin . . . simply because its Representatives are not called together in accordance with the authority vested in its Chief Executive, and forced to remove from the Statute Books the law which is eating away the vitals of American honesty, of American credit, and casting into a great abyss a century of financial honor." [1]

President Cleveland, who had been during his previous Administration a strong opponent to the heavy coinage of silver required by the Bland-Allison Act, was from the beginning of his second Administration also outspoken in his opposition to the Sherman Act. On June 30, 1893, only four days after the closing of the Indian mints, he called for an extraordinary session of Congress to be convened on August 7, "to the end that the people may be relieved through legislation from present and impending danger and distress," a condition which "is largely the result of a financial policy which the executive branch of the Government finds embodied in unwise laws, which must be executed until repealed by Congress."

The day after Congress opened Cleveland sent to it a clarion call for the repeal of the Sherman Act and for other legislation that would "put beyond all doubt or mistake the intention and the ability of the Government to fulfill its pecuniary obligations in money universally recognized by all civilized countries." In explaining the breakdown of confidence resulting from the heavy silver purchases, he said:

> "Between the 1st day of July, 1890, and the 15th day of July, 1893, the gold coin and bullion in our Treasury decreased more than $132,000,000, while during the same period the silver coin and bullion in the Treasury increased more than $147,000,000. Unless Government bonds are to be constantly sold to replenish our exhausted gold, only to be again exhausted, it is apparent that the operation of the silver-purchase law leads in the direction of the entire substitution of silver for the gold in the Government Treasury, and that this must be followed by the payment of all Government obligations in depreciated silver."

This, he pointed out, would constitute abandonment of the gold standard. He then continued:

[1] Quoted by Barnes, *idem*, p. 259.

"The knowledge in business circles that our Government cannot make its fiat equivalent to intrinsic value nor keep inferior money on a parity with superior money has resulted in such a lack of confidence that capital refuses its aid to new enterprises, while millions are actually withdrawn from the channels of commerce to become idle in the hands of timid owners. Foreign investors, equally alert, not only decline to purchase American securities, but make haste to sacrifice those which they already have."

The fight for repeal was a hard one, and both political parties were badly split. Broadly speaking, the division of public sentiment was more territorial than political. In the East both Republican and Democratic sentiment were strong for repeal. The West was strongly pro-silver, the Middle West was divided, while the South, except for the large planters and the commercial population of the cities, was generally opposed to repeal. The House, in which the representation of the populous Eastern states dominated, passed the repeal bill promptly on August 21 by a vote of 239 to 108; but the Senate, with its large representation from silver-producing states and from agricultural states, continued to resist. The spread of the panic from the East to the West, however, with widespread failures of Western banks, somewhat weakened the silver enthusiasm in a number of the Western states.

In the latter part of October the Democrats in the Senate, 37 out of 44, sought a compromise according to which the silver purchase clause should be extended to July 1, 1801, the seigniorage in the Treasury should all be coined, and further issues of Treasury notes should be limited to the denominations of ten dollars and above. In this effort the Democrats were joined by a group of silver Republicans. Cleveland was indignant over the proposal and on October 23, after a Cabinet meeting in which he expressed his opposition in vigorous language, he authorized a statement to the press given out by Secretary Carlisle, that: "The President adheres to the position that the purchasing clause of the Sherman silver law should be unconditionally repealed. . . ." [1]

The President finally won his fight and on October 30 the Senate voted for repeal by the vote of 43 to 32.

After Repeal

The repeal of the silver purchase clause, however, did not bring the financial crisis to an end. The crisis had altogether too much

[1] Cf., Nevins, *Grover Cleveland*, pp. 545 and 546.

momentum to be stopped so easily. Moreover, the agitation for bimetallism, both in Congress and out, continued unabated. In fact, it was soon to be greatly strengthened under the powerful political leadership of William Jennings Bryan.

The gold reserve continued to decline in response to heavy demands for hoarding and for export, and by February 1, 1894, it had reached the low figure of $65 million. Again the Secretary of the Treasury replenished it by the issue of bonds under authority of the Resumption Act of 1875. Two such issues added to the gold reserve over $117,000,000, but as fast as the reserve was replenished it was depleted by the presentation of Treasury notes and greenbacks for redemption in gold, and the so-called "endless chain" continued in full operation. In the words of President Cleveland's message of December 2, 1895: "Again disappointment awaited the anxious hope for relief. There was not even a lull in the exasperating withdrawals of gold. On the contrary, they grew larger and more persistent than ever." On January 28, 1895, the President again sought authority from Congress to issue gold bonds at low interest rates for replenishing the reserve, but again there was no response.

The Syndicate Bond Issue

By February the situation had become critical, with the reserve at less than $42 million, and with a breakdown of the gold standard imminent. To meet the situation a new device was adopted. Instead of selling the bonds in the open market for gold that was in large part withdrawn from the Government's gold reserve by the public to pay for the bonds, the Government made a special agreement with a syndicate of large financial interests. This agreement provided that 4 per cent thirty-year bonds, of a type authorized by the Resumption Act of 1875, amounting to about $62 million, should be exchanged for gold receivable by weight, to an amount a little over $65 million. The gold was to be delivered in installments over a period of six months, and at least one-half of it was to be obtained from abroad. It was stipulated that during the continuance of the contract the members of the syndicate would use every means in their power to protect the Government against gold withdrawals.

In view of the National Government's repudiation in 1933 of the gold clause in its bond obligations, it is significant that in the case of this bond issue of 1895 the confidence of the public in the integrity of the gold clause was so great that the Government could have borrowed, it was alleged, at a substantially lower interest rate, if Congress had been willing to authorize the issue of bonds payable in gold coin, instead of merely "in coin." On this subject President Cleveland said in his message of December 2, 1895:

> "The contract also provided that if Congress would authorize their issue, bonds payable by their terms in gold and bearing interest at the rate of 3 per cent per annum might within ten days be substituted at par for the 4 per cent bonds described in the agreement.
>
> "On the day this contract was made its terms were communicated to Congress by a special Executive message, in which it was stated that more than $16,000,000 would be saved to the Government if gold bonds bearing 3 per cent interest were authorized to be substituted."

Congress failed to grant the authority to issue gold bonds requested by the President and the syndicate operation for "coin" bonds was carried through as planned. As a result of this operation, the gold reserve was raised to about $108 million by early July, 1895. Confidence was temporarily improved, but the syndicate was not able to prevent a further serious depletion in the reserve and in a short time the reserve had again fallen to a dangerously low figure.

Although Congress had refused the President authority to issue bonds payable in gold, the proponents of silver in both houses attacked him vigorously for this issue of bonds for gold bullion through a syndicate of bankers. The critics claimed that such an issue lacked legal authority, and that in making it the President had been subservient to the dictates of Wall Street.

A Fourth Bond Issue to Replenish Gold Reserve

At the end of 1895 the reserve was so low and the situation was so threatening, apprehension having been recently increased by the fear of war with England over the Venezuelan affair, that a fourth bond issue was authorized to replenish the gold reserve. In view of the opposition aroused by the previous syndicate issue, this fourth issue, which was for $100 million 30-year 4 per cent bonds, was offered directly to the public. It was greatly oversubscribed and yielded a premium of approximately $11 million. However, according to careful estimates, something like forty million of the bonds were purchased with gold that was withdrawn from the United States Treasury for the purpose through the presentation of notes for redemption.

Despite the replenishment of the reserve through this fourth bond issue, the hoarding and exportation of gold continued to deplete the reserve, and this depletion was stimulated by the free silver campaign which culminated in the defeat of William Jennings Bryan and the election of William McKinley in November, 1896.

Confidence in Gold Standard Restored

After the election confidence was restored, gold came out of hoards and was turned into the Government Treasury in large volume, while the heavy net exports of gold which characterized the period 1891 to 1896 (except for the year 1892) were soon transformed into a strong flow of gold into the country. By 1897 prices began to move upward under the influence of the heavy outpourings of gold from the newly developed gold fields of South Africa, and the country entered upon another period of prosperity which continued until the panic of 1907.

The Gold Standard Act of 1900

Although the closing of the American mints to the free coinage of the standard silver dollar in 1873 provided the legal basis for a gold standard currency which would become effective whenever specie payments should be resumed, and although the currency was actually and lawfully on the gold standard after the resumption of specie payments on January 1, 1879, there was no clear-cut and definitive statutory establishment of the gold standard until the so-called Gold Standard Act of 1900. This act declared that the dollar consisting of 25.8 grains of gold .900 fine should be the standard unit of value, and provided that "all forms of money issued or coined by the United States shall be maintained at a parity of value with this standard, and it shall be the duty of the Secretary of the Treasury to maintain such parity." United States notes and Treasury notes were specifically made redeemable in gold coin on demand and a redemption fund of $150,000,000 was established to be "used for such redemption purposes only." For maintaining the redemption fund at an adequate figure the Secretary of the Treasury was given liberal powers of borrowing money on terms and conditions that would have fully met the wishes of President Cleveland during the long years of his valiant fight to obtain authority from Congress to issue bonds on satisfactory terms for the maintenance of the gold reserve. Not only was the Secretary of the Treasury authorized by this law to sell bonds to replenish the gold reserve fund whenever necessary to maintain the gold standard, but he was positively required to do so.

The Act of 1900 provided for the cancellation and retirement of Treasury notes to an amount equal to the value of standard silver dollars and subsidiary silver coins minted from the bullion purchased with these notes, it being contemplated that the notes themselves would be replaced in circulation chiefly by silver certificates. By 1912 all the Treasury notes had been retired, except about $3,000,000 and the few struggling notes still outstanding have long since ceased to be a factor in the monetary circulation.

The silver legislation of the years 1933–1935 and its results are tied up with the currency and banking problems of this critical depression period. They will be discussed in Volume II of this book as a phase of our current monetary problems.[1]

NOTE

The second volume of this book, which is now in preparation, is devoted mostly to the subjects of credit and banking. Inasmuch as our current monetary problems are closely interwoven with our problems of credit and banking and cannot be adequately discussed except in their interrelationship with those problems, the chapter dealing specifically with our present-day monetary controversy is being placed at the end of Volume II instead of in the present volume on Money.

Until the publication of Volume II, any reader interested in the author's views on the monetary controversy of the depression period 1930–1935 will find them given in popular form in his book *Kemmerer on Money*,[2] which was first published in January, 1934 and is being currently revised.

BIBLIOGRAPHY

Barnes, James A., *John G. Carlisle—Financial Statesman;* New York, Dodd, Mead and Company, 1931.

Carothers, Neil, *Fractional Money;* New York, John Wiley & Sons, 1930.

Cleveland, Grover, *Presidential Problems;* New York, The Century Company, 1904.

[1] A brief discussion of these developments will be found in the author's *Kemmerer on Money*, Second Edition, Chaps. VII and VIII.

[2] Kemmerer, E. W., *Kemmerer on Money*, Second Edition; Philadelphia, The John C. Winston Company, 1934.

Dewey, Davis R., *Financial History of the United States;* New York, Longmans, Green and Company, 1928.

Eckenrode, H. J., *Rutherford B. Hayes, Statesman of Reunion;* New York, Dodd, Mead & Company, 1930.

"Gold and Silver Controversy," Essays from the *Political Science Quarterly;* New York, Ginn & Company, 1896.

Hepburn, A. Barton, *A History of Currency in the United States;* New York, The Macmillan Company, 1915.

Kemmerer, Edwin Walter, *Kemmerer on Money*, Second Edition; Philadelphia, The John C. Winston Company, 1934.

——, *Modern Currency Reforms;* New York, The Macmillan Company, 1916.

de Knight, William F., and Tellman, J. F., *History of the Currency of the Country and of the Loans of the United States;* Washington, Government Printing Office, 1900.

Laughlin, J. Laurence, *The History of Bimetallism in the United States*, New York, D. Appleton & Company.

McElroy, Robert M., *Grover Cleveland, the Man and the Statesman*, 2 volumes; New York, Harper and Brothers, 1923.

Nevins, Allan, *Grover Cleveland, A Study in Courage;* New York, Dodd, Mead and Company, 1932.

——, *The Letters of Grover Cleveland, 1850–1908;* Boston, Houghton Mifflin Company, 1933.

Noyes, Alexander Dana, *Forty Years of American Finance;* New York, G. P. Putnam's Sons, 1909.

Report of the Monetary Commission of the Indianapolis Convention; Chicago, University of Chicago Press, 1898.

Reports of the Secretary of the Treasury, Annual, Especially the Report for 1897; Washington, Government Printing Office, 1897.

Sherman, John, *John Sherman's Recollections of Forty Years in the House, Senate and Cabinet—An Autobiography*, 2 volumes; Chicago, The Werner Company, 1895.

Thorp, Willard Long, *Business Annals;* New York, National Bureau of Economic Research, Inc., 1926.

Walker, Francis A., *International Bimetallism;* New York, Henry Holt and Company, 1897.

INDEX

DATE DUE
GAYLORD
PRINTED IN U.S.A.